Grounded in Grace

Essays to Honour Ian M. Randall

Grounded in Grace

Essays to Honour Ian M. Randall

Edited by
Pieter J. Lalleman, Peter J. Morden
and Anthony R. Cross

Foreword by
David W. Bebbington

WIPF & STOCK · Eugene, Oregon

Wipf and Stock Publishers
199 W 8th Ave, Suite 3
Eugene, OR 97401

Grounded in Grace
Essays to Honour Ian M. Randall
By Lalleman, Pieter J. and Morden, Peter J.
Copyright © 2013 by Lalleman, Pieter J. All rights reserved.
Softcover ISBN-13: 978-1-7252-8822-5
Hardcover ISBN-13: 978-1-7252-8824-9
eBook ISBN-13: 978-1-7252-8823-2
Publication date 9/22/2020
Previously published by Spurgeon's College, 2013

This edition is a scanned facsimile of the original edition published in 2013.

Contents

Contributors ix

Preface and Acknowledgements xi

Foreword
David W. Bebbington..xv

Ian Randall: Biographical Sketch
Keith G. Jones and Peter J. Morden xix

Chapter 1
Are we all Hussites now?
Michael Bochenski 1

Chapter 2
Election and Predestination in Baptist Confessions of the
Seventeenth Century
Nigel G. Wright 16

Chapter 3
John Bunyan: A Seventeenth-Century Evangelical?
Peter J. Morden... 33

Chapter 4
Abraham Booth's Defence of Believer's Baptism by Immersion
Sharon James 53

Chapter 5
Undenominationalism in Britain, 1840–1914
Tim Grass... 69

Chapter 6
Baptists in the Czech Lands
Lydie Kucová 85

Chapter 7
Adam Podin: An Estonian Baptist with International Links and
Pan-Evangelical Vision
Toivo Pilli... 103

Chapter 8
Sarah Terrett, Katherine Robinson and Edith Pearce: Three Nonconformist Women and Public Life in Bristol, 1870–1910
Linda Wilson 118

Chapter 9
Baptists from East and West at the World Missionary Conference in Edinburgh, 1910
Brian Stanley 133

Chapter 10
Dynamics versus Mechanics: Baptists and the Welsh and Lowestoft Revivals
Timothy B. Welch 147

Chapter 11
Jews in the Mindset of German Evangelicals
Erich Geldbach 164

Chapter 12
A Moment of Transformation: The European Baptist Federation and the Collapse of the Soviet Union and its European and Central Asian Empire, 1989–92
Keith G. Jones 180

Chapter 13
Mainstream: 'far greater ambitions' – An Evaluation of Mainstream's Contribution to the Renewal of Denominational Life, 1979–1994
Derek Tidball 202

Chapter 14
What is truth?: Evangelicalism, Foundationalism and a Hermeneutic of Witness
John E. Colwell 223

Chapter 15
Sapientia Experimentalis: 'Knowledge by experience' – Aspects of a Baptist Baptismal Spirituality
Anthony R. Cross 235

Chapter 16
Bringing Good News to the Poor: An Evangelical Imperative
J. Andrew Kirk 260

Chapter 17
Struggling with Female Happiness: God's Will and God's Blessing in Primary Evangelical Theology
Lina Andronovienė 277

Chapter 18
Hearing what is Written to Recover our Future
Simon Jones 292

Select Bibliography of the Writings of Ian M. Randall 309

General Index 317

Contributors

Lina Andronovienė is Course Leader in Applied Theology at the International Baptist Theological Seminary, Prague, Czech Republic.

David W. Bebbington is Professor of History, University of Stirling.

Michael I. Bochenski is Pastor of Rugby Baptist Church. He was previously Rector of the Warsaw Baptist Theological Seminary, Poland.

John E. Colwell is Pastor of Budleigh Salterton Baptist Church, Devon, and a Senior Research Fellow of Spurgeon's College. He previously served as Tutor in Christian Doctrine and Ethics at Spurgeon's.

Anthony R. Cross has served as a minister of two Baptist churches, lectured in Church History and Theology at the University of Roehampton, and is a Member of the Faculty of Theology and Religion, University of Oxford.

Eric Geldbach taught in Marburg and Kiel; between 1997 and 2004 he was Professor of Ecumenical Studies and Director of the Ecumenical Institute of the Faculty of Protestant Theology of the Ruhr-University Bochum.

Timothy G. Grass is an Associate Tutor of Spurgeon's College and an assistant editor for the Ecclesiastical History Society.

Sharon A. James is a conference speaker and author, who gained her PhD through Spurgeon's College.

Keith G. Jones is Rector of the International Baptist Theological Seminary, Prague.

Simon M. Jones is Pastor of Bromley Baptist Church and an Associate Tutor of Spurgeon's College.

J. Andrew Kirk taught for many years in institutions of higher education in the UK and Argentina. He is a Senior Research Fellow at the International Baptist Theological Seminary, Prague.

Pieter J. Lalleman is Academic Dean and Tutor of New Testament, Spurgeon's College.

Lydie Kucová is Acting Course Leader in Biblical Studies at the International Baptist Theological Seminary, Prague.

Peter J. Morden is Tutor in Church History and Spirituality, Spurgeon's College.

Toivo Pilli is Associate Professor of Free Church History and Identity, Tartu Baptist Theological Seminary, Estonia, and Pastor of Tartu Salem Baptist Church.

Brian Stanley is Professor of World Christianity and Director of the Centre for the Study of World Christianity at the University of Edinburgh. He is a former Tutor in Church History at Spurgeon's College.

Derek J. Tidball was formerly Principal of London Bible College/London School of Theology. He is currently a Visiting Scholar at Spurgeon's College.

Timothy B. Welch is Pastor of Cambray Baptist Church, Cheltenham, and a graduate of Spurgeon's College.

Linda Wilson is a Senior Lecturer with the Open Theological College, University of Gloucestershire, teaching Church History.

Nigel G. Wright is Principal of Spurgeon's College where he also teaches Theology and Practical Ministry.

Preface and Acknowledgements

The title of this book, *Grounded in Grace: Essays to Honour Ian Randall*, was first mooted by the Principal of Spurgeon's College, Nigel G. Wright, as discussions about a possible Festschrift for Ian began to take shape in May 2011. It was quickly adopted. The subtitle states our most obvious aim, which is to honour Ian on the occasion of his sixty-fifth birthday. Our desire to do this was, we soon discovered, widely shared. Ian has been and continues to be a colleague, spiritual guide and friend to many, a man whose influence is both broad and deep. We hope this Festschrift represents a fitting tribute to him. Yet, from the project's inception we have also had another complementary aim: to produce a book which serves the cause of Christ today, contributing especially to a greater understanding of evangelicalism and to its ongoing renewal. We think Ian will appreciate this. Not only is he a distinguished exemplar of the evangelical tradition, he has consistently worked for its renewal by helping evangelicals recover their past in ways that help inform present and future thinking and practice. It would have been inappropriate, therefore, had this book lacked a practical cutting edge. We offer this Festschrift as a mark of our esteem for Ian and also in the hope it will play a part in his continuing work. The title of the book, *Grounded in Grace*, seemed highly appropriate, for both the man and the evangelical tradition at its best are rooted in the grace of God.

The eighteen main chapters are written by women and men who have all been influenced by Ian, most of them significantly so. There is rich diversity. There are chapters from those associated with the International Baptist Theological Seminary (IBTS), Prague (Andronovienė, Keith Jones, Kirk, Kucová, and Pilli), and from those connected with Spurgeon's College (examples include Colwell, Grass, Morden, and Wright). In addition, there is a contribution from someone who knew Ian in his pre-Spurgeon's days (James) and another by one of his former pastors (Simon Jones). There are chapters from long-established scholars (for example, Geldbach and Stanley) and from others whose PhDs Ian supervised to completion (Bochenski, James, Keith Jones, Morden, and Pilli). Some of this latter group (for instance, Pilli) are well on the way to establishing solid scholarly reputations themselves. The presence of some emerging writers (for example, Kucová and Welch) is especially appropriate given that Ian has consistently sought to encourage the next generation. There is further diversity in the way the different chapters cover a wide range of topics. The themes of spirituality (for example, Cross and Wilson) and history (for example, Morden and Tidball) are well represented, and this will be of little surprise to those who know Ian's work. But there are also theological reflections (for example, Colwell) and missiological studies (for example, Kirk). Thus, what you will find here are writers from different contexts specialising in a range of disciplines and offering a variety of perspectives.

Yet, alongside this diversity, we believe there is much coherence and unity. All the authors are united behind the two aims of the Festschrift: to honour Ian and provide resources to help renew evangelicalism. All the essays provoke the reader to reflect on contemporary thought and practice. Taken as a whole, we believe this volume has the potential to inform and shape the present and future of evangelicalism, as well as contributing to other debates. We hope that it will be read widely, by scholars, pastors and students, indeed by any thinking Christian who is serious about living faithfully and creatively for God in today's world.

Many people have helped make this volume a reality. The different contributors readily accepted invitations to be involved and have taken time out of busy schedules to produce quality work to tight deadlines. The Baptist Historical Society (BHS) agreed to publish the Festschrift in conjunction with Spurgeon's College. The President of the BHS, John H.Y. Briggs, and the Secretary, Stephen Copson, have been unfailingly enthusiastic and helpful. It is appropriate that the BHS are involved in this volume, given Ian's service on the Society's management committee and as editor of the *Baptist Quarterly*, roles he has valued greatly. A significant grant from the Whitley Trust, established in honour of the Baptist historian, W.T. Whitley, helped defray the costs of publication. The close involvement of both the BHS and Whitley, together with of course Spurgeon's and IBTS, help remind us that Ian is both a warm-hearted evangelical with broad sympathies and also a committed Baptist. Micky Munroe worked hard to produce the splendid cover. In addition to writing the Foreword, David W. Bebbington gave helpful advice at a number of points. To all the individuals and organisations mentioned in this paragraph we are most grateful. Any errors that are present remain the responsibility of the editors.

It is worth offering some comment on the order in which the chapters appear. After the Foreword and a biographical sketch, the chapters that are primarily historical come first arranged in chronological order depending on the periods of history analysed. After these we have grouped the contributions that engage in broader theological, biblical and contemporary reflection. However, and as already noted, many of the 'historical' chapters have a strong contemporary edge and the 'contemporary' chapters are often earthed in historical reflection. Too much should not be made of the order of the chapters, therefore. The volume closes with a bibliography of Ian's publications. He has been astonishingly prolific although, as will be stated at more length in the biographical sketch, it is the consistently high quality of his work which is most remarkable. In this, as in much else, he is a hard act to follow.

Finally, it should be noted that we have been careful in this Preface to refer to Ian's 'continuing' work! Whilst we give thanks for his life and ministry up to this point, our prayer is for him to be given strength and vision to continue serving for many years to come. So, in the words of one of the evangelical hymns Ian knows so well,

Preface and Acknowledgements

> We'll praise [God] for all that is past,
> And trust him for all that's to come.[1]

Pieter J. Lalleman, Peter J. Morden, Anthony R. Cross
Spurgeon's College, November 2012

---

[1] Joseph Hart, 'No prophet, nor dreamer of dreams', No. 75 in *Hymns Composed on Various Subjects* (London: M. Jones, 1811 [1759]). The lines are from the seventh and final stanza. Later this stanza was amended and popularised as 'How good is the God we adore'.

Foreword

Wilkie Collins, a contemporary and close friend of Charles Dickens, published his novel *Armadale* in 1864–66. In the book, set some fifteen years earlier, Miss Gwilt, the anti-heroine, visits Mrs Oldershaw, formerly her sponsor in crime, and discovers the older woman at home on Sunday, allegedly too ill to attend church. 'There sat mother Jezebel', writes Collins, 'with the air of a woman resting on the high-road to heaven, dressed in a slate-coloured gown, with grey mittens on her hands, a severely simple cap on her head, and a volume of sermons on her lap. She turned up the whites of her eyes devoutly at the sight of me, and the first words she said were – "Oh, Lydia! Lydia! Why are you not at church?"' Mrs Oldershaw had turned Evangelical. As she puts it, 'her connection with the pomps and vanities of the world was at an end for ever. "I have been born again, Lydia," said the brazen old wretch. … she had found it to her advantage – everybody in England finds it to their advantage – to cover the outer side of her character with a smooth varnish of Cant.'[1] Mrs Oldershaw is crafted to condemn herself in the eyes of the reader as a sanctimonious charlatan. Like Dickens, whose portrayals of Evangelicals were rarely less contemptuous, Collins represents Evangelical Christianity as a bogus form of religiosity.

The depiction of Mrs Oldershaw is worth dissecting. In the first place she is hypocritical. She presents herself as a confident believer, somebody 'on the high-road to heaven', and yet she is not at worship herself. Her absence from church, we are made to suspect, is based on a sham excuse of poor health. She may have a volume of sermons on her lap, but it is not said to be open. It is evidently part of the image she wishes to project to her visitor, an elaborate form of deception. Then, secondly, Mrs Oldershaw is unattractive. Her description as Jezebel, the most abhorrent female character in Scripture, prepares the reader to see her as obnoxious. Her dress is the ugly colour of slate, her hands are shrouded in mittens of a similar grey and her headwear, in Puritan fashion, is 'severely simple' rather than in any way decorative. Here is a figure who presents no visual appeal whatsoever. She is also, in the third place, censorious. Her conversational gambit is not a greeting but an expostulation. Why is her visitor not doing her duty by attending church? It is not only Lydia Gwilt whom she censures. The public at large, with its 'pomps and vanities', is subject to her dismissive blanket judgement. And fourthly, Mrs Oldershaw indulges in 'Cant', a pretentious and self-righteous form of jargon. She turns up the whites of her eyes, as though to heaven, and claims to have been born

---

[1] Wilkie Collins, *Armadale* (London: Penguin, 1995), 582-83.

again. Her language is no more than surface deep, proclaiming her piety while underneath she remains a 'brazen old wretch'. Mrs Oldershaw is utterly repulsive.

In the middle years of the nineteenth century, when Collins was writing, society at large in the English-speaking world was permeated with Evangelical religion. The novelist could write of 'everybody in England' adopting similar ways. The Evangelical Revival of the eighteenth century had continued to gather force during the early nineteenth century so that its values had risen to a position of dominance. It is perhaps not surprising that authors of the time should wish to protest against the prevailing style of manners. Subsequently, however, that cultural hegemony fell gradually into decay, so that by the twenty-first century Evangelical assumptions are widely contested and have become marginal in many domains of life. It is no longer a social advantage to profess the Christian faith in its Evangelical form. Yet the image of Evangelical Christianity as hypocritical, unattractive, censorious and canting persists. The Evangelical Alliance even pondered changing its name so as to avoid the popular connotations of the title. The gospel seems compromised by the way in which its adherents are perceived.

Much of the work of Ian Randall has been designed to dispel such misapprehensions of the nature of Evangelical faith. While he was in Aberdeen, the guidance of William Still, the doughty minister of Gilcomston South Parish Church, pointed him towards resolute defence of gospel values. Subsequently in Sussex, he helped to edit the journal *Reformation Today* as an outlet for the assertion of a Reformed Baptist standpoint. As he came under charismatic and wider Baptist influences, Ian adopted a broader position which saw the record of past Christian achievements as a way of vindicating the value of authentic faith. History, he came to believe, was the best apologetic. Accordingly his master's thesis was on the life of F.B. Meyer, the distinguished Baptist minister at the turn of the twentieth century, demonstrating that his subject, while highly spiritual in his preoccupations, was also strongly committed to social reform. His doctoral thesis showed that Evangelicals of all types in the inter-war period cultivated forms of spirituality that were well thought out and gradually developed over time. Both theses, firmly founded on primary sources, soon appeared in print. A wealth of other publications followed, revealing that Evangelical institutions were often forward-looking, that Baptists were commonly outstanding figures and that, as Ian highlighted in his first editorial as editor of the *Baptist Quarterly*, there were innumerable 'links between Baptist life and wider evangelicalism'.[2] As he served in Prague, his own writings, and those of authors he fostered, revealed comparable themes working themselves out in the setting of central and eastern Europe. Those who read Ian's books and articles (and there are many) found that Evangelicals in general, and Baptists in particular, were frequently noble characters who, by any standard, lived out a vibrant interior faith in long years of dedicated commitment. While avoiding hagiography, Ian portrayed instances of practical spirituality that could hardly fail to command admiration.

---

[2] Ian M. Randall, 'Editorial', *Baptist Quarterly* 43.1 (January, 2009), 3.

The contributors to this tribute volume make a similar collective point. Evangelicals, and especially the Baptists among them, have often been straightforward rather than hypocritical, appealing rather than unattractive, irenical rather than censorious and frank rather than canting. The authors of the essays assembled here do not pretend that their subjects have always combined depth of conviction with largeness of heart. Yet many of the people discussed in the contributions to this book do reveal qualities that deserve respect. These individuals have nurtured a robust spirituality, founded on the Bible and encouraging a revival temper. They have ornamented their faith with good works by pursuing varieties of social commitment. They have shown a capacity for warm co-operation with Evangelicals of very different types. And they have explained their identity with candour even in extremely difficult times. The essays in this volume show something of the range of Ian's academic interests, embracing spirituality and social involvement, broad sympathies and Baptist convictions, Britain and Europe. They are also intended to display many of the typical characteristics of Evangelical Christians that Wilkie Collins missed.

David Bebbington
November 2012
University of Stirling

Rev. Dr Ian M. Randall.

Ian Randall: Biographical Sketch

Keith G. Jones and Peter J. Morden

Ian Maurice Randall hails from the Highlands and Islands of Scotland. He was born in Wick, Caithness, on 9 January 1948.[1] Until the age of nine he lived in a small cottage in John O'Groats where his father was an evangelist with the Christian Brethren. He then moved to the Shetland Isles where he lived for a year on Trondra, an island with a total area of 1.06 square miles. The school's teacher had to row across from the mainland every day to reach his young charges. The highlight was when the weather was too bad for the crossing to be attempted and so there was no teacher and therefore no school that day.

Ian moved to the seaside town of Nairn on the Moray Firth when he was ten. He did well at school, showing academic prowess from an early age. He loved books, often reading into the early hours of the morning by the use of a torch. He left Nairn Academy, where he gained the prestigious Dux Medal, to study Economics at Aberdeen University. His Scottish MA was in Economics and Economic History. Whilst at University he developed an interest in theology, and his personal commitment to Christ deepened. At that time he attended a large Church of Scotland congregation in the centre of the city, Gilcomston South Church. The minister was the redoubtable William Still, who remained at his post from 1945 to 1997. Through a regular diet of no-frills expository preaching, Willie Still helped shape generations of Scottish evangelicals, communicating a love for the Bible and for Christ. During Ian's summer vacations he would volunteer as a lay-preacher for remote churches in the Highlands of Scotland. That was the only time he put on weight, as the hospitable congregations were inclined to feed him too many cakes.

Ian met Janice whilst at University. They married and moved to London, and later lived in Haywards Heath and Maidenhead. During this time his church commitment shifted away from the Brethren assemblies of his childhood and the Presbyterianism of his University days. He attended an Independent Baptist church which experienced a real measure of revival under the leadership of Errol Hulse. In 1970 Hulse took over the editorship of a magazine, *The Christian Pathway*, and changed its name to *Reformation Today*. Ian was involved in the production of the magazine

---

[1] The authors are grateful to Ian's children, Ailsa and Moragh, who provided much of the information included in the first three paragraphs of this sketch to Keith Jones, hopefully without guessing the reason it was required! We are also grateful to Linda Campbell for giving advice on Scottish geography.

and contributed a number of articles.² As his thinking developed he became increasingly warm towards the Baptist Union of Great Britain (BUGB) and also experienced charismatic renewal. Ian and Janice remained united during this time of change and their relationship was and remains one of the bulwarks of his life. They have two daughters, Ailsa, married to Jiři and living in Brno, Czech Republic, and Moragh, married to Skander and living in Gothenburg, Sweden. Ian and Janice are now proud grandparents of Theodor, Iona and Ella.

After graduation, Ian first worked as a planner with British Telecom, then as a personnel manager for the South Eastern Electricity Board (SEEB). In 1980 he sensed a call from God to Baptist ministry within the BUGB. He began theological education at Regent's Park College, Oxford, in 1983, continuing his personnel work and studying alongside this on a part-time basis. He gained his University of Oxford Certificate in Theology with distinction in 1986. During this time he came under the influence of Dr Barrie R. White, the then Principal of Regent's. White's love of church history, and his convictions regarding its relevance for those training for ministry, made a deep impact on his student, whose own love for such history – especially Baptist and evangelical history – grew. White was also, as Ian later recalled, 'passionately concerned for the health of the [Baptist] denomination'.³ Once again, the student was decisively influenced. Themes that would become central to Ian's life and ministry were beginning to emerge.

Ian served as Pastor at Wraysbury Baptist Church, near Staines, from 1986 to 1990 and then at Dedworth Green Baptist Church, Windsor, from 1990 to 1992. At this point his ministry was bi-vocational and he pastored whilst continuing his demanding work for SEEB. Despite the long hours this arrangement entailed, his commitment to study was growing. He and Janice had an extension built on their house in Maidenhead so he could have an office at home. Once this was completed, he was often to be found there working from 5 a.m., an example of evangelical activism of which Ian's historical heroes would have been proud! This habit of an early start to the day – meeting with God, reading, writing articles and sermons – became a noted feature of his ministry and helps explain how he has been able to achieve so much.

Ian finally left SEEB in 1992, when he became full-time Tutor in Church History at Spurgeon's College, London. One of the panel who interviewed him, Professor David Killingray of Goldsmith's College, regards arguing for the recruitment of this relatively inexperienced candidate as 'one of the best decisions [he has] ever made',⁴ whilst Nigel Wright, who became Principal in 2000, believes Ian's appointment was

---

[2] Cf. Ian's comments in his 'Connecting Radical Church Life to the Riches of the Past', in Alan Kreider and Stuart Murray (eds), *Coming Home: Stories of Anabaptists in Britain and Ireland* (Kitchener, ON: Pandora, 2000), 115.

[3] Interview with Ian Randall, 'History's Lessons for the Great Leap Forward', in Simon Jones (ed.), *Talk: The Mainstream Magazine* 5.2 (Summer, 2005), 6.

[4] Personal recollection, Peter J. Morden. Confirmed by email correspondence, David Killingray to Peter J. Morden, 21 October 2012.

one of the most significant the College has made in its long history.[5] At this point Ian did not have a research qualification, but he was already studying hard for this. Later in 1992 he gained a Master of Philosophy degree for an excellent thesis on the career of Frederick B. Meyer (1847–1929), the noted Baptist pastor whose wide sympathies and interests led him to bring together a range of different people and movements, building bridges between those who had formerly looked with suspicion on one another. Meyer also engaged in vigorous mission, both social and evangelistic.[6] The thesis combined an interest in history and spirituality, a dual focus which Ian was to maintain in much of his later writing.

Not everyone was immediately aware of Ian's suitability for his new role at Spurgeon's. One temporary member of the teaching staff appeared especially puzzled, telling a class of bemused students that the new church history tutor 'presently works for the electricity board', with no further word of explanation given![7] Yet it soon became evident that Ian was wonderfully well suited to the role of tutor. Not only was he an astute teacher with a keen eye for the more amusing moments in church history, he was also highly approachable and sympathetic. It was entirely appropriate that in due time he added the subject area of spirituality to his duties as a lecturer, and became the College Chaplain too. In this latter role, Ian supported numerous students, and as a spiritual advisor and director he continues to help to shape the ongoing discipleship of many.

As well as serving as Chaplain, Ian continued to press forward with his academic studies. After completing his MPhil he almost immediately began PhD research, looking at evangelical spirituality in inter-war England. This groundbreaking study was successfully concluded in 1997 and published in 1999 to considerable acclaim.[8] Although he had already written a number of scholarly articles, this was the first of his book length studies to be published. After this date the books and articles started to appear at a rapid rate and the years 2000 to 2010 were astonishingly productive. During this time he authored or co-authored ten further books, and the same period saw the appearance of a staggering fifty-five articles or chapters in books edited by others. (For good measure he also edited or co-edited four multi-author volumes himself.) Never, since the days of its founder has someone at Spurgeon's College had so much work appear in print. As already noted, Baptist and evangelical history were Ian's special areas of interest. He was particularly at home in the nineteenth and twentieth centuries, but was able to write penetratingly about the eighteenth century too. By the end of the decade he had established himself as a historian of the first rank, someone who combined careful and thorough analysis of primary sources with an awareness of the wider context which was both wide and deep. His work was

---

[5] Email, Nigel G. Wright to Peter J. Morden, 19 October 2012.

[6] Later published as *Spirituality and Social Change: The Contribution of F.B. Meyer (1847–1929)* (Carlisle: Paternoster, 2003).

[7] Personal recollection, Peter J. Morden. Peter was a ministerial student at Spurgeon's from 1991–95.

[8] *Evangelical Experiences: A Study in the Spirituality of English Evangelicalism, 1918–1939* (Carlisle: Paternoster, 1999).

both scholarly and readable. He was not only prolific, therefore, but also produced work of an extremely high standard, illuminating people and movements in church history so they could inform contemporary debates about theology and practice.

This written output is all the more remarkable given that Ian was extremely active in other ways too. From 1999 to 2003 he was dividing his time between Spurgeon's College and the International Baptist Theological Seminary (IBTS) in Prague, where he worked as Director of Baptist and Anabaptist Studies. He developed the work of IBTS and was a prime mover in establishing the *Journal of European Baptist Studies*, editing many of the early issues himself. Formally Ian was 'seconded to' IBTS by Spurgeon's College but he and Janice were based mainly in Prague during this period, living in a flat on the IBTS campus. Whilst there, he involved himself in wider Christian life, lecturing at the Institute of Ecumenical Studies for the Czech Brethren and travelling to various Baptist and evangelical seminaries in Europe as a visiting lecturer. His lecturing style, full of passion and enthusiasm, was widely appreciated by students from Eastern Europe who were accustomed to a much more sober, formal approach and his laughter became legendary on the IBTS campus, as it had been at Spurgeon's.

Ian and Janice always felt able to contribute to IBTS community social events. On one occasion he played a highly effective 'ugly sister' in a Christmas pantomime rendition of 'Cinderella' and with the Rector, both wearing kilts, performed a spirited adaptation of 'Donald where's yer troosers' to revised wording composed by the Rector's wife. Janice and Ian were noted for their hospitality and friendship, especially to those finding themselves in a new land and very different circumstances. He twice served as Moderator of the Šárka Valley Community Church (Baptist) in Prague, of which Janice and he were founding members. Countless were the strangers turning up to worship who were immediately embraced and invited to their apartment for a cup of tea and cakes.

From 2003 he was based at Spurgeon's again, and served as Deputy Principal from 2003 to 2006, although he continued to work for IBTS as Senior Research Fellow, travelling regularly to the Czech Republic. Many PhD students at both institutions had their theses supervised to completion by Ian. His supervision combined vigorous attention to detail with an awareness of the need for a clear, progressing argument. A further hallmark of his work was the way penetrating comment was blended with liberal doses of encouragement. In one outstanding academic year he saw no fewer than nine students through to the successful completion of their doctoral dissertations. Although he 'semi-retired' from Spurgeon's in 2008 he continued as part-time Director of Research until 2011, and remained extremely active at IBTS. In 2009 he also took on the editorship of the *Baptist Quarterly*, the flagship journal of the British-based Baptist Historical Society.

As if this activity was not sufficient, Ian was also involved in various pan-evangelical concerns. He was a member of the Keswick Convention Council and he chaired the Evangelical Alliance Commission on Unity and Truth among Evangelicals (ACUTE). David Hilborn, former head of theology at the Evangelical

Alliance (EA), regards Ian's time as chair of ACUTE as especially significant, stating, 'In many ways he embodied the irenic, generous pan-evangelical approach we were seeking to model.'[9] It was not easy to chair some of these discussions, which covered topics such as homosexuality and the nature of the atonement,[10] but Ian gave himself to this work and to much else besides.

Thus, Ian's most productive decade of writing coincided with him taking on a range of different responsibilities. Yet he never seemed to give the impression of a man in a hurry or under pressure. He always had time for people and appeared to operate out of a deep spirituality which was rooted in evangelicalism and open to the riches offered by other traditions of the church. Great energy flowed from a quiet centre sustained by great spiritual discipline. At least that is the view of the authors of this chapter; close family might have another story to tell!

In 2008 he and Janice moved to Histon near Cambridge, and from this new base he continues to write, supervise and teach. He is also involved in pastoral ministry, on the staff team of a local church and exercising a role as a hospital chaplain.

Much detail has been left out of this brief survey, and many important themes have been given scant treatment. Yet hopefully the sketch gives a flavour of a life lived to the full for God and the gospel with, we hope, many more fruitful years of service ahead.

Summing up such a rich and varied life is no easy task. Surveying the whole of Ian's sixty-five years, one of the themes is certainly that of change. His life can be viewed as a series of journeys. Firstly, there have been literal journeys, those he has undertaken with Janice as they have moved from Scotland to England and then to the Czech Republic before returning to the British Isles. There have been many other such journeys, for example those he has made to speak in places such as the Keswick Convention in the English Lake District, Wheaton College in the USA, the Baptist Theological Seminary of Armenia and countless other places besides. A man whose early years were spent in the beautiful yet remote Highlands and Islands of Scotland became someone who, whilst particularly influential in Europe, is known around the globe. Ian has been on a vocational journey too. He was called as a minister and then received a further calling into theological education, continuing to operate as a pastor but in a different sphere.

Finally, there have also been a number of faith journeys. The mature Ian has embraced thought and practices which, we suspect, would have surprised and even alarmed his younger self. His commitment to working within the Baptist Union of Britain and sister conventions in Europe, with all their diversity, would be one example; his discovery of radical Anabaptism and some of the devotional practices associated with Eastern Orthodoxy, such as the Jesus prayer, would be others. Ian's understanding of Christian faith and discipleship has not remained static. He has been on a pilgrimage, one that has led him to traverse much exciting and varied terrain.

---

[9] Email, David Hilborn to Peter J. Morden, 29 August 2012.
[10] Email, David Hilborn to Peter J. Morden, 27 October 2012.

Yet although his life and ministry have been characterised by considerable change, there is much that has remained constant. He has been on a journey yet he has remained grounded. So, even though Ian is a man whose ministry transcends national boundaries, he remains a proud Scot. And while he is a man of broad sympathies, whose faith and practice is enriched by a range of different traditions, he remains rooted in evangelicalism. Indeed, the impression gained is that these roots have deepened and strengthened over the years as he has explored the rich heritage of the evangelical movement. In a recent conversation he was vigorously declaring the need for 'full blooded gospel churches'.[11] These convictions are propounded with generosity and winsomeness, but there should be no mistaking the fact that they are strongly held. Ian Randall has always been a committed evangelical.

The island of Trondra on which Ian spent some his childhood is no longer as isolated as it once was. It now has two road bridges, one connecting it to the neighbouring islands of East and West Burra and the other to mainland Shetland. It is possible to see an image of Ian's life and ministry here. He has remained rooted in the warm-hearted, Christ-centred evangelicalism of his youth and early ministry, nurturing those roots in a way that has enabled him to reach out and explore widely without ever losing a sense of what is most important. He has also been, like F.B. Meyer before him, a bridge builder, bringing together different people and encouraging them to work together for the sake of the gospel. Nigel Wright highlights Ian's ability to work 'harmoniously and cooperatively' with others as one of the hallmarks of his ministry,[12] something he has maintained whilst continuing to be at the cutting edge of thinking about discipleship and mission.[13] Consequently there has been both continuity and change, development and consistency. And, flowing out from this, there has been a remarkable fruitfulness. We might sum up by saying Ian has remained 'grounded in grace'. Many have been helped through Ian's personal encouragement and example to remain similarly rooted. Our hope and prayer is that through this book still more might be challenged to be firmly grounded in the grace of God, in life and in ministry.

---

[11] Personal recollection, Peter J. Morden.
[12] Email, Nigel G. Wright to Peter J. Morden, 19 October 2012.
[13] As an example of this latter trait, see the interview conducted with Ian by Simon Jones, 'History's Lessons for the Great Leap Forward', 4-7.

CHAPTER 1

Are we all Hussites now?

Michael Bochenski

After consideration of the influence of the fifteenth-century Czech reformer Jan Hus had on the Lutheran reformation in Germany, an overview of his life and teachings[1] will be followed by an exploration of the ongoing impact they had in Bohemia and on the emerging sixteenth-century Anabaptist movements. Finally an attempt to answer this essay's title question will be made.

Martin Luther discovered an unexpected ally whilst reading some of the surviving works of the Bohemian reformer Jan Hus:

> When I was at Erfurt I found in the library of the convent a volume of *The Sermons of John Hus.* When I read the title I had a great curiosity to know what doctrines that heresiarch had propagated, since a volume like this in a public library had been saved from the fire. On reading I was overwhelmed with astonishment. I could not understand for what cause they had burnt so great a man, who explained the Scriptures with so much gravity and skill. But as the very name of Hus is held in so great abomination that I imagined the sky would fall and the sun be darkened if I made honourable mention of him, I shut the book and went away with no little indignation. This, ever, was my comfort, that perhaps Hus had written these things before he fell into heresy. For as yet I knew not what was done at the Council of Constance.[2]

Luther later wrote to Georg Spalatin,[3] his friend and advocate at the court of Elector Frederick: 'I have hitherto taught and held all the opinions of Hus without knowing it

---

[1] The main sources for this section are T.A. Fudge, *Jan Hus: Religious Reform and Social Revolution in Bohemia* (London: I.B. Tauris, 2010); the introductory material in H.B. Workman and R.M. Pope (eds), *The Letters of John Hus* (London: Hodder and Stoughton, 1904; Bibliolife reproduction, 2009); and D. MacCulloch, *Reformation: Europe's House Divided 1490–1700* (Harmondsworth: Penguin Books, 2004).

[2] From Luther's Preface to a 1537 edition of Hus' letters, quoted by Workman and Pope, *Letters of Hus*, 1. The extract can also be found in Emile de Bonnechose (ed.), *Letters of John Huss written during his exile and imprisonment* (Edinburgh: W. Whyte, 1846), 9; this book is available on line at http://books.google.co.uk/books?id=bU6mxnnH6k0C&pg=PA1&source=gbs_toc_r&cad=4#v=onepage&q&f=false (accessed 15 October 2012).

[3] The humanist Georgius Burkhardus de Spalt was a spiritual advisor to the Elector Frederick and served as archivist, librarian and historian at the University of Wittenberg in the formative years of what became the Protestant Reformation.

... We are all of us Hussites without knowing it. I do not know what to think for amazement.'[4]

One of the many legends that came to be associated with Hus (a name that means 'goose' in the Czech language) was a prophecy he is said to have given anticipating Luther's reforms.[5] In the future, he wrote, his accusers will have to answer to God because 'other birds' would appear to sing which could not be so easily cooked.

> At first they laid their gins, their citations, and anathemas for the Goose, and now they are lying in wait for some of you; but since the Goose, a tame creature and a domestic fowl with no power to reach great heights in his flight, hath yet broken through their nets, we may the more confidently expect that other birds, which by God's word and by their lives soar to high places, will break their traps in pieces ... And it is this same Truth Who hath sent to Prague, in the place of one feeble, weakly Goose, falcons and eagles, which surpass all other birds in the keenness of their sight. These by God's grace, soar high and seize other birds for Christ Jesus, Who will strengthen these His servants and confirm all His faithful ones.[6]

Hus clearly envisioned here future reformers whom the authorities would be unable to silence. Luther and his supporters appropriated his prophecy.

> God wanted finally to terminate this and sanctify again His name, so that finally His kingdom could come and His will be done. Jan Hus has prophesied about me when he wrote from his prison in Bohemia: 'Now they roast a goose ... but in a hundred years they shall hear a swan singing, which they will not be able to do away with.'[7]

Luther's fascination with Hus deepened when, later in life, he came across his *Letters* – widely recognised now as '... a classic within the literature of Christian spirituality'.[8] Realising their significance for the ecumenical debates of his day, Luther moved quickly to have them published for the German public. In 1536 and 1537 several editions in Latin and in German, all with a preface by Luther, emerged from the Leipzig and Wittenberg presses. In the Preface, he wrote,

> Observe how firmly Hus clung in his writings and words to the doctrines of Christ; with what courage he struggled against the agonies of death; with what patience and humility he suffered every indignity, and with what greatness of soul he at last confronted a cruel death in defence of the truth; doing all these things alone before an imposing assembly of the great ones of the earth, like a lamb in the midst of lions and wolves. If such a man is to be regarded as a heretic, no person under the sun can be

---

[4] Quoted by Workman and Pope, *Letters of Hus*, 1-2. Letter from Luther to Spalatin, February 1529.

[5] For an analysis of the prophecy see Fudge, *Jan Hus*, 195-97.

[6] Letter of October 1412 to the people of Prague, in Workman and Pope, *Letters of Hus*, 95.

[7] Quoted by L. Batka, 'Jan Hus' Theology in a Lutheran Context', *Lutheran Quarterly* 23 (2009), 1-28 (2), from Luther's 'Commentary on the Alleged Imperial Edict' (13 April 1531).

[8] Fudge, *Jan Hus*, 87.

looked on as a true Christian. By what fruits then shall we recognise the truth, if it is not manifest by those with which John Hus was so richly adorned?[9]

Luther's words here serve as a helpful introduction to the life, thought and legacy of Jan Hus.

'Observe how firmly Hus clung in his writings and words to the doctrines of Christ'

Hus' high profile attacks on the contemporary Roman Catholic Church, from within Bohemia, led inexorably to his execution in 1415. The roots of this conflict lie, however, in the previous century and in the lives of earlier reformers such as Waldhauser, Milicz, Matthias of Janov and Wyclif. Conrad Waldhauser, an Augustinian monk, had come to Prague in 1363 from Austria. His provocative sermons, railing against clerics and others who loved comforts more than the gospel, inevitably created enemies. Following a 'failed' defence of his views in the then papal capital of Avignon, he was executed there in 1369. Jan Milicz of Kromeriz was among the many who were inspired by Waldhauser's preaching and by reading the Bible. In 1364 his own preaching career began – one which sounded many distinctively patriotic Czech notes. Among the practical outcomes of his preaching was the transforming of a brothel into a community ('Jerusalem') of God's poor. Milicz was also summoned to Avignon to defend himself but died before a verdict was reached. Matthias of Janov, who had been attracted to Milicz's preaching in 1372, continued his reforming work. He was an early advocate of the view that communion should be given with greater frequency to the laity and not just to priests. Clerical opposition forced him to recant many of his views; Milicz died in 1394.

It was, however, John Wyclif who proved to be the most significant influence on Hus' doctrinal thinking. Wyclif, 'sometime Master of Balliol College',[10] had dissented from traditional Catholic teaching in Britain. His translation of the Latin Vulgate into English proved ground-breaking and paved the way for the many vernacular translations of the Reformation period. Hus himself worked as a copyist of Wyclif's work and was inspired by what he read. His loyal friend, Jerome of Prague, was similarly enthused and travelled to England in 1401 to find out more, bringing back with him copies of Wyclif's theological writings. These were soon to grip the University of Prague. From 1402, Hus preached regularly from the pulpit of the newly built (1391) Church of the Holy Innocents at Bethlehem ('the Bethlehem Chapel') – still one of the many delightful tourist attractions in Prague's Wenceslas Square. As Fudge observes, 'It was his sermons to popular audiences which galvanized a reform movement in Prague.'[11] His congregation there has been

---

[9] Workman and Pope (eds), *Letters of Hus*, 2-3, from Luther's Preface to a 1537 Wittenberg edition of Hus' letters.
[10] N. Davies, *Europe: A History* (Oxford: Oxford University Press, 1996), 403.
[11] Fudge, *Jan Hus*, 58.

estimated at around 3,000 people and included women, children, servants, magistrates, university lecturers, political and military figures, tradesmen, merchants and artisans as well as the queen and the archbishop's sister. While rector of the Bethlehem Chapel, Hus preached over 3,000 sermons or one a day for nearly ten years.[12] In the process, his pulpit became the focal point of a Czech nationalistic movement. When in 1403 German nationals at the Charles University began making attacks on Wyclif and his adherents, Hus led the struggle against them. In one sermon in 1401, for example, Hus referred to the recent German invasion of Bohemia:

> They seize all of the state offices and we do not say a word. According to every law, including the law of God, and the natural order of things, Czechs in the kingdom of Bohemia should be preferred in the offices of the Czech kingdom. This is the way it is for the French in the French kingdom and for the Germans in the German lands. Therefore a Czech should have authority over his own subordinates as should a German. What would be the point of a Czech who knew no German becoming a priest or a bishop in Germany? He would be about as useful to a herd as a dog who cannot bark. And just as useless to us Czechs is a German. Knowing that this is contrary to the law of God and the regulations, I declare it to be illegal.[13]

As MacCulloch observes, 'Wyclif's message shaped his growing dissatisfaction with existing Church institutions, which mirrored the discontent of other leading Czech church men ... Hus' movement became an assertion of Czech identity against German speakers in the Bohemian Church and commonwealth.'[14]

The battle moved to the University precincts. At the instigation of Hus and others, King Wenceslas IV issued a decree that the Bohemian nation should have three votes in all affairs of the Charles University, and foreign nations (Bavarian, Saxon and Polish) only one. As a consequence, thousands of non-Czech students, masters and doctors left the University in protest in 1409.

The emergence of such Czech nationalism reflected wider disputes in the era of three contemporaneous popes. A brief summary of a somewhat tangled web may prove helpful here. In 1377, Pope Gregory XI had moved the papal capital from Avignon, France (where it had been located for some sixty-eight years), back to Rome. After his death, in 1378, the College of Cardinals in Rome elected an Italian as Pope, Urban VI. His relentless determination to reform the College was a thinly disguised attempt to further reduce the French influence on the papacy. Urban was succeeded by Boniface IX, Innocent VII and then Gregory XII (1406–15). Several disaffected cardinals, angered by what they perceived as Italian bias, formed their own conclave and elected a second Pope, Clement VII – a cousin to the French king – who in 1394 was succeeded by Benedict XIII. Finally, as a strong conciliar movement grew in response to this, the Western Schism, a third Pope, Alexander V,

---

[12] Fudge, *Jan Hus*, 59.
[13] Quoted by Fudge, *Jan Hus*, 96.
[14] MacCulloch, *Reformation*, 36-37.

was appointed in 1409. The ridiculousness of this state of affairs helped to create a climate of anti-Catholic discontent in Prague.

In 1409, Hus, his followers and the king transferred their allegiance from Gregory XII to Alexander V and under royal pressure Archbishop Zajic reluctantly did the same. In the process Bohemia became embroiled in the schism of the period. It was to Alexander V that Zajic appealed in an attempt to stop Hus from propagating Wyclifism in the Czech Church. His papal bull of 20 December 1409 empowered the Archbishop to proceed against Hus and his followers in Bohemia. All Wyclif's writings were to be given up, his doctrines repudiated and confrontational preaching discontinued. Hus counter-appealed in vain. Many books and valuable manuscripts of Wyclif were destroyed, Hus and his adherents were excommunicated for endorsing his views and the churches of Prague were collectively put under a papal ban. Riots ensued with the royal government taking the side of Hus who continued to preach defiantly in the Bethlehem Chapel. Zajic himself fled Prague in 1411 and died soon after. Alexander V also died in 1411 and was succeeded by the deeply flawed John XXIII[15] who, in May 1412, sent a representative to Bohemia as the crisis there deepened.

To finance John XXIII's armies for the battles with his papal rival Gregory, a trade in indulgences burgeoned. The people of Prague were pressured into giving their offerings in return for indulgences – pledges of present and future divine forgiveness. Hus had previously preached against indulgences but never while they were actually being sold. When Hus was asked by the king and the new archbishop (Albik) to keep quiet, he refused. This caused not only his relationship with them to collapse, but also the profits of the indulgence sellers. Popular demonstrations against the indulgences continued. In 1412, a University dispute took place, at which Hus spoke, using arguments clearly reflecting Wyclif's writings. He stated that no pope or bishop had the right to take up the sword in the name of the Church; that God's forgiveness cannot be bought but comes only after repentance and confession; and that a papal excommunication or ban could only be valid if a country's sovereign supported it.[16] Hus, it seems, convinced many people not to purchase indulgences and in the process made some powerful enemies.[17]

Hus' teaching on the pope, however, caused still more consternation. Hus had by this time come to question 'the idea of absolute obedience to ecclesiastical authority'.[18] The true test of Church leaders was that their lives must mirror that of Jesus: 'Live like Christ and you will know Christ well.'[19] Some words attributed to Dietrich von Niem, a contemporary of Hus, capture well the mood of Prague at this time:

---

[15] This antipope has the same number as 'good pope' John XXIII (1958–63).
[16] Workman and Pope (eds), *Letters of Hus*, 68-70.
[17] Fudge, *Jan Hus*, 62.
[18] Fudge, *Jan Hus*, 32
[19] From Hus' Commentary on James, quoted by Fudge, *Jan Hus*, 44.

> What is a pope? A man! The son of a man, clay from clay, a sinner who is likely also to sin. Two days prior he was just the son of a poor peasant now he is made pope. Is he no longer in need of confession, penance and contrition? Or has he become as an angel and incapable of sin? The pope is human and can sin just as a man may err.[20]

In a later letter to the Charles University rector in April 1414, Hus clearly expressed his attitude to the then papacy:

> I abide by this: whatever the Holy Roman Church or the Pope along with the cardinals shall decree or order to be held or done according to Christ's law, that in a humble spirit, as a faithful Christian, I wish to respect and reverently accept. But not whatever the Pope along with the cardinals hath laid down or ordered universally.[21]

The king made determined efforts to reconcile the opposing parties by ordering a synod to be held. Yet Hus was excluded from participation and, after it had ended, was summoned to trial but refused to go. He left Prague for exile in October 1412 and lived in southern Bohemia, protected by some friendly nobles. His preaching there sowed the seeds for what would later become a Hussite movement.

> Hitherto I have preached in towns and market places; now I preach behind hedges, in villages, castles, fields, woods. If it were possible I would preach on the seashore, or from a ship, as my Saviour did ... By the help of God, I have preached, still am preaching, and if His grace will allow, shall continue to preach; if perchance I may be able to lead some poor tired, blind, or halting soul into the house of Christ to the King's supper.[22]

Hus also took the opportunities exile gave him to write and, in the process, helped to consolidate the graphics of the Czech language – by inventing diacritical signs to aid alphabetical recognition.[23] His largely Wyclifite and derivative *De Ecclesia* was published in June 1413. A comparative examination of the two texts suggests that Hus lifted some 1,602 lines, or twenty-three per cent of his text, almost verbatim.[24] Plagiarism in those days, it seems, was leniently received!

In his surviving letters, Hus can be seen clinging to 'the doctrines of Christ'. A beautiful Christmas Day 1413 letter to the congregation from which he had been exiled, for example, remains one of the spiritual treasures of the mediaeval church:

> Rejoice with great joy that to-day is born unto us a King, to bestow in its fullness upon us the heavenly kingdom, a Bishop to grant His eternal benediction, a Father of the ages to come, to keep us as His children by His side for ever: yea, there is born a

---

[20] Fudge, *Jan Hus*, 36.
[21] Workman and Pope (eds), *Letters of Hus*, 130-31.
[22] Workman and Pope (eds), *Letters of Hus*, 86-87.
[23] Workman and Pope (eds), *Letters of Hus*, 86.
[24] H. Vilem, 'Jan Hus, A Heretic, A Saint or A Reformer?', *Communio* 45.1 (2003), 5-23 (17).

Brother beloved, a wise Master, a sure Leader, a just Judge, to the end that there may be glory to God in the highest ... Rejoice that the rich Lord of the Universe lies in a manger, like a poor man, that he may make us rich. Rejoice, dearly beloved, that what the prophets prophesied has been fulfilled, that there may be glory to God in the highest, etc. Oh, dear friends, ought there, to be but a moderate rejoicing over these things? Nay, a mighty joy! Indeed, the angel saith: I bring you good tidings of great joy, for that there is born a Redeemer from all misery, a Saviour of sinners, a Governor of His faithful ones; there is born a Comforter of the sorrowful, and there is given to us the Son of God that we may have great joy, and that there may be glory to God in the highest and on earth peace to men of goodwill. May it please God, born this day, to grant to us this goodwill, this peace, and withal this Joy.[25]

Throughout Hus' writings and sermons five core responsibilities of a priest are encouraged: preaching the gospel, prayer, the ministry of the sacraments, the study of the scriptures, and good works.[26] His lectures on the *Sentences* of Peter Lombard in autumn 1407 reveal an understanding of the power of God's Word to change the human heart and the Church. In them Hus saw himself in continuity with Augustine's understanding of the Catholic faith.[27]

The need for good eucharistic practice also features regularly in Hus' writings and sermons, especially his conviction that communion should be distributed more frequently to the laity.[28] After his death, Hus' followers developed his teachings on the eucharist into a practice that became known as utraquism[29] – whereby the laity were allowed to receive both the bread and the wine on a regular basis. These Hussite themes – the duties of a pastor, the power of the Scriptures to transform lives and faith communities, the need to challenge abuses of power by church hierarchies, and the importance of good sacramental practice – recur in the writings of Luther, in Anabaptist literature[30] and, for example, centuries later, in the pastoral theology of Eugene H. Peterson.[31] It is little surprise then that Davies and others describe Hus and Wyclif as 'pioneer Protestants'.[32]

'Observe ... with what courage he struggled against the agonies of death'

Hus appealed to a council rather than the pope to judge his case. In 1414 a council had been called in Constance at which, in fact, his trial was something of a footnote. The council's main task was to resolve the anomalies resulting from having three

---

[25] Workman and Pope (eds), *Letters of Hus*, 108-10.
[26] Fudge, *Jan Hus*, 14.
[27] Fudge, *Jan Hus*, 30.
[28] Fudge, *Jan Hus*, 51.
[29] From the Latin *sub utraque specie*, 'in both kinds'.
[30] See the Schleitheim Confession of 1527, for example in J.H. Yoder (ed.), *The Legacy of Michael Sattler* (Pasadena, CA: Herald Press, 1973), 27-45.
[31] Especially E.H. Peterson, *Working the Angles – the shape of pastoral integrity* (Grand Rapids, MI: Eerdmans, 1987).
[32] Davies, *Europe*, 404.

popes and to seek to end this malpractice.³³ As Cohn observes, the council which condemned Hus to death because of his challenge to the authority of the Church of his day, merely dismissed Pope John XXIII for simony, murder, sodomy and fornication(!): 'Never an extremist or rebel Hus offended by simply refusing blind obedience to his ecclesiastical superiors, but that was enough to cost him his life'.³⁴ The council had been called at the insistence of Sigismund, King of Germany and Hungary and heir to the Bohemian crown, who was anxious to put an end to religious dissension within his territories. Hus departed Bohemia for Constance in October 1414, encouraged – somewhat naively as it turned out – by promises of safe conduct from Sigismund. Promises of safe conduct were invalidated in medieval law by the charge of heresy.³⁵ Initially, Hus was at liberty but, after a few weeks, his opponents succeeded in imprisoning him on the strength of a rumour that he intended to flee. He was delivered to the Archbishop of Constance, suffering inhumane treatment in his castle.³⁶ His situation became worse still after the downfall of John XXIII. In February 1415 he wrote to a friend,

> The articles which they have extracted from my book *De Ecclesia* by false omissions and additions shall be brought to light by God's grace, and also the reply which I wrote in prison, though I had not a single book to help me.³⁷

On 5 June 1415, Hus was tried formally for the first time, after being transferred to a Franciscan friary where he spent the last weeks of his life. During the interrogations, Hus declared himself willing to recant if his errors should be proven to him from the Bible. Skilful interrogators persuaded him to affirm his support for Wyclif, thereby condemning himself in their eyes. Hus wrote feverishly between hearings and several moving letters have survived.³⁸ His piety breathes through his final letters which indeed reach 'serene heights of resignation and conviction'.³⁹

> O loving Christ, draw me, a weakling, after Thyself; for if Thou drawest me not, I cannot follow Thee. Grant me a brave spirit that it may be ready. If the flesh is weak, let Thy grace prevent, come in the middle, and follow; for without Thee I can do nothing, and, especially, for Thy sake I cannot go to a cruel death. Grant me a ready spirit, a fearless heart, a right faith, a firm hope, and a perfect love, that for Thy sake I may lay down my life with patience and joy. Amen.⁴⁰

Hus also wrote to a friend outlining the defence he was making.

---

³³ MacCulloch, *Reformation*, 39.

³⁴ N. Cohn, *The Pursuit of the Millennium: Revolutionary Millenarians and Mystical Anarchists of the Middle Ages* (London: Pimlico, rev. edn, 2004), 206-207.

³⁵ Davies, *Europe*, 419.

³⁶ Workman and Pope (eds), *Letters of Hus*, 167-69.

³⁷ February 1415, to John of Chlum, in Workman and Pope (eds), *Letters of Hus*, 175-76.

³⁸ See Workman and Pope (eds), *Letters of Hus*, XXXIII to LXXXII.

³⁹ Workman and Pope (eds), *Letters*, 250.

⁴⁰ June 1415, in Workman and Pope (eds), *Letters of Hus*, 253.

> I, John Hus, a servant of Christ in hope, refuse to state that any one of the articles taken from my book is erroneous, lest I condemn the opinion of the holy doctors, and especially of the blessed Augustine. Secondly, I refuse to confess that I asserted, preached, and held the articles with which I have been charged by false witnesses. Thirdly, I refuse to abjure, lest I commit perjury.[41]

As his trial progressed, and was clearly going badly, Hus took the extraordinary step of an appeal to Christ. As Fudge observes, this represented 'an ultimate rejection of canon law and all forms of ecclesiastical authority including papal and conciliar'.[42] The council records reveal how this appeal to Christ became a liability in practice; it was legally incomprehensible. One Pierre d'Ailly expressed this succinctly: 'We are unable to judge matters according to your conscience. We can only proceed in terms of what has been proven and concluded against you and on what you have confessed'.[43] In effect, then, Hus' stance amounted to offering no defence.

The condemnation of Hus took place on 6 July 1415 in the cathedral, in the presence of the assembly of the council. He was led into the church and, following a speech on the duty of eradicating heresy, his trial report was read. Hus' final humiliation then began – with curses, de-frocking and the placing on his head of a paper hat bearing the inscription *Haeresiarcha*.[44] He was then immediately escorted under guard to the stake where he was undressed, bound and chained. Given one last opportunity to recant, Hus declined with the words, 'God is my witness that the evidence given against me is false. I have never thought nor preached save with the one intention of winning men if possible, from their sins. In the truth of the gospel I have written, taught and preached, today I will gladly die'.[45] His ashes were thrown into the Rhine to prevent, it seems, any possible future veneration of his remains.

'By what fruits then shall we recognise the truth, if it is not manifest by those with which John Hus was so richly adorned?

The news of Hus' execution as a heretic antagonised much of Bohemia. In September 1415, 452 nobles of Bohemia affirmed in a signed document that the sentence of heresy passed on Hus – and by implication on Bohemia itself – was both unjust and insulting. A Hussite League was formed with the tacit support of the king whose queen, Sophie, was an open supporter of the Hussites. Between 1420 and 1431, the Hussite forces defeated five consecutive papal crusades against them – conflicts that became known as the Hussite Wars. For nearly two centuries afterwards, and as a direct result of Hus' execution, a high proportion of those who lived in Bohemia remained avowedly non-Roman Catholic as the Hussites established themselves within Charles University, Prague itself and across Bohemia.

---

[41] June 1415, to John of Chlum, in Workman and Pope (eds), *Letters of Hus*, 210.
[42] Fudge, *Jan Hus*, 129
[43] Fudge, *Jan Hus*, 130-31.
[44] I.e., the leader of a heretical movement.
[45] From his Final Declaration, in Workman and Pope (eds), *Letters of Hus*, 279.

Only when a remnant of Hussite forces was finally defeated in 1620 at the Battle of the White Mountain (an early battle in what became the Thirty Years War), was Catholicism restored as the majority religion in Bohemia. Davies' summary of these subsequent events is a helpful one:

> The Hussites, who founded a national Czech Church, survived repeated attempts to suppress them. They appeared at a juncture when the Papal schism was at its height and when Bohemia was rent by conflicts between Czechs and Germans, between kings and nobles, between the clergy and the Pope, the University and the Archbishop of Prague. Their demands soon exceeded the theological and political propositions advanced by Hus. They were so infuriated by the news of his death, and by the excommunications hurled at the whole Czech people by the Council of Constanz, that they launched what in effect was a national rising and 'the first Reformation'. They were divided into groups: the Utraquists, who took over the established Church from its largely German, Catholic hierarchy, and the radical Taborites, who founded separate evangelical communities centred on their fortified camp or 'Tabor'.[46]

Maag continues the story, noting that by the 1540s Taborite importance had dwindled as 'they were replaced on the more radical wing by the Bohemian Unity of Brethren who advocated strict discipline, rejected oaths, focusing on the importance of faith, but placing equal stress on the role of works'.[47] Hus' teachings lived on growing deep roots across the land of his birth.

The Anabaptists

The inspiration of Hus' story for Luther and therefore for the course of the Protestant Reformation has already been observed. What is less well known is the influence of his teachings and courage on some of the first Anabaptists. Though not explicitly mentioned by the Anabaptist pioneer Balthasar Hubmaier, his work *Heretics and Those Who Burn Them*[48] was published in the place where Hus was burned at the stake, Constance.[49] Hubmaier (1480–1528) was an Anabaptist theologian who knew both the Scriptures and patristic writers well, and who was also well versed in scholastic thought.[50] His *Heretics* is one of the earliest pleas for religious pluralism and tolerance in European history. In it, he declared that heretics are those who resist the Bible's teachings, not godly believers. Heretics, he argued, should be gently

---

[46] Davies, *Europe*, 428.

[47] K. Maag (ed.), *The Reformation in Eastern and Central Europe* (Aldershot: Ashgate, 1997), 9.

[48] Balthasar Hubmaier, *On Heretics and Those who Burn Them* (1524), in W.H. Pipkin and J.H. Yoder (eds), *Balthasar Hubmaier: Theologian of Anabaptism* (Scottdale, PA: Herald Press, 1989), 58-66.

[49] Pipkin and Yoder (eds), *Hubmaier*, 59.

[50] For an account of his life, see C. Windhorst, 'Balthasar Hubmaier: Professor, Preacher, Politician', in H.J. Goertz (ed.), *Profiles of Radical Reformers* (Scottdale, PA: Herald Press, 1982), 144-57.

instructed not persecuted, quoting for proof the parable of the wheat and the tares in Matthew 13. Those who burn heretics do not follow the teachings of Christ, he insisted. Instead they become heretics themselves, because they attempt to separate the wheat from the tares, which is God's task, not that of human powers. Secular authorities have the right to punish the wicked but they do not have the right to punish heretics – that is for God alone to do. Was Hus in mind as Hubmaier penned Article 20: 'Nor is it an excuse for them (as they babble) that they turn the godless over to the secular authority, for whoever in this way turns someone over is even more guilty of sin John 19:11'?[51]

The Martyrs' Mirror[52] contains accounts and testimonies of many of the first Anabaptist martyrs. The *Mirror* began as a small book published in 1562 and called *The Sacrifice of the Lord*. Revised versions in 1566, 1570 and 1615 added accounts of many more martyrs before, in 1660, Thieleman J. van Braght, a Dutch Mennonite elder, completed the work. Its ongoing popularity was assured when it was powerfully illustrated by Jan Luiken in or around 1685.[53] Rooted deeply as it is in early Anabaptist history, Van Braght recalls some reflections of an Anabaptist pioneer, Sebastian Franck, concerning Hus: 'John Huss, a disciple and fellow believer of this Wickliffe, received the Wickliffite doctrine from Jerome of Prague, who carried it with him from England to Bohemia as a sacred treasure.'[54] The articles of faith which Hus had learned and adopted from Wyclif's writings are then approvingly listed.

> 1. That the Roman church has no right to divide the sacrament, and has wrongfully deprived the laity of one form. 2. That the Roman bishop is just like other (ordinary) bishops. 3. That under all circumstances there is no purgatory. 4. To pray for the dead is vain and unavailing, and is invented by the avarice of the priests. 5. Images of God and the saints are not to be tolerated, and should be abolished. 6. The wicked devils have invented the unspiritual mendicant orders. 7. The priests ought to be poor, and live only from alms. 8. Outward, auricular confession is altogether false and man's invention. It is sufficient to confess one's sins in the closet to God. 9. The ceremonies and usages of the (Roman) church are vain things. 10. Touching several things concerning the sacrament, etc. 11. The time is uselessly consumed by the seven hours.[55] 12. There is no merit in the fasts instituted by the church, and in many other errors.[56]

A core Anabaptist practice, opposition to oaths, is also attributed to Hus in *The Mirror*: 'Here we certainly clearly see that the doctrine of not swearing in any wise, was an article of his faith; and if it was the case that he was requested to abjure his

---

[51] Pipkin and Yoder (eds), *Hubmaier*, 63.

[52] T.J. van Braght (ed.), *The Martyrs' Mirror: The Bloody Theater or Martyrs' Mirror of the Defenseless Christians* (Scottdale, PA: Mennonite Publishing House, 1950).

[53] A.O. Swartzentruber, 'The piety and theology of the Anabaptist martyrs in van Braght's Martyrs' Mirror', *Mennonite Quarterly Review* 28 (1954), 5-26, 128-42.

[54] Van Braght (ed.), *Martyrs' Mirror*, 336.

[55] I.e., the Catholic times of prayer.

[56] Van Braght (ed.), *Martyrs' Mirror*, 336-37.

faith or religion, he refused to abjure it, not only because he would not forsake his faith or religion, but also because he held that one ought not to swear at all, as the 13th article declares : "Men shall not swear in any wise", that is, not at all'.[57]

Another seminal Anabaptist work also looks back affirmatively to the stance Hus took in the fifteenth century.[58] The Hutterian *Chronicle*, one of the earliest source documents of the Anabaptist movement, contains this brief account of Hus' times.

> A man called Jerome of Prague returned from England with books and teachings that he passed on to John Huss (named after the village of Huss). Huss accepted Wycliff's teachings as the truth. Nearly all Bohemia renounced the papacy and became his followers. Because of these articles of faith, the emperor Sigismund summoned Huss to a council at Constance, granting him safe-conduct both ways. But because he refused to follow the teachings of Rome, he was condemned to death and burned.[59]

In *The Chronicle* the ministries of Wyclif and Hus are seen as beginning the restoration of the Church, after some 1,400 years, by paving the way for reformers such as Zwingli and Luther.[60]

It is also interesting to note, in this context, that many of the earliest Anabaptist Hutterite communities settled in areas where Hussite battles had long been fought.

Under benign rulers, sixteenth-century Moravia, part of the kingdom of Bohemia, became a place of refuge and inspiration for many religious radicals, including Anabaptists. Moravia had often been drawn into the Hussite disputes and wars flowing from the execution of Hus.[61] One outcome was a tradition of religious diversity and tolerance there, not then widespread in Europe.[62] These late fifteenth-century wars had left many parts of Moravia unpopulated and therefore open to economic immigration. Packull has traced the origins of the Hutterite communities and has also outlined the key role played by Moravian rulers in their development.[63] The Moravian feudal lords, it seems, offered the Anabaptists refuge in return for significant economic benefits. As Packull comments,

> The vagaries and fluctuations of Anabaptist fortunes in the promised land are best understood against the larger canvas of the political realities that prevailed in the host society. Whether the Anabaptists were conscious of it or not, their fragile fortunes clearly were linked to those of their patrons, the nobility of Moravia. Any history of

---

[57] Van Braght (ed.), *Martyrs' Mirror*, 337.

[58] K. Braitmichel (ed.), *Chronicle of the Hutterian Brethren* (New York, NY: Plough Publishing, 1986).

[59] Braitmichel, *Chronicle*, 37.

[60] G.H. Williams, *The Radical Reformation* (Kirksville, MO: Truman State University Press, 3rd edn, 2000), 1077.

[61] Cohn, *Pursuit of the Millennium,* 205-14.

[62] Ian M. Randall, 'Unity Truly of the Universal Christian Faith', *Anabaptism Today* 26 (Spring 2001), 5-12.

[63] See W.O. Packull, *Hutterite Beginnings* (Baltimore, MD: Johns Hopkins University Press, 1995).

Anabaptist communities in Moravia must take cognisance of this historic fact. For good or ill, the Anabaptist communities became part of the Moravian political economic landscape.[64]

Places of refuge were offered in return for conscientious work and new skills.

Imperial attempts to wipe out the Anabaptists were frustrated, in part, because of this context of toleration: 'the nobles insisted that the quiet and industrious "heretics" constituted no threat to the land; indeed they were sometime deemed absolutely essential to the economic welfare of the lord's holdings'.[65] The nobles repeatedly answered demands for repression by using pleas for freedom of conscience which echoed Hus' self-defence a century or so earlier. Rothkegel quotes two instances.

> In 1538, the Moravian Diet agreed on the formula that people cannot be forced to believe, for faith is nothing else than a gift of God, and cannot be given by anybody else than by God himself. One year later, the influential Lord Jan z Pernstejna wrote to the king: 'Faith, most gracious king, is a gift of God, and nobody can give it to those who do not receive it from God.'[66]

Braitmichel notes the significance of this for Anabaptism.

> It was then here in Bohemia, in 1528, that the Hutterian communitarian movement was given its birth. Although there was persecution throughout the country in 1535 and again in 1545–1551, political and religious freedom were possible here for decades afterwards. Over a hundred Hutterian communities flourished during this time, scattered throughout Moravia and Slovakia.[67]

In the eyes of the Moravian nobles these early Anabaptists had become, as it were, honorary Hussites.

'If such a man is to be regarded as a heretic, no person under the sun can be looked on as a true Christian'

Are we all Hussites now? Luther's indebtedness to Hus is clear. Batka draws attention to the ongoing legacy of Hus for world Lutheranism as a whole.[68] The inspirational impact of Hus' legacy on some of the pioneer Anabaptists and its positive influence on their survival in Bohemia have also now been described. An

---

[64] Packull, *Hutterite Beginnings*, 75.

[65] P.J. Klaasen, *The Economics of Anabaptism, 1525–1560* (The Hague: Mouton, 1964), 113.

[66] M. Rothkegel, 'Benes Optát, On Baptism and the Lord's Supper: An Utraquist Reformer's Opinion of Pilgram Marpeck's *Vermahnung*', *Mennonite Quarterly Review* 82 (2005), 359-81 (360).

[67] Braitmichel, *Chronicle*, 'Appendix 1: Political and Economic Context', 802.

[68] Batka, 'Jan Hus' Theology'.

early exponent of Hus' relevance for the contemporary Church, Enrico Molnar, has written a series of articles outlining something of Hus' ecumenical legacy. Molnar makes the case that, whilst always challenging the Roman Catholicism he knew, Hus remained, in many ways, an orthodox and loyal Catholic to the end.[69] Similarly, Vilem quotes 'the Polish Pope', John Paul II, who, at a specially convened International Symposium at the Papal Lateran University in Rome in December 1999, met with representatives of those lobbying for the charge of heresy against Hus to be overturned. The pontiff's reply stopped short of that, but was nonetheless charitable.

> Hus is a noteworthy figure for many reasons. It is however most particularly his moral courage face to face with enmity and death which make him a person of special significance for the Czech nation, also heavily tested in the course of the centuries ... I feel the duty to express a deep sorrow over the cruel death to which Jan Hus had to submit, and over the resulting wound, which opened in the minds and hearts of the Czech people and became the source of conflicts and divisions.[70]

In his articles, Molnar also traces something of the ecumenical legacy of utraquism[71] and tells the fascinating story of 'the English Hussite and Bohemian Lollard', Peter Payne, whose attempts to build ecumenical bridges with the Greek orthodox communion in the early fifteenth century 'made him a unique link and bridge between England, Bohemia and Greece'.[72] More generally, Hus helped to forge a paradigm shift in the way Church power and authority were viewed and understood. This shift came to characterise most Church-State relationships across the continents and denominations in subsequent centuries.[73] In that sense we *have* all become Hussites.

But can more be said? Dr Ian Randall, for some years a respected tutor at the International Baptist Seminary in Prague,[74] is a scholar deeply conscious of the significant place the Czech capital holds in the history of evangelical reform. To see that outstandingly beautiful city through his eyes is to enjoy living history. Those of us seeking the renewal of contemporary evangelicalism would do well to look again to the Prague of Jan Hus because many of the varied emphases Randall has brought to evangelical scholarship can be said to have had their origins in the life and teachings of Hus, the Czech pastor, preacher and scholar. The courage needed to tackle overweening ecclesial authority in the light of the Bible; the power of

---

[69] E.C.S. Molnar, 'Catholicity of the Utraquist church of Bohemia', *Anglican Theological Review* 41.4 (1959), 260-70.

[70] Vilem, 'Jan Hus', 21.

[71] Molnar, 'Restoration of Holy Communion', 104.

[72] E.C.S. Molnar, 'The strange ecumenical story of Peter Payne the English Hussite', *Anglican Theological Review* 35 (1953), 189-97.

[73] Fudge, *Jan Hus*, 245.

[74] After Dr Bochenski had submitted his text, the decision was made to move the Seminary from Prague to Amsterdam [editors].

sustained evangelical preaching to change lives and churches; the spirituality which undergirds true reformers across the centuries; the importance of freedom of conscience to the history of Europe; the emergence of Anabaptism and its ongoing legacy; and the remarkable place central Europe has in any study of Protestant reform, have all been features of Ian Randall's research and writings. All of these emphases can in fact be traced back to medieval Prague and to the ministry of the very remarkable Jan Hus. In his life and ministry the past, present and future of a renewed evangelicalism converge.

CHAPTER 2

Election and Predestination in Baptist Confessions of the Seventeenth Century

Nigel G. Wright

Introduction

One of Ian Randall's stories of his early years in the Scottish Highlands concerns certain types of conservative Presbyterians. The identity of the elect being known only to God, they were unsure whether they were going to heaven but were 'absolutely certain that nobody else was!' Whatever their lack of assurance, it is in such otherwise doctrinally and theologically confident circles of Reformed Christianity that Ian's Christian foundations were laid. Though he may have been broadening his spirituality ever since, no-one can doubt that this Calvinistic foundation was a solid one and has stood him in good stead. The combination of the so-called 'doctrines of grace' and a generous and gracious spirit, of which Ian is an example, is one worth pondering.

An article entitled 'Young, Restless, Reformed' appeared in the September 2006 edition of *Christianity Today*. Subtitled 'Calvinism is making a comeback – and shaking up the church', it described how in the United States, while much attention is being given to the conversation about 'Emerging' church, a very different movement is also under way among young people, one which represents a resurgence of Calvinist doctrine and may in the long run prove more significant.[1] At the heart of this resurgence is Dr John Piper, pastor for preaching and vision at Bethlehem Baptist Church, Minneapolis, and author of the best selling book, *Desiring God*.[2] The New Calvinism is one which is also leaving its mark in the British Isles in large measure through the numerous, and often profitable, writings of those such as Piper, Mark Driscoll, Don Carson and Wayne Grudem.[3] Significant

---

[1] Collin Hansen, 'Young, Restless, Reformed: Calvinism is making a comeback – and shaking up the church', *Christianity Today* (September, 2006), 32-38; see also Hansen's later book, *Young, Restless, Reformed: A Journalist's Journey with the New Calvinists* (Wheaton, IL: Crossway, 2008).

[2] John Piper, *Desiring God: Meditations of a Christian Hedonist* (Leicester: IVP, 2004).

[3] Mark Driscoll, *The Radical Reformission: Reaching Out Without Selling Out* (Grand Rapids: Zondervan, 1974); Don Carson, The *Difficult Doctrine of the Love of God* (Nottingham: IVP, 2004); Wayne Grudem, *Systematic Theology: An Introduction to Biblical Doctrine* (Leicester: IVP, 1994).

Christian movements such as New Frontiers and the Universities' and Colleges' Christian Fellowship often show enthusiasm for the combination of biblical, theological and experiential concerns that these names represent.

Whatever one's response to Calvinism, it is hard not to be impressed by Piper. In many ways he is a model minister. Educated at Wheaton and Fuller Theological Seminary, with a doctorate from Munich and experience as a theological teacher at Bethel Seminary, St Paul, Minnesota, his pastorate at Bethlehem Baptist Church has been long, thorough and diligent. His personal life is exemplary and disciplined. He defines his and the church's purpose as 'spreading a passion for the supremacy of God in all things for the joy of all peoples'. His preaching demonstrates a straightforward commitment to engaging with the text of Scripture. He does not shirk but rather addresses head on the suffering which he encounters in his pastoral ministry and is unashamed in declaring it to be ordained by God for the ultimate benefit of the elect. His almost twenty books are widely read and appreciated. His addresses at pastors' conferences are hugely popular. He is clearly loved and admired by his own people. Most significantly, he combines deeply-felt passion for the glory and supremacy of God with an unwavering commitment to doctrinal, specifically Calvinist, Christianity. At the core of this is the commitment to the doctrines often summarised under the acronym TULIP, specified by the Synod of Dort in 1619 as total (radical) depravity, unconditional election, limited (particular) atonement, irresistible (efficacious) grace, and the perseverance of the saints.[4] To these Piper is willing to add the doctrine of double predestination, the doctrine that God has decreed whom he will save and whom he will damn from before the foundation of the world, as a logical corollary of these theological principles.[5] He conveys the impression that much contemporary Christianity is 'content-lite', but at the same time his own expression of the faith is both experiential and charismatic. In this he reflects his own clearly identified theological mentor, Jonathan Edwards.

British Christians, especially British Baptists, do not commonly identify the more Reformed wings of their movement with passionate and warm-hearted Christianity. They are more likely, for instance, to think of Strict Baptists as a declining and introspective movement than as a wave of the future, although it is certainly possible to identify exceptions to this rule. Their judgement might be that those who call themselves 'Grace Baptists' are generally more likely than other Christians to exhibit a notable lack of grace rather than a fullness of it: Christians who would rather be inclined to be anti-ecumenical and even separatist in approach. Furthermore, the progress of the mainstream Baptist cause in this country is arguably one in which, for the sake of unity, strong convictions about the doctrines of election and predestination have been sublimated rather than emphasised. The Baptist Union of Great Britain is drawn from two original traditions, the General and Particular Baptists, who were distinguished from each other primarily at this point, one

---

[4] Paul K. Jewett, *Election and Predestination* (Grand Rapids, MI: Eerdmans, 1985), 15.

[5] Piper's website, <www.desiringgod.org>, contains a number of references to his version of 'seven-point' Calvinism.

espousing Arminian and the other Calvinist convictions. Growth into unity has therefore come as a result of diminishing these distinctive doctrinal positions and merging them into a more general evangelical identity, as happened in the joining of the Calvinistic Baptist Union and the New Connexion of General Baptists in 1891. The joining of these two movements is itself an indication that the debate had, in Alan Sell's words, 'run into the sand' and that henceforth people would agree to disagree.[6] It is to be wondered whether any significant proportion of Baptist church members would today be equipped to discuss the doctrines of election and predestination knowledgeably, and how many older churches have any memory at all as to whether they are, if of sufficient age, of General or Particular Baptist origin. Conversely, a resurgence of Calvinist doctrine, should it happen, might be thought to threaten the unity of Baptist churches by bringing to the fore an ancient fault line which has been successfully suppressed for some years.

What is not to be denied is that the apparent Calvinist resurgence in the United States is quite properly able to appeal to at least one major strand of Baptist history to authenticate itself. In particular, it is in part able to draw upon early Particular Baptist confessions to establish its position. This chapter therefore aims to revisit the seventeenth-century confessions to elucidate and understand their respective General and Particular positions and to detect signs of development over the century. Since all of these confessions have been drawn together into one volume by W.L. Lumpkin, his book will be prominent in this chapter. To allow the confessions to speak for themselves, that being our current concern, the chapter will also rely heavily on direct quotations. The subject under discussion will be pursued by close attention to the confessions that Lumpkin identifies. Beyond that the chapter is concerned with the general articulation of the doctrine of election, agreeing and disagreeing as necessary with the seventeenth-century confessions and with their modern day representatives, and with contributing to a constructive theology of divine election for today.

The Doctrine of the Early General Baptists

It can quite properly be claimed that the seventeenth century is the century of debate and development as far as the doctrine of predestination is concerned, and also concerning the allied subjects of providence, original sin, the status of children, human depravity, and the extent of the atonement. It is not surprising, therefore, that these themes figure large, both in the agreement and the disagreement within the writings we shall examine.

In investigating the very earliest Baptists it is clear that we cannot in the first instance look for association confessions or the general confessions of a national assembly. Neither such bodies existed at that point. Of necessity the first confessions are either those of individuals, churches or factions within churches since it is with

---

[6] Alan P.F. Sell, *The Great Debate: Calvinism, Arminianism and Salvation* (Worthing: H.E. Walter, 1982), 95.

these small beginnings and the inclination towards self-definition that the movement began.

Jacob Arminius, the Dutch antagonist to mainstream Calvinism, died in 1609, the same year in which the first Baptist church was founded by John Smyth in Amsterdam.[7] As we shall note, the contexts of both time and place are significant for this enquiry. Immediately we confront in Smyth's *Short Confession of Faith in XX Articles* (1610) a clear rejection of orthodox Calvinism. 'God has created and redeemed the human race to his own image, and has ordained all men (no one being reprobated) to life' (Article 2). With this comes the rejection of original sin, all sin being actual and voluntary (Article 5), the affirmation that the grace of God is to be offered to 'all without distinction and that not feignedly but in good faith' (Article 8), and that by the grace of God and the prevenient work of the Holy Spirit it is possible for all to repent and believe. On the other hand people can resist the Spirit and perish forever (Article 10).[8]

Smyth's position is regarded by Lumpkin not so much as thoroughgoing Arminianism as a rejection of high Calvinism.[9] As such it fits well, we may note, into its immediate geographical and theological contexts. Smyth and his companions were emerging from within Calvinistic Separatism and finding themselves now in some tension with it. Within the same church Thomas Helwys was to lead a faction that would eventually return to England to establish in Spitalfields the first Baptist church on English soil in 1612. Despite tensions in other areas, the Helwys group shared with Smyth a clear rejection of double predestination. In their *A Declaration of Faith of English People Remaining at Amsterdam in Holland* (1611), Article 5 argues,

> That God before the Foundation off the World hath Predestinated that all that believe in him shall-be saved, Ephes. 1.4, 12; Mark 16.16 and al that beleeve not shalbe damned. All this is the Election and reprobacion spoken of in the Scripturs, concerning salvacion, and condemnacion, and not that GOD hath Predestinated men to be wicked, and so to be damned, but that men being wicked shallbee damned, for GOD would have all men saved, and come to the knowledg of the truth, 1 Tim. 2.4 and would have no man to perish, but would have all men come to repentance. 2 Pet. 3.9. and willeth not the death of him that deith. Ezec. 18.32. And therefore GOD is the author of no mens comdemnacion, according to the saieing of the Prophet, Osæa 13. Thy destruction O Israel, is off thy selfe, but thy helpe is off mee.

The *Declaration* appears to retain a Calvinistic realism about human depravity, while affirming the human ability to receive or reject grace and insisting that there is

---

[7] A comprehensive account of Arminius' life and theology can be found in Carl Bangs, *Arminius: A Study in the Dutch Reformation* (Nashville, TN: Abingdon, 1971); see also W.A. den Boer, *God's Twofold Love: The Theology of Jacobus Arminius (1559–1609)* (Göttingen: Vandenhoeck & Ruprecht, 2010).

[8] W.L. Lumpkin, *Baptist Confessions of Faith* (Valley Forge, PA: Judson Press, 1959), 100-101.

[9] Lumpkin, *Baptist Confessions*, 16.

no room for complacency about perseverance in grace. So Article 4, 'even so now being fallen, and having no disposition or will unto anie good, yet GOD giving grace, man may receive grace, or may reject grace'; and Article 7,

> And therefore let no man presume to thinke that because he hath or had once grace, therefore he shall always have grace: But let all men have assurance, that iff they continew unto the end, they shalbee saved: let no man then presume; but let all worke out their salvacion with feare and trembling.[10]

Clearly then, the very first formal Baptist utterances are to be seen as rejecting high Calvinism and tending towards an Arminian position. After the death of Smyth in 1612 and the departure of Helwys and his group for London, Smyth's followers, still trying to prove their *bona fides* to the Waterlander Mennonites with whom they hoped to join (finally accomplished in 1615), issued *Propositions and Conclusions concerning True Christian Religion* (1612–1614), in which they affirmed,

> Article 10. That God is not the Author or worker of sin (Psal. v. 4; James i.13), but that God only did foresee and determine what evil the free will of men and angels would do; but He gave no influence, instinct, motion or inclination to the least sin.
> Article 15. That Adam sinning was not moved or inclined thereto by God, or by any decree of God but that he fell from his innocency, and died the death alone, by the temptation of Satan, his free will assenting thereunto freely (Gen. iii. 6).

Rejecting in Article 18 both the term and the concept of original sin it goes on therefore to assert,

> Article 20: That infants are conceived and born in innocency without sin, and that so dying are undoubtedly saved and that this is to be understood of all infants under heaven (Gen v.2; 1.27 compared with 1 Cor. xv. 49) for where there is no law there is no transgression, sin is not imputed where there is no law (Rom. 1v.15 and v.13), but the law is not given to infants, but to them that could understand (Rom. v.13; Matt. Xiii.9; Neh viii.3).
> Article 26. That God before the foundation of the world hath determined the way of life and salvation to consist in Christ, and that he hath foreseen who would follow it (Eph. i.5; 2 Tim i.9), and on the contrary hath determined the way of perdition to consist in infidelity, and in impenitency, and that He hath foreseen who would follow after it (Jude, 4th verse).[11]

Accordingly, all that bear the image of God are capable of receiving the redemption of God (Article 27). The earliest Baptists then, like the Anabaptists who preceded them, had a clearly anti-Calvinistic stance and had themselves understood with some degree of clarity what they were rejecting, they themselves as English Separatists once having shared it.

---

[10] All citations from Lumpkin, *Baptist Confessions*, 118-19.
[11] All citations from Lumpkin, *Baptist Confessions*, 125-28.

The Confessions of Early Baptist Associations

From the beginnings we move on to examine some of the early association confessions, the first of which is the *London Confession* of 1644, the product of seven Particular Baptist London churches writing at a time of great opportunity. Particular Baptists emerged from Separatism in the 1630s and became visible through their involvement with the Parliamentary party and the army in the 1640s. Amongst the charges against which this new movement was defending itself were those of anarchy, Anabaptism and Pelagianism, alongside the need to distinguish themselves from the General Baptists. What results is a clear but still moderate statement of Calvinist opinion. The Calvinism was to be further softened in later editions of the confession as the debate shifted towards that with emergent Quakerism, which included many former Baptists.[12] An example of the moderation is the omission of the decree of reprobation. Article III can therefore assert,

> And touching his creature man, God had in Christ before the salvation of the world, according to the good pleasure of his will, foreordained some men to eternall life through Jesus Christ, to the praise and glory of his grace, leaving the rest in their sinne to their just condemnation, to the praise of his Justice.

Accordingly, Article XXI asserts an atonement for the elect alone, but also that the gospel is to be preached to all.

> That Christ Jesus by his death did bring forth salvation and reconciliation onely for the elect, which were those which God the Father gave him; & that the Gospel which is to be preached to all men as the ground of faith, is that Jesus is the Christ, the Son of the ever-blessed God ...

Faith is wrought in the hearts of the elect by the Spirit of God (Article XXII) and so Article XXIII states,

> Those that have this pretious faith wrought in them by the Spirit, can never finally nor totally fall away ... but shall be kept by the power of God to salvation ...[13]

The first General Baptist associational confession appears as *The Faith and Practice of Thirty Congregations* in 1651 and was the product of a meeting in Leicester of thirty widely scattered congregations. It is the first General Baptist statement representing more than one church. Lumpkin judges that it reveals no consistent Arminian system and that it retains some Calvinist features.[14] In Article 17 it affirms 'That Jesus Christ, through (or by) the grace of God, suffered death for all mankind, or every man; Heb. 2.9'. However Article 25 is a strong repudiation of human free will.

---

[12] Lumpkin, *Baptist Confessions*, 150-51.
[13] All citations from Lumpkin, *Baptist Confessions*, 157, 162, 163.
[14] Lumpkin, *Baptist Confessions*, 173.

> That there is not, neither ever was any man endued with any abilities and power to do the revealed will of God, but it was given him from above. Iam 1.17.

It is the prior love of God for humanity that enables any person to respond to God in loving obedience (Article 37). However, Article 38 clarifies that faith and obedience are not in themselves meritorious works since they do not 'procure salvation as eternal life, neither are they any cause at all to move God to bestow it'. The confession imagines the grace and light of God being given to all (Article 28), but that such gifts need to be 'improved upon' by human appropriation of grace to lead to eternal life.

> Article 45: That all those who refuse to improve the gifts of grace which God hath afforded them, so that they repent not, neither turne to him in obedience to his commands made manifest unto them, they do despise the goodness of God or his free grace, denying the Lord that bought them and so are liable to destruction, 1 Pet. 2.1, 2.

Consistent with this, steadfast perseverance in faith leads to eternal glory.

> Article 43: That all those that continue stedfastly unto the end of their lives, pressing forward to the mark (Jesus Christ) that is set before them, shall not only have the comfort and joy which is a part of their portion in this life, but they shall also have a Crown of eternal glory in the life to come; Rev. 22.24. 2 Tim. 4.8.

Also in the Midlands was a gathering of seven churches of Particular Baptist conviction at Warwick in 1655. In the *Midland Confession*, they approved sixteen articles which were to be influential upon the later 1689 *Second London Confession*. Lumpkin describes this short 1655 confession as 'a careful and praiseworthy summary of Calvinistic doctrine of the middle of the seventeenth century'.[15] The three articles which justify this statement are:

> 5th. That God elected and chose, in His eternal counsel, some persons to life and salvation, before the foundation of the world, whom accordingly He doth and will effectually call, and whom he doth so call, He will certainly keep by His power, through faith to salvation. Acts xiii.48; Ephesians i.2-4; II Thessalonians ii.13; I Peter i.2, etc.
> 6th. That election was free in God, of His own pleasure, and not at all for, or with reference to, any forseen works of faith in the creature, as the motive thereunto. Ephesians 1.4; Romans xi.5, 6.
> 8th. That all men until they be quickened by Christ are dead in trespasses – Ephesians ii.1; and therefore have not power of themselves to believe savingly – John xv.5. But faith is the free gift of God, and the mighty work of God in the soul, even like the rising of Christ from the dead – Ephesians 1.19. Therefore consent not with those who hold that God hath given power to all men to believe to salvation.[16]

---

[15] Lumpkin, *Baptist Confessions*, 197.
[16] Lumpkin, *Baptist Confessions*, 198-99.

Similarly mild in its Calvinism is the *Somerset Confession* of 1656 which Lumpkin sees as an attempt to comprehend Baptists of both persuasions within the area.[17] Articles IX and XI therefore strike Calvinist notes:

> Article IX: THAT God in his son did freely, without respect to any work done, or to be done by them as a moving cause, elect and choose some to himself before the foundation of the world (Eph. 1:3, 4; 2 Tim. 1:9), whom he in time hath, doth, and will call, justify, sanctify and glorify (Rom. 8:29, 30).
>
> Article XI: THAT those that are chosen of God, called and justified, shall never finally fall from him, but being born from above are kept by the power of God through faith unto salvation.

Yet these articles are balanced by Article XXXIV which Lumpkin characterises as 'one of the clearest statements on the missionary obligation of a church to be heard before the time of William Carey'.[18]

> Article XXXIV: THAT as it is an ordinance of Christ, so it is the duty of his church in his authority, to send forth such brethren as are fitly gifted and qualified through the Spirit of Christ to preach the gospel to the world (Acts 13:1,2,3; 11:22; 8:14).[19]

Baptist General Confessions

As the seventeenth century drew on so it became possible for national gatherings of Baptists to take place and for more general confessions to be produced. It is in these that the work of previous generations came to fruition and that the most mature confessional statements of the century are to be found. The General Baptist *Standard Confession* of 1660 affirms that Christ has made propitiation for all, that God is not willing that any should perish and that the gospel should be preached to every creature so that no-one suffers in hell (Articles III and IV). Article IV continues,

> Unbelief therefore being the cause why the just and righteous God will condemn the children of men; it follows against all contradiction, that all men at one time or other, are put into such a capacity, as that (through the grace of God) they may be eternally saved, John 1.7. Acts 17.30. Mark 6.6. Heb. 3.10, 18, 19. I John 5.10. John 3.17.

Election is the election of those who believe, but it should not be understood that this constitutes any degree of merit in those who do believe.

> Article VIII. That God hath even *before the foundation of the world chosen,* (or elected*) to eternal life such as believe,* and so are in Christ, *John 3.16. Ephes. 1.4, 2 Thes. 2.13.* yet confident we are, that the purpose of God according to election, was not

---

[17] Lumpkin, *Baptist Confessions*, 202.
[18] Lumpkin, *Baptist Confessions*, 202.
[19] Lumpkin, *Baptist Confessions*, 205, 212-13.

in the least arising from fore-seen faith in, or works of righteousness done by the creature, but only from the mercy, goodness, and compassion dwelling in God, and so *it is of him that calleth*, Rom. 9.11. whose purity and unwordable holiness, cannot admit of any unclean person (or thing) to be in his presence, therefore his decree of mercy reaches only the godly man, whom (saith *David*) God *hath set apart for himself*, Psal. 4.3.

Furthermore, we may entertain great hope about children who die.

> Article X. That all Children dying in Infancy, having not actually transgressed against the Law of God in their own persons, are only subject to the first death, which comes upon them by the sin of the first *Adam*, from whence they shall be all raised by the second *Adam*; and not that any of them (dying in that estate) shall suffer for *Adams* sin, eternal punishment in Hell (which is the second death) *for of such belongs the Kingdome of Heaven*, 1 Cor. 15: 22. Mat. 19. 14, not daring to conclude with that uncharitable opinion of others, who though they plead much for the bringing of children into the visible Church here on earth by *Baptism*, yet nevertheless by their Doctrine that Christ dyed but for some, shut a great part of them out of the Kingdome of God for ever.[20]

On the ascension of William and Mary to the throne in 1689, 107 Particular Baptist churches sent messengers to the first Particular Baptist General Assembly in London. They approved the *Second London Confession* which had been issued first in 1677 and reaffirmed it as what has come to be known as the *1689 Confession*, probably the most famous of all Baptist confessions and one which is still adhered to by Strict Baptists and those of like conviction. The *1689 Confession* is based upon the *Westminster Confession* of 1646 and as such is a display of solidarity with Congregationalists and Presbyterians. As with the Congregationalist adaptation of the *Westminster Confession* at the Savoy Conference of 1658, the *1689 Confession* modifies Westminster's Presbyterian doctrine of the church whilst otherwise following its pronounced Calvinism. Yet even here there are modifications towards a more moderate Calvinist position, notably in the omission of the decree of reprobation[21] and the substitution of the following article for it as Chapter III:3:

> By the *decree* of God, for the manifestation of his glory, some men and Angels are predestinated, or fore-ordained to Eternal Life, through Jesus Christ, to the praise of his glorious grace; others being left to act in their sin to their just condemnation, to the praise of his glorious grace.

---

[20] Lumpkin, *Baptist Confessions*, 225-27, 228.

[21] 'By the decree of God, for the manifestation of his glory, some men and angels are predestinated unto everlasting life, and others foreordained unto everlasting death': Chapter III:3: J.H. Leith (ed.), *Creeds of the Churches* (Louisville, KY: Westminster/John Knox Press, 1982), 198.

The Calvinism of the document is then reinforced in the articles that follow which themselves mirror the *Westminster Confession* precisely.

> 4. These Angels and Men thus predestinated, and fore-ordained, are particularly, and unchangeably designed, and their number so certain, and definite, that it can not be either increased, or diminished.
> 5. Those of mankind that are predestinated to life, God, before the foundation of the world was laid, according to his eternal and immutable purpose and the secret Counsel and good pleasure of his will, hath chosen in Christ unto everlasting glory, out of his meer free grace and love; without any other thing in the creature as a condition or cause moving him thereunto.
> 6. As God hath appointed the elect unto glory, so he hath by the eternal and most free purpose of his will, fore-ordained all the means thereunto, wherefore they who are elected, being faln in Adam, are redeemed by Christ, are effectually called into faith in Christ, by his spirit working in due season, are justifyed, adopted, sanctified, and kept by his power through faith unto salvation; neither are any other redeemed by Christ, or effectually called, justified, adopted, sanctified and saved, but the Elect only.
> 7. The Doctrine of this high mystery of predestination, is to be handled with special prudence, and care; that men attending the will of God revealed in his word, and yielding obedience thereunto, may from the certainty of their effectual vocation, be assured of their eternal election; so shall this doctrine afford matter of praise, reverence, and admiration of God, and of humility, diligence, and abundant consolation, to all that sincerely obey the Gospel.

Further chapters of the confession take a high view of God's providential rule, as in Chapter V:2:

> Although in relation to the foreknowledge and *Decree* of *God*, the first cause, all things come to pass immutably and infallibly; so that there is not any thing, befalls any by chance or without *his Providence*; yet by the same *Providence* he ordereth them to fall out, according to the nature of second causes, either necessarily, freely, or contingently.

Later chapters affirm that humans are 'wholly defiled' in all their parts (Chapter VI:2), that guilt and sin are imputed to the posterity of Adam (VI:3), that the fallen will is unable to incline towards the good (IX:3). The consequent dependence on God's intervening grace is total (X:2). The confession affirms the salvation of 'Elect Infants' dying in infancy and of other elect persons who are 'uncapable of being outwardly called by the Ministry of the Word' (X:3). Those are incapable of being saved who are not 'effectually called' even if they are called by the ministry of Word and are what the confession elsewhere calls 'temporary believers' (XIV:3). Likewise, those who do not receive the Christian religion (X:4) are excluded from salvation. Christ's perfect sacrifice and obedience avails, however, for 'all those whom the Father hath given unto him' (VIII:5), which Elect

> can neither totally nor finally fall from the state of grace; but shall certainly persevere therein to the end and be eternally saved, seeing the gifts and callings of God are

without Repentance ... they shall be sure to be kept by the power of God unto Salvation ...[22]

Parallel to the confession of 1689 (first issued in 1677) is the General Baptist *Orthodox Creed* of 1678, compiled by fifty-four messengers of the Buckinghamshire, Hertfordshire, Bedfordshire and Oxford Associations and once more modelled on the *Westminster Confession*, although less closely than the *1689 Confession*. According to Lumpkin, it 'approaches Calvinism more closely than any other General Baptist Confession' and indeed should be seen as 'an early attempt at compromise between the two great systems of theology, thus anticipating the work of Andrew Fuller and others of the latter eighteenth century'.[23] The language is interesting and subtle. So, in Article IX we read,

> Now predestination unto life, is the everlasting purpose of God, whereby before the foundation of the world was laid, he hath constantly decreed in his counsel secret to us, to deliver from curse and damnation, those whom he hath chosen in Christ, and bring them to everlasting salvation, as vessels made to honour, thro' Jesus Christ, whom he elected before the foundation of the world, and is called God's elect ... and God the father gave this his elected and beloved son, for a covenant to the people, and said, that his covenant shall stand fast with him; and his seed shall endure for ever ... And so God the father, that he might bring about the salvation of his elect, chose the man Christ, with respect to his human nature, out of the fallen lump of mankind ... Therefore Christ, the second Adam, was a fit mediator between God and man ... according to God's eternal purpose in electing of Christ, and of all that do, or shall believe in him ... Now faith is necessary as the way of our salvation, as an instrumental cause; but the active and passive obedience of Christ, is necessary as a meriting cause of our salvation ... Now here is a great mystery indeed, for God so administereth his absolute decree that he leaveth us much place for an efficacious conditional dispensation, as if the decree itself were conditional.

The Christological focus of this article is reinforced in the one that follows.

> We do believe, that known unto God are all his works from eternity; therefore he foresaw Adam's fall, but did not decree it, yet foreseeing it in his eternal counsel and wisdom, did elect and chuse Jesus Christ, and all that do or shall believe in him, out of that fallen lump of mankind. And hath manifested his love and grace by Jesus Christ, his elect or beloved son, thro' the gospel means, to all; and hath given us his word and oath to assure us that he desires not the death of the wicked, but rather that they repent, or return to him and live, and if any do perish, their destruction is of themselves: and hath decreed to punish all those wicked, or ungodly, disobedient, and unbelieving or impenitent sinners, that have, or shall despise his grace, love and woings, or strivings of the holy ghost, or longsuffering, whether by a total and continued rejection of grace, or by an universal and final apostacy ...

---

[22] All citations from Lumpkin, *Baptist Confessions*, 234-95.
[23] Lumpkin, *Baptist Confessions*, 296.

In Article XV, the *Orthodox Creed* affirms the doctrine of original sin and of human depravity (reasserted in Article XX), but Article XVIII contains a robust statement of universal atonement.

> God the father, out of his royal bounty, and fountain of love, when all mankind was fallen by sin, in breaking of the first covenant of works made with them in Adam, did chuse Jesus Christ, and sent him into the world to die for Adam, or fallen man. And God's love is manifested to all mankind, in that he is not willing, as himself hath sworn, and abundantly declared in his word, that mankind should perish eternally, but would have all to be saved, and come to the knowledge of the truth. And Christ died for all men, and there is sufficiency in his death and merits for the sins of the whole world, and hath appointed the gospel to be preached unto all, and hath sent forth his spirit to accompany the word in order to beget repentance and faith: so that if any do perish, it's not for want of the means of grace manifested in Christ to them, but for the non-improvement of the grace of God, offered freely to them through Christ in the gospel.

Similar notes are struck when writing of effectual calling in Article XXI.

> Vocation, or calling, general, or common, is, when God by the means of his word and spirit, freely of his own grace and goodness, doth ministerially acquaint mankind with his gracious good purpose of salvation, by Jesus Christ; inviting and wooing them to come to him, and to accept of Christ revealing unto them the gospel covenant, and those that with cordial hearts do improve this common grace, he in time worketh unfeigned faith, and sincere repentance in them; and by his grace they come to accept of Christ, as their only Lord and Saviour, with their whole heart; and God becomes their father in Christ, and they then being effectually called, are by faith united to Jesus Christ by grace unto salvation.

The creed goes on to reject the idea that children dying without baptism cannot be saved (Article XXVIII) and to assert the converse in Article XLIV.

> We do believe, that all little children, dying in their infancy, viz. before they are capable to chuse either good or evil, whether born of believing parents, or unbelieving parents, shall be saved by the grace of God, and merit of Christ their redeemer, and work of the holy ghost, and so being made members of the invisible church, shall enjoy life everlasting; for our Lord Jesus saith, of such belongs the kingdom of heaven. Ergo, we conclude that opinion is false, which saith, that those little infants dying before baptism, are damned.[24]

A Sign of Convergence

The last confession to which we draw attention is *A Short Confession or a Brief Narrative of Faith* (1691) and therefore towards the end of our period. This represents a confession of a number of Particular Baptist churches in the West

---

[24] Citations from Lumpkin, *Baptist Confessions*, 297-331.

Country influenced by Thomas Collier, the so-called 'Apostle to the West', and it is particularly notable in that it reveals a current away from Calvinism. This perhaps reflects Collier's desire to unite Particular and General Baptist churches in his locality. In Chapter VI it affirms that Christ was sent into the world 'to give himself a ransom for all mankind; for the world, the whole world' such that if salvation is not attained 'it is not for want of grace in the father, nor a sacrifice in the son'. Chapter XVIII:1 contains the words,

> Concerning God's decrees we believe, that the word of God is his decreed will; and that there is no secret will or decree in God, contrary to his revealed word and will; and that his decree is that whosoever believeth and obeyeth him, persevering therein to the end, shall be saved; and he that believeth not shall be damned.

Whatever God has absolutely decreed shall come to pass, but

> 3. We believe, that many things that do come to pass are not decreed of God, For it seems to us not only unscriptural, but also altogether irrational, to imagine, that the righteous and holy God should decree any sin, or unholiness, either in angels or men, tho' God doth permit them to come to pass, yet there is no decree of his that do necessitate the being of them. It might suit the nature of the Devil, or of wicked men, to decree wickedness; but far be it from the righteous God so to do; shall not the judge of all the earth do right?

On election the confession affirms in Chapter XX,

> 2. And affirmatively we do believe, that the infinitely wise and holy God, suitable to his name and nature, did elect or choose unto himself from eternity, and (merely of his own good pleasure) out of the whole body and bulk of mankind, an entire species, or sort of men, namely those that in time do believe, and sincerely obey him, patiently continuing in the way of well doing unto the end.
> 3. We believe this election to be in Jesus Christ, of God's eternal purpose and grace, before the foundation of the world.
> 4. We do believe that God's electing grace doth extend itself to the whole number of the godly in all nations, throughout all ages, under the various dispensations, under which they live.

Concerning reprobation this means, according to XXI:1

> that God hath not decreed from eternity, the reprobation of any person of mankind, considered as such, who may not very possibly be saved, notwithstanding any decree in God; much less do we hold a decree of reprobation from eternity, of the greatest part of mankind, excluding a possibility of their being saved; for we believe that God doth not hate or reprobate any man, as his creature, before he considers him as an actual sinner.

It is not God's intention to reprobate but to save and 'if ever the Lord does finally reprobate any person or persons, it is for their final rejecting him, in his many calls, and gracious invitations'. This leads to two final conclusions:

4. From whence we conclude, that those that own personal election, and personal reprobation before time, so as to deny the love of God to the world, do not own the faith of the gospel.

And

5. We believe, that God hath not decreed the reprobation of any infant, dying before the commission of actual sin.[25]

We might conclude that for Calvinists Collier and his companions make very good Arminians. It is no surprise that the London Particular Baptists sought to persuade Collier of his error.

Conclusions

Having reviewed these various confessions, what might we then conclude? Firstly, it is clear that in the first century of their life, Baptists of both kinds were active in seeking to give doctrinal, confessional expression to their faith. We find them immersed in, engaged with and contributing to the general theological debates which were particularly characteristic of their day and age.

It is sometimes claimed that Baptists are non-creedal people. The sense in which this is true is open to debate. Certainly they had suffered from the attempt to impose a creed upon them as an act of political and social conformity and had objected. Like other Protestants, whatever confessions they produced were 'subordinate standards' in the sense that they themselves were subject to Scripture. But there were good political and ecclesial reasons why they needed and wished to define themselves doctrinally, both to fend off the distorted criticisms that came their way and to demonstrate their essential soundness, and to clarify the precise ways in which, when it came to ecclesiology, they were actually saying something different from others. The evidence of the confessions is that they were doctrinally competent. It is also worth noting that at least one of the confessions we have examined, namely the *Orthodox Creed*, explicitly affirms that the *Nicene Creed*, the *Athanasian Creed* and the *Apostles' Creed* 'ought thoroughly to be received and believed' (Article XXXVIII).[26]

If in our own day there is a new concern with the doctrinal expression of Christianity this is surely to be welcomed in principle, whilst at the same time it should be guarded so that the doctrinal does not slip over into the doctrinaire. The kind of Christian faith espoused by these early Baptists has intellectual content and was identified in the confessions themselves. Contemporary Christian movements need intellectual content at the heart of their faith, but the integration of the 'grace and truth'[27] which are to be found in Christ is a proper and major challenge so that

---

[25] All citations from Lumpkin, *Baptist Confessions*, 336-39.
[26] Lumpkin, *Baptist Confessions*, 326.
[27] John 1:17.

the doctrine of divine grace is matched by gracious behaviour towards others. It might accurately be maintained that the charismatic movements of the second half of the twentieth century served the church well in emphasising that Christianity is an experiential faith concerned to realise communion with God. A reverse side to such experientialism is a generation of Christians more used to emoting than thinking their faith. Here lies the attraction of the New Calvinism. Not for the first time,[28] those who seek an intellectual challenge in their Christian discipleship are able to fall back upon one of the traditions in which such Christianity has been expressed, the resources of the Reformed tradition. In doing so they may not be immediately aware of the varied forms in which that strand of the faith has expressed itself and of the spectrum of intellectual options open to them.[29]

Secondly, within the theological discussions of the seventeenth century election and predestination figured prominently both in affirming and denying the contested versions of these doctrines. In this the Baptists were reflecting the debates taking place within the Reformed tradition for most of the century and beyond, and clearly believed that a great deal was at stake. On the one hand the Particulars were concerned to exalt the greatness of God as the one who was the first and final cause of all things, whether salvation or damnation. On the other hand the Generals were concerned to exalt the goodness of God in the light of which it was unthinkable that God should create any human beings with the intention of damning them. The debate between these opposing positions is clearly one which continues today and fundamentally at stake is how we are to think of God.[30] A new literacy in these areas of the tradition is called for and I for one would argue that a reconsideration of these themes is (for Baptist at least) one of the ways in which it becomes possible to wrestle with matters at the heart of the faith. Conversely their neglect is a sign of a weakened theology.

Thirdly, it is reasonably clear that although election and predestination figure within the seventeenth-century Baptist doctrinal tradition, there is a marked tendency to avoid extremes. Seventeenth-century Particular Baptist confessions represent at the most a moderate Calvinism. This is evidently so in the avoidance on the side of the Particulars of the doctrine of double predestination. Not only is this not asserted (God predestines to life but does not actively reprobate, rather God leaves sinners in their sin), it is also edited out of non-Baptist sources in favour of milder statements within the Baptist versions. The adaptation of the *Westminster Confession* in the confession of 1689 is an example. It is also probably true of the 1644 *London Confession* in so far as it draws from the Separatist *True Confession* of 1596.[31] It is

---

[28] The resurgence led by Martyn Lloyd-Jones in the 1950s would be an earlier example accompanied by the significant publishing work of the Banner of Truth Trust.

[29] Kenneth J. Stewart, *Ten Myths About Calvinism: Recovering the Breadth of the Reformed Tradition* (Nottingham: Apollos, 2011), 270-71.

[30] On this tension, see in particular Roger Olson, *The Mosaic of Christian Belief: Twenty Centuries of Unity and Diversity* (Leicester: IVP, 2002), chapter 5, '**God** Great *and* Good'.

[31] Lumpkin, *Baptist Confessions*, 146; cf. the *True Confession*, Article 3, in Lumpkin, *Baptist Confessions*, 82.

as though the framers of these documents were aware that to go further than they do would begin to sound like determinism and lose the element of the dynamic.

Conversely, the General Baptist confessions avoid the charge of Pelagianism by making it progressively clearer that human beings are unable to save themselves and are completely dependent upon prevenient grace before they are able to respond in faith to God's gracious approach. Early rejections of the doctrine of original sin are, therefore, modified in later sources by an acceptance of human inability, although notions of the imputation of original guilt are absent, as is clear from the clauses that deal with those who die as infants. Although it is undoubtedly true that in the eighteenth century the Particulars were to fall into hyper Calvinism and the Generals into rationalism and Unitarianism, the seventeenth century itself gives evidence of moderation and that in itself might serve the present generation well as it retrieves its traditions. Perhaps this moderation was sustained because of the mutual and reciprocal critique of General and Particular Baptists.

Fourthly, as the century progresses so does the theology. The century's Baptist confessional project reaches its peak in the *1689 Confession* and in the *Orthodox Creed* of 1678. The 1689 benefits from its ability to draw upon the carefully crafted *Westminster Confession* and is confident in the more moderate Calvinism it espouses. The *Orthodox Creed* is Calvinian in its anthropology but robustly assigns final loss to human resistance rather than to divine reprobation. Significantly, it crafts a doctrine of election with reference to Christ as the Elect, in whom those who are his are also elect, and speaks of the 'wooings' of the Holy Spirit towards all people, the rejection of which is the final cause of damnation. In this construct it anticipates the re-working of the doctrine of election to be found in such later theologians as Karl Barth[32] and perhaps indicates that Barth's position is not so much a novelty as is sometimes claimed. In my judgement, this is the perspective which will best serve the re-articulation of a constructive doctrine of election in our day.[33]

---

[32] Karl Barth, *Church Dogmatics* (Edinburgh: T. and T. Clark, 1957), Volume II/2, Chapter VII, 'The Election of God'. A useful summary of Barth's reworking of the doctrine can be found in T.H.L. Parker, 'Predestination', in Alan Richardson (ed.), *A Dictionary of Christian Theology* (London: SCM Press, 1969), 264-72. Parker, 270, likens Barth to a landscape gardener: 'There is the same place; it has the same name; the same prominent natural features still confront us. But the whole view has been changed by readjustments, trees planted, undergrowth torn up, a stream diverted, new vistas, a new scene.' He continues, 272, 'Barth has transformed the scene from severity and even gloom into a place of joyfulness and light. He has brought about a scene that even Capability Brown could not achieve – he has made the sun shine on the scene.'

[33] See my attempts in this direction in *The Radical Evangelical: Seeking a Place to Stand* (London: SPCK, 1996), chapter 3, 'God's Universal Outreach'.

Application

The New Calvinism represents in many ways a welcome hunger for coherent and stretching intellectual content to Christian faith to strengthen rather than replace its experiential realities. The Calvinist tradition, however, 'contains a complex of convictions, some of which prove highly difficult'.[34] We have seen that one of the most difficult of these, the idea of double predestination, cannot in fact appeal to Baptist confessions of the seventeenth century for support. It is studiously avoided. It should be avoided today, but not by means of editing out the hugely significant doctrines of election and predestination from our discourse and proclamation. Instead, these should be articulated in a way which shows them to be the good news that they are. As Karl Barth puts it, 'The doctrine of election is the sum of the Gospel because of all words that can be said or heard it is the best'.[35]

Although this study has concentrated on the Baptist tradition, its conclusions are of wider relevance. Baptists are a species of evangelical. The evangelical tradition stands in constant need of renewal. Sustained attention to election and predestination gives shape and purpose to evangelical action, placing it within the enduring ways of the faithful God who is working out a beneficent, merciful and eternal redemption. These doctrines enable us to understand what kind of God we serve and how this God is working out the divine purpose as year succeeds to year.

---

[34] Stewart, *Ten Myths*, 270.
[35] Barth, *Church Dogmatics* II/2, 3.

CHAPTER 3

John Bunyan: A Seventeenth-Century Evangelical?[1]

Peter J. Morden

Introduction

On 3 March 1847 the pioneering Baptist missionary Hannah Marshman lay on her deathbed in Serampore, India. One of those in attendance was W.H. Denham, fellow missionary and Principal at the Serampore College which Hannah's late husband, Joshua, had helped to found. Though dying, Hannah managed to summon the strength to say, 'Where is Bunyan's Pilgrim?' A copy of *The Pilgrim's Progress* by John Bunyan was close by and Denham held it in front of her so she could see it. According to him, Hannah asked him to read from the section which describes how 'Christian' crosses the 'River of Death'. This he proceeded to do. At Hannah's funeral service, which took place on 14 March, Denham spoke of this incident, saying that the passage from *The Pilgrim's Progress*

> which seemed to affect her most was the [one] where Christian begins to sink and Hopeful encourages him ... As I read I paused, for she occasionally spoke on the circumstances recorded ... At her wish we turned to Christian's removal and the remaining characters. That of Steadfast and his last words appeared to interest her greatly ... I could read no more. I knelt down and prayed that her feet like his might stand fast in that dread hour.[2]

Bunyan's allegory of the Christian life provided the concepts, characters and imagery which helped the evangelical missionary face death with confidence and which shaped the prayers of the man who ministered to her.

It is no surprise that *The Pilgrim's Progress* was close at hand when Hannah Marshman needed it. The work, originally published in 1678 with a second part following in 1684, was highly prized by a wide range of eighteenth- and nineteenth-

---

[1] I am grateful to David Bebbington and Crawford Gribben for reading drafts of this chapter and making helpful comments which I have incorporated. Of course, I alone am responsible for the views I have expressed.

[2] W.H. Denham, 'Memoir of the Late Mrs Marshman ... From the Funeral Address Delivered March 14, 1847', *Baptist Magazine* 39 (August, 1847) (London: Houlston and Stoneman, 1847), 481-82. She died on 5 March.

century evangelicals.³ Indeed, by the beginning of the nineteenth century it had become a 'key evangelical document',⁴ regarded by many as second only to the Bible in importance.⁵ As such, it had a significant shaping effect on evangelical spirituality. Those like Hannah Marshman who engaged in transcultural missionary service invariably carried this treasured book with them and they had it translated into languages and dialects as varied as Xhosa, Yoruba, Fanti, Chinese and Japanese so those they were ministering among could read it too.⁶ Other works by Bunyan did not enjoy the same transnational circulation but were nonetheless still revered by English-speaking evangelicals, with the nineteenth-century Baptist preacher Charles Haddon Spurgeon declaring, 'All Bunyan's books are precious.'⁷ Spurgeon never tired of commending the numerous different editions of these works as they poured forth from the Victorian presses.⁸ Other writers, such as one of Bunyan's biographers, John Brown, encouraged their readers to reflect on his life as well as his books.⁹ His theology and spirituality were alike worthy of emulation; indeed, according to the editor of a three-volume edition of Bunyan's collected works, George Offor, 'he was deeply versed in the mysteries of godliness'.¹⁰ Evangelicals were more than happy to acknowledge their indebtedness to Bunyan and they believed him to be a kindred spirit.

Bunyan and the Debate on the Emergence of Evangelicalism

For the reader who is conversant with recent debates concerning the origins of evangelicalism, the close connection between Bunyan and these later eighteenth- and nineteenth-century figures might well provoke reflection. David Bebbington, in his landmark study of 1989 entitled *Evangelicalism in Modern Britain*, argues that

---

³ For examples from the eighteenth century see, for instance, George Whitefield's 'Recommendatory Preface' to *The Works of that Eminent Servant of Christ, Mr John Bunyan ...* (2 vols; London: Johnston and Dilly, 1767–68), I, iii; William Cowper, 'Tirocinium; Or, a Review of Schools' (composed 1784) in *The Task* (London: John Sharpe, 1825), 194.

⁴ Isabel Hofmeyr, *The Portable Bunyan: A Transnational History of The Pilgrim's Progress* (Princeton: Princeton University Press, 2004), 1.

⁵ See, e.g., Joseph Ivimey, *A History of the English Baptists ...* (4 vols; London: Button *et al.*, 1811–30), II, 42.

⁶ Richard L. Greaves, *Glimpses of Glory: John Bunyan and English Dissent* (Stanford, CA: Stanford University Press, 2002), 612; Hofmeyr, *Portable Bunyan*, *passim*. Greaves' work is the outstanding scholarly biography. I have written an accessible introduction entitled *John Bunyan: The People's Pilgrim* (Farnham: CWR, 2013).

⁷ C.H. Spurgeon (ed.), *The Sword and The Trowel: A Record of Combat With Sin and Labour For The Lord* (London: Passmore and Alabaster, 1865–92), October 1882, 542.

⁸ See, e.g., Spurgeon (ed.), *Sword and Trowel*, December 1873, 566; January 1874, 37; May 1877, 234.

⁹ John Brown, *John Bunyan (1628–88): His Life, Times, and Work* [1885] (Frank M. Harrison; London: Hulbert, rev. edn, 1928), xxiv; cf. George Offor's 'Preface' to *The Works of John Bunyan* [*Works*] (ed. George Offor; 3 vols; London: Blackie and Son, 1856), I, v-vii.

¹⁰ Offor, 'Preface', *Works*, I, vii.

evangelicalism is a 'popular Protestant movement which has existed in Britain since the 1730s'.[11] In his view it was the eighteenth-century Evangelical Revival which heralded the emergence of the movement. He is careful to note that there was significant continuity between this evangelicalism and its immediate Protestant past. Nevertheless, he emphasises that there was enough discontinuity for the Evangelical Revival to constitute a new beginning, a position he has recently affirmed (with some qualifications). 'Not withstanding the weighty legacy from the past', he insists, 'the emergence of evangelicalism did represent a revolutionary development in Protestant history.'[12]

Bebbington's defence and restatement of his basic thesis is made in the final chapter of a multi-author work entitled *The Emergence of Evangelicalism: Exploring Historical Continuities* which was published in 2008. Other contributors, in different ways and to various degrees, seek to argue that there was more continuity between the evangelical movement of the eighteenth and nineteenth centuries and its Protestant antecedents than Bebbington allows. Garry Williams is one of the authors who strongly contends that Bebbington's argument for the dating of the movement 'does not hold', arguing the case for 'seeing Puritanism and the Reformation as themselves authentically evangelical movements'.[13] In this volume and elsewhere, the origin of evangelicalism is a subject for much debate and disagreement.

A study of Bunyan will certainly not settle this debate, but it ought to illuminate it. If the seventeenth-century Bunyan was held in such high esteem by later evangelicals and if he provided, particularly through *The Pilgrim's Progress*, language and imagery they used to describe their spiritual experience, we might expect there to be a fundamental continuity between his thinking and praxis and theirs. Conversely, if it can be shown that there was significant discontinuity then that surely strengthens the case for 'revolutionary development'. If even Bunyan, an iconic figure in modern evangelicalism, was qualitatively different from the later movement in important ways, then perhaps a major shift did indeed take place at the beginning of the eighteenth century. This study will seek to show that, whilst there were many similarities between Bunyan and later evangelicals, there were real differences in some crucial areas. The similarities will be considered first.

---

[11] D.W. Bebbington, *Evangelicalism in Modern Britain: A History from the 1730s to the 1980s* (London: Unwin Hyman, 1989), 1, cf. 21. Throughout this study I am using the word 'evangelical' in this sense.

[12] David W. Bebbington, 'Response', in Michael A.G. Haykin and Kenneth J. Stewart (eds), *The Emergence Of Evangelicalism: Exploring Historical Continuities* (Leicester: IVP, 2008), 432.

[13] Garry J. Williams, 'Enlightenment Epistemology and Eighteenth-Century Evangelical Doctrines of Assurance', in Haykin and Stewart, *Emergence of Evangelicalism*, 347.

Continuities

Bebbington defines the distinctive hallmarks of evangelicalism as 'biblicism', 'crucicentrism', 'conversionism' and 'activism'.[14] These four 'special marks' form a 'quadrilateral of priorities which is the basis of Evangelicalism'.[15] Although this approach has attracted some criticism[16] it has also gained widespread support, not least from the contributors to *The Emergence of Evangelicalism*, as Bebbington himself notes.[17] This four-dimensional model, then, seems a good place to start in discussing whether Bunyan can be regarded as a 'seventeenth-century evangelical'. Three of the four points of the quadrilateral will be analysed at this juncture, namely the stress on the Bible, the importance of the cross and the imperative for conversion.

BIBLICISM

Bunyan's attitude to the Bible is set out in his various works. The Scriptures, both Old and New Testament, constituted God's 'true sayings' and were his trustworthy 'counsel'.[18] In Bunyan's writings he always sought to pay close attention to the biblical text, as the title of his first published work, *Some Gospel Truths Opened According to the Scriptures*, suggests.[19] Moreover, for him it was insufficient just to know the Scriptures thoroughly and be able to argue a case from them. The Bible – God's word – needed to be trusted, 'reverenced' and lived out on a personal level. He challenged those of his readers who believed the Bible to live in a way which was consistent with that belief.[20] There is ample evidence to support the conclusion of his pastor until 1655, John Gifford, that his *modus operandi* as an author was to 'magnify' and 'exalt' the Bible, showing its 'worth, excellency, and usefulness'.[21]

As Bunyan expounded the Scriptures, there was an almost ubiquitous focus on Christ and his gospel. He believed that the whole of the Bible pointed to Christ, a commitment which could lead to some fanciful typologising of Old Testament passages. In his *Solomon's Temple Spiritualized* he related even the tiny details of the temple to Christ. For example, some of the 'golden nails' referred to in 2 Chronicles 3:9, fastened as they were to the Most Holy Place, represented 'Christ Jesus our Lord as fixed in his mediatory office in the heavens'.[22] The subtitle of *Solomon's Temple Spiritualized* was *Gospel Light Fetched out of the Temple at*

---

[14] Bebbington, *Evangelicalism in Modern Britain*, 5-17.

[15] Bebbington, *Evangelicalism in Modern Britain*, 2-3.

[16] See, e.g., Don A. Carson, *The Gagging of God: Christianity Confronts Pluralism* (Leicester: IVP, 1996), 449-450.

[17] Bebbington, 'Response', 425-426.

[18] J. Bunyan, *A Few Sighs From Hell, or the Groans of a Damned Soul* [1658] in *Works*, III, 720.

[19] J. Bunyan, *Some Gospel Truths Opened According to the Scriptures* [1656] in *Works*, II, 129-175.

[20] Bunyan, *A Few Sighs From Hell*, 720.

[21] John Gifford, 'Preface', *A Few Sighs From Hell*, 672.

[22] J. Bunyan, *Solomon's Temple Spiritualized* [1688] in *Works*, III, 499.

Jerusalem.²³ In this particular work, as elsewhere, references to 'Christ' and 'gospel' were never far away.

As far as Bunyan's personal appropriation of Scripture is concerned, his 'spiritual autobiography', *Grace Abounding to the Chief of Sinners*, is important evidence.²⁴ This foundational Bunyan work, which especially covers the years 1650–60, is peppered with biblical quotations and allusions, including twenty-five references to the book of Hebrews alone.²⁵ These references include a number to Hebrews 12:22-24, verses which were important in leading him to a more confident assurance.²⁶ *Grace Abounding* as a whole reveals Bunyan wrestling with the text of Scripture, seeking to base his life upon it. His intense struggle for assurance will be analysed in more detail in the second half of this chapter, but the point to note here is that he was a thoroughgoing 'biblicist', someone who immersed himself in the text of Scripture. Evangelicals recognised this and celebrated it. Although the more sober of them might baulk at the way he spiritualised Old Testament passages,²⁷ his experiential biblicism was perceived as being congruent with their own. In 1814 Joseph Ivimey observed with approval, 'All his arguments and illustrations are drawn from the Scriptures, and prove his extensive knowledge and deep penetration.'²⁸ Spurgeon pointed to Bunyan's biblicism as a model for his own generation:

> Oh, that you and I might get into the very heart of the Word of God, and get that Word into ourselves! ... I would quote John Bunyan as an example of what I mean ... Prick him anywhere; and you will find that his blood is Bibline, the very essence of the Bible flows from him. He cannot speak without quoting a text, for his soul is full of the Word of God.²⁹

Bunyan shared the basic evangelical commitment to live out of the text of Scripture; indeed, he was perceived as exemplifying this and providing a standard to aim at.

CRUCICENTRISM

Bunyan's work also exhibits a thoroughgoing commitment to the cross of Christ. True, his epic allegory, *The Holy War*, has surprisingly little place for the cross, a

---

²³ Bunyan, *Solomon's Temple Spiritualized*, 460.
²⁴ J. Bunyan, *Grace Abounding to the Chief of Sinners* [1666] in *Works*, I, 1-46.
²⁵ The paragraphs in *Grace Abounding* are numbered. The references occur in paragraphs 116, 121, 141, 148, 173, 196 (three references), 203, 208, 209, 216, 221, 223, 224, 225, 229, 239, 262, 263, 322 (two references), 332.
²⁶ Bunyan, *Grace Abounding*, 40 (paragraphs 262 and 263).
²⁷ Even Spurgeon was cautious about *Solomon's Temple Spiritualized*. See C.H. Spurgeon, *Lectures To My Students* (3 vols; London: Passmore and Alabaster, n.d.), I, 112-13.
²⁸ Ivimey, *History of English Baptists*, II, 41.
²⁹ C.H. Spurgeon, *Autobiography: Compiled from his Diary, Letters, and Records ...* (4 vols; London: Passmore and Alabaster, 1899), IV, 268.

point which has drawn criticism from evangelical writers.[30] But elsewhere he insists that the cross is the place where sin is dealt with. Those who received salvation did so only through the sacrifice of Christ; they were justified only by his blood and reconciled to God only by his death.[31]

The Pilgrim's Progress can be cited as an example of this crucicentrism. One of the pivotal passages sees Christian losing his heavy burden of sin at the cross. He comes to a place 'somewhat ascending' upon which stands a cross and, a little below it, a 'sepulchre'. The narrative continues,

> So I saw in my dream, that just as Christian came up with the cross, his burden loosed from off his shoulders, and fell from off his back, and began to tumble, and so continued to do till it came to the mouth of the sepulchre, where it fell in, and I saw it no more.
>
> Then was Christian glad and lightsome, and said with a merry heart, 'He hath given me rest by his sorrow, and life by his death.' Then he stood still a while, to look and wonder; for it was very surprising to him that the sight of the cross should thus ease him of his burden. He looked, therefore, and looked again, even till the springs that were in his head sent the waters down his cheeks.[32]

The cross is the place where sin is decisively dealt with. Paradoxically, life for the sinner came only through Christ's death. Bunyan skilfully evokes deep feeling in his imaginative description of Christian's response to his burden coming loose and 'tumbling' out of sight. Christian was first 'glad', 'lightsome' and 'merry' and then, as he continued to contemplate the cross, wept tears of gratitude to his saviour. As with his approach to the Bible, the atonement was not just a doctrine to be believed, it was to be appropriated by the believer so it became part of his or her experience.

Such crucicentrism was ubiquitous in later evangelicalism. Just one example can be cited here, that of Andrew Fuller, the eighteenth-century Baptist pastor and missionary statesman. In a sermon, entitled 'Conformity to the Death of Christ', he declared, 'The death of Christ is a subject of so much importance in Christianity as to be essential to it ... It is not so much a member of the body of Christian doctrine as the life blood that runs through the whole of it. The doctrine of the cross is the Christian doctrine.'[33] In another message, entitled 'Preaching Christ', he urged gospel ministers to 'hold up Christ's atonement and mediation as the only ground of a sinner's hope'.[34] The saving work of Christ on the cross had to be believed by the minister and preached with conviction, for without it there was no salvation.

---

[30] For a recent example, see Faith Cook, *Fearless Pilgrim: The Life and Times of John Bunyan* (Darlington: Evangelical Press, 2008), 382. For the text of *The Holy War, Made by Shaddai upon Diabolus ...* [1682], see *Works*, III, 244-373.

[31] J. Bunyan, *Christ a Compleat Saviour* [1692], in *Works*, I, 207.

[32] J. Bunyan, *The Pilgrim's Progress* [1678], in *Works*, III, 102.

[33] Andrew Fuller, 'Conformity to the Death of Christ' (n.d.), in *The Complete Works of the Rev Andrew Fuller ...* (ed. Andrew Gunton Fuller; ed. J. Belcher; 3 vols; Harrisonburg, VA: Sprinkle Publications, 3rd edn, 1988 [rev. edn, 1845]) I, 310.

[34] Andrew Fuller, 'Preaching Christ' (n.d.), in *Fuller's Works*, I, 501-504.

Bunyan was an important writer for Fuller, as we will see. The two men stood in the same essential tradition of experimental crucicentrism. Spurgeon also lauded Bunyan for his focus on the atonement. As well as commending other reprints of Bunyan works, he himself republished the treatise *The Water Of Life*, making it clear in his Preface that he had taken this step because it was a 'precious' work, pointing readers to Christ and his cross.[35] As with biblicism, here there is evidence of continuity.

CONVERSIONISM

Bunyan's own conversion experience is covered in the second half of this study, but it is important to establish here that what Bebbington calls conversionism was important to him. He was a Puritan and a Calvinist, but he combined a commitment to strict Calvinism with a vigorous evangelistic ministry which was carried on through preaching and in print. In his very first book, *Some Gospel Truths Opened*, he addressed those who had not put their personal faith in Christ, saying, 'In a word, you that have not yet laid hold on the Lord Jesus Christ, for eternal life, lay hold upon him; upon his righteousness, blood, resurrection, ascension, intercession, and wait for his second coming to "judge the world in righteousness".'[36] The title of one of his later works, *Come and Welcome to Jesus Christ*, aptly sums up his applied, invitational approach.[37] He remained a lifelong proponent of a thoroughgoing Calvinism, declaring in *Come and Welcome* that, 'Coming to Christ is by virtue of the gift, promise, and drawing of the Father.' Yet sinners who wanted to trust in Christ should be encouraged for, he reasoned, the very fact that they wanted to come to Christ was *prima facie* evidence that God was drawing them. '[T]hou art a coming', Bunyan said, 'therefore God hath given thee, promised thee, and is drawing thee to Jesus Christ.'[38] *Come and Welcome* was based on Jesus' words as recorded in John 6:37, 'Him that cometh to me I will in no wise cast out.' Bunyan believed this verse was a great encouragement to sinners to 'come' to Christ. He was also sure it gave him the mandate to apply himself unstintingly to evangelistic ministry.

Conversionism such as this was characteristic of eighteenth- and nineteenth-century evangelicalism. Indeed, Bunyan's approach was influential in encouraging some later figures to adopt invitational evangelistic preaching for themselves. Andrew Fuller belonged to a church where the dominant theology was the high Calvinism associated with the early eighteenth-century Particular Baptist theologian John Gill. As a result, Fuller's minister, John Eve, 'had little or nothing to say to the unconverted'.[39] By his own testimony, Fuller was helped to a more evangelical position at least in part through his reading of Bunyan. When he compared Bunyan's

---

[35] J. Bunyan, *The Water Of Life ... With Preface By C.H. Spurgeon* (London: Passmore and Alabaster, 1868), vi. The *Water of Life* was written in 1688.

[36] J. Bunyan, *Some Gospel Truths Opened* [1656] in *Works*, II, 169.

[37] Bunyan, *Come and Welcome*, 240-99.

[38] Bunyan, *Come and Welcome*, 284.

[39] See Peter J. Morden, *Offering Christ to the World: Andrew Fuller (1754–1815) and the Revival in Eighteenth Century Particular Baptist Life* (Carlisle: Paternoster, 2003), 16.

approach to that of Gill, he recognised their theological systems were 'not the same' for, whilst both were Calvinists, Bunyan 'held with the free offer of salvation to sinners without distinction', something that Gill did not.[40] Fuller was influenced in theology and practice by a whole host of factors,[41] the most important single figure being the eighteenth-century New England Congregationalist Jonathan Edwards.[42] Bunyan's influence was, comparatively speaking, not great. Nevertheless, Fuller does mention Bunyan and believed he was standing in the same tradition as he, so that when the expansive evangelical Calvinism represented by Fuller's theological treatise *The Gospel Worthy of All Acceptation* came to be dubbed 'Fullerism' its author protested in the following terms: why not call it 'Bunyanism' instead?[43] Fuller was sure that in moving towards a more evangelical position and espousing conversionism he was standing in a tradition which included Bunyan, a man whose writings had assisted his own theological development.

REFLECTIONS ON THE CONTINUITIES

It comes as little surprise that Bunyan's approaches to the Bible, the cross and conversion were fundamentally congruent with later evangelicalism. Bebbington always argued that, as far as these three points of his quadrilateral were concerned, there was much common ground between evangelicals and earlier movements such as Puritanism, the tradition in which Bunyan broadly stands.[44] Indeed, in *Evangelicalism in Modern Britain* he explicitly notes that *The Pilgrim's Progress* was beloved of the eighteenth-century Methodist preachers.[45] The similarities between Bunyan and later evangelicalism set out in the first half of this study are striking.

Another parallel can be adduced, for Bunyan also evinced a certain irenic spirit, a 'catholicity' which led him, for example, to espouse open communion principles: both credobaptists and dissenting paedobaptists were welcome to the Lord's Table in Bedford. This was a view he defended in debate with the London Particular Baptist, William Kiffin, who advocated closed communion.[46] Bunyan maintained friendships with paedobaptist Dissenters such as the Congregationalist John Owen, who is reputed to have declared he would 'gladly relinquish all his learning' in return for

---

[40] John Ryland, Jr., *The ... Life and Death of the Rev. Andrew Fuller* (London: Button and Son, 1818), 36.

[41] See Morden, *Offering Christ to the World*, 23-51.

[42] As shown by Chris Chun, *The Legacy of Jonathan Edwards in the Theology of Andrew Fuller* (Leiden: Brill, 2012), 32-65.

[43] John W. Morris, *Memoirs of the Life and Death of the Rev. Andrew Fuller* (London: Wightman and Cramp, 1826). Fuller also suggested 'Owenism' as a possible epithet, after John Owen.

[44] Bebbington, *Evangelicalism in Modern Britain*, 34-35; 'Response', 427-48.

[45] Bebbington, *Evangelicalism in Modern Britain*, 35.

[46] J. Bunyan, *Differences in Judgement About Water Baptism, No Bar to Communion* [1673] in *Works*, II, 616-47.

Bunyan's abilities as a popular preacher.[47] Such a 'peaceable' approach in some ways prefigures the evangelical ecumenism of the eighteenth and nineteenth centuries. (His 'catholic spirit' was noted with approval by none other than George Whitefield.[48]) Yet such an argument should not be pushed too far. Bunyan was more interested in questions of church order than many evangelicals,[49] he was a staunch opponent of the Church of England of the Restoration, and he engaged in weighty polemic against the Quaker, Edward Burroughs.[50] Nevertheless, his overall approach was more conciliatory than the norm for his times. Yet, when the continuities are noted (and doubtless more could have been highlighted), I want to contend that there were significant differences between Bunyan and 'modern evangelicalism', however much evangelicals may have revered him and drawn from him. It is to the theme of discontinuity, then, that this study now turns.

Discontinuities

ASSURANCE OF SALVATION

One of the discontinuities centres around the issue of assurance of salvation. Indeed, Bunyan's 'conversion narrative', the aforementioned *Grace Abounding*, exhibits a number of features which do not fit with what became the evangelical norm. He relates how he experienced some conviction of sin when still a child of 'but nine or ten'. He was afflicted, he said, both 'night and day', trembling as he thought of the impending day of judgement and the 'fearful torments of hell fire' which would surely follow.[51] Although these 'terrible dreams' did leave him for a while,[52] doubt regularly returned, and with increasing force, particularly following his reading of two Puritan books, Arthur Dent's *The Plain Man's Pathway to Heaven* (1601) and Lewis Bayly's *The Practice of Piety* (3rd edn, 1613), which his first wife brought into their marriage as her dowry.[53]

As he fought his way to some resolution, Bunyan tried conformity to religious and moral standards, but this 'outward reformation' only brought temporary relief.[54] He overheard some women from John Gifford's dissenting congregation in Bedford talking in the street about their faith.[55] Impressed by the spiritual tenor of their

---

[47] Ivimey, *History of English Baptists*, II, 41.

[48] J. Bunyan, *Peaceable Principles and True* [1674], in *Works*, II, 648; Whitefield, 'Recommendatory Preface', iv.

[49] See, e.g., the letter he and other leaders wrote to Mary Tilney, a member of the Bedford meeting who had moved to London, in Ivimey, *History of English Baptists*, II, 37-40.

[50] For examples of Bunyan's opposition to Anglicanism, see Greaves, *Glimpses of Glory*, 152-58, 496-97; for his debate with Burroughs, see *A Vindication of Gospel Truths* [1657], in *Works*, II, 176-214.

[51] Bunyan, *Grace Abounding*, 6 (paras 6-7).

[52] Bunyan, *Grace Abounding*, 6 (para. 8).

[53] Bunyan, *Grace Abounding*, 7 (para. 16).

[54] Bunyan, *Grace Abounding*, 9 (para. 30).

[55] Bunyan, *Grace Abounding*, 9 (paras 37-38).

conversation, he started to attend their meetings. At this time, he says, 'I began to look into the Bible with new eyes, and read as I never did before; and especially the epistles of the apostle Paul were sweet and pleasant to me; and, indeed, I was never out of the Bible, either by reading or meditation ...' We might assume this marked his conversion, but as far as Bunyan was concerned this was not the case, for he insisted that he was 'still crying out to God' that he might 'know the truth, and way to heaven and glory'.[56] *Grace Abounding* continues in this vein; indeed, the moment of Bunyan's conversion is difficult to identify. As Crawford Gribben states, the reader cannot be sure when God's work in Bunyan's life becomes 'saving': the moment of his regeneration 'is a closely guarded secret'.[57] Bunyan wrote that at one point he

> could have spoken of [God's] love, and have told of His mercy to me, even to the very crows, that sat upon the ploughed lands before me, had they been capable to have understood me: wherefore I said in my soul, with much gladness, Well, I would I had a pen and ink here, I would write this down before I go any farther; for surely I will not forget this forty years hence.

But if he believed this was the moment of conversion he does not say so. Moreover, his joy was not to last forty years, for 'within less than forty days' he began 'to question all again'.[58] Later evangelicals tended to speak of their conversions in much more definite terms. Here, then, there is a difference.

Allied to these doubts about the moment of conversion is Bunyan's protracted struggle for assurance of salvation. He feared he was a 'reprobate', was plagued by doubts, and terrified he had committed the unforgiveable sin of Mark 3:39.[59] In between these times of agony and despair there were occasional moments of relief,[60] but the dominant motifs are those of struggle and fear. There are no dates in *Grace Abounding*, so it is hard to know exactly how long these struggles lasted, although his period of conviction and uncertainty spanned at least the years 1650–57,[61] lasting long after Bunyan had been admitted into fellowship in Gifford's church.[62] His battles over assurance were long and deep.

The uncertainties which characterise *Grace Abounding* have been recognised by Bunyan scholars. Gribben speaks of how the work oscillates between 'hope and despair', exhibits a 'cyclical', repetitive pattern and 'refuses to offer closure',[63]

---

[56] Bunyan, *Grace Abounding*, 10 (para. 46).

[57] Crawford Gribben, *The Puritan Millennium: Literature and Theology, 1550–1682* (Milton Keynes: Paternoster, 2008), 208.

[58] Bunyan, *Grace Abounding*, 17 (para. 93). He does say, 'at times, I was helped to believe that it was a true manifestation of grace unto my soul', 17 (para. 94).

[59] Bunyan, *Grace Abounding*, 16 (para. 87); 21 (paras 122-24); 24 (para. 148).

[60] Bunyan, *Grace Abounding*, 20 (para. 117).

[61] See Morden, *John Bunyan*, chs 3 and 4.

[62] See, for example, Bunyan, *Grace Abounding*, 31 (para. 198); 39 (para. 253).

[63] Gribben, *Puritan Millennium*, 209.

whilst Anne Hawkins writes that Bunyan's conversion narrative has 'little sense of structure', and is a 'kind of conversion which is by definition diffuse, repetitive, and cumulative'.[64] We might counter that there is a measure of closure: Bunyan does at last attain some assurance,[65] and although the book is cyclical there is a discernible trajectory from despair to hope, albeit one that unfolds only by painful, incremental steps with many false starts and dramatic falls. Nevertheless, the cumulative impression given by *Grace Abounding* to many readers is one of uncertainty. Sure knowledge of salvation is hard to come by.

Bunyan's writing in *Grace Abounding* was influenced by wider Puritan thinking. Gribben writes,

> Bunyan's continued uncertainty as to whether or not he was saved simply enacted William Perkins' teaching that 'every new act of sin requires a new act of faith and repentance'. Perkins viewed conversion as more of a cyclical process than a linear teleology: the converted could always be reconverted.[66]

Much Puritan spirituality emphasised that assurance of salvation would only be attained after a long and painful struggle, with the outcome of that struggle far from certain.[67] According to Thomas Brooks, the Christian who wanted to know he was truly saved 'must work, and sweat and weep ... He must not only dig, but he must dig deep before he can come to the golden mine. Assurance is such precious gold, that a man must win it before he can wear it.'[68] Only the elect would be saved, and if people were truly one of that number then once they had exercised faith there would be signs that God was working in their lives, leading them to holiness and good works. Through regular, rigorous self-examination, these signs might be discerned and individuals could potentially inch their way towards assurance of salvation. Brooks, in his *Precious Remedies Against Satan's Devices*, offered a checklist of ten marks of grace an anxious person should look for, and other preachers supplied similar lists, often with a strong emphasis on 'works'.[69] This 'experimental

---

[64] Anne Hawkins, 'The Double-Conversion in Bunyan's *Grace Abounding*', *Philological Quarterly* 61 (1982), 259.

[65] See especially, Bunyan, *Grace Abounding*, 40 (para. 262).

[66] Gribben, *Puritan Millennium*, 209, citing William Perkins, *The Art of Prophesying* (Edinburgh: Banner of Truth, 1996 [1606]), 62.

[67] John Coffey has shown that Puritan views on assurance were more diverse than has often been supposed, whilst accepting the view I am describing in this paragraph as the mainstream one. See his 'Puritanism, Evangelicalism and the Evangelical Protestant Tradition', in Haykin and Stewart (eds), *Emergence Of Evangelicalism*, 265-66.

[68] Thomas Brooks, *Heaven on Earth* (London: Banner of Truth, 1961 [1654]), 139.

[69] See David K. Gillett, *Trust and Obey: Explorations in Evangelical Spirituality* (London: Darton, Longman and Todd, 1993), 43; Bebbington, *Evangelicalism in Modern Britain*, 44.

predestinarianism'[70] combined in Bunyan with a tendency to depression to produce the agonised soul-searching which fills page after page of *Grace Abounding*.[71]

Here there are contrasts with later evangelicalism. Evangelical conversion narratives tended to be clearer and more linear than Bunyan's and, most importantly, evangelicalism exhibited a much more confident view of assurance. In the eighteenth century, Arminians such as the Wesley brothers and Calvinists such as George Whitefield and Howell Harris habitually spoke of *knowing* they were children of God.[72] Moreover, in evangelical teaching such assurance was normal for all believers and would most likely accompany conversion or follow on soon after. Rather than spending a lifetime pressing on to make their 'calling and election sure', those who had exercised faith in Christ could have assurance of salvation grounded on their felt experience and the objective promises of God to save all who turned to him.[73] It is true that some eighteenth-century evangelicals, such as John Newton, exhibited a more typically 'Puritan' approach to assurance,[74] and these may have been more numerous than previously thought, especially in Calvinistic Dissent.[75] Nevertheless, they were still in the minority and a more confident doctrine of assurance increasingly became the norm. Bunyan's approach was out of step with the new, more confident thinking.

C.H. Spurgeon provides an example of this more certain attitude to assurance from the nineteenth century. As already noted, Spurgeon was a devotee of Bunyan, but he did not follow him or other Puritans such as Brooks in their approach to assurance. He had a decisive, clearcut conversion experience in January 1850 and came to a confident assurance of salvation within a few months. 'I felt as sure that I was forgiven as before I felt sure of condemnation', he said.[76] His mature approach to assurance was that it was the birthright of every believer.[77]

---

[70] John Coffey and Paul C.H. Lim, 'Introduction', in John Coffey and Paul C.H. Lim (eds), *The Cambridge Companion to Puritanism* (Cambridge: Cambridge University Press, 2008), 4.

[71] Bunyan's proclivity for depression is described and analysed by Greaves, *Glimpses of Glory*, 51-60, 174-76.

[72] See Bebbington, *Evangelicalism in Modern Britain*, 45.

[73] See the evidence amassed by Bebbington, *Evangelicalism in Modern Britain*, 45-46. 1 Peter 1:10 was an important text in much Puritan spirituality.

[74] D. Bruce Hindmarsh, *John Newton and the English Evangelical Tradition* (Oxford: Clarendon Press, 1996), chapter 6.

[75] See David W. Bebbington, 'Evangelical Conversion, c. 1740–1850', *Scottish Bulletin of Evangelical Theology* 18.2 (2000), 122-24.

[76] Spurgeon, *Autobiography* 1, 111, cf. 112.

[77] See, e.g., C.H. Spurgeon, 'The Blessings Of Full Assurance', *Metropolitan Tabernacle Pulpit* [*MTP*] (London: Passmore and Alabaster, 1861–1917), 34, Sermon No. 2023, 1 John 5:13, delivered 13 May 1888, 273-76.

How was this certainty to be achieved and sustained? Although there was some development in Spurgeon's thought,[78] his mature approach was to reject the Puritan attitudes which mark *Grace Abounding*. Any kind of self-examination which would take a believer away 'from the cross-foot' was to be eschewed, for it proceeded in entirely the 'wrong direction'.[79] Spurgeon declared that those who felt 'very poor' would not get rich by looking through their 'empty cupboards'. 'No, no; if our graces are to be revived, we must begin with a renewed consciousness of pardon through the precious blood.' The only way to get this, said Spurgeon, was to go to the cross again, as believers had done 'at first'.[80] They were not to look inside themselves for evidence of their salvation; rather they were to look away from 'self' towards Christ and his substitutionary death. Assuming this focus on Christ and the cross was maintained, assurance of salvation would be maintained as well.[81]

One of the sources shaping this evangelical doctrine of assurance was the eighteenth-century Enlightenment. It is increasingly recognised that the Enlightenment was a complex and diverse phenomenon,[82] and consequently it is difficult to nail down a precise definition of what it meant to be 'enlightened'. Nevertheless, it certainly involved an assertion of 'the ability of human reason to discover truth'. Enlightenment empiricism encouraged free enquiry in an effort to ascertain the facts of whatever the matter under examination might be. That which had been 'found by investigation' could then 'be known with confidence'.[83] Bebbington has shown how the Enlightenment impinged on eighteenth-century evangelical thinking about assurance.[84] It is not difficult to see similar connections between Spurgeon's approach and 'enlightened' patterns of thinking. Take the following from his *Autobiography* as an example:

> Has Jesus saved me? I dare not speak with any hesitation here; I know He has. His word is true, therefore I am saved. My evidence that I am saved does not lie in the fact

---

[78] For an extended discussion of Spurgeon and assurance, see my *'Communion with Christ and his People': The Spirituality of C.H. Spurgeon* (Oxford: Regent's Park College, 2010), 71-75.

[79] Spurgeon, *Autobiography*, I, 161-62.

[80] C.H. Spurgeon, 'Redemption Through Blood, The Gracious Forgiveness Of Sins', *MTP* 37, S. No. 2207, Ephesians 1:7, n.d., 311.

[81] Spurgeon, 'The Blessings Of Full Assurance', 270-73.

[82] See, e.g., Bruce K. Ward, *Redeeming the Enlightenment: Christianity and the Liberal Virtues* (Grand Rapids, MI: Eerdmans, 2010), 2-3.

[83] David W. Bebbington, *Holiness in Nineteenth-Century England* (Carlisle: Paternoster, 2000) 33, 35; cf. Bebbington, *Evangelicalism in Modern Britain*, 48.

[84] This association has been challenged, see, e.g., Williams, 'Enlightenment Epistemology', 344-74. Nevertheless, although the Enlightenment was perhaps 'less the inspiration' for the typical evangelical view of assurance than was previously thought, it was still important, see Bebbington, 'Response', 422. Mark Noll has written that 'evangelicalism revealed its closest affinities to the Enlightenment … in a dramatically heightened concern for the assurance of salvation'. See his *The Rise of Evangelicalism: The Age of Edwards, Whitefield and the Wesleys* (Leicester: IVP, 2004), 141.

that I preach, or that I do this or that. All my hope lies in this, that Jesus Christ came to save sinners. I am a sinner, I trust Him, then He came to save me, and I am saved; I live habitually in the enjoyment of this blessed fact, and it is long since I have doubted the truth of it, for I have His own word to sustain my faith.[85]

Spurgeon's argument reveals an Enlightenment confidence that truth can be known. The particular truth in question, assurance of salvation, was based on Christ and his word and verified in Spurgeon's own experience. Even more 'enlightened' is the following: 'True Christian assurance is not a matter of guesswork, but of mathematical precision. It is capable of logical proof, and is no rhapsody or poetical fiction.'[86] By speaking in this way Spurgeon showed himself to be significantly influenced by Enlightenment patterns of thinking.

It ought to be noted that although Bunyan did attain a real measure of personal assurance, he never repudiated the uncertain and protracted approach to the issue that stood behind his experience as chronicled in *Grace Abounding*, and his spiritual autobiography was revised and reprinted with his approval on five separate occasions before his death in 1688.[87] Moreover, although he encouraged anxious sinners to trust in Christ in books such as *Come and Welcome*, he also instructed them to engage in self-examination. In his *Mapp of Salvation*, published in 1663, he set out pictorially the respective ways of the elect and the reprobate. According to the *Mapp*, the elect experience many workings of grace in their lives, including 'humility at the sight of sin' and 'watchfulness against it', together with growth in 'holinesse', prayer and love for the law of God. Eventually, the 'weary saint' is welcomed into eternity. Bunyan was explicit in challenging the reader to study this part of the *Mapp* and then 'look into thy heart, as in a book, and see if thou canst read the same'. This promoted self-examination which was likely to be protracted, detailed and introspective. Those who sensed that their own experience did not tally with that side of Bunyan's chart were told to be afraid and to look at the other side, which set out the progress of the reprobate to the 'everlasting fire'.[88] On the issue of assurance, Bunyan's Puritan casuistry diverged from the approach typical of later 'enlightened' evangelicalism.

ESCHATOLOGY, ACTIVITY AND MISSION

I want to argue that eschatology, activity and mission represent further points of divergence. This might seem surprising. In respect of eschatology, were not the Puritans postmillennial, and did not this 'Puritan hope' help fire the evangelical missionary movement, of which Hannah Marshman was such a distinguished

---

[85] Spurgeon, *Autobiography*, I, 112.

[86] Spurgeon, 'The Blessing Of Full Assurance', 268.

[87] The sixth edition of *Grace Abounding* appeared in 1688: see Greaves, *Glimpses of Glory*, 640.

[88] J. Bunyan, *Mapp of Salvation, Shewing the Order and Causes of Salvation and Damnation* in *Works*, III, n.p.

representative?[89] It is certainly true that one of the distinguishing features of Puritanism was a heightened interest in the millennium, and it is further the case that Bunyan shared this stress. But Puritan eschatology was more complex and multi-faceted than has often been supposed and straight lines cannot be drawn between Bunyan's approach and that of the eighteenth-century postmillennial evangelicals. In his posthumously published *Exposition of the First Ten Chapters of Genesis*, he wrote of the 'glory' the church would have in the 'latter day' when 'Christ shall set up his kingdom on earth'.[90] World history as a whole would last seven thousand years and Christ's reign on earth would take place in the seventh millennium. But where does the second coming fit into this schema? As Gribben shows, Bunyan is not clear on this question in this *Exposition*, hovering 'ambiguously between pre- and postmillennialism'. 'He never informs the reader whether Christ's reign is spiritual – *through* the saints – or physically *with* them.'[91] *The Holy War* is no clearer on this question. Gribben writes that,

> far from demonstrating a linear historiography culminating in a millennium and an apocalypse, as we might expect from a text purporting to be an allegory of universal history, *The Holy War* mirrors the more cyclical experience of *Grace Abounding*'s protagonist.[92]

In short, it is far from certain that Bunyan was postmillennial in the way that later generations would understand the term. Overall, his eschatology is ambivalent.

Eighteenth-century evangelical eschatology tended to be quite different. The postmillennialism of Jonathan Edwards was robust. One of his treatises, the short title of which was *An Humble Attempt*, was rooted in the movement to establish regular prayer meetings for revival which had begun in evangelicalism in the 1740s and which criss-crossed the Atlantic.[93] Noteworthy for us is the way Edwards' appeal to his readers was grounded in an optimistic postmillennial eschatology. At the beginning of Part 2, in which Edwards set out what he believed to be the biblical basis for the so-called 'Concert of Prayer', he stated,

> It is evident from Scripture, that there is yet remaining a great advancement of the interest and the kingdom of Christ in this world, by an abundant outpouring of the Spirit of God, far greater and more extensive than ever yet has been. 'Tis certain, that

---

[89] See Iain H. Murray, *The Puritan Hope* (Edinburgh: Banner of Truth, 1971).

[90] J. Bunyan, *An Exposition of the First Ten Chapters of Genesis* [1691], in *Works*, II, 456.

[91] Gribben, *Puritan Millennium*, 213.

[92] See Gribben, *Puritan Millennium*, 213.

[93] Jonathan Edwards, *An Humble Attempt to Promote Explicit Agreement and Visible Union of God's People in Extraordinary Prayer* [1747] in *The Works of Jonathan Edwards* 5 (ed. Stephen J. Stein; New Haven, CT: Yale University Press, 1977), 309-436.

many things, which are spoken concerning a glorious time of the church's enlargement and prosperity in the latter days, have never yet been fulfilled.[94]

As the argument proceeded, Edwards sought to show how both the Old and New Testaments pointed forward to this latter day glory. Texts he cited include Isaiah 11:9, 'The earth shall be full of the knowledge of the Lord, as the waters cover the seas', and Romans 11:32, 'God hath concluded them all in unbelief, that he might have mercy upon all', a verse which he applied to the conversion of both the Jewish and the Gentile nations, not a part of each, but 'the fullness of both, the whole lump'.[95] Overall, he believed it was 'very evident, that the main fulfilment of those prophecies, that speak of the glorious advancement of Christ's Kingdom on earth, is still to come'.[96] An enlightened confidence can be discerned – 'it is evident', ''Tis certain', 'very evident'; so can postmillennialism – the glorious time would take place 'in this world, by *an abundant outpouring of the Spirit of God*'.[97] Here was sure and certain knowledge which, together with a particular reading of the signs of the times, Edwards believed should 'animate Christians with hopes of imminent 'success' as they joined together in prayer for revival.[98] Whilst there is a measure of continuity between Bunyan and Edwards, important dimensions of their respective eschatologies and their practical outworkings stand in sharp contrast.

It was this optimistic Edwardsean eschatology which played a significant role in animating the late eighteenth- and early nineteenth-century English Baptists who gave themselves unstintingly to intercessory prayer for the conversion of the world. Edwards' *An Humble Attempt* was read with excitement in the 1780s by Andrew Fuller and his colleagues, John Ryland, Jr, and John Sutcliff, who were spurred on to issue their own 'Call to Prayer' in 1784.[99] They reprinted *An Humble Attempt* themselves in 1789, and were open and explicit about the debt they owed to Edwards' work.[100] Indeed, the eschatology of Fuller, the premier English Baptist theologian, was remarkably similar to that of Edwards, as Chris Chun has shown.[101]

Crucially, the English Baptists combined this eschatology and commitment to prayer with a similarly Edwardsean emphasis on the use of 'means', a stress which

---

[94] Edwards, *Humble Attempt*, 329.

[95] Edwards, *Humble Attempt*, 334.

[96] Edwards, *Humble Attempt*, 335.

[97] My italics. Because Edwards' view is recognisably 'postmillennial' as later generations would understand it, I believe it is legitimate to apply it to Edwards, even though, as Crawford Gribben shows, the term itself did not become current until later. See his 'Evangelical Eschatology and the "Puritan Hope"', in Haykin and Stewart (eds), *Emergence of Evangelicalism*, 379.

[98] Edwards, *Humble Attempt*, 351. For some of Edwards' speculations on contemporary history, see 422-24.

[99] Morden, *Offering Christ to the World*, 120-26.

[100] Sutcliff's 'Preface' to the English edition is included in *The Works of Jonathan Edwards* (ed. E. Hickman; 2 vols; Edinburgh: Banner of Truth, 1974 [1834]), II, 278-79.

[101] Chun, *Legacy of Jonathan Edwards*, 66-83.

led to prayer being combined with vigorous, sustained action.[102] There were many strenuous and successful efforts for evangelism at home, and in 1792 the Baptist Missionary Society (BMS) was founded with William Carey as its most prominent missionary. Carey and his party arrived in Bengal in November 1793, to be joined by the Marshmans six years later. Carey's famous maxim, 'Expect great things [from God]; attempt great things [for God]' encapsulates the Baptist evangelicals' approach.[103] Suffused with an optimistic eschatology, fired with a passion for revival, and committed to an energetic, pragmatic programme of missionary expansion which embraced the use of all appropriate 'means', they were ready to take on the world.

It should be noted that Bunyan was 'active' too. He gave himself to preaching and pastoring, and travelled widely as an itinerant. True, he was imprisoned for twelve years of his life for refusing to conform to the Church of England and preaching at an illegal conventicle, but it is hardly fair to take this as an example of lack of activity! Indeed, he used this time to write, and his output was prodigious.[104] Evangelicals recognised this, with Joseph Ivimey – himself a product of the revival in eighteenth-century Baptist life – lauding the Bedford man for his 'labours' which were 'very great'.[105] 'Activism', the fourth point of Bebbington's evangelical quadrilateral, seems characteristic of Bunyan too.

Yet even if Bunyan's activity is properly acknowledged, the activism of later evangelicals such as those who formed the BMS was still different from his in some important respects. Firstly, their activism was different in nature. It was more confident, grounded (as has already been argued) on full assurance of salvation and driven by an optimistic postmillennial hope. In addition, they enthusiastically embraced the use of 'means' and pursued a revivalist agenda with remarkable energy, praying, preaching, visiting, itinerating, writing, publishing, networking, engaging in social action and generally working unstintingly. Their pragmatic approach led them to eschew doctrinal speculation and aim for a theological simplicity which cleared away all obstacles to passionate, invitational gospel preaching, an approach exemplified by Fuller's modified evangelical Calvinism.[106] This dynamic, creative, practical activism became ingrained in the evangelical psyche and continued on into the nineteenth century, even as millennial expectations shifted. By contrast a significant amount of Bunyan's activity, when viewed in the round, was directed to introspective soul-searching and questions of church order

---

[102] See Fuller's comments in a letter to John Fawcett, 28 January 1793, in John Fawcett, Jr, *An Account of the Life, Ministry and Writings of the Late Rev John Fawcett, DD* (London: Baldwin, Craddock and Joy, 1818), 294.

[103] Morden, *Offering Christ to the World*, 128.

[104] For a complete list of his publications, see Greaves, *Glimpses of Glory*, 637-41.

[105] Ivimey, *History of English Baptists*, II, 41.

[106] See Peter J. Morden, 'Biblical Renewal for Mission: Andrew Fuller and Eighteenth-Century Baptist Life', *Bulletin of the Strict Baptist Historical Society* 38 (Autumn, 2011), 1-20.

and discipline.[107] Bunyan and later evangelicals were both active, but there was a difference in the nature of their activism.

Secondly, there was discontinuity in the scope of their activity. This is seen most clearly in respect of transcultural mission. Bunyan did not engage in this, and neither did the Puritans, although a few did express the desire.[108] Part of the difference can be explained by context. Fuller believed that the 'improvement of navigation' and the 'maritime and commercial turn of this country [i.e., Britain]' made engagement in vigorous cross-cultural mission a 'duty peculiarly binding' on Christians of his generation.[109] But the difference in the scope of activity was also driven by the particular nature of evangelical activism. Compare for example the differences in millennial expectation and the way this was worked out practically. Bunyan was interested in the millennium, but his expectations of a future day of great blessing were unfocused and unclear and, crucially, they did not orient and drive his activism towards the vigorous pursuit of world mission. Fuller's activism was of a different temper. His use of the word 'duty' in the quotation just cited is especially suggestive. If the millennium was at hand and God was opening the way for action, then Fuller and Carey alike believed it was their duty to be involved up to the hilt and 'attempt great things'. For these and the countless other men and women who dedicated themselves to global mission, the desire to spend and be spent in God's service was overwhelming. A postmillennialism which envisaged a worldwide outpouring of God's Spirit combined with revivalist fervour and a commitment to use means to produce an explosion of cross-cultural activity. (Following the founding of the BMS, other societies soon followed, with the interdenominational London Missionary Society, begun in 1795, especially significant.[110]) Mission 'at home' was pursued with no less vigour by both ministers and an army of committed laypeople. This was a new, evangelical era. There was continuity with previous Protestantism of course, a continuity which is arguably more evident in respect of the outstanding popular evangelist Bunyan than it would have been if another Puritan (John Owen or Thomas Brooks?) had been the focus of this study. But for all the continuity between the seventeenth and the eighteenth centuries there was real discontinuity as well, even where Bunyan – hallowed as he was by the later movement – was concerned.

Conclusion

This study has compared the seventeenth-century John Bunyan with the 'modern evangelicalism' associated with the eighteenth-century Evangelical Revival and

---

[107] See, e.g., Bunyan, *Solomon's Temple Spiritualized*, 495, and *A Discourse of the Building ... of the House of God* [1688] in *Works*, III, 577-90.

[108] Michael A.G. Haykin, 'Evangelicalism and the Enlightenment', in Haykin and Stewart (eds), *Emergence of Evangelicalism*, 52.

[109] Andrew Fuller, *Pernicious Consequences of Delay* [Preached at a Ministers' Meeting, 27 April 1791] in *Fuller's Works*, I, 147.

[110] Brian Stanley, *The History of the Baptist Missionary Society, 1792–1992* (Edinburgh: T. & T. Clark, 1992), 21.

beyond. In many ways the seventeenth-century man prefigures this later movement. His life and ministry exhibit biblicism, conversionism and crucicentrism and there is good evidence of activism too. Along with Richard Baxter he stands as one of the Puritans most in tune with later evangelicalism and it is not surprising that he was such a hero for many within the movement. Evangelicals themselves tended to emphasise this continuity, even when they were dealing with an area of dissonance. On the linked issues of conversion and assurance, Spurgeon somehow managed to hold up Bunyan's experience in *Grace Abounding* as a sort of ideal for his own day without recognising that it was significantly different both from his own experience and from the pattern of conversion and immediate assurance he consistently preached.[111] He probably interpreted the struggles chronicled in *Grace Abounding* as having occurred before conversion, which had also been Ivimey's way of handling the material.[112] But this is the narrative viewed through an evangelical lens. Other evangelicals recognised more clearly that Bunyan's experience did not mesh so easily with the way they saw things. George Offor described Bunyan's spiritual narrative as a 'very extraordinary case' and sought to assure his readers that these 'terrors' are not necessary 'prerequisites to faith' (again there is the inference that Bunyan's struggles were pre-conversion rather than post).[113] Assurance, Offor affirmed, was freely available for all through trust in Christ and his word 'without an inquiry into the means by which we are called'.[114] Bunyan was not criticised and *Grace Abounding* was still praised as a work of genius, but on the specifics of spiritual experience Offor (perhaps unconsciously) distanced himself from the book he was commending. In a short memoir of Bunyan, the evangelical Anglican Bible commentator Thomas Scott skated quickly over the events recorded in *Grace Abounding*, providing a brief gloss on his subject's experience of conversion/assurance, effectively presenting it as a cautionary tale which would 'teach others', helping them avoid similar 'temptations' and 'perplexities'.[115] Bunyan was reinterpreted and repackaged for an evangelical age, even as these later authors claimed to be following him.

Yet the areas of discontinuity should not be downplayed, even if evangelicals in the eighteenth and nineteenth centuries sidestepped them. There is a certainty and confidence about 'modern evangelicalism' which is absent in Bunyan. Not only in respect of assurance, but also with regards to eschatology and the nature and scale of activism, I hope I have shown that the differences between him and those who came later were real and substantial. Hannah Marshman illustrates some of that discontinuity, even as she lay dying and listening to her treasured *The Pilgrim's Progress*. Although she was present in Bengal as a 'missionary wife' as far as the

---

[111] Spurgeon (ed.), *Sword and Trowel*, February 1883, 60.
[112] Ivimey, *History of English Baptists*, II, 40.
[113] Offor, 'Advertisement by the Editor [to *Grace Abounding*]', *Works*, I, 3.
[114] Offor, 'Advertisement by the Editor', 1.
[115] Thomas Scott, 'The Life of John Bunyan' in *The Pilgrim's Progress ... with Original Notes by the Rev. Thomas Scott* (London: Henry Bohn, 1857), xviii.

BMS was concerned, she more than deserves the epithet 'missionary'. She had arrived in India in October 1799, and served with distinction for nearly forty-eight years, despite the indifferent health which necessitated her one and only return to England in 1820–21. Her work in women's education is quite rightly described as 'pioneering' by George Howells.[116] This began in 1820 and by 1824 there were 160 Indian girls attending six schools, a ministry she developed whilst continuing to have a lead role in the running of the large and complex missionary household in Serampore.

It is important not to claim too much for this present study, which represents a modest attempt to make a small contribution to the wider debate about evangelical origins. Yet I hope I have shown enough to call into question some of the confident assertions of continuity between the Reformed and Puritan traditions and the eighteenth century evangelicals in *The Emergence of Evangelicalism*. Certainly, whilst Hannah Marshman's life and ministry were rooted in the Protestant past represented by her favourite author, her efforts and those of her colleagues were groundbreaking and a truly 'revolutionary development'.

---

[116] George Howells, *The Story of Serampore and its College* (Serampore: The College, 1927), 11.

CHAPTER 4

Abraham Booth's Defence of Believer's Baptism by Immersion

Sharon James

It seems appropriate in a volume honouring Ian Randall's life and ministry to include a contribution on Abraham Booth. Like Ian, Booth was a leader who was firmly committed to baptistic principles, yet one who also maintained warm fellowship with believers of other persuasions.[1]

The baptism of believers by immersion following profession of faith is a distinctive Baptist practice, which has now gained recognition – even acceptance – among many Christians. Worldwide, the Baptists form one of the largest denominations. In addition, Pentecostals and Charismatics generally practise believer's baptism (and, with it, the gathered church principle).

Thus, from our twenty-first century perspective, it is almost impossible to grasp how radical and dangerous it was to advocate believer's baptism in England during the seventeenth century (outside of the Commonwealth period). Even fellow Independents often regarded Baptists as fanatical. The great Puritan Richard Baxter – who along with them suffered persecution following the Restoration of Charles II to the throne in 1662 – dismissed baptism by immersion as 'a heinous sin' and 'flat murder'.[2]

Opposition to Believer's Baptism

The 1689 settlement secured a measure of freedom for Baptists but they continued, into the following century, to be regarded as second-class citizens. Believer's baptism by immersion was still regarded by the great majority of Christians as unbecoming, unhealthy, and an affront to the traditions of both Church and State. John Wesley insisted on calling Baptists 'anabaptists', as a deliberate slur. His

---

[1] I was delighted to be asked to contribute this chapter, as I have probably known Ian longer than any other contributor to this volume. Ian and Janice were my youth leaders at the time of my own baptism. Much more recently, I enjoyed the privilege of having Ian supervise my doctoral studies.

[2] Richard Baxter, *Plain Scripture proof of infants Church-membership and baptism* (London: John Wright, 1656), 134.

brother Charles described them as 'a carnal, cavilling, contentious sect'.³ Matthew Henry (1662–1714) was hugely influential during the eighteenth century and beyond.⁴ His *Treatise on Baptism* was published, posthumously, in 1783. In it, those who failed to baptise their infants were said to 'deliver their children to Satan, as members of his visible kingdom'.⁵ Challenging the *status quo* on infant baptism was 'a device of Satan, to perplex ignorant and to delude unstable souls'.⁶ He gave three reasons to oppose baptism by immersion:

> 1. It unavoidably occasions a very great distraction and discomposure of mind, in the management of a solemn ordinance; and is therefore evil. Putting an adult person, unused to bathing, over head in water, must needs, for the present, unfit him for any thoughts suitable to such a solemnity ...
> 2. In many cases, this mode is very perilous to the *health,* and even the *life* of the body: and God hath taught us that he will have *mercy and not sacrifice,* Matt. vii, 7. In so cold a climate as ours, especially to some people at some seasons, bathing in cold water would be almost certainly fatal.
> 3. To baptize naked, or next to naked, (which is supposed, and generally practised, in immersion,) is against the law of modesty; and to do such a thing in public solemn assemblies, is so far from being tolerable that it is abominable to every chaste soul, and especially to baptize women in this manner.⁷

At the time that this work was published, Abraham Booth (1734–1806) had been ministering at Prescot Street Baptist Church (near the Tower of London) for fifteen years. He had studied the arguments for and against believer's baptism by immersion, and, for his own interest, had compiled lists of quotations from paedobaptist authors which supported the Baptist position. When Henry's *Treatise on Baptism* appeared, Booth was encouraged to publish his own compilation. *Paedobaptism Examined* was published in 1784. The first edition rapidly sold out, and Booth expanded and reprinted it in 1787 in two volumes (443 pages and 342 pages respectively). The work provoked a flurry of interest. One reviewer noted, 'He sets them [i.e., paedobaptists] together by the ears and leaves them to overthrow the very cause in defence of which they professed to take the field.'⁸ The author of Booth's *Memoir* noted,

---

³ Quoted in Michael A.G. Haykin, *One Heart and One Soul: John Sutcliffe of Olney, his friends and his times* (Darlington: Evangelical Press, 1994), 28.

⁴ Matthew Henry, *Commentary on the Bible* (1708–10) was widely read and respected, and still is.

⁵ Matthew Henry, *Treatise on Baptism,* in *The Miscellaneous Works of the Rev. Matthew Henry* ..., Volume 2 (London: Joseph Ogle Robinson, 1833), 1145-1204 (1160).

⁶ Henry, *Treatise on Baptism,* 1176.

⁷ Henry, *Treatise on Baptism,* 1175.

⁸ *Monthly Review* September 1784, quoted in the (anonymous) *Memoir* which appeared in the three-volume edition of his *The Works of Abraham Booth in Three Volumes* (3 vols; London: W. Button, 1813), I, xvii-lxxx.

The performance, in its present state, may, almost without a hyperbole, be said to have exhausted the controversy on the Baptist side of the question, and the simple inquirer after truth who is not convinced by Mr Booth's volumes can hardly be expected to yield his judgement to anything that man can say upon this long contested point.[9]

Paedobaptism Examined presented what was, to date, the most detailed and comprehensive defence of believer's baptism ever written.[10] The strength of the work lay in the mastery of the paedobaptist authors, including those who wrote in other languages, but also in the good humour and grace maintained throughout, in contrast to the tone of the debate as pursued by many at the time. Although little-known today, the publication of this work was a landmark in Baptist theology.

Remarkably, its author, along with so many Baptist leaders of his time, was an autodidact. He had, by sheer hard work, risen from a wretchedly poor background. Poverty had compelled him to go out to work from a young age. His father had taught him to read and thereafter he launched on an extensive programme of study carried out in the hours after his long working days. For many years after his conversion he carried out gospel ministry alongside supporting himself and his family by means of the stocking trade and teaching at a village school. When he became minister at the Prescot Street church, a leading Particular Baptist church in London in 1768, the change in situation for Booth (then aged twenty-four) and his family was immense. No more weaving, no more lessons for village boys. He engaged a tutor, an ex-priest, to further his knowledge in Latin and Greek. He read voraciously in theology and church history, including many works in Latin. He formed a life long habit of reading a chapter of the Greek New Testament every morning. His own books – and notably *Paedobaptism Examined* – quote extensively from a vast range of other works.

Roy Porter has argued that a feature of the Enlightenment period was that 'reading proffered an admission into the cultural magic circle, even for those of no great wealth or social status'. He suggested that the

> key polarity in Georgian England [was] ... between those swimming in the metropolitan culture pool created by print, and those excluded, those whose culture was still essentially oral.[11]

Booth, a labourer's son, rising to take his place as a respected London denominational leader, is a perfect illustration of Porter's thesis.

---

[9] *Memoir*, I, xlvi.

[10] With regard to the theology of baptism, Booth was not a sacramentalist. He laid out his convictions in a written testimony at the time when he was ordained to the ministry at Prescot Street in 1769: Abraham Booth, *Confession of Faith*, in M.A.G. Haykin and A.E. Haykin (eds), *The Works of Abraham Booth: Volume 1. Confessions of Faith and Sermons* (Springfield, MS: Particular Baptist Press, 2006), 25-32.

[11] Roy Porter, *Enlightenment: Britain and the Creation of the Modern World* (London: Penguin, 2000), 76.

After a biographical introduction to Abraham Booth, this chapter will provide a (necessarily brief) summary of his massive *Paedobaptism Examined*.

The Life and Ministry of Booth

Abraham Booth was born in 1734 in the village of Blackwell, Derbyshire. When his father became a tenant farmer on the estate of the Duke of Portland, the family moved south to Annesley Woodhouse in Nottinghamshire. From childhood, Abraham had to help on the farm, but after his father taught him to read he showed an insatiable appetite for books. By the time of his tenth birthday, in 1744, the area had been affected by the Evangelical Revival. Abraham's family heard gospel preaching from a group initially encouraged by Selina, Countess of Huntingdon. The preachers sometimes braved vicious attacks but many hearers were converted. Groups of believers began meeting in several villages. A meeting house was built at Barton and an Independent church constituted in 1745.[12] Ten years after the church was formed, in 1755, the group had become convinced of believer's baptism, and sixty or so, including Abraham aged twenty-one, were baptised by immersion. By now, Abraham was accepting preaching invitations in villages up to forty miles away from his home. Since the age of sixteen he had been working for a stocking maker, rather than on the farm, as this gave him greater opportunities for private study. He worked immensely hard, eventually owning his own stocking frames. Often he studied through much of the night and then travelled long distances preaching at weekends. When the many groups of converts, loosely attached to Barton, were constituted into a number of separate churches, Booth was asked to take pastoral oversight of the church at Kirkby Woodhouse.

At the age of twenty-four Abraham married Elizabeth Bowman, a farmer's daughter. Her family had managed to provide her with a better education than was usual for girls in her situation and she had the skills to help Abraham set up a school in the small weaving community of Sutton in Ashfield. Elizabeth taught the girls and Abraham the boys: He also continued with his stocking making.

Abraham Booth's persistent study ultimately led to a complete change in doctrinal conviction. Having been converted and discipled by Arminian teachers, and taught to despise Calvinism, he found himself compelled to embrace what he had abhorred. He admitted to his own church, as well as the other churches he preached in, that he had changed his view. He resigned his pastorate and stopped preaching. But a group of supporters rented premises in Sutton in Ashfield where he could continue his ministry as the pastor of a Calvinistic Baptist church.

---

[12] John Todd, *By the Foolishness of Preaching: Leicestershire and the 18th Century Evangelical Revival, with particular reference to the 'Barton Preachers'* (Barton-in-the Beans: Baptist Church Publication, rev. edn, 2003).

For some time, Booth taught school and continued weaving during the week to support his family, as well as preaching three times each Sunday.[13] A series of sermons on the doctrines of grace formed the basis for his book *Reign of Grace* (1768).[14] Booth had no prospects of publishing this but a friend who read it enthused about it to Henry Venn (1725–97), an evangelical minister in Huddersfield. Venn, an educated Church of England man, paid for the manuscript to be published. (Since that time this book has never been out of print.) Venn also took the time to travel south to meet with Booth; the start of a long friendship. Venn admitted that one of the spin-offs he hoped for from the publication of *Reign of Grace* was that it would lead Booth to a more advantageous situation, liberated from the need to support his family by manual work.

That is exactly what happened. April 1768 was the month that *Reign of Grace* appeared; it was also the month when pastor Samuel Burford, of Little Prescot Street, Goodman's Field, London, died. *Reign of Grace* made such an impression on some of the Prescot Street members that three of them travelled immediately to Nottinghamshire to hear Booth preach. As a result, he was invited to preach at Prescot Street several times and a unanimous call to the pastorate was extended. The induction service was held in February 1769. Booth would minister at Prescot Street for the remaining (nearly) thirty-seven years of his life.

The little rural community which the Booths had left behind was made up of ninety-five families. By contrast, the population of London 'was about to burst its bounds completely and become the first metropolis of the world'.[15] By Booth's death, the population had hit one million.

Booth had come to a historic church in a fashionable area. During his first ten years there were 122 baptisms. Over the whole period of his pastorate, there were a total of 452 baptisms. Booth tried to preach at Prescot Street every Sunday, only taking engagements elsewhere during the week. He was closely involved in the pastoral work of the church, he wrote up all the minutes of the monthly and other church meetings, kept the records of membership and was dearly loved by his congregation. He was also closely connected with the variety of evangelistic enterprises engaged upon by Particular Baptists at this time. As he had already demonstrated in practice, he was a passionate supporter of village itinerant preaching, and took the lead in initiating the London Society for Itinerancy, formed in 1797. He was an enthusiastic supporter of the new Baptist Missionary Society (f.1792) and introduced William Carey to his colleague John Thomas. He was foremost among the London ministers at the time in voicing opposition to the slave trade. He took a lead in promoting the Particular Baptist Fund and members of his

---

[13] As well as preaching in his own church, he continued to walk long distances to preach in needy village situations.

[14] In response to the overstating of the doctrines of predestination and election on the part of some Particular Baptists, *Reign of Grace* shows that a biblical understanding of sovereign grace should encourage gospel preaching to sinners rather than inhibit it.

[15] Peter Ackroyd, *London: The Biography* (London: Vintage, 2001), 517-18.

congregation gave generously to this cause. A member of the London Baptist Board, he was *de facto* one of the leaders of Dissent during this period.

As one who had suffered the want of education in his youth, he was fully behind the efforts of one of his members, William Fox, in initiating Sunday schools for poor children.[16] Also, having lacked formal ministerial training, he was keen to promote the training of young ministers. Shortly before his death he worked to re-establish the London Education Society. One of his deacons became treasurer, and another endowed the Society with the funds to purchase what would in 1810 become the Baptist College at Stepney. (The College later moved to Oxford, as Regent's Park College.) In addition to all this, he published a number of books.

In the last years of his life he struggled with asthma, and the church took on two successive assistants to help out with the work. He died at the age of seventy-one in January 1806.

Booth never forgot his humble origins. He had moved from the rigours of manual work in a village situation to a secure income in London – which could at that time be described as 'a gorgeous, chaotic theatre of eye-popping spectacle and greedy consumption'[17] Yet one of the most appealing aspects of his character was his insistence on a simple lifestyle, as well as a transparent humility. He refused to adopt a more fashionable appearance: one visitor to Prescot Street noted that before he ascended the rostrum he could be mistaken for a poor layman.[18] His extant correspondence with relatives shows a pastoral, generous concern for their welfare.[19] He was a loving husband and father. Preaching at the induction of a new pastor he gave a touching appeal on behalf of neglected ministers' wives, exposing the hypocrisy of men who were assiduous in caring for their congregations while failing to spend time with their 'second self'. 'Spend your evenings at home!', he urged.[20] His complete integrity and godliness always commanded respect.

> Such a degree of majesty attended him, plain as he was in exterior, that if he sat down with you but a few minutes you could not help feeling that you had a prince or a great man in the house.[21]

---

[16] In 1785, Fox established a society which encouraged all churches (dissenting and Church of England) to establish Sunday schools.

[17] Simon Schama, *A History of Britain: The British Wars, 1603–1776* (London: BBC, 2001), 365.

[18] Quoted in Ernest A. Payne, 'Abraham Booth, 1734–1806', *The Baptist Quarterly* 26.1 (January, 1975), 28-42 (41).

[19] The Booth Collection, The Angus Library, Regent's Park College, The University of Oxford.

[20] Abraham Booth, *Pastoral Cautions*, in Haykin and Haykin (eds), *The Works of Abraham Booth*, I, 67.

[21] *Memoir*, lxxix.

A Summary of Paedobaptism Examined

Booth begins his treatise with a definition of baptism. It is a 'positive institution'. Moral duties are universally binding on all humans because they may be seen by the light of reason and conscience. By contrast, a 'positive institution' is a command of God, known only by means of his Word. Booth gives twenty citations from paedobaptist writers, concluding that,

> positive institutions originate entirely in the sovereign will of God, that the obligation to observe them arises not from the goodness of the things themselves, but from the authority of God, that they admit of no commutation, mutilation or alteration by human authority, that our obligation to observe them does not result from our seeing the reasons for them but from the command of God; that it is great presumption to make light of them.[22]

Booth then gives eighty-two citations from paedobaptist writers indicating that immersion is the obvious meaning of the term 'baptism', that the word baptism is nowhere used in Scripture to signify sprinkling, that the manner of baptism should correspond to the significance or meaning of the ordinance, and that neither pouring nor sprinkling is warranted by the word 'baptism'. He concludes,

> Paedobaptism as practised in the northern parts of Europe [i.e., by sprinkling] is not agreeable to the native, obvious and common acceptation of the word baptism ... It opposes the grand rule of interpretation, that the ordinary and most usual signification of words must not be deserted except for cogent reasons ... Paedobaptism, however, has nothing to plead for departing from this rule but – its own existence.[23]

Next seventy-five citations from paedobaptist writers are given, indicating that immersion represents union with Christ in his death, burial and resurrection. 'We have reason to conclude on their own principles and concessions that there neither is nor can be any valid plea for pouring or sprinkling as a proper mode of administration.'[24] Booth then offers ninety-six quotations from paedobaptist writers to show that John the Baptist, the apostles and the Church in later ages all practised immersion. He demonstrates that immersion was the general and almost universal course of action for centuries; that the churches of Helvetia [Switzerland] and the Church of England required immersion (except in cases of illness); he quotes two paedobaptist writers who admitted that the custom of sprinkling is indefensible, and others who admitted that a restoration of the 'primitive' custom of immersion would be desirable.[25]

---

[22] Abraham Booth, *Paedobaptism Examined, with Replies to the Arguments and Objections of Dr Williams and Mr Peter Edwards in Three Volumes* (3 vols; London: Ebenezer Palmer, 1829 [1784–87]), I, 16-17.

[23] Booth, *Paedobaptism Examined I*, 72.

[24] Booth, *Paedobaptism Examined I*, 170.

[25] Booth, *Paedobaptism Examined I*, 201.

Booth cites those paedobaptists who saw no problem in the 3,000 converts in Acts 2:41 being baptised by immersion in one day.[26] He allows that some paedobaptists found it hard to think of such large numbers being baptised in one day and wonders why they had no problem with the Old Testament accounts of large numbers being circumcised in one day (Genesis 17:23-24), which is even more time-consuming. If you reduce immersion to sprinkling because of a supposed difficulty in timing, why not suppose that circumcision did not involve '*cutting off*' the foreskin but just 'making *a slight incision* in that pellicle'?[27]

While talking about the mode of baptism, Booth replies to Matthew Henry, who, as mentioned above, in his *Treatise on Baptism* had accused Baptists of baptising candidates naked.

> When in perusing the treatise, I came to these words, I paused, I was astonished, I was almost confounded. What, thought I, is this the language of the amiable and excellent Mr Henry? Does immersion SUPPOSE the subject of the ordinance naked or next to naked? Is this practised, generally practised, practised in public solemn assemblies, and that upon women too? ... On the word of an author who has long been held in a high degree of esteem ... we have often committed the most enormous outrage on the laws of decorum ... I shall only add a salutary prohibition, a gentle reprehension and a candid extenuation: 'Thou shallt not bear false witness against thy neighbour.'[28]

At an earlier time, the Puritan Richard Baxter had been even more intemperate than Matthew Henry in his attacks on immersion. Booth quotes him:

> the ordinary practice of baptizing over head in cold water is no ordinance of God, but an heinous sin ... the magistrate *ought to restrain it,* to save the lives of his subjects. ... That it *is flat murder* ... is undeniable to any understanding man ... covetous physicians, methinks, should [encourage it] ... Catarrhs and obstructions, which are the two great fountains of most mortal diseases in man's body, could scarce have a more notable means to produce them where they are not, or to increase them where they are. Apoplexies, lethargies, palsies, and all comatous diseases, would be promoted by it. So would ... debility of the stomach, crudities, and almost all fevers, dysenteries, diarrhoeas, colics ... convulsions, spasms, tremors, and so on ... it is good for nothing but to despatch men out of the world that are burdensome ... I conclude, if murder be a sin, then dipping in cold water over head, in England, is a sin.[29]

Booth's good humoured response was

> Poor man! He seems to be afflicted with a violent hydrophobia! For he cannot think of anyone being immersed in cold water but he starts, he is convulsed, he is ready to die

---

[26] Booth, *Paedobaptism Examined I*, 222-23.

[27] Booth, *Paedobaptism Examined I*, 225 (italics original).

[28] Booth, *Paedobaptism Examined I*, 231-32.

[29] Booth, *Paedobaptism Examined I*, 234-35.

with fear ... What a pity it is that the celebrated *History of Cold Bathing* by Sir John Floyer were not published half a century earlier.[30]

Turning to the practice of the Greek and Oriental churches, ten paedobaptist writers are quoted showing that the Greek and Russian churches immerse babies, and Booth concludes,

> These paedobaptist writers show immersion has been uninterruptedly continued as general mode in all Greek and oriental churches. These include about half the Christians in the world ... Therefore why do opponents of immersion treat it as novel and singular?'[31]

The English Prayer Book indicated that the priest should dip the infant in water, unless the godparents certify it to be weak.[32] Booth wonders why all the infants in England, at that time, seemed to be afflicted with weakness.

Booth quotes sixteen paedobaptist writers who agreed that the meaning of baptism is more clearly expressed by immersion than by pouring or sprinkling. For example, Dr Wall admitted

> That [sprinkling] is sufficient for the essence of baptism; but [he] could not deny the other (except in the case of danger of health) to be the fittest ... The immersion of the person, whether infant or adult, in the posture of one that is buried and raised up again, is much more solemn, and expresses the design of the sacrament and the mystery of the spiritual washing much better, than pouring a small quantity of water on the face. And that pouring of water, is much better than sprinkling, or dropping a drop of water on it.[33]

Booth reflects that all these paedobaptist writers admit that immersion, compared with pouring or sprinkling, has the honour of priority in respect of time, it is more significant and it is more certain of being right. He finds twenty-four paedobaptist writers to show that pouring was first used in the case of invalids; when Christianity spread to cold countries, pouring was sometimes used instead of immersion. In addition, when infants began to be baptised instead of adults, because of their weakness, pouring was used instead of immersion. He suggests that the most ancient instance on record of pouring or sprinkling is recorded by Novatian in AD 251. The supposed necessity arose either from bodily weakness or from lack of water. But water was poured or sprinkled not on the face only but on the whole body. This

---

[30] Booth, *Paedobaptism Examined I*, 236-37. Sir John Floyer (1642–1734), a physician based in Lichfield, was famous for his research into asthma and as an advocate of cold-bathing and vigorous exercise.

[31] Booth, *Paedobaptism Examined I*, 241.

[32] Booth, *Paedobaptism Examined I*, 242. The reference is, as Booth puts it, to 'The first common prayer book' of Edward VI, 1662.

[33] Booth, *Paedobaptism Examined I*, 248.

pouring or sprinkling was considered an imperfect administration of the ordinance, and so was called sprinkling, not baptising.

Paedobaptist writers were used to show that in England, while the practice of sprinkling commenced during the reign of Elizabeth I, immersion was still the more common practice until the time of James I. Booth concludes,

> The practice of pouring and sprinkling makes but a poor figure in the eyes of a consistent protestant, for ... it had no existence until many corruptions had taken deep root in the church.[34]

Primitive immersion had been laid aside upon a 'supposition of it being dangerous and indecent'.[35] Booth accepts that many paedobaptist writers say that immersion in cold water is not merciful and that it is kinder to sprinkle instead. But, he asks, would not that have had much more relevance to the practice of circumcision? And he argues that plenty of (even) non-Christian people advocate cold bathing for the benefit of health. Anyway, Booth writes, 'How strange it is that Protestant authors should ever talk of dispensing with divine laws or of mitigating their severity!'[36]

Moving to the subjects of baptism, Booth quotes thirty-one paedobaptist writers who accepted that there is no clear command or example of infants being baptised in the New Testament. For example, Cellarius for whom 'infant baptism is neither commanded in Sacred Scripture, nor is it confirmed by apostolic examples'.[37] Booth concludes that infant baptism rests on the same foundation as diocesan episcopacy: it is a human tradition. He argues that when children are present in various New Testament narratives, it is made explicit. Children were present at the feeding of the 4,000 (Mt. 14:21; 15:38); they were presented to Christ (Mt. 19:13; Mk 10:13; Lk. 18:15); and they were present at the farewell to Paul (Acts 21:5). If children were baptised in the New Testament, it would have been even more important to make it clear that they were present and included than in those cases. In Acts 21:21, Christian Jews were told *not* to circumcise their children. They were *not* told to baptise them instead. Booth shows that the argument for infant baptism from inference or intimation is exactly the methodology used by Catholic writers to justify other human traditions. For example, Mr Walker wrote,

> Where the authority of Scripture fails, there the custom of the church is to be held as a law ... who can say but that among those many *unwritten* sayings of his [Christ] there might be an express plea for infant baptism?[38]

This, says Booth, is the exact method used to justify Catholic rituals. He mentions the meeting of Oxford Divines in 1647 who concluded that 'Without the

---

[34] Booth, *Paedobaptism Examined I*, 263.
[35] Booth, *Paedobaptism Examined I*, 291.
[36] Booth, *Paedobaptism Examined I*, 295-96.
[37] Booth, *Paedobaptism Examined I*, 309.
[38] Booth, *Paedobaptism Examined I*, 307.

consentaneous judgement of the universal church, they should be at a loss when they are called upon for proof, in the point of infant baptism.'[39] The most paedobaptists could do was show that infant baptism is not forbidden. He then quotes paedobaptist writers to show that the Bible alone is our source of authority, not tradition, and who argues that 'the silence of Scripture' is sufficient ground for rejecting Roman Catholic practices such as the sign of the cross or the adoration of images of Christ?[40]

Booth quotes twelve paedobaptist writers to show that there is no evidence of paedobaptism before the end of the second or the beginning of the third century. Tertullian was the first person to speak expressly of infant baptism, saying that some in his day were baptising infants because they were afraid they might die before baptism. He opposed them in *De Baptismo* (written about AD 204) because one who has no understanding of the faith should not be baptised. Although Tertullian allowed various other rites, such as the making the sign of cross, he considered infant baptism a novel invention, not enjoined by divine command nor warranted by apostolic example.[41]

Booth concludes:

> As it appears from this and the preceding chapter, that the NT contains neither express precept for, nor plain example of infant baptism, and that no substantial evidence can be produced from ecclesiastical authors, of its being a prevailing custom, till about the middle of the third century; we may with great propriety (*mutatis mutandis*) adopt and apply to Paedobaptism, the reasonings of Protestants against the peculiarities of Popery.[42]

Booth then quotes a series of paedobaptist authors who argued against rituals such as consecrating water, prayers for the dead, candidates for baptism wearing white robes for a few days, candidates carrying lighted tapers and the baptising of bells. All these practices, like baptising infants, were not introduced until about the time of Tertullian. He quotes paedobaptist writers who explained that the belief grew up that without baptism there would be no salvation. When John 3:5 ('except a man be born of water and the spirit he cannot enter the kingdom of heaven') began to be understood as referring to baptism, infants were baptised. If an infant was critically ill, it would be presented for baptism. Episcopius wrote, 'Paedobaptism was not accounted a necessary rite, till it was determined so to be in the Milevitan council, held in the year 418.'[43]

At this point Booth argues that Scripture does not teach that baptism took the place of circumcision. 'Admitting the succession pretended, how came it that Paul

---

[39] Booth, *Paedobaptism Examined I*, 309.
[40] Booth, *Paedobaptism Examined I*, 317-19.
[41] Booth, *Paedobaptism Examined I*, 384.
[42] Booth, *Paedobaptism Examined I*, 394.
[43] Booth, *Paedobaptism Examined I*, 415.

circumcised Timothy after he had been baptized?'[44] 'It is obvious that the primitive Jewish Christians did not consider baptism a substitution for circumcision, or as coming in its place, because they circumcised their children' (Acts 21:21).[45]

Moving to a discussion of particular passages of Scripture, Booth begins with the Great Commission (Mt. 28:19). Converts are first to be instructed, then baptised. Booth gives twenty-eight citations from paedobaptist writers showing that this text argues against infant baptism.[46] With regard to the text 'Suffer the little children to come to me and forbid them not for of such is the kingdom of heaven' (Mt. 19:14), Booth quotes a number of paedobaptist writers who admit that Christ did *not* baptise children here. He accepts that it is appropriate to recommend an infant to God in solemn prayer and that this text

> wears a smiling aspect on the final state of such as die in their infancy, and that without any restriction in reference to carnal descent. But hence to infer that infants are entitled to baptism any more than to the holy supper is a conclusion wide of the mark.[47]

With regard to the text 'The promise is to you and your children and to all that are far off, even to as many as the Lord our God shall call' (Acts 2:39), Booth gives eight paedobaptist citations indicating that this text does not infer infant baptism. The promise is of the Holy Spirit or his extraordinary gifts. The term 'children' signifies 'posterity' not infants. Repentance is needed for enjoyment of these blessings. The text refers to 'those who are called', not to all offspring without exception. Similarly with regard to the 'household baptisms' (e.g., Acts 16:15, 33; 1 Cor. 1:16), Booth uses paedobaptist writers to show that we have no evidence that infants were baptised. For example, Dr Hammond,

> I think it unreasonable that the apostle's bare mention of baptizing his household should be thought competent to conclude that infants were baptized by him, when it is uncertain whether there were any such in the house.[48]

The noted paedobaptist Dr Philip Doddridge had quoted 1 Corinthians 16:15, where the household of Stephanus 'were the first converts in Achaia, and they have devoted themselves to the service of the saints: submit to such as these.'[49] This household could not have included infants for the Corinthians could not be expected to submit to children. And it is explicitly stated that the household of Crispus *all believed* (Acts 18:8).

With regard to 1 Corinthians 7: 14, 'the unbelieving husband is sanctified ... else were your children unclean, but now they are holy', Booth gives eighteen

---

[44] Booth, *Paedobaptism Examined II*, 86.
[45] Booth, *Paedobaptism Examined II*, 88.
[46] Booth, *Paedobaptism Examined II*, 107.
[47] Booth, *Paedobaptism Examined II*, 161.
[48] Booth, *Paedobaptism Examined II*, 177.
[49] Booth, *Paedobaptism Examined II*, 178.

paedobaptist citations which argued that 'sanctified' indicated that the marriage is legitimate and the children are legitimate; but that the text says nothing about baptism or the Lord's Supper.

Booth shows, next, that many paedobaptist writers agreed that infant baptism and infant communion were introduced at about the same time and supported by similar arguments. For example, Venema wrote,

> in the ancient church these two sacraments, in respect of the subjects were never separated the one from the other ... Infants in the third century were generally admitted to baptism and the Lord's supper ... In the thirteenth century baptized infants ceased to be admitted to the eucharist, because it began to be administered after one kind.[50]

And Dr Joseph Priestley admitted that 'no objection can be made to this custom [infant communion] but what may with equal force be made to the custom of baptizing infants'.[51] Bishop Jeremy Taylor accepted that

> for above six hundred years the church of God did give the holy communion to newly baptized infants ... The primitive church had all this to justify their practice, that the sacraments of grace are the great channels of the grace of God; that this grace always descends upon them that do not hinder it, and therefore certainly to infants ... It was confessed that the communion would do them benefit, yet it was denied to them then when the doctrine of transubstantiation entered; upon pretence lest, by *puking up* the holy symbols, the sacrament should be dishonoured.[52]

All these paedobaptist writers agreed that the Lord's Supper was given to infants when infant baptism was introduced, that the custom first prevailed in the African churches and then became more general. There is no express mention of infant baptism before that of infant communion and the practice of giving communion to infants first arose from a misunderstanding of John 6:53 ('unless you eat the flesh of the son of man and drink his blood you have no life in you'). Giving infants communion followed immediately on them being baptised and in point of right these two positive ordinances cannot be separated, as indeed in the ancient church baptism and the Lord's Supper were never separated. In conclusion, once the Lord's Supper was considered necessary for salvation, then when infants were sick the Lord's Supper was privately administered to them in the same way as to sick adults, and infant communion was the general practice for 600 years.

Booth then gives an overview of the arguments put forward by paedobaptist authors in favour of believer's baptism by immersion, and concludes,

> It is very observable, that so many Paedobaptists themselves have admitted the facts on which we reason, and that they have either expressly rejected the texts usually pleaded against us, as having nothing to do in the controversy; or so explained them, as renders

---

[50] Booth, *Paedobaptism Examined II*, 256-57.
[51] Booth, *Paedobaptism Examined II*, 257.
[52] Booth, *Paedobaptism Examined II*, 257-58, 260.

their application in support of infant baptism quite impertinent. *They have admitted the facts on which we reason.*

In a word, there is not, that I recollect, one topic of argument, nor one scripture, usually pleaded in favour of infant baptism, even by the more judicious of our opponents; but it is either expressly cashiered, as having nothing with the controversy, or so understood, as to be of no service to the cause.

We have the honour, therefore, to agree with many of them, as to a great part of our premises; and with some of them, respecting the whole.

Yes, amazing as it may seem, we are honoured with having some of them for our associates in everything except the conclusion. Here indeed we are utterly deserted by them.[53]

Booth then demonstrates that paedobaptists are divided between themselves on the question of which infants should be baptised. Should baptism be for infants of communicant church members (or should at least one parent to be so); for infants of true believers, whether church members or not; or for any children (e.g., children of 'infidels' if they fell into 'Christian' hands during times of war, or orphans left by unbelieving parents)? He shows that paedobaptists are also divided on what the grounds for infant baptism are: is infant baptism based on the universality of divine grace; on the necessity of baptism for salvation; or on the profession of faith made on behalf of infants by sponsors (as in the Church of England)? In other words, are the children of believers being included in the covenant of grace by virtue of birth or are the children of believers brought into the covenant of grace by virtue of baptism? Do children have a right to baptism because of the profession of faith of their parent/s? And so on. Booth concludes,

Now, reader, what think you of these efforts and struggles to support the reputation of paedobaptists? Are they not plain indications that the obvious meaning of divine law, and the natural import of New Testament facts, are inconsistent with the modern prevailing practice?[54]

Finally, Booth reflects on Bishop Taylor's assertion that the paedobaptists have 'more truth than evidence on our side'. He is pleased to hear the Bishop's admission that the Baptists have evidence on their side. But how can anyone discover truth without evidence? Booth is even more perplexed to think of truth and evidence taking opposite sides in an argument. He insists that the Baptists would continue to go where the biblical evidence led them.

On the other hand, we need not wonder if the Paedobaptists exult in the possession of truth, because it is a precious jewel; and such truth especially as it is obtained without evidence must be precious indeed, it being so extremely scarce. Despairing therefore of

---

[53] Booth, *Paedobaptism Examined II*, 289, 292.
[54] Booth, *Paedobaptism Examined II*, 304.

putting an end to any controversy where truth and evidence take different sides, I must here lay down my pen.[55]

No wonder that after writing what comes to 785 closely printed pages, Booth would wish to lay down his pen! He planned to write no more on the subject.

Reception

Booth's work produced one published paedobaptist response. Dr Edward Williams (1750–1813) wrote *Antipaedobaptism Examined* which proved to be embarrassingly badly written, peppered with grammatical errors and aggressive in tone. One writer commented, 'We can scarcely imagine two combatants more unequally matched.'[56] Booth did not at first consider it worth publishing a reply.[57] But Dr Williams was heard to boast that his book had won Booth over to the paedobaptist position, which was why no response had been published. On hearing this claim, Booth produced *A Defence of Paedobaptism Examined or Animadversions on Dr Edward Williams's Antipaedobaptism Examined* (474 pages), a good humoured response to a bad-tempered book. There are pleasant allusions to the various insults which had been directed against Booth sprinkled throughout. Booth could afford to be relaxed: his opponent had not produced anything especially threatening.

> A repeated perusal of *Antipaedobaptism Examined,* far from producing that strong conviction, of which Dr Williams was pleased to boast, had an effect quite the reverse. For the principles on which he endeavours to support infant sprinkling, are many of them so novel, so paradoxical, and so extremely foreign from every idea suggested by the law and practice of baptism as recorded in the New Testament, that I received additional confirmation of my avowed sentiments. Nay, so far from being convinced ... I could not forebear suspecting, that even many Paedobaptists themselves ... must be ashamed to see their cause defended on such principles ... I have endeavoured to convince him ... that I am NOT a paedobaptist *incog*. ... I am no more convinced by the force of my Opponent's arguments than I am charmed with the modesty of his pretensions, the consistency of his sentiments, the perspicuity of his meaning, the accuracy of his language, or the elegance of his composition, on all which I have made some animadversions, that would certainly have been spared ... if he had not considered me as *captivated* by his performance ...[58]

At this point a Mr Peter Edwards wrote *Candid Reasons for Renouncing the principles of Antipaedobaptism*. He found it hard to make his mind up on this issue. Originally a paedobaptist, he became a Baptist and was baptised by immersion, but

---

[55] Booth, *Paedobaptism Examined II*, 304.
[56] William Jones, *Essay on the Life and Writings of the Rev. Abraham Booth* (Liverpool: James Smith, 1808), 47.
[57] Abraham Booth, *A Defence of Paedobaptism Examined*, in *Paedobaptism Examined II*, 347.
[58] Booth, *A Defence of Paedobaptism Examined*, 349-50.

then changed back again to be a paedobaptist; at this point he penned *Candid Reasons*. This work should have been entitled *Candid Reason* as Edwards triumphantly produces one single point. Where is the scriptural 'proof' that women should take the Lord's Supper? There is none! So, why demand 'proof' that infants were baptised in the New Testament? The likelihood for infants being baptised is about equal to the likelihood of females taking the Lord's Supper.

In addition, Edwards descends to the most scurrilous personal abuse of Booth. A reply was published by 'James Dore' in 1795, with the unwieldy title *The Principles of Antipaedobaptism and the Practice of Female Communion completely consistent. In answer to the arguments and objections of Mr Peter Edwards in his Candid Reasons: with Animadversions on his temper and conduct in that Publication.* It was, in reality, written by Booth. It was easier to answer the numerous examples of personal invective against himself when using the third person. And then, finally, he did lay down his pen on this subject.

Booth's defence of believer's baptism by immersion was provoked by the intemperate but widespread attacks on the practice by other Christians at the time. He was not driven to write out of any love of controversy and he maintained warm relations with believers of other convictions.

> I acknowledge it as my indispensable duty to cultivate a friendly freedom, and brotherly affection, with all those who love our Lord Jesus Christ in sincerity, and bear his image. Such of whatever denomination they be, I desire to esteem as my brethren ...[59]

Throughout his life, Abraham Booth's driving motivation was obedience to Christ. The decision to be baptised by immersion had been costly; years of walking significant distances to preach the gospel in needy villages (outside of long working hours) had been even more costly. Accepting Calvinist principles had meant severing ties with his church and resigning his pastorate. But, he believed, when dealing with God's commands in Scripture humans are not at liberty to dilute them in any way. 'When God speaks we should be all attention, and when he commands we should be all submission.'[60]

---

[59] Booth, *Confession of Faith*, 31.

[60] Abraham Booth, *An Apology for the Baptists in which they are vindicated from the imputation of laying an unwarrantable stress on the ordinance of baptism; and against the charge of Bigotry in refusing Communion at the Lord's Table to Paedobaptists* (Boston, MA: Manning and Loring, 1808 [1778]), 68.

CHAPTER 5

Undenominationalism in Britain, 1840–1914

Tim Grass

Introduction

It is a commonplace of writing about Evangelicals to say that to whatever denomination they belong, they are Evangelicals first and Baptists (Anglicans, or whatever) second.[1] Throughout the movement's history, as with its continental Pietist relatives, there has been a strong strand of belief that it is possible to overleap denominational boundaries and to give visible ecclesiological expression to the fellowship of true (i.e., converted) believers. The nineteenth century saw a whole succession of what might be termed 'radical evangelical' movements coming into being as those exercised about the state of contemporary churches sought a purer form of Christianity and a broader fellowship embracing all true believers in Christ. Grayson Carter's work on early nineteenth-century evangelical seceders from the Church of England has delineated the variety of such groups,[2] and that of Timothy Stunt has highlighted the international aspects of the radical impetus.[3] Some of these groups were avowedly sectarian; others just as avowedly non-sectarian, claiming (in the words of the ecumenically-minded Richard Baxter) to be nothing other than 'mere Christians'. The Brethren were a prime example of the latter group, although in them the two tendencies of sectarianism and non-sectarianism struggled for mastery.

But there were a number of prominent evangelical pastors who, while sharing aspects of Brethren thought and practice, nevertheless believed that the pastoral office remained in the church as something to be formally and publicly recognized, and not simply something to which individuals might choose to devote themselves on an informal basis. Many had been trained for the ministry, and after seceding from their denominations continued as pastors in chapels provided specially for them. The usual view of these men and their congregations has been that they represented a reaction against preoccupation with denominational interests and a

---

[1] Ian Randall, to whom this essay is dedicated, has always been interested in the whole spectrum of evangelical spirituality.

[2] Grayson Carter, *Anglican Evangelicals: Protestant Secessions from the* Via Media, *c.1800–1850* (Oxford: Oxford University Press, 2001).

[3] Timothy C.F. Stunt, *From Awakening to Secession: Radical Evangelicals in Switzerland and Britain 1815–35* (Edinburgh: T&T Clark, 2000).

breaking down of sectarian outlooks in the wake of the 1859 revival.[4] However, there is more to be said than that, and a more nuanced picture to be presented.

Although several of these pastors gathered large congregations and wrote prolifically, they have rarely received much scholarly attention, and certainly have not often been considered as a group. The only work to have treated them at length has been E.J. Poole-Connor's *Evangelical Unity*, which appeared many years ago. This essay therefore is a 'think piece' offering some arguments for testing, introducing the men and their churches, and sketching some potentially fruitful lines of inquiry for more detailed research. We shall consider who the undenominationalists were, their convictions regarding the church and the pastoral office, and the churches they built. The focus will be on the period up to 1914, in order to avoid the complications presented by the impact of Fundamentalism (which was at its peak in Britain during the 1920s) and the formation in 1922 of what became the Fellowship of Independent Evangelical Churches (FIEC).[5] Further research could, however, usefully explore how the undenominational impulse was modified under the influence of the modernist threat, a development which is evident by the time of the 'Downgrade' controversy. Geographically, the scope of this essay is necessarily restricted to Britain; the American context, in which undenominationalism has attained a higher profile, makes for several significant differences and requires separate treatment.[6]

What do we mean by 'Undenominational'?

In spite of a recurrent tendency to use one term where the other is meant, 'undenominational' is not the same as 'interdenominational'. We may explain the difference by reference to the founding in 1846 of the Evangelical Alliance (EA), an organization which has been seen as the primary expression of the evangelical impulse to fellowship and which sought to surmount the barriers presented by different denominational camps.[7] The EA did not found churches nor did it seek (during the period under review here) to bring them together as churches. So it can

---

[4] E.g., E.J. Poole-Connor, *Evangelical Unity* (London: Fellowship of Independent Evangelical Churches, 2nd edn, 1942), x.

[5] On these topics, see especially Poole-Connor, *Evangelical Unity*; D.W. Bebbington, 'Baptists and Fundamentalism in Inter-war Britain', in Keith Robbins (ed.), *Protestant Evangelicalism: Britain, Ireland, Germany and America, c.1750–c.1950* (Studies in Church History, Subsidia 7; Oxford: Basil Blackwell, 1990), 297-326; David Bebbington and David Ceri-Jones (eds), *Evangelicalism and Fundamentalism in Britain* (Oxford: Oxford University Press, forthcoming).

[6] On North America, see Hartford Institute for Religion Research, 'Nondenominational Congregations Study', <http://hirr.hartsem.edu/cong/nondenom.html>. Note that the phenomenon discussed in this essay is to be distinguished from the use of the designation 'undenominational' by the denomination known in the United States as the Church of Christ.

[7] See Ian Randall and David Hilborn, *One Body in Christ: The History and Significance of the Evangelical Alliance* (Carlisle: Paternoster Press, 2001).

be argued that the formation of undenominational congregations was an attempt to go further than the EA had done, to give ecclesiological expression to that sense of united fellowship, to take principles manifested in the para-church sphere, such as the unity of true believers in Christ in a fellowship which unconverted church members could not share, and to apply them to the church sphere. (It would be worth investigating how many undenominational leaders were involved with the EA in any meaningful sense.) Such congregations came to be known as undenominational rather than interdenominational because the objective was not so much to seek to unite believers in existing denominations as to leave them behind in the quest for a fellowship which was as comprehensive, and yet as pure, as that believed to have been practised in the New Testament. Certain churches shared the undenominational breadth of outlook but did so from within a denominational tradition where they were happy to remain; but undenominational churches saw such ties as hindering the full realization of the impetus to fellowship. Possibly in some cases they also feared that the requirement to remain faithful to particular denominational traditions and ways of doing things hindered a church from being free to submit to whatever light might be given to it from the teaching of Scripture.

The reasons for adopting an undenominational standpoint fell into three main categories. The first was ecclesiological: there was concern to make visible in the form of local congregations the unity of evangelical believers who shared a heart experience of Christ, as well as disapproval of denominational traditions which allowed people to be members who were regarded by the undenominationalists as unbelievers. The other side of this coin was a desire to realize true catholicity among believers. Of William Fuller Gooch, founder of Lansdowne Hall, West Norwood, his son wrote, 'increasingly as his friendships and fellowships developed and his influence widened, he felt that denominationalism as such fettered the catholicity of the one Church of Christ and threatened its witness to revealed Truth'.[8]

The second was evangelistic: there was a desire to be free to reach the unchurched without the hindrance of denominational traditions of worship and polity, and to establish a pattern of church life which was oriented towards evangelism rather than the maintenance of a pattern of church life suited to the churched classes. The activism which David Bebbington has highlighted as one of the hallmarks of evangelicalism[9] fuelled this desire, particularly in the wake of the revival of 1858–62 and the British mission of Moody and Sankey in 1873–75.

The third category, which became increasingly significant later in the nineteenth century, was doctrinal. Some who became undenominational leaders seceded from a denomination because of their concern at the rise of apostasy. Fuller Gooch was a close friend of Charles Spurgeon and supported his stand during the Downgrade controversy, and according to Gooch's son 'there can be little doubt that the effects

---

[8] Henry Martyn Gooch, *William Fuller Gooch: A Tribute and a Testimony* (London: The World's Evangelical Alliance, 1929), 51.

[9] D.W. Bebbington, *Evangelicalism in Modern Britain: A History from the 1730s to the 1980s* (London: Unwin Hyman, 1989), 10-12.

of this Controversy had much to do with my father's subsequent decision to sever connection with all denominational ties'.[10] Factors in his resignation from Chatsworth Baptist Church, West Norwood, included his wish to be free to express his convictions regarding church government, in view of the trend of church systems and the perceived downgrade among existing denominations.[11] Likewise, Worthing Tabernacle was founded in 1896 after a minister in the town, Douglas Crouch (d.1938), who had trained at Spurgeon's Pastor's College, withdrew from the Baptist Union over the Downgrade.[12] In time, this opposition to apostasy acquired a confirmatory eschatological tinge: true believers should come out of 'Babylon' (interpreting Revelation 18:4 as portraying *inter alia* apostate mainstream Christendom) lest they share in its downfall. During his later career, Fuller Gooch, for example, was a noted exponent of biblical prophecy. In one conference address, he managed to tie together all three motivations for undenominationalism: 'It does seem that we are in the last days, for we are in perilous times, and God is not only gathering sinners out of the world, but is gathering His own children out of an apostate Christendom that they may be brought closer together.'[13]

All three of these categories derived their power from the desire to be wholly faithful to the teaching of the Bible, which many undenominationalists saw as impossible within existing denominational structures.

Who were the Undenominationalist Leaders?

Considerable research would need to be done to determine the extent to which undenominationalism was a lay movement, but it is likely to prove less so than might be thought, given the influence exercised by high-profile pastors. These men (and they were all men) can usually be distinguished from the host of itinerant evangelists and founders of para-church agencies, settled or itinerant, male or female, who did not possess particular denominational allegiances and few of whom sought to plant churches, although they founded many mission halls which did not observe baptism or the Lord's Supper and did not usually see themselves as providing a complete diet of corporate worship for Christians. Among the best-known evangelists were men such as R.C. Morgan, Reginald Radcliffe and Lord Radstock.[14]

Few undenominational pastors have received sustained attention in recent years, so it is worth introducing some of them here, looking at those who became

---

[10] Gooch, *A Tribute and a Testimony*, 40-41, quotation at 41.

[11] Gooch, *A Tribute and a Testimony*, 51.

[12] 'Church Profile', <http://www.worthingtab.org.uk/churchprofile.htm>, accessed 25 January 2012.

[13] 'South Coast United Christian Convention', *Footsteps of Truth* 10 (1892), 235-42, at 237.

[14] See George E. Morgan, *'A Veteran in Revival': R.C. Morgan: His Life and Times* (London: Morgan & Scott, 1909); [Jane Radcliffe], *Recollections of Reginald Radcliffe, by his wife* (London: Morgan & Scott, 1896); 'Mrs Edward Trotter', *Lord Radstock: An Interpretation and a Record* (London: Hodder and Stoughton, 1914).

undenominationalists primarily for ecclesiological reasons, those who did so for evangelistic reasons, and finally those who seceded for doctrinal reasons.

Robert Govett (1813–1901) was a Fellow of Worcester College, Oxford,[15] and an Anglican clergyman, grandson of the evangelical cleric William Romaine. His preaching as curate of St Stephen's, Norwich, drew large audiences, but in 1844 he declared that he could no longer baptize infants, and seceded.[16] Soon after, he witnessed a service of believers' baptism and requested it for himself; in the next few years several hundred persons were in turn baptised by him.[17] As so often, many of his congregation left with him and he began services in what was known as the Bazaar Chapel, building its successor, Surrey Chapel, in 1854. He remained pastor until his death, at the same time producing a stream of works, many on eschatological questions and advocating a distinctive approach to the question of rewards for believers. Of Govett's expository output it was once alleged that he 'extracted great gleaming wealth out of the New Testament by turning it into a book of Euclid'.[18]

Arthur Augustus Rees (1814–84)[19] served in the navy and then experienced an evangelical conversion. He trained for the Anglican ministry at Lampeter, playing a leading role in a group of radical Evangelicals known as the 'Lampeter Brethren'. Another was H.J. Prince (1811–99), whose sister Rees married and who became notorious as the founder of the sect of the Agapemonites, whose combination of sexual immorality, intense piety and devotion to Prince as the mouthpiece of God is evidence that from a historical perspective radicalism and unorthodoxy cannot always be rigidly distinguished. Ordained in 1841, Rees took a curacy in Sunderland, where his forthright evangelistic preaching soon attracted large numbers of the working classes. However, complaints about his sermon when he preached in another church nearby led the Bishop of Durham to forbid him to preach outside his

---

[15] The Strict Baptist seceder J.C. Philpot (1802–69) had been a fellow of the same college, though he appears to have seceded on different grounds from Govett.

[16] Govett was typical in asserting that the practice of infant baptism was a principal means by which the world had infiltrated the church: Robert Govett, *Of whom does the Church Consist?* (Norwich: Fletcher and Son, 1874), 16.

[17] Norwich, Norfolk Record Office, MS 4260, Maurice F. Hewett, 'Collection of material in preparation for a Historical Record of the Baptists of Norfolk and their Churches', vol. 2, typescript [1940s], 'Norwich, The Bazaar Church and Surrey Road, Ebenezer'.

[18] Thomas Phillips, 'A Man who was never Insulted by a Stipend', *Baptist Times* 24 August 1923, reprinted in John Wilmot and James H. Pizey, *God's Work in God's Way: A Memoir of the Life and Ministry of James Stephens, M.A.* (London: Highgate Road Chapel, 1934), 115-16, quotation at 115. Euclid was an ancient mathematician.

[19] On Rees, see James Everett, *The Midshipman and the Minister: The Quarter Deck and the Pulpit* (London: Adams, 1867); Comtesse Héloïse de Manin, 'Our Friends in Heaven: VIII. Arthur Augustus Rees', *Footsteps of Truth* 2 (1884), 349-52, 427-32, 547-52, 610-15; Sydney E. Watson, *Bethesda Free Chapel Centenary* (Sunderland: Bethesda Chapel, 1945); Timothy C.F. Stunt, 'The Early Development of Arthur Augustus Rees and his Relations with the Brethren', *Brethren Archivists' and Historians' Network Review* 4.1 (2006), 22-35.

own parish. Rees formed a church within a church, composed of spiritually awakened members of his congregation, and was given notice to leave by his rector, apparently because of his views on divine sovereignty and his assertion on the basis of Matthew 7:13-14 that only a few would be saved. (This implies that Rees may have been a fairly high Calvinist, as were many other seceders during the first half of the nineteenth century.[20]) He was then appointed to a charge in Bath but was turned out because his previous bishop would not provide the requisite testimonial. Rees finally seceded from the Church of England, returned to Sunderland and planted a congregation whose nucleus was drawn from his earlier ministry there. Bethesda Chapel was built for them and unlike most chapels of the period no seat rents were charged; Rees appears to have borne the running expenses himself, as well as foregoing any stipend, although he soon placed boxes in the chapel for voluntary contributions.

At the start, Rees was emphatic that he would 'not be a dissenter on *principle*, but by *compulsion*, for I was conscientiously a minister of the church', and that he was leaving behind not the doctrines of the Church of England but its 'misgovernment and bad administration'.[21] He regarded himself as a nonconformist but not a dissenter, and continued to use the Book of Common Prayer and to wear a gown when conducting worship, but abandoned both practices after being baptized as a believer in 1845 by the Brethren leader George Müller; 1,200 of his flock followed his example and were immersed. His views continued to evolve; in 1848 he also adopted the Brethren practice of holding communion each week on Sunday morning. Yet he refused to align himself exclusively with Brethren, offering his reasons in *Four Letters to the Christians called 'Brethren' on the Subject of Ministry and Worship*, the first two of which appeared in 1868.[22] Rees' critique focused on the Brethren notion that the Holy Spirit rather than any human being presided at corporate worship, coupled with the claim to quasi-charismatic inspiration for contributions to open worship and the allegation by some Brethren that congregations whose practice differed from this did not truly meet in the name of Christ. At the back of Rees' mind was undoubtedly the story of Prince, whose deviation from theological orthodoxy and moral rectitude had begun with similar claims to immediate inspiration.[23] The ecclesiological motivation for Rees' secession was evident in the reasons he gave for refusing to co-operate in revivalist meetings held in Sunderland in 1859. These included the use of women as preachers, which he regarded as contravening Pauline injunctions (1 Cor. 14:34; 1 Tim. 2:10-14); the

---

[20] Arthur Augustus Rees, *Solemn Protest, before the Church and Nation, of the Rev. Arthur A. Rees, Late Minister of Thomas Street Episcopal Chapel, Bath, against his Virtual Ejection from the Ministry of the Church of England* (Bath: T. Noyes, 1844), 3-4 (citing a report in the *Sunderland and Durham County Herald*), 12.

[21] Rees, *Solemn Protest*, 10.

[22] A.A. Rees, *Four Letters to the Christians called 'Brethren' on the Subject of Ministry and Worship* (London: Passmore & Alabaster, 2nd edn, [1875]).

[23] A.A. Rees, *The Rise and Progress of the Heresy of the Rev. H.J. Prince* (Weymouth: Benson and Barling, n.d. [1846]).

deployment of techniques such as encouraging inquirers to go forward to the 'penitent form'; and the general failure to observe Paul's command that everything be done decently and in order (1 Cor. 14:40).[24]

William Fuller Gooch (1843–1928), to whom I am related, was unusual in having a Baptist background, his father having pastored churches in East Anglia. The first half of William's ministry was spent in Baptist churches (apart from a year at Bethesda, Sunderland), but the second half was devoted to an undenominational congregation which he founded – Lansdowne Hall, West Norwood. One of Gooch's sons, Henry Martyn Gooch, served in the interdenominational rather than undenominational setting as secretary of the Evangelical Alliance. Fuller Gooch's pamphlet *Undenominationalism* set out his fundamental convictions:

1. Differences on secondary issues among believers do not require separation into rival sects or parties.
2. It is wrong for Christians and congregations to take the names of individuals or ordinances.
3. The Bible and church history show that that the Holy Spirit's working is always on the side of such principles.
4. Denominationalism is a great hindrance to the spread of the gospel.[25]

E.J. Poole-Connor (1872–1962) pastored Lansdowne Hall, West Norwood (1910–12), and Talbot Tabernacle (1913–21, 1933–43); his chief significance, though, was as the main begetter of the Fellowship of Independent Evangelical Churches, which falls outside the timescale of this paper.[26]

Of those who became undenominationalists primarily for reasons connected with evangelistic effectiveness, several did so during the 1858–62 revival. J. Denham Smith (1817–89) was a Congregational minister in Kingstown, Dublin, who resigned his pastorate in the wake of the 1859 revival, 'in order to take his stand as a servant of the Church at large'.[27] His friends had a large hall built for him in Dublin, Merrion Hall (now part of a luxury hotel), which although linked with Brethren was more of an undenominational place of worship in that it welcomed the ministry of speakers from the denominations and did not necessarily follow Brethren ecclesiological thinking or practice.

---

[24] A.A. Rees, *Reasons for not Co-operating in the alleged 'Sunderland Revivals': in an Address to his Congregation* (Sunderland: Wm Henry Hills, 1859).

[25] Reproduced in Gooch, *A Tribute and a Testimony*, 67-74. I have been unable to consult an earlier address of his entitled *Our Distinctive Position as a Denomination: A Paper read at the Annual Meeting of the Suffolk and Norfolk Baptist Home Missionary Union* (1868). This body had been founded in 1846, effectively replacing the previous association, and became the Suffolk Baptist Union.

[26] On Poole-Connor, see D.G. Fountain, *E.J. Poole-Connor (1872–1962): 'Contender for the Faith'* (Worthing: Henry E. Walter, 1966).

[27] C. Russell Hurditch, 'Our Friends in Heaven: XXX. Mr. Denham Smith', *Footsteps of Truth* 7 (1889), 237-69; quotation at 245.

The Scottish advocate and erstwhile deist Gordon Forlong (1819–1908), although known as an evangelist in Britain and (from 1876) New Zealand, was also the founder (in 1866) and first minister of Talbot Tabernacle in London's Notting Hill, which along with its founder maintained loose Brethren links.[28]

Henry Varley (1835–1912)[29] was converted at John Street Chapel in London[30] under B.W. Noel, a seceder from the Church of England who in time became a Baptist minister. After a few years in Australia, Varley returned to London and became a successful butcher as well as superintending a Congregational mission in Notting Dale. As the mission's converts were not sufficiently 'respectable' for the mother chapel, Varley formed a church for them and in 1860 he and his father-in-law paid for a new chapel to be built, the Free Tabernacle, later the West London Tabernacle. He was advised to join the Baptist Union and to seek denominational ordination but saw no need for human ordination and feared that denominational allegiance would restrict the congregation's freedom. His friend Spurgeon once called him 'a bad Baptist and a half-bred Plymouth Brother', not a bad description of a number of these men![31]

Although the chapel developed a full programme of outreach activities, Varley travelled more and more, feeling that his first calling was to be an evangelist. Belief in the doctrine of election, coupled with adherence to dispensationalist eschatology, drove him to seek to gather in the full number of the elect in view of the approaching End. Like several other undenominationalists, he wrote on eschatology, *Christ's Coming Kingdom* (1885). From the 1870s, his lectures to youths and men regarding sexual purity became famous and were widely published. Visiting Australia again 1877–79 (during his absence trustees were appointed and a committee formed to manage chapel affairs), he resigned his pastorate in 1886 and moved there in 1888. His style of evangelism, as well as his particular ministry to younger men, ensured wide publicity: Paproth has shown just how controversial his Australian activity was,

---

[28] On Forlong, see Henry Pickering, *Chief Men among the Brethren (Acts 15.22): 100 Records and Photos of Brethren Beloved* (London: Pickering & Inglis, 2nd edn, [1931]), 67-69; Poole-Connor, *Evangelical Unity*, 163-64; G. Forlong, *The Life of Gordon Forlong* (Te Puke: H.G. Forlong, 2nd edn, 1975); Peter Lineham, *There we found Brethren: A History of Assemblies of Brethren in New Zealand* (Palmerston North: Gospel Publishing House, 1977).

[29] On Varley, see his biography, *Henry Varley's Life Story by his Son*, H. Varley (London: Alfred Holness, [1913]); Darrell Paproth, 'Henry Varley and the Melbourne Evangelicals', *Journal of Religious History* 25 (2001), 173-87.

[30] John Street had been built in 1818 by the banker, MP and later Catholic Apostolic apostle, Henry Drummond, for the ministry of James Harington Evans (1785–1849). Evans' ministerial career began in the Church of England; he seceded as part of the high Calvinist 'Western Schism' around 1815 and after flirting with trinitarian unorthodoxy during the early 1820s settled down to minister at John Street to a congregation which gradually adopted more of a Baptist complexion; cf. James Joyce Evans, *Memoir and Remains of the Rev. James Harington Evans, late minister of John-Street Chapel* (London: James Nisbet, 1852); Carter, *Anglican Seceders*, chapter 4.

[31] Varley, *Life Story*, 74.

marked as it was by militancy and anti-clericalism, and has even argued that Varley may be seen as a forerunner of more recent charismatic individualists who are motivated by a will to power. This argument, if extrapolated to others discussed here, could prove as contentious as Varley's own pronouncements.

C. Russell Hurditch (1839–1918) joined the Brethren during the early 1860s,[32] but in many ways he fits the undenominational mould rather better. He ran a chain of missions across North London, a number of which did observe baptism and the Lord's Supper, and he founded a periodical, *Footsteps of Truth*, which included articles by and about Evangelicals of all denominations.

F.E. Marsh began his ministry as one of the workers in Hurditch's Evangelistic Mission, becoming an itinerant evangelist before succeeding Fuller Gooch as pastor of Bethesda, Sunderland; from 1910–12 he pastored Unity Chapel, Bristol.[33]

D.J. Findlay (1858–1938) founded St George's Cross Tabernacle, Glasgow. He was primarily an evangelist, in an era when evangelical church services were aimed primarily at evangelism and fitting Christians to evangelize as the focus of an activist spirituality. Linked with the vigorous programme of evangelism was the prominence given to overseas mission in Findlay's church as in many others.

Some were what we might term 'doctrinal undenominationalists'. B.W. Newton (1807–99) had been a leading light among the early Brethren at Plymouth. However, after being virtually cast out in 1848 because his church practice and theological views clashed with those of John Nelson Darby, he founded a small congregation at Bayswater in West London.[34] He could be described as undenominational in the sense of meeting apart from existing denominations (the Brethren included), but he would probably be one of the most sectarian of undenominational leaders in his outlook and his practice of fellowship. Between the mid-1850s and 1872 he pastored a chapel in Duke Street, St James's Park, and then one in Queen's Road, Bayswater (the latter being his personal property), but after a physical breakdown he gave up his charge and closed the chapel; he had never allowed anyone else to preach there except his cousin, the biblical critic and erstwhile Brethren member S.P. Tregelles (1813–75).

James Stephens (1846–1932) was a United Presbyterian minister at Berwick-upon-Tweed. Having adopted George Müller's practice of 'living by faith' without any guaranteed stipend, he later became convinced of believers' baptism and seceded in 1876. He became a Baptist minister at the newly founded Highgate Road Chapel in 1878, but withdrew from the London Baptist Association in 1887, his church following him shortly afterwards. (It had already withdrawn from the Baptist

---

[32] 'Septima' [Grace Hurditch], *Peculiar People* (London: Heath Cranton, 1935), 27.

[33] *Footsteps of Truth* 9 (1891), 273; K. Linton and A.H. Linton, *'I will Build my Church': 150 Years of Local Church Work in Bristol* (Bristol: C. Hadler, [1982]), 213.

[34] On Newton, see George H. Fromow, *B.W. Newton and Dr. S.P. Tregelles: Teachers of the Faith and the Future* (London: Sovereign Grace Advent Testimony, 2nd edn, 1969); Jonathan D. Burnham, *A Story of Conflict: The Controversial Relationship between Benjamin Wills Newton and John Nelson Darby* (Carlisle: Paternoster Press, 2004), esp. chapter 8.

Union.³⁵) In 1896 Thomas Spurgeon pressed Stephens to accept the principalship of the Pastor's College, where he was already lecturing each week, but he refused. His views on prophecy, on which he was a noted exponent, accorded with those of B.W. Newton and S.P. Tregelles (being what nowadays we would call post-tribulational pre-millennialism). Stephens later wrote and spoke extensively on behalf of the Sovereign Grace Advent Testimony, founded in 1918.

Frank H. White (d.1915) studied at Spurgeon's Pastors' College (1861–62).³⁶ After pastoring Paradise Chapel (later Lower Sloane Street Chapel), Chelsea, a Baptist work, from 1862, he succeeded Forlong at Talbot Tabernacle in 1874, remaining there until 1903. He too wrote on prophetic and typological themes. White does not seem to have seceded from the Baptist Union so much as drifted out of it, an example of those whose ministries overlapped the porous boundary between denominational and undenominational churches.

Undenominationalism was not always easy to distinguish by sight: the careers of some of the men we have referred to illustrate that it shaded off at its edges into Brethren and Baptist churches which sat relatively lightly to traditional group loyalties and pursued a somewhat independent path. Other men, therefore, could perhaps be seen in an undenominational light, among them George Müller, who functioned as the pastor of Bethesda, Bristol, and was accorded the title 'Rev.' in reports of his itinerant ministry; the ex-Anglican William Lincoln (1817–88) of Beresford Chapel, Walworth, in South London, which shared many of the features of Brethren assemblies but was under his care; Spurgeon, especially once he withdrew from the Baptist Union in 1887; and the Brethren itinerant G.H. Lang (1874–1958), who served briefly as pastor of Unity Chapel, Bristol, and whose thinking helped to mould that of some early Restorationist pioneers.

Undenominational Churches

As we have intimated already, a distinction may be drawn between the lay-orientated mission-hall movement which grew out of the 1859 revival and which saw evangelistic works being initiated all over the county in unpretentious halls in urban and rural locations, and the churches of the undenominational movement. Undenominational churches may be differentiated from preaching places or mission halls *tout simple* by two things in particular: their observance of the ordinances of baptism and the Lord's Supper, and (often) their having a recognized pastor, although ordination as conferring exclusive rights to administer the sacraments was rejected.³⁷ Mission halls, and the Christian Unions in Scotland and Ulster, were not intended to provide a complete diet of worship and teaching for the Christian,

---

³⁵ On Stephens, see 'Pastor James Stephens, M.A., of Highgate', *Footsteps of Truth* 10 (1892), 150-51; Wilmot and Pizey, *God's Work in God's Way*.

³⁶ Poole-Connor, *Evangelical Unity*, 164; Judy Powles to the author, 30 July 2012.

³⁷ Cf. R. Govett, *The Church of Old in its Unity, Gifts, and Ministry; or, An Exposition of 1 Corinthians XII, XIII, XIV* (3 parts; Norwich: Josiah Fletcher, 1850), III, 31.

whereas undenominational churches were. Of course, many mission halls in time became undenominational churches as a nucleus of converts was gathered together and provision needed to be made for their spiritual growth.

It is impossible to establish a comprehensive list of all such congregations, since many were little known beyond their immediate locality, but some of the main undenominational churches were very well known in evangelical circles. In his chapter on 'The Independent Evangelical churches', which is still the most accessible overview of them, Poole-Connor discusses Unity, Bristol; Bethesda, Sunderland; Surrey Chapel, Norwich; West London Tabernacle; Wattville Street Undenominational Church, Handsworth, Birmingham; Talbot Tabernacle; and Lansdowne Hall, West Norwood.[38] Below I have attempted to provide, in chronological order, a list of the main undenominational causes. It will show that the same mix of factors was at work in their foundation as was evident in the men who led them.

Surrey Chapel, Norwich (1844), moved into its own premises in 1854, the building of which was almost entirely financed by its founder.[39] The ministries of Govett and his successor, D.M. Panton (1870–1955),[40] were marked by distinctive eschatological views, however, which must have narrowed the range of people finding fellowship there, in spite of Govett's insistence (over against the Brethren especially) that it was unscriptural to exclude people from church fellowship on doctrinal grounds.[41]

Bethesda Chapel, Sunderland (1845) was built to provide a home for the continuing ministry of A.A. Rees, but unlike many such chapels it continued to prosper, with a succession of notable ministers and an effective evangelistic outreach.

Unity Chapel, Bristol (1850) was founded by a member of the Brethren assembly at Bethesda, Bristol, but is pointedly described by Poole-Connor as 'not *quite* a Brethren assembly'.[42] The chief difference was that for a number of years until 1915, it had stated ministers. Perhaps Lang (1900–1908) is the best known nowadays, but F.E. Marsh also served here (1910–12).[43]

West London Tabernacle (1860) was intended by Varley to be a church for the unchurched but once he resigned as pastor it lost its momentum. Eventually it passed into the hands of the Disciples of Christ, but before too many decades had passed it

---

[38] Poole-Connor, *Evangelical Unity*, 145-73.

[39] Poole-Connor, *Evangelical Unity*, 153.

[40] On Panton, an ex-Anglican and close friend of Fuller Gooch, whose teaching was indirectly influential on Watchman Nee, see Keith Ives, 'Keiths Histories: David Morrieson Panton', <www.keithshistories.com>, accessed 3 August 2012.

[41] R. Govett, *Exclusion of Believers for Doctrine, Unscriptural* (Norwich: Fletcher & Son, 2nd edn, 1873).

[42] Poole-Connor, *Evangelical Unity*, 147.

[43] Linton and Linton, '*I will Build my Church*', 212-13.

was being used as a warehouse. Poole-Connor's judgement is that the decline was due to Varley's failure to set up any kind of church organization.[44]

Beresford Chapel, Walworth, London (1862), was originally an Anglican proprietary chapel; as Roy Coad explains, 'The lease of the chapel was in the minister's name, and the congregation (or as many as followed him) continued to use it after his accession to Brethren.'[45] Some who wished to see a more thoroughgoing outworking of Brethren principles withdrew to found daughter assemblies but after Lincoln's death Beresford became more typically Brethren.

Talbot Tabernacle, Notting Hill, London (1869), saw a succession of undenominational men lead it, including Forlong, White and Poole-Connor. Its foundation had been primarily for evangelistic reasons.

Wattville St, Birmingham (1871), was founded as a mission work by David Wright, whose family ran it for many years. They had associated with Brethren and the morning services followed the Brethren pattern, but the congregation moved out of the Brethren orbit because it did not accept Brethren eschatology.[46]

Edinburgh Castle People's Mission Church, London (1872), represents a striking example of an undenominational congregation founded for evangelistic reasons. It was started by Thomas Barnardo, who had spent some years among Brethren in Dublin. Once again, Barnardo wanted to provide for converts from the lower classes who needed a church home where they would not feel out of place, and an alternative to the 'fellowship' which had been offered in the building when it was a gin palace.

St George's Cross Tabernacle, Glasgow (1874), was another congregation whose founding impetus was evangelistic. It has been suggested that the choice of the name 'Tabernacle' reflects the nomenclature adopted by the Scottish evangelists James and Robert Haldane at the beginning of the nineteenth century, who manifested both evangelistic and ecclesiological concerns in their careers.[47] However, the name was also adopted widely among contemporary revivalists in America as well as Britain, and there does not seem to have been any specific link with the churches founded by the Haldanes.[48]

Highgate Road Chapel, London (1878), was not only open communion but open membership; believers' baptism was taught but not required for membership. The ethos of the church does seem to have been more explicitly separatist, perhaps

---

[44] Poole-Connor, *Evangelical Unity*, 160.

[45] F. Roy Coad, *A History of the Brethren Movement* (Exeter: The Paternoster Press, 2nd edn, 1976), 177.

[46] Poole-Connor, *Evangelical Unity*, 160-62.

[47] Alexander Gammie, *Pastor D.J. Findlay: A Unique Personality* (London: Pickering & Inglis, 1949), 28.

[48] On the Haldanes, see Alexander Haldane, *The Lives of Robert Haldane of Airthrey, and of his Brother, James Alexander Haldane* (London: Hamilton, Adams, 2nd edn, 1852; reprinted); Deryck W. Lovegrove, 'Unity and Separation: Contrasting Elements in the Thought and Practice of Robert and James Alexander Haldane', in Robbins (ed.), *Protestant Evangelicalism*, 153-77.

because by now the nonconformist landscape was changing and the chief enemy was increasingly seen to be doctrinal error rather than entanglement with the world.

Lansdowne Hall, West Norwood (1878), home to the ministries of Fuller Gooch and Poole-Connor, came into being for ecclesiological reasons, as Fuller Gooch sought a wider fellowship. Nevertheless, once established, it maintained an active evangelistic concern and is one of the minority of churches surveyed here which are still in existence today.

Finally, let me offer two examples of a host of smaller undenominational congregations, often in villages or small towns, whose existence is much more difficult to track down. The first is in the town where I live, Ramsey on the Isle of Man. The notice board of the Bethel Chapel there proclaims that the church is 'undenominational'. It has often had a recognized pastor, practises baptism and communion, and grew out of a mission to seamen which was around by the 1880s. The second is in Kent: Samuel Morley, a Congregationalist, founded several 'undenominational' mission halls in the area west of Tonbridge from 1870 onwards. Some at least of these grew into churches practising baptism and communion, and one had a settled evangelist attached to it.[49]

Although the churches thus formed were individual congregations, responsible to no outside agency, it would be misleading to regard them as congregational in polity. Some undenominational congregations seem to have adopted a modified form of Presbyterianism, but in many the pastor exercised a firm leadership, even if elders or deacons existed – and sometimes they did not. Indeed, in some cases there was no recognized officer apart from the pastor (e.g., Findlay, Varley, Govett) which gave rise to problems when he retired or died. Govett came under fire from the Scottish itinerant John Bowes for his dictatorial style.[50] Even Findlay's admiring biographer admits that his subject was a dictator in the church! He received no salary, served as its treasurer and dealt with all administration.[51] Just after Govett's death, his church had to meet to elect a committee of management.[52] Such strong leadership differentiated them to some extent from Brethren, although some Brethren congregations had *de facto* pastors. Furthermore, some of these pastors wrote to take

---

[49] Coad, *History of the Brethren*, 175-77.

[50] [John Bowes] (ed.), *Important Correspondence between Messrs. R. Govett and J. Dean: The Latter Suspended by the Former for his Sympathy with the Norwich Conference of Nonconformists* (Cheltenham: John Bowes, 1853). John Bowes (1804–74), who had a Methodist background, planted a number of Brethren-style congregations, although he never fitted easily into the Brethren scene because of his independence of outlook and his tendency to ride hobbyhorses. He could be seen as manifesting some features evident in later undenominationalists: see Neil Dickson, *Brethren in Scotland 1838–2000* (Carlisle: Paternoster Press, 2002).

[51] Gammie, *Findlay*, 10, 28.

[52] Rosamunde Codling, *150 Years at Surrey Chapel, Norwich, 1854–2004* (Norwich: Surrey Chapel, [2004]), 11.

issue with Brethren views on stated ministry and pastoral office (e.g., Rees and Govett).[53]

Buildings might be the personal property of their founders. After Rees' death, his chapel in Sunderland was purchased from his executors by its elders and deacons and a trust deed and constitution were drawn up.[54] Newton's chapel in Bayswater was his personal property and when he could no longer minister in it, he closed it. Lincoln's chapel was leased in his name, and provides an unusual example of movement of a building across denominational boundaries.

Some of these churches had no formal membership; Findlay's Tabernacle was one.[55] This was true of a number of Brethren assemblies, too, although I doubt whether the reasons were always the same. Some Brethren at least resisted any formal church organization because of a belief that the church on earth was irreparably ruined and all that believers now could do was to meet together on the basis of Matthew 18:20, trusting in God's promised presence with the 'two or three'. I have not come across any undenominationalists who held such views, and think it more probable that their lack of organization is simply an extreme example of evangelical pragmatism and aversion to religious bureaucracy; many Brethren would have shared this.

As for the ordinances, most practised baptism of believers by immersion but refused to make it a condition of communion; Govett, indeed, criticized the Strict Baptist position on this score.[56] The Lord's Supper in such churches was open to all born-again believers in Christ. The introduction of communion seems to have been the point at which Findlay's meetings in Glasgow metamorphosed into a church fellowship[57] and this was likely the case elsewhere.

As in the Brethren, the undenominational impetus could be seen as leading to separatism and secession (Poole-Connor), but also to ecumenism (Fuller Gooch). The evangelist and revival publicist R.C. Morgan's son George, in his father's memoir, felt it necessary to reject as 'pre-eminently unsound' the idea that American evangelists were 'instrumental in creating a vogue for undenominational missions – indeed, almost a new sect of "undenominationalists" – admittedly devoted and eager in soul-winning, but seeking isolation rather than unity of heart and purpose in the wider life of the churches'.[58] In George Morgan's view, his father was pan-denominational instead. But he was writing half a century afterwards, when the trajectory of the movement could be traced over time.

---

[53] E.g., Rees, *Four Letters*; Govett, *The Church of Old*.
[54] Watson, *Bethesda*, 18.
[55] Gammie, *Findlay*, 106.
[56] [R. Govett], *Open or Strict Communion? Judgment pronounced by the Lord Jesus himself* (Norwich: Fletcher & Son, 1845).
[57] Gammie, *Findlay*, 24.
[58] Morgan, *R.C. Morgan*, 190.

Interestingly, some congregations gave birth to daughter churches in distant locations. Findlay's church in Glasgow was the progenitor of one in Bradford; Lansdowne in West Norwood produced Worthing Tabernacle.[59]

Conclusion

We have discussed the main leaders and churches, noting three types of undenominationalism: evangelistic, ecclesiological and doctrinal. Our sketch has indicated that strong leadership was a key feature, perhaps because many of these churches were the result of individual initiative. What can be said about their strengths and weaknesses? Poole-Connor, writing as an apologist for the Fellowship of Independent Evangelical Churches, which sought to draw such congregations together, considered that they had a bigger vision, they were less liable to the inroads of modernism and they were better suited to planting in new districts. On the other hand, they were also liable to become self-centred and insular, and there was a lack of suitable ministers for them; there was no external source of help when needed, it was difficult to know how to describe or label them, and it was harder for ministers to secure exemption from military service (an important issue earlier in the twentieth century). Perceptively, he noted that they were well supported in times of revival, when their principles were in accord with the prevailing outlook, but when that faded the practical difficulties of their position became more evident.[60] The history of these congregations seems to bear out many of his assertions, especially the last one. Undenominational churches, like many denominations birthed in times of spiritual revival and intense evangelistic activity, seem to have gone through a phase of institutionalization from which some did not emerge. Further research is needed to test out Poole-Connor's opinions and to explore the range of outcomes evident in the histories of these churches and hence the futures open to similar congregations today.

Other issues, too, call for serious thought. Many large evangelical Baptist churches have in effect functioned as undenominational ones, even if nominally remaining within the Baptist Union of Great Britain or similar bodies. Is undenominationalism a function of an evangelical congregation's size as well as its theology and polity? Does congregational church order encourage a sense of self-sufficiency?

What types of foreign mission agency did these churches found or support? Did the undenominational impulse in its various forms have a 'knock-on effect' on the foreign mission field, whether in terms of working relationships with personnel from denominational missions or the churches founded by missionaries? How much were undenominational pastors involved with the newer societies through serving on councils and committees? Conversely, did mission-field realities influence the way

---

[59] Gammie, *Findlay*, 49-50; Gooch, *A Tribute and a Testimony*, 63.
[60] Poole-Connor, *Evangelical Unity*, 170-73.

in which key figures in Britain viewed the issues addressed by undenominationalism?

What degree of continuity was there between pre-1859 and post-1859 undenominationalism? A similar question has been asked regarding the Brethren, whose church life has sometimes been seen as metamorphosing from a primary orientation towards Bible study to a much more evangelism-orientated pattern. Related to this is the question of the role played by *The Revival* (later *The Christian*) and other similar periodicals in funding and spreading news of undenominational work. How much did undenominationalism owe to the evangelism-orientated revivalist network whose development Morgan did so much to foster?

Finally, we have not looked at the links between undenominationalism and interdenominationalism, and particularly at the kind of interdenominationalism represented by conventions such as Keswick, which were intended to deepen the spiritual experience which Evangelicals shared in common and which impelled them to reach hands across denominational barriers. Ian Randall has written illuminatingly on Keswick spirituality in particular and evangelical spirituality in general, and his work will be an indispensable starting-point for exploration of these questions.

CHAPTER 6

Baptists in the Czech Lands[1]

Lydie Kucová

The Czech Baptist movement emerged in the second half of the nineteenth century and was diverse at its beginning.[2] Three major streams of Baptist witness are identifiable in Bohemia, Moravia, and Silesia, and among Czechs living in Europe outside the Austro-Hungarian borders.[3] All three have their roots in the Baptist missionary movement, initiated in Germany in the first half of the nineteenth century by Johann Gerhard Oncken. This movement experienced rapid growth in its early days and spread from Germany to other European countries with a strong German presence.[4]

---

[1] An earlier version of this paper was given at the meeting of the Baptist World Alliance History and Heritage Commission in Prague, Czech Republic, in 2008. I would like to thank Jan Bistranin and Pavel Vychopeň for their helpful comments on that version of the paper, and Astrid van der Poel, whose initial study of the subject in the 1990s was beneficial to my own research. I gladly offer the paper in honour of Ian M. Randall, a noted Baptist historian, who has spent a significant part of his teaching career in the country whose Baptist heritage is explored in this paper.

[2] For an older comprehensive study of the Czech Baptists and their beginnings, see Vaclav Vojta, *Czechoslovak Baptists* (Minneapolis, MN: Czechoslovak Baptist Convention in America and Canada, 1941).

[3] Bohemia, Moravia and Silesia are three geographical regions of the Czech Republic that are traditionally occupied by Czechs, although in the past people of other nationalities, especially Germans, were also strongly present in these lands. The Czech Lands of the nineteenth century belonged to the Habsburg monarchy that is known by its official names Austrian Empire (1804–67) and Austria-Hungary (1867–1918) for the periods considered here.

[4] For a recent treatment of Oncken's missionary movement see Andrea Strübind, '"Mission to Germany". Die Entstehung des Deutschen Baptismus in seiner Verflechtung mit der internationalen Erweckungsbewegung und den Schwesterkirchen in den USA und England', in Andrea Strübind and Martin Rothkegel (eds), *Baptismus: Geschichte und Gegenwart* (Göttingen: Vandenhoeck & Ruprecht, 2012), 163-200. For a survey of the Baptist movement across the mainland of Europe emanating from German Baptist mission work, see Ian M. Randall, *Communities of Conviction: Baptist Beginnings in Europe* (Schwarzenfeld: Neufeld Verlag, 2009); and Richard V. Pierard, 'Germany and Baptist Expansion in Nineteenth-Century Europe', in David W. Bebbington (ed.), *The Gospel in the*

The Beginnings

The earliest stream of Baptist witness in the Czech Lands is associated with the German missionary Magnus Knappe, who started mission outreach in Prussian Silesia, close to the borders with Bohemia. Knappe was called as a volunteer for mission outreach in Silesia at the regional conference of German Baptist churches in Stettin in 1858.[5] After having based his mission first in Voigtsdorf and later in Freiburg, he travelled regularly across the border to the Bohemian towns of Broumov (Braunau) and Šonov (Schaunau) for evangelistic outreach among the German-speaking population. The conditions for missionary work were very difficult in this Catholic region under the Austrian authorities. They were worsened by the fact that Knappe commuted to Bohemia from Prussian Silesia, a region that belonged to the Kingdom of Prussia which at that time had strained relations with Austria.[6] The early missionary efforts of Knappe in Bohemia bore no fruit. He persevered, though, and after several years of continuous mission endeavour the first convert from Bohemia was baptised by Knappe in his church. The baptism took place in 1863 and was followed by more baptisms in succeeding years, which led to the formation of a small group of Baptist believers in the Broumov region in 1868. The group experienced steady growth over the years and eventually, in 1893, became a mission station of the Baptist church in Prague.[7]

The second centre of Czech Baptist beginnings is found among the Czech-speaking population of Russian Poland. The Baptist witness to the German communities in Russian Poland and in the Volhynia province is part of the general story of German Baptist extension. This witness soon spread among Czechs and other Slavs who shared the land with German settlers. A major figure among the Baptists in Russian Poland was a German school teacher, Gottfried F. Alf,[8] who founded the first Baptist church on Polish soil in Adamow in August 1861. The second Baptist church was established just weeks later in Kicin and became a centre of Baptist life in Poland during the nineteenth century. The Baptist congregation in Kicin soon experienced considerable growth that led to the foundation of new

---

World: International Baptist Studies (Studies in Baptist History and Thought, 1; Carlisle: Paternoster, 2002), 189-208.

[5] Joseph Lehmann, *Geschichte der deutschen Baptisten II* (Hamburg: J.G. Oncken Nachfolger, 1900), 195-96; Samuel Knappe, *Magnus Knappe, ein von Gott zubereitetes Werkzeug zur Verbreitung evangelischer Wahrheiten in Schlesierlande* (Kassel: J.G. Oncken Nachfolger, n.d.), 20.

[6] The conflict between Prussia and the Austrian Empire culminated in the Austro-Prussian war (1866) that took place near Hradec Králové in eastern Bohemia, not very far from the place of Knappe's mission outreach.

[7] Knappe, *Magnus Knappe*, 34-41; cf. Rudolf Donat, *Das waschende Werk: Ausbreitung der deutschen Baptistengemeinden durch sechzig Jahre, 1849 bis 1909* (Kassel: Oncken Verlag, 1960), 388.

[8] On Gottfried F. Alf, see the biography by Albert W. Wardin, Jr., *Gottfried F. Alf: Pioneer of the Baptist Movement in Poland* (Brentwood, TN: Baptist History and Heritage Society, 2003).

churches in the 1870s.⁹ One of these, the church founded in Kurówek in 1870, played a significant role in spreading the Baptist witness among the Czech-speaking community in Zelów. The first Czech convert from Zelów was baptised in Kurówek in 1870 and two years later a first Czech Baptist church was organized in Zelów with Jan Jersák as its first pastor. This earliest Czech Baptist church, founded in 1872, is also regarded as the earliest Slavic church in Poland.[10]

The third stream of Baptist witness among Czechs is linked with two influential names in Czech Baptist history, August Meereis and Henry Novotný. August Meereis was the son of Bohemian immigrants with a Lutheran and Catholic background who lived in Volhynia. Due to an epidemic his parents had died when he was only ten years old. As an orphan he was taken care of by Karl Ondra, whose son, also called Karl, later became a significant minister in Volhynia and in Russian Poland. The young Meereis attended Baptist meetings in his village, which were decisive in his conversion. He was baptised upon confession of his faith in a little pond on a dark night in 1863. As a person subject to Austro-Hungarian laws, Meereis was sent to Bohemia to undertake three years of military service in the late 1860s. On completion of the service in 1872 he did not return to Russia but remained in Bohemia and became a colporteur of the British and Foreign Bible Society. Travelling from one place to another in the Czech Lands, he worked as a missionary and conducted the first baptisms of Czechs in Brandýs nad Orlicí in April 1877. However, he never stayed long in one location; after a few conversions and baptisms he would move on. In 1879 he was called to be a minister of the Baptist church in Vienna. Though living in Vienna, Meereis did not lose sight of the work in Bohemia. He kept ties with scattered converts in the Czech Lands through letters and visits, by means of which the groundwork was laid for the formation of the first Baptist church on Czech soil a few years later.[11]

Henry Novotný and the First Baptist Church in Bohemia

The pioneering work of August Meereis paved the way for a stronger Baptist presence in Bohemia which is now linked with the name of Henry Novotný, the leading person in the early Czech Baptist movement. Novotný was born in 1846 to a

---

[9] On the earliest German speaking Baptist churches in Russian Poland, see G.L. [Gottfried Liebert], *Geschichte der Baptisten in Russisch-Polen umfassend den Zeitraum von 1854 bis 1874* (Hamburg: J.G.Oncken, n.d. [c.1874]), 77-95; Lehmann, *Geschichte II*, 300-307; Eduard Kupsch, *Geschichte der Baptisten in Polen, 1852–1932* (Zdunska-Wola: Kupsch, n.d. [c.1932]), 44-64; Donat, *Das waschende Werk*, 145-56.

[10] G.L., *Geschichte der Baptisten in Russisch-Polen*, 142, 144; Kupsch, *Geschichte der Baptisten in Polen*, 109-12, 400-402; Edita Štěříková, *Zelów: Česká exulantská obec v Polsku* (Praha: Kalich, 2002), 257-58; J.H. Rushbrooke, *The Baptist Movement in the Continent of Europe* (London: Kingsgate Press, rev. edn, 1923), 66; M.S. Lesik, 'The Baptists in Poland', *Baptist Quarterly* 7.2 (1934–35), 79-84 (81).

[11] August Meereis, *Šedesát let apoštolem* (Praha-Brno-Bratislava-New York: Bratrská Jednota Chelčického, 1922), 3-19; Vojta, *Czechoslovak Baptists*, 39-41.

moderate Roman Catholic family in a village near the city of Náchod, in a part of Bohemia known as a hidden fortress of secret Protestantism. The young Novotný came under the influence of pious readers of the Bible, which led him to abandon Roman Catholicism and to join the Reformed Church. He began his career as a businessman, and his job caused him to travel considerably. On one of his trips to Prague he met Adrian van Andel, a missionary of the Free Church of Scotland,[12] who encouraged him to begin religious training. After some hesitation, Novotný accepted the offer and went to St Chrischona near Basel in Switzerland for a four-year theological training programme. On his return to Bohemia in 1874, he became involved in a mission in Prague led by American Congregationalist missionaries.[13] It was at this time that Novotný made the first contact with the travelling missionary August Meereis and from him learned about Baptist emphases. In 1881 Novotný received a scholarship to study at the Free College in Edinburgh, where he went with his wife and two children. While staying in Great Britain he met and heard the sermons of Victorian preachers, such as C.H. Spurgeon, and encountered a wider Baptist witness. The stay in the free and religiously attractive nation of Scotland had a lasting impact on Novotný, so much so that he formed long-term friendships and returned to Britain later in his life on a number of occasions.[14]

On completion of his theological studies in Scotland, back in Prague Novotný became involved with a new church founded by Congregationalist missionaries.[15] In March 1884 he became the first ordained Czech minister of the Congregational church, but he did not stay long in that post because difficulties soon arose in the relationship between him and the missionaries. Novotný desired more independence for Czech mission work but the Congregationalist missionaries regarded him as a difficult and strong-willed character who was dividing the congregation. His view of baptism began to change in this period and he leaned more and more towards the baptism of believers, which also affected his relationship with the missionaries. The

---

[12] In the second half of the nineteenth century there was heightened interest in the Czech Lands by missionaries from abroad (Scotland, England, United States and others). See Alois Adlof, *Nástin dějin svobodných církví křesťanských zvláště pak svobodné reformované církve české* (Praha: Křesťanský spolek mladíků v Čechách, 1905), 51-109.

[13] The missionaries were sent to Bohemia by the American Board of Commissioners for Foreign Missions, a mission agency linked with the American Congregational Churches.

[14] Joseph Novotný, *The Baptist Romance in the Heart of Europe (Czechoslovakia): The Life and Times of Henry Novotny* (New York, NY: Czechoslovak Baptist Convention in America and Canada, 1939), 46-61; Joseph Novotný, 'Pilný život: Ze života Jindřicha Novotného', in *Chelčický, rodinný kalendář československý* 5 (1924), 75-84 (75-80); Meereis, *Šedesát let*, 10.

[15] Originally the missionaries had no intention to form a new church and they encouraged new converts to join existing Protestant churches. However, disagreements gradually arose between the missionaries and the existing Reformed Church in Prague which led to the formation of a new church, which later gave rise to a whole new denomination, the Free Reformed Church. The denomination changed its name in 1919 to the Czech Brethren Union and in 1967 to the Evangelical Brethren Church (Czech: Církev Bratrská).

conflict resulted in the dismissal of Novotný from the mission work by the missionaries in October 1884; not long afterwards he left the Congregational church.

In early 1885 Novotný's name became known to Karl Ondra, a Baptist minister in Poland, who invited him to his church in Lodz. By this time Novotný had become convinced of believer's baptism and on his arrival he asked Ondra to baptise him. He was baptised in February 1885 and in March 1885 was ordained in the church in Żyrardow for Baptist work in Bohemia. His task was to gather the scattered Baptists and to lay the foundations for a permanent Baptist presence in the Czech Lands. On his return to Bohemia, Novotný, Meereis and a handful of other Baptist believers gathered on 25 March 1885 in the village of Hleďsebe, near Prague, and formed the first Baptist church in Bohemia. The members numbered sixteen, including some who were formerly members of the Baptist church in Vienna. During earlier visits by Meereis, Baptist believers had already been meeting in Hleďsebe. These gatherings now received anchorage in the newly formed Baptist church, which elected Henry Novotný as its minister.[16]

Henry Novotný built the first Baptist chapel in Prague in the garden of his own house. The first worship service was held in this chapel in the autumn of 1886 but in the following year the chapel was closed down by the Austrian authorities. The authorities of Austria-Hungary were opposed to new religious movements. The Protestant Patent of 1861 allowed for state recognition of two hitherto tolerated churches, the Reformed and the Lutheran, and later of other religious groups (Orthodox, Old Catholic Church, Moravian Church, Jews and Muslims) but the new free Protestant churches that arose in the last quarter of the nineteenth century were not recognised by the state. Baptists and Free Reformed churches did not seek state recognition because of their insistence on the separation of church and state. They existed legally under the association law. As unrecognised churches they could not own property and their meetings could not be open to the public but only to invited guests. Religious work outside the limits of the state and the recognised churches was at times difficult, even dangerous. Fearing the hostility of Catholic priests and of the public, the Baptists initially held baptismal services in secret during the night. Novotný was often called to appear before the police, was arrested several times and accused of crimes against religion in the high court. Despite this persecution, Novotný experienced success in his ministry and his congregation grew in number. He remained the minister of the Baptist church in Prague till his death in 1912.[17]

The early days of Baptist missions on Czech soil had close ties with similar developments in Slovakia. August Meereis, who helped to found the first Baptist church in Bohemia, also helped to organise the first Baptist church in Slovakia in

---

[16] Novotný, *Baptist Romance*, 63-65, 74-76; Novotný, 'Pilný život', 80-82; Adlof, *Nástin dějin*, 141-51; Meereis, *Šedesát let*, 20-21.

[17] Novotný, *Baptist Romance*, 77-95; Rudolf Říčan, *Od úsvitu reformace k dnešku* (Praha: YMCA, 1948), 315-16, 329-30; Vratislav Bušek, 'Historický vývoj poměru státu k církvím v zemích Koruny české', in *Československá vlastivěda, V. stát* (Praha: Sfinx, 1931), 246-83 (276-82).

1888.[18] Novotný developed further relations with Baptists in Slovakia by organising joint Czechoslovak conferences of Baptist churches – long before Czechoslovakia existed as a state – to discuss systematic mission work in Bohemia, Moravia and Slovakia.[19] Besides Slovakia, Novotný developed most important and lasting relations with Anglo-Saxons. His friends in Scotland formed a society, called the Bohemian Baptist Mission, which for a number of years supported Novotný and his two sons Henry and Joseph.[20] Henry Novotný laid lasting foundations for Baptist work among the Czechs in the Austro-Hungarian Empire. At the time of his death in 1912, Baptist churches and mission stations existed in Bohemia, Moravia and Slovakia as well as among Czech immigrants and minorities in America and other countries.

Earliest Baptist Developments (1885–1918)

The formation of the first Baptist church in Prague in 1885 provided the Baptists in the Czech Lands with the organisational means to promote their cause more effectively. Despite the difficult political and social conditions of the late nineteenth century, with Baptists facing opposition from the Austrian authorities, the established churches and the public, the early missionary work grew. It expanded from the capital city to other places in Bohemia. Thus, mission stations were founded in Rovné u Roudnice in 1889 and in Bělá pod Bezdězem in 1893. After ten years of existence, the Baptist church in Prague had 180 members who were dispersed over several places in Bohemia. The membership also included a number of Germans, particularly from the Broumov area, where Baptist missionary Knappe had initiated the mission work in the late 1850s. The group of believers in Broumov joined the Baptist church in Prague in 1893 and remained its mission station until 1908, when Broumov became a church with its own minister. Another Baptist church that became independent of the church in Prague was formed in Roudnice nad Labem in 1899.[21]

The Baptist work in Moravia, the eastern region of the Czech Lands, is linked with the name of Norbert Čapek, who was converted while attending services in the Baptist congregation in Vienna. In 1890 he went to study theology at the Baptist Seminary in Hamburg. After completing his studies and a short period of pastoral experience in Saxony he moved to the major Moravian city of Brno (Brünn) with the

---

[18] Henry Procházka, *Obrazy z dějin baptistů* (Praha: Svaz mládeže čsl. baptistů, 1938), 79; Ján Jančuš, 'Baptisti pod Tatrami', in Ján Šaling and Vladimír Dvořák (eds), *Niesli svetlo evanjelia* (Bratislava: Bratská jednota baptistov v SSR, 1988), 25-90 (43-44).

[19] Jančuš, 'Baptisti pod Tatrami', 51-52.

[20] Novotný, *Baptist Romance*, 126-28. Henry junior, Novotný's oldest son, died at a very young age after contracting an incurable disease on one of his missionary travels. Novotný's son Joseph later became his successor in the ministry in the Baptist church in Prague; see Novotný, *Baptist Romance*, 135.

[21] *Historie sborů BJB v ÈR* (Praha: BJB, 1994), 16, 65-66; Rushbrooke, *Baptist Movement*, 69.

intention to initiate Baptist missionary work. In 1898 Čapek founded a Baptist church in Brno and remained its minister for more than a decade. Although he was a gifted preacher and organiser, the editor of several journals and the composer of Christian hymns, he later left the Baptists and after the First World War founded the Unitarian Church in Czechoslovakia. Under Čapek's ministry the church in Brno initiated missionary work in the Moravian region of Wallachia, from which Karel Vaculík came, who later helped to develop Baptist churches in Slovakia. The Baptists in the Wallachia region first did mission outreach under the leadership of the church in Brno. They held regular meetings in Rokytnice u Vsetína until 1913, when they organised themselves into a Baptist church of eighty-one members.[22]

The last town to be mentioned in connection with the pre-war presence of Baptist believers in the Czech Lands is Jablonec nad Nisou (Gablonz an der Neisse)[23] in northern Bohemia. At the end of the nineteenth century Jablonec was heavily populated by Germans. Two members of the Baptist Church in Vienna moved there in 1894. Because they had an influential Christian witness in their neighbourhood in Jablonec, the church in Vienna recognised the need for a pastor in Jablonec to further the mission work. Hence in 1907 Gerhard Peters was sent to Jablonec, supported by the church in Vienna. He worked fruitfully in the church till the beginning of the First World War when he was called to service in the Austrian army; he did not see the end of the war as he died a few months before it was over.

The situation of Peters as a minister at the outbreak of the First World War was not unfamiliar to many members of Baptist and other churches in the Austro-Hungarian Empire. Men under fifty years of age were called to service; among them were also active members of Baptist churches. The churches were weakened during the war as they lost many young men who left behind widows and orphans. The remaining church members looked forward with hope towards the end of the war, which came in 1918.[24]

Baptists in Czechoslovakia between the Wars (1918–39)

The end of the First World War brought liberation to the Czech Lands as the old Austro-Hungarian Empire collapsed and the new political situation brought significant changes to the life of the churches. The dispersed Baptist churches reassembled in the newly formed state of Czechoslovakia. In 1918, the Lutheran and the Reformed Churches united to form the Evangelical Church of Czech Brethren.[25] In the early years of Czechoslovakia the so-called Transfer Movement, also known

---

[22] Vlastimil Pospíšil, '100 let baptistické práce v Čechách a na Moravě', in Vladimír Dvořák and Vlastimil Pospíšil (eds), *100 let života víry: jubilejní sborník BJB v ČSSR* (Praha: Ústřední církevní nakladatelství, 1990), 75-82 (79); cf. Petr Tvrdek, *Norbert Fabian Čapek: život a dílo* (Hronov: Unitária, 1995), 7-17.

[23] For simplicity, the town is referred to as Jablonec from here.

[24] Cf. Pospíšil, '100 let', 79; Rushbrooke, *Baptist Movement*, 71.

[25] The Czech name of the church (Českobratrská církev evangelická) is in some English literature translated as the Protestant Church of Czech Brethren.

as the 'Away from Rome' movement, led a number of Catholic believers to leave the Roman Catholic Church and to form the Czechoslovak Church.[26] The Protestant churches, including some small churches, to some extent benefited from this national movement. The First Czechoslovak Republic (1918–38) with its president T.G. Masaryk (until 1935) fostered civic and religious freedoms. The atmosphere in the new state was one of religious tolerance and autonomy, which affected the Baptists in their new enthusiasm for preaching and missionary endeavours. They felt the need to organise the work more structurally in order to deal effectively with the new opportunities.[27]

In 1919 the first Czechoslovak Baptist conference took place in Vavrišovo, Slovakia, with delegates of Czech, Moravian and Slovak as well as German and Hungarian churches present, representing twenty-five churches and mission stations.[28] At this conference the Baptist Union of Czechoslovakia was constituted under the name of Brethren Union of Chelčický. The Baptists in Czechoslovakia put Chelčický into the name of their Union in order to express continuity with the Czech reformation. They found the thoughts of Petr Chelčický, the fifteenth-century spiritual father of the Czech Brethren, closest to their distinctives.[29] The leadership of the Baptist Union consisted of able young men, among whom Joseph Novotný, son of Henry Novotný, was elected as president. He was asked by the churches to travel abroad and to renew the contacts with Baptists in other countries which had been interrupted by war. He was particularly sent to churches in Great Britain and the United States, but he also visited Czechoslovak legionnaires in Siberia.[30]

In July 1920 the leaders of the Union attended a conference in London that played an important part in the post-war developments in relationships among Baptists worldwide. The conference consisted of representatives of the Baptist World Alliance (BWA), the American Foreign Mission Boards and Baptist leaders from European countries, all of whom came to London to consider two major issues: the immediate needs of the Baptist congregations in countries devastated by the war and the wider needs for effective Baptist witness in Europe. As a result of the conference, a relief effort was established for a period of three years, with Henry Rushbrooke as the administrator. He administered the funds that came from richer Baptist unions to the unions of needy European countries through special committees formed for that purpose. The conference also helped to establish cooperation between the younger Baptist unions of European countries afflicted by the war and the older and stronger Baptist unions of the wider world in order to meet the continuing missionary needs. It was agreed that assistance to the newly formed Baptist Union in Czechoslovakia would be given by the Northern Baptist

---

[26] The Czechoslovak Church changed its name to Czechoslovak Hussite Church in 1971.

[27] See Václav Müller, *Náboženské poměry v Československé republice* (Praha: Státní nakladatelství, 1925), 21-22, on the religious situation of the first years of Czechoslovakia.

[28] Procházka, *Obrazy*, 79.

[29] Procházka, *Naše zásady. Pro náboženskou výchovu dospělých i mládeže ve sborích Bratrské Jednoty čs. Baptistů (Chelčického)* (Lipt. Sv. Mikuláš: Čas. Rozsievač, 1930), 15.

[30] Novotný, *Baptist Romance*, 137.

Convention and by the Baptist Union in Great Britain.[31] This cooperation bore significant fruit for the Baptist churches in Czechoslovakia over a number of years.

The second conference of the Brethren Union of Chelčický was held in Klenovec, Slovakia, in the autumn of 1920. At that time the Baptist Union consisted of churches with a total of some 1,200 members and twenty-two ministers, missionaries and colporteurs. Seven hundred more members belonged to the Czech and Slovak Baptist churches outside Czechoslovakia, in Hungary and Yugoslavia, and about the same number lived in Poland and Ukraine. Those leaders of the Union who had attended the London conference reported on the plans for assistance from abroad for the poor, widows, orphans, mission workers and Sunday school teachers. Further assistance was promised for literature and building funds. In 1920 the Union also formed several boards for the new tasks which lay ahead: the Foreign Board, the Economic Board, the Literature and Publishing Board, and the Education Board. The boards were created to facilitate communication with the Foreign Mission Boards and between Baptist churches in and outside Czechoslovakia; they also assisted in the administration of the various funds created by the Union, in publishing Christian literature and in the training of missionary workers.[32]

In connection with their enthusiastic missionary work, the Baptists in the young Czechoslovak Republic felt the need for better training of those entering the ministry. Some ministers had previously received their training at the theological seminary of the German Baptists in Hamburg. Henry Rushbrooke, while visiting Czechoslovakia in 1920, envisioned establishing a Baptist University for the Slavic nations in Prague, but his idea did not come to fruition. Instead, several national seminaries were founded: in Estonia, Latvia, Hungary, Romania, Spain, Portugal and one in Czechoslovakia.[33] The seminary in Prague was opened in the autumn of 1921 with the financial support of Baptist funds in the United States and Great Britain. Twelve students entered the seminary in its first year, including one female. Henry Procházka, who had studied at a Baptist college in London (Regent's Park) and had obtained his doctorate in Philosophy at the Charles University in Prague, became the principal of the seminary. He led the seminary for the entire time of its existence (the war years excepted) until the mid-twentieth century, when it was closed down by the communist regime. Besides his leading role in the seminary, Procházka also served as the Secretary of the Brethren Union of Chelčický from 1920 and also on various boards of the Union for a number of years.[34]

The seminary played a leading role in providing training for Baptist ministers in the first half of the twentieth century. It consisted of a four-year programme and its

---

[31] See Rushbrooke, *Baptist Movement*, 199-206; and Bernard Green, *Tomorrow's Man: A Biography of James Henry Rushbrooke* (Didcot: Baptist Historical Society, 1997), 80-87, for the details of the London conference in 1920.

[32] Minutes of the conference of the Brethren Union of Chelčický, 29 October 1920. The Minutes are held in the Archive of the Baptist Union in the Czech Republic (BUCR), Na Topolce 14, Prague 4, Czech Republic.

[33] Green, *Tomorrow's Man*, 73-77, 82-83.

[34] On Henry Procházka, see the biographical notes in the Archive of the BUCR.

students were also associate students of the Huss Theological Faculty of the Charles University. In its curriculum the seminary emphasised holistic personal development so that the students received a basic education in humanities and science besides their training in theological subjects. A significant number of the Baptist ministers who studied in the seminary later pastored Baptist churches in Czechoslovakia and Czech-speaking churches in Poland, Ukraine and North America.[35]

A special concern of the Baptists in the early years of Czechoslovakia was a social ministry. Joseph Novotný gave a programmatic speech on 'The Social Involvement of the Churches' at the Union's conference in 1920, which stirred a lively debate among the conference delegates. At Novotný's initiative, Peabody-Montgomery Children's Home for orphans was founded in Podhořany near Prague in 1922. The Baptist church in Brno ran its own aid programme called Tabita, which supported women's social work. Another children's home was founded in Čeklís near Bratislava in Slovakia. These and other projects were maintained through sustained financial support from Baptists abroad. Funds that were raised came, among others, from American women of the Northern Baptist Convention, Czech and Slovak Baptist churches in the United States and, significantly, from Baptists in Scotland.[36]

Baptist ministry to children and young people was carried out not only through the work of orphanages but also through Sunday schools. Children's Sunday schools experienced growth, especially immediately after the First World War. In 1921 the Association of Sunday Schools was founded, in which Baptists played a part. The significance of Sunday schools was promoted particularly by Henry Procházka, who had a lifelong interest in religious education and published books and articles on the subject. Sunday schools were seen by Baptists as playing an important part in the life of churches which wanted to fulfil their missionary and educational tasks.[37]

Similarly, the Baptists in the First Czechoslovak Republic recognised the value of producing good religious and educational literature. For this purpose, they formed the Czechoslovak Baptist Publication Society, the first fruit of which was the publication of a Baptist hymnal in 1923. Long before that, however, in Bohemia, Henry Novotný had begun with the production of *Posel pokoje* (*Messenger of Peace*) in 1892, which was followed in 1912 by Chelčický. In Slovakia the periodical *Rozsévač* (*Sower*) was produced from 1914. Baptist writers also contributed to interdenominational periodicals and published literature, tracts and

---

[35] Henry Procházka, 'Deset let Semináře čs. baptistů', in *Z naší brázdy: sborník Semináře čs. baptistů k prvnímu desítiletí 1921–1931* (Praha: nákl. vlastním, 1931), 74-77.

[36] Minutes of the conference of the Brethren Union of Chelčický, 29 October 1920, Archive of the BUCR; Henry Procházka, *Po deseti letech: Přehled činnosti Bratrské Jednoty čsl. Baptistů (Chelčického) 1919–1929* (Lipt. Sv. Mikuláš, nákl. vl., 1929), 7, 12-13; Brian Talbot, 'Fellowship in the Gospel: Scottish Baptists and their relationships with other Baptist Churches, 1900–1945', in David W. Bebbington and Anthony R. Cross (eds), *Global Baptist History* (Milton Keynes: Paternoster, forthcoming).

[37] Procházka, *Po deseti letech*, 16.

pamphlets on various religious and educational issues. Among these, specific attention was paid to issues of Baptist identity and distinctives.

The first decade of Czechoslovakia witnessed a vibrant Protestant scene, and publication activity was instrumental to Baptists in consolidating their position in this exuberant environment.[38] The Baptist work at this time experienced its most fruitful years in terms of mission endeavours and growth. Eight new churches came into existence in Bohemia and Moravia in the 1920s;[39] all of these, with the exception of the church in Vikýřovice which was founded by Czechs returning from Poland, began through home mission activity. Baptists also met in more than forty other places which were known as mission stations. There was space and freedom for Baptist mission initiatives in a number of areas in the interwar period. This was helped by favourable social conditions with the increased power of liberalisation and secularism and the decrease of Catholicism, although the Roman Catholic Church remained the largest church in Czechoslovakia.[40]

The constitution of the first Czechoslovak Republic guaranteed the right of every person to freedom of conscience and religion. Its laws in relation to religious bodies, however, continued the former legal system of Austria-Hungary, in which churches in Slovakia and Subcarpathian Ruthenia had a different legal status than churches in Bohemia, Moravia and Silesia. While in Slovakia some Baptist congregations were recognised by the state, following the association law of 1867 in Bohemia and Moravia the Baptist churches were not recognised but organised themselves as charitable associations. However, this state of affairs was unsustainable in the long term so that church-state relations were discussed at almost every gathering of Baptists, yet without a satisfactory outcome. The Baptists in Czechoslovakia, keeping to their distinctives, were not in favour of state recognition. They strived for some form of corporation law. Efforts were made on the side of both the state and the Baptist churches to resolve the issue, but an acceptable solution was not found and the legal position of the Baptist churches remained problematic in the interwar years.[41]

The era of the 1930s brought challenges to Baptist life. The world economic crisis badly hit members of the Baptist congregations and they struggled to support their ministers. The help and support from Baptist bodies abroad also decreased in the years of economic crisis. All this affected Baptist ministers and their families, who were forced into virtual poverty.[42] The Baptist Publication Society was in significant

---

[38] Procházka, *Po deseti letech*, 13-15.

[39] The churches were founded in Brno Husovice, Kroměříž, Lipová, Ostrava, Pardubice, Praha Pankrác, Vikýřovice and Vysoké Mýto; some others (Bělá pod Bezdězem or Zlín) were considered as mission stations despite having their own ministers.

[40] Pospíšil, '100 let', 80.

[41] Procházka, *Po deseti letech*, 2-3; Müller, *Náboženské poměry*, 22-23.

[42] See the correspondence of the ministers with the office of the Baptist Union in the 1930s, Archive of the BUCR.

financial difficulties as well.[43] The publication of the Baptist periodical *Chelčický* had to stop in the mid 1930s and was not renewed. The more difficult years, however, were yet to come with the outbreak of the Second World War. Baptist churches and mission stations that in 1938 found themselves in the German occupied zone were disbanded; their members moved and joined churches inland.[44] One Baptist minister was arrested by the Gestapo and eventually died in the concentration camp in Auschwitz.[45] The Second World War had devastating effects on both society and the churches. Church buildings were damaged, lives were destroyed and vital resources were not available. For six years the distress was felt everywhere. Hopes for restoration of normal church life came only in May 1945 with the capitulation of Hitler's Germany.

The Renewal of Baptist Life (1945–48)

The early post-war years saw the revitalisation and renewal of Baptist life in Czechoslovakia. Significant demographic changes took place in Central Europe immediately after the Second World War, which also impacted the Baptist congregations. After the post-war deportation of the German minority from Czechoslovakia, the Czechoslovak government called upon Czech minorities living abroad to return to Czechoslovakia to settle in the regions the Germans had left. The first families began to return to their old homeland in the autumn of 1945. Among them were Baptist families of Czech minorities living in Poland. In 1947 Czech Baptists from the Volhynia region in Ukraine were allowed to return. Another foreign group of Czech Baptists returned from Romania, and a few Czech Baptists came back to their homeland from Yugoslavia. This momentous return of former migrants to Czechoslovakia in the post-war years significantly strengthened the Baptists in the Czech Lands and six new Baptist churches were formed in Bohemia and Moravia by Czech Baptists who returned from abroad. Other churches saw significant growth through repatriated members who joined them.[46] The Brethren Union of Chelčický increased by more than one-third in Bohemia and Moravia

---

[43] The situation of the Publication Society is discussed in the letter of W.O. Lewis to H. Rushbrooke, 18 April 1935: Angus Library, Oxford, BWA files, Czechoslovakia (1921–1946).

[44] This concerned the church in Vikýřovice and the mission station in Suchdol nad Odrou; on Vikýřovice see Dobroslav Stehlík, 'Kořeny a první období sboru Bratrské jednoty baptistů ve Vikýřovicích', *Exulant* 30 (2010), 15-27 (22-24).

[45] Reverend Theofil Malý of Vikýřovice Baptist Church died in Auschwitz on the 5 April 1943; see his biographical notes in the Archive of the BUCR.

[46] The new churches originated in Cheb, Liberec, Lovosice, Šumperk, Teplá and Žatec. They had their mission stations in more than twenty places. For brief histories of these churches, see *Historie sborů BJB v ÈR*. The German-speaking Baptist churches in Broumov and Jablonec were transformed into Czech-speaking churches by the migrations of Germans and Czechs.

through this influx and this had an impact on the Union as a whole.[47] The Baptists from abroad brought with them new forms of piety and spirituality, fresh traditions of Bible reading and specific expressions of worship. The period of post-war renewal of Baptist life, however, did not last long. In 1948 the communist regime came to power and with it the climate in society changed notably.

The Era of the Communist Regime (1948–89)

The policy of the regime that came to power in 1948 was to gain power over the ecclesial sphere which was perceived as a threat and adversary to the communist government. In 1949 the regime imposed religious laws which seemingly should have led to the equality of churches before the state. The laws, however, became instruments of state control over the churches, allowing state officials to interfere with all aspects of church life. State control took place through the Office of Religious Affairs and through church secretaries in regional and district city councils whose job was to monitor the churches. A system of government-issued licenses was introduced, by which only those granted state permission could deliver sermons and become ministers. Any religious activity without state permission was seen as a breach of the law and was punishable with imprisonment. The religious legislation imposed a state salary on priests and ministers and included an oath of loyalty by those who took any such position of church leadership.[48]

Initially the Baptists were reluctant to submit to these laws. They understood that accepting the imposed policies meant that they would have to give up some of their key principles such as the autonomy of the local congregation, freedom of conscience, and the separation of church and state. Rejecting submission to the laws meant that they would be disbanded, since acceptance of the laws was a necessary condition for the legal existence of a church.[49] Seeing no other alternative as a viable option, Baptists subjected themselves to the laws and reluctantly became a church recognised by the state.[50]

One of the deliberate communist policies against the churches was the implementation of a law in 1950 which dissolved the denominational schools of the small Protestant churches. This affected the theological seminary in Prague, the prime institution of Baptist theological thought, which was closed down in the year the law was enacted. Another measure of repression of the Baptists was the

---

[47] See the church statistics from 1949 in the Archive of the BUCR.

[48] On the church-state relationship in the early years of the communist regime in Czechoslovakia, see Karel Kaplan, *Stát a církev v Československu v letech 1948–1953* (Brno: Doplněk, 1993).

[49] Some other non-recognised religious communities were not given recognition as religious denominations and were disbanded; this was, for example, the case with the Salvation Army.

[50] The attitude of the Baptists towards the new religious laws of 1949 is documented in the materials related to two trials of Baptist ministers in 1953, V-1170 HK and V-1020 HK, the Security Services Archive, Prague, Czech Republic.

dissolution of the Young People's Society that had existed since the 1920s. The communist regime also took measures against the churches' press and publication activities, and this also affected the Baptists. The last issue for a long time of their denominational periodical *Rozsévač* came out in December 1951.[51]

At first the communist regime focussed heavily on restricting and persecuting the Catholic Church as the largest ecclesial body in Czechoslovakia. A few years after 1948, the pressure also started to grow against small religious communities such as the Seventh Day Adventists, the Baptists and the Jehovah's Witnesses. In the early 1950s the Baptists, alongside the Catholics and other religious communities, experienced harsh persecution. The leaders of the Baptist Union, who had been freely elected before the communist regime came to power in 1948, were imprisoned in 1952 and with them a number of Baptist ministers. This severely affected the churches in Bohemia and Moravia, since half of them had their ministers in custody by the end of 1952.[52] Baptist leaders and ministers were accused of espionage, disclosing state secrets to the imperial West and conspiring against the People's Democratic Republic. Under severe psychological pressure the imprisoned ministers were forced to memorise texts which they were to recite at the constructed trials. They were judged in two trials in the summer of 1953. The first trial was of four Baptist leaders: the president of the Baptist Union, Jan Řičař, the Union secretary, Cyril Burget, the leader of Slovak Baptist churches, Michal Kešjar, and the principal of the seminary, Henry Procházka. They were sentenced to between five and eighteen years imprisonment. The second trial related to the remaining pastors who were given from one to four years imprisonment. A further Baptist minister was tried on similarly fabricated accusations in 1955. The Union secretary, Cyril Burget, died in prison; others were released after some years under an amnesty law.[53]

As a consequence of these events the Baptists in Czechoslovakia experienced the most distressing and difficult times in their history. Under these adverse conditions with the serious loss of leadership the Baptist churches were shattered. This created a critically weak position, which led the Baptist churches to a public renunciation of the convicted Baptist leaders and ministers at their annual conference in December 1953.[54] The new Baptist leadership that was appointed at the conference was put under enormous pressure by the communist officials to distance themselves from the

---

[51] See the correspondence between the office of the Baptist Union and the churches in the years 1950–52, Archive of the BUCR. On the Protestant churches in the first years of the communist regime in general, see Jiří Piškula 'Protestantské církve v prvním roce režimu', in Pavel Hlaváč and Peter C.A. Morée (eds), *Cesta církve III* (Praha: Českobratrská církev evangelická, 2011), 19-33.

[52] Nine Baptist churches out of the total of eighteen were without a minister during the imprisonments of ministers in 1952 and their trials in the summer of 1953.

[53] On the trials see V-1170 HK and V-1020 HK, the Security Services Archive.

[54] Minutes of the conference of the Brethren Union of Baptists in CSR, 12 December 1953, Archive of the BUCR; *Conference of the Baptist Unity in Czechoslovakia* (Prague: Baptist Unity, n.d. [c.1954]): Angus Library, Oxford, BWA files, Czechoslovakia (1949–1955).

previous leadership, in order not to cause even more severe persecution. The destruction of the entire Baptist denomination was in the air. Eventually the dilemma was resolved by sacrificing a few, the former leadership, for the sake of the many in order to satisfy the regime. In the late 1960s attempts were made to rehabilitate unjustly convicted ministers of the previous decade, but in the end this did not happen. These ministers only received full rehabilitation after the fall of the communist regime in 1990, by which time many of them were no longer alive.[55]

The difficult years of harsh persecution in the 1950s were followed by a period of softer communist pressure which culminated in the Prague Spring in 1968. The political and economic reforms introduced under the government of Alexander Dubček had a positive impact on society, including the life of the church. The door opened for Baptists to work towards the repair of some of their structures. The constitution of the Baptist Union was revised with the view to strengthen Baptist distinctives, particularly the autonomy of local congregations. Young people's conferences were renewed and the conferences for women were launched. The publication of the Baptist periodical *Rozsévač* resumed after a seventeen year absence. The door also opened for the construction of new church buildings and for repairs and adaptations to the older ones. In the area of theological training, a two-year distance learning theological course was launched for lay people. As theological education was very limited during the communist regime, those who could not study at the Comenius Protestant Theological Faculty in Prague received some theological training from this distance learning course.[56]

In August 1968 the armies of the Warsaw Pact invaded Czechoslovakia and the atmosphere in the country changed again. The years following the invasion are known as the years of normalisation, at which the political circumstances returned to what they had been before the political reforms of the Prague Spring. In some areas, Baptists could maintain the structures that had recently been introduced, but in other areas the regime tightened its restrictive measures. For example, in the area of literature production stricter censorship was introduced in the period of normalisation and this negatively affected Baptist publications.[57]

The religious conditions began to improve slightly in the 1980s. More opportunities cautiously started opening up for churches to be more visible in society. An event of wider societal and religious significance for the Baptists in Czechoslovakia was the visit of the evangelist Billy Graham in 1982.[58] This and other foreign visits and contacts were made possible through the significant involvement of Stanislav Švec, the secretary of the Baptist Union. He was a

---

[55] Resolution of the conference of the Brethren Union of Baptists in CSFR, 12-14 October 1990, Archive of the BUCR.

[56] *Rozsévač* 39 (1969), 19, 36-37, 59; *Rozsévač* 40 (1970), 3, 93-94.

[57] E.g., the Baptist periodical *Rozsévač* was not free to publish whatever the churches wanted during the era of normalisation. It also had to include political statements on world peace.

[58] Pavel Titěra (ed.), *Volání na cestu pokoje: Billy Graham v Československu* (Praha: Ústřední církevní nakladatelství, 1987).

respected leader among Baptists in Czechoslovakia who had borne the burden of the pressure of communist authorities for a considerable period of time, and had been the secretary of the Baptist Union for almost thirty years (1956–84). Despite the adverse political conditions of the time, he kept churches aware of Baptist distinctives and did the maximum possible for Baptist congregations within the restrictions of the totalitarian regime.[59] The measures against churches softened in the final years of the regime up to the arrival of the political dawn for Czechoslovakia in November 1989, when the course of the country changed towards democracy.

Chances in the Era of Democracy

The fall of the communist regime in 1989 brought fundamental changes to political life and society in Czechoslovakia. Baptist churches, alongside other denominations, experienced freedom which they had lacked in the previous forty years. In a politically free country new opportunities arose for Baptist witness. The Baptists particularly put their renewed energy into the areas of mission, social engagement and diaconal ministry. Most importantly, work started on rectifying those things from the Baptist tradition that had been deformed and twisted under the totalitarian regime. The new leadership of the Baptist Union soon initiated the process of reflection and return to the Baptist principles as they are known among Baptists elsewhere in the world. In 1994 the Baptist Union of Czechs and Slovaks divided into two unions following the peaceful division of Czechoslovakia into the separate Czech and Slovak Republics. The fact that the relationships between the two unions have remained warm after the division can be documented by referring to events in which both unions participate. Perhaps the strongest common bond is the continuing publication of the shared monthly periodical *Rozsévač* by the two Unions. Finally, the constitution of the Czech Baptist Union was adopted in 1995 after several years of work and with it other key documents reflecting Baptist ecclesiology.[60]

Baptists in the Czech Lands have had a most moving history throughout the 150 years of their existence. In this brief contribution it has only been possible to show the main contours of their story. Each historical period of the Czech Baptists still awaits full historical treatment and analysis in the future.

---

[59] On Stanislav Švec, see the biographical notes in the Archive of the BUCR.

[60] The constitution of 1995 replaced the constitution of 1988 and remains valid to the present.

Baptists in the Czech Lands

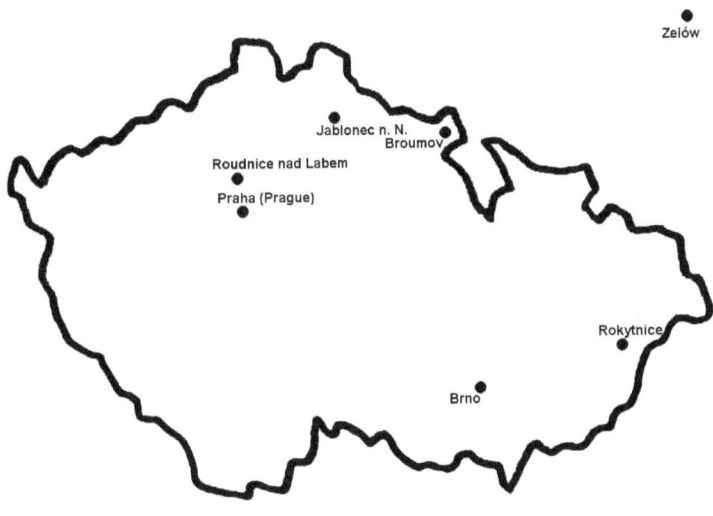

The Earliest Baptist Churches to 1918. (Border of the current Czech Republic.)

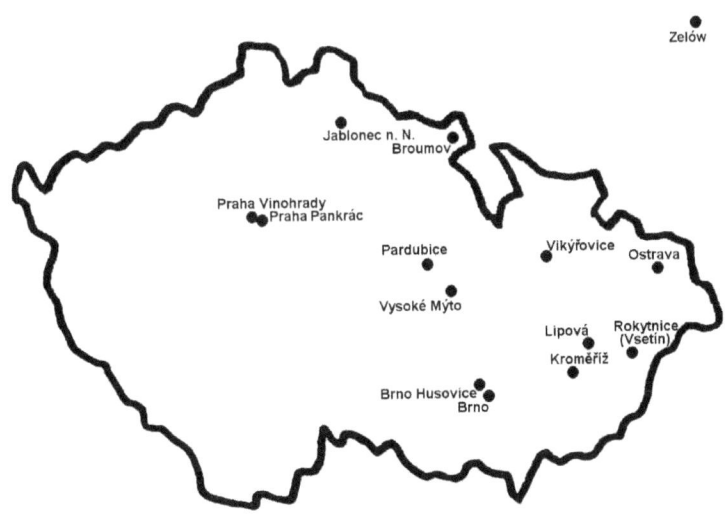

Baptist Churches in the Interwar Period, 1918–39.

Baptist Churches in the Post-Second World War Period, 1945–48.

Baptist Churches in the Period of Renewed Democracy (as of 1994).

CHAPTER 7

Adam Podin: An Estonian Baptist with International Links and Pan-Evangelical Vision

Toivo Pilli

This article focuses on the work and mission of Adam Podin, an Estonian Baptist pastor with Latvian background and with wide international relations. In his ministry and person, Podin exemplifies the openness and broad contacts of Baltic evangelical life, both geographically and theologically, in the late nineteenth and the first half of the twentieth century. I will tell Podin's story and discuss his contribution to tsarist Russia and later Estonia, as an evangelical and a Baptist, in the areas of pastoral work, theological education and social ministry. I will argue that Podin also contributed in a fourth area: as a person with international links he broadened the vision of the Estonian Baptists with pan-evangelical awareness and influences, and – looking at the story from another perspective – he enriched the European evangelical context with the example of his vivid and inspiring ministry.

The Baptist expansion in tsarist Russia and in the Baltic region in the nineteenth century had strong German dimensions.[1] In addition, local influences helped to shape early Baptist life in continental Europe. In Estonia, the early Baptists were heavily influenced by the so-called West Coast revival, which conveyed the Scandinavian version of Lutheran pietism to the Baltic context and prepared the way for the emerging Baptist movement.[2] Recent research, however, has also brought to light other aspects of this religious narrative in Russia and the Baltics. For example, the role played by holiness spirituality and Keswick influences in the beliefs and practices of the early Russian evangelicals has been convincingly demonstrated by the research of Gregory Nichols into Johann Kargel, one of the important early Baptist – or perhaps it is more accurate to say 'baptistic' – figures in Eastern

---

[1] See, e.g., Ian M. Randall, 'Every Apostolic Church a Mission Society: European Baptist Origins and Identity', in Anthony R. Cross (ed.), *Ecumenism and History: Studies in Honour of John H.Y. Briggs* (Carlisle: Paternoster Press, 2002), 281-301; Richard V. Pierard, 'Germany and Baptist Expansion in Nineteenth-Century Europe' in David W. Bebbington (ed.), *The Gospel in the World* (Carlisle: Paternoster Press, 2002), 189-208.

[2] Riho Saard, 'Baptismi Viron ja Pohjois-Liivinmaan kuvernementeissa 1865–1920' (Pro gradu thesis, Helsinki University, 1994).

Europe.³ Kargel had a significant impact on Russian and Ukrainian, Baltic and Bulgarian evangelicals. The wider evangelical perspective was clearly brought out in this research.

The role of Adam Podin is similar to that of Kargel, in this case in an Estonian setting. His biography reveals not only the surprising variety of countries and places he visited and persons he knew, but it also gives evidence of pan-evangelical influences on his ministry. Through the lens of his life story one not only becomes aware of the dynamics of Estonian Baptist history, but also learns how wider evangelical ideas – such as compassion-driven social ministry – spread internationally and incarnated in a local setting. Because Podin was a Baptist preacher in Estonia, these influences became intertwined into the Estonian Baptist canvas.

Unfortunately, Adam Podin was not a man of writing. He could tell stories, he could preach, he could deliver deeply moving fundraising addresses, he was an able administrator, but little of his theology exists in written form. This is a drawback and an opportunity at the same time. In the absence of written sources, the researcher is challenged to concentrate on Podin's Christian activity and service as a set of lived out convictions and beliefs.

Europe is Attractive: The Early Life of Podin

Adam Podin (Adams Podins) was born 31 December 1862 (old style) in the Braslava region of northern Latvia. (The *Global Anabaptist Mennonite Encyclopedia Online* mistakenly says that he was born in Lithuania.⁴) His parents' names were Karlis and Lize.⁵ The family had a small piece of land, and farming was the main source of income. Spiritual questions emerged in Adam's life comparatively early. He was twelve or thirteen years old when he decided to go to worship services in the local Lutheran church every Sunday, 'in order to find blessedness'. He took Lutheran confirmation more seriously than his companions who 'shared beer and tobacco in the confirmation class'.⁶ Later, Podin studied at Cimze Seminary in Valga, a town on the border between Estonia and Latvia, and he graduated with excellent results.⁷ In the 1880s Cimze Seminary was a forward-looking pedagogical institution, operating

---

³ Gregory L. Nichols, *The Development of Russian Evangelical Spirituality: A Study of Ivan V. Kargel (1849–1937)* (Eugene, OR: Pickwick Publications, 2011).

⁴ Helmut Huebert and Susan Huebert, 'Podin, Adam K. (1862–1940s?)', October 2009, in *Global Anabaptist Mennonite Encyclopedia Online* (http://www.gameo.org/encyclopedia/contents/podin_adam_k._1862_1940s), accessed 14 August 2012.

⁵ Latvian State Archives, F-235, 7, 157.

⁶ 'Adam Podini 100. sünniaastapäev' (31 December 1962), typewritten manuscript. Eesti Evangeeliumi Kristlaste ja Baptistide Koguduste Liidu Arhiiv (= EEKBLA) [Archive of the Union of the Evangelical Christian and Baptist Churches of Estonia].

⁷ Richard Kaups (ed.), *50 aastat apostlite radadel* (Keila: E.B.K. Kirjastus, 1934), 58; Mikk Vaikla, 'Elu Keila koguduses', in *Keila Baptistikogudus 100* (Keila, 2003), 8.

in the spirit of Pestalozzi; and a number of future Estonian school teachers, composers, writers and other cultural figures received their education there.

However, the Baltic province of tsarist Russia was much too small for a youthful and adventurous spirit. It was probably in the summer of 1884 that Podin boarded a ship, chosen almost randomly, and travelled to England. His educational interests and an inner need to see the world and find new experiences were mixed with a religious quest. In London he visited revivalist evangelical meetings in a mission house, but the personal form of faith that he saw there did not impress him at all. With mixed feelings he listened to sermons about the prodigal son and talents for good stewardship. It must have been a surprise for him to see a female preacher, who obviously belonged to the aristocracy. Podin later remembered his vanity and arrogance as he was thinking, sitting there at the meeting: 'You old maid know nothing. I have 60 roubles in my pocket and more in the bank.'[8] But ultimately, what seemed economic security for a young world traveller, did not offer existential peace. In November 1884, Podin experienced spiritual conversion at an evangelical meeting in London,[9] though he was only baptised upon his confession of faith many years later in Estonia. His spiritual journey clearly took place in a wider evangelical context.

Initially, the focus of the young Estonian-Latvian convert was on evangelism and activism rather than on confessional-denominational identity. In the second half of the 1880s Podin worked in the Seamen's Mission Society, which allowed him to combine his thrust for evangelism with his interest in travelling: he visited Africa, India, Burma and other parts of the world. At the beginning of the 1890s, most probably in 1891, he studied at a Missionary Training Home in London, and a couple of years later he briefly worked as a pastor in Great Yarmouth, a fishing port in Norfolk. It must have been his Seamen's Mission commitment that soon took him to Smyrna (Izmir in present day Turkey), but he did not stay long in this city either. In these years the events in Podin's life and the countries where he lived changed as quickly as the colours in a kaleidoscope; the restlessness may be a sign that the young man, then in his early thirties, had not yet found his main calling in life.

The disjointed information allows us to conclude that from Smyrna Podin returned to England in 1894, and then travelled through Switzerland to the Baltics. On his way, he visited Otto Stockmayer, who resided in Hauptweil, Thurgau, in Switzerland.[10] Stockmayer, a leading figure in the European holiness-movement, developed a prayer-and-healing-ministry, and was a frequent speaker at Keswick meetings.[11] This fact again shows Podin's broad evangelical openness as well as his personal contacts that, no doubt, influenced his spiritual preferences. In 1896, after

---

[8] 'Adam Podini 100. sünniaastapäev' (31 December 1962), typewritten manuscript. EEKBLA.
[9] Kaups, *50 aastat apostlite radadel*, 58.
[10] 'Adam Podini 100. sünniaastapäev', EEKBLA.
[11] Biography of Otto Stockmayer in *Healing and Revival* (www.healingandrevival.com/BioOStockmayer.htm), accessed 15 August 2012.

stopping for a while in Latvia, Podin arrived to Estonia, the country that was going to be his permanent home. But not yet ...

In the years 1896–98 Podin commuted between Latvia and Estonia, preaching at different evangelistic and Bible study meetings, yet it was still a rather hectic life. For a while he worked in Riga under the auspices of the Seamen's Mission. Then he returned once more to Britain and was involved in Seamen's Mission work in Cardiff, an important coal and transport hub. A clearly defined and peaceful streambed was still to be found. However, one factor was going to influence Podin's future years and it is possible that this was the reason why he finally settled in Estonia: in December 1897 he married Emilie Tammik, a housekeeper at Laitse (Laitz) manor in northern Estonia. At that time the manor belonged to another colourful Estonian Baptist, Baron Woldemar von Üxküll, who was obviously interested in employing evangelical believers for different jobs on his property. Podin had met his future wife during one of his preaching trips to Laitse, which in the 1890s, due to Baron von Üxküll's contacts and interests, was an important centre where evangelistic work was conducted in a pan-evangelical spirit.[12]

Pastoral Work in Keila

In May 1900, after yet more travelling, the Podin family returned to Estonia, and they began pastoral work in Keila (Kegel). Keila manor and its surroundings, also owned by Woldemar von Üxküll, had recently experienced a small-scale local evangelical awakening. Podin had already preached in Keila in 1896. In 1901–02 Üxküll arranged the conversion of the manor distillery into a chapel, a 'prayer house' as locals preferred to say. In 1903 Adam Podin was officially registered by the tsarist Russian authorities as the preacher of Keila Baptist Church.[13] Being Baptists was probably not essential to these believers, but as the Baptists were an official denomination in tsarist Russia, it was easiest and most logical to register the new church under this name. Podin himself had been baptised by immersion only in October of 1900 in the Keila River. The person who conducted the ceremony had been Nicolaus von Stackelberg, a Lutheran pastor who had moved towards holiness and Evangelical Alliance spirituality. This episode is symbolic of Podin's life as it emphasises his links across denominational borders and across social ranks.[14]

Adam Podin considered the chapel in the former distillery unsuitable because the building was damp. Energetic and action-orientated, he decided to start building a new chapel, despite the fact that the small congregation did not have any spare funds. He was able to give publicity to his project, even if there were no special appeals or fundraising campaigns. Baron von Üxküll was not overly enthusiastic about the new project, as he had only recently renovated the distillery, and he refused to give a piece of land for the new chapel. But this did not stop Podin, who built the chapel on

---

[12] Vaikla, 'Elu Keila koguduses', 9.

[13] Kaups, *50 aastat apostlite radadel*, 58.

[14] Vaikla, 'Elu Keila koguduses', 9-10.

his own property. When the new wooden building was opened in 1904 it was free of debt; the building costs, 1,813 roubles, had been covered by donors. As a preacher who valued a good dramatic narrative, Podin emphasised that the whole project ended with a 'profit' of two roubles and twenty-four kopecks. It is worth mentioning that some builders came from southern Russia (Ukraine) to help with the construction. Their names – Schmidt, Dick and others – reveal that they were German Mennonites. With a number of Allianz-minded Mennonites, including Peter Schmidt (1860–1910) from Steinbach Estate, Molochna Colony, and the Dick family of Apanlee, Podin had personal contacts.[15]

As a pastor, Podin worked steadily, without explosive growth in membership. In 1920 Keila church had thirty-eight full members; together with children and youth the 'total number of souls' was sixty-three.[16] Perhaps the slow growth can partly be explained by the reality that Podin continued to travel extensively as his vision for Christian work was broader than Estonia. While the pastor was away, his co-workers such as Ludvig Luther and others helped in ministry. After 1922, when the Baptist theological seminary was opened in Keila, the students also practiced their skills in preaching, youth work, as well as a choir, in the local church. It is probably not unfair to argue that Podin did not enjoy the routine pastoral tasks: he needed new challenges. However, the church membership continued to grow and by the end of 1932, when Podin retired from the pastor's role after serving for almost thirty years, there were ninety-two full members in the 'flock'.[17] This was the average size for a Baptist church in these years. In 1934, when Richard Kaups, the new pastor, had been inaugurated into ministry, the Keila church was active in mission work in surrounding locations; it had three Sunday school classes, an active youth and women's ministry, and growing music life.[18]

Besides responsibilities in the local church, Adam Podin was a member of numerous committees and boards, where he contributed through his life experience as well as his international contacts. His skills as a fundraiser and public-relations person were appreciated by his colleagues. As Baptist Union annual reports reveal, Podin was a member of the Estonian Baptist Union board in the periods 1903–08, 1912–14 and 1920–37, thus influencing Estonian Baptist life and strategic decisions over almost four decades. In 1920–28 he was on the board of the Estonian Baptist Literature Society and for a couple of years, beginning in 1935, he offered his leadership as the chairman of the Estonian United Evangelical Believers' Educational Society. His work as director of the Estonian Baptist Preachers' Seminary (Baptist Theological Seminary) will be touched upon later in this article.

---

[15] See David Sudermann, '*Allianz* in Ukraine: More Pieces of the Puzzle', *Mennonite Historian* 1–2 (1997), 1-2, 6-7; Vaikla, 'Elu Keila koguduses', 10.

[16] Eesti Baptisti koguduste aruanne 1920.

[17] Eesti Baptisti Usuühingute Liidu aruanne 1932.

[18] Kaups, *50 aastat apostlite radadel*, 59.

Years Devoted to Prison Ministry

Adam Podin was a long-term pastor of the church in Keila and an active figure in Estonian Baptist leadership. He also channelled wider Allianz or Evangelical Alliance spirituality into Estonia. Nevertheless, from the local perspective he is better known for his social ministry, both prison ministry and work among lepers. In this field, as in other areas of his work, he crossed borders, initiated new paths and made effective use of his international contacts.

Podin was a pioneer of systematic social work among the Baptists of Estonia, who combined compassion and mission, and he helped to contextualise the beliefs and practices of wider European evangelicalism into the local culture. Also, in a way, he continued the social sensitivity of Pashkovism, though in a changed cultural framework.[19]

There are clear connections between Podin's prison ministry, the ideas of late Pashkovism and wider evangelical alliance principles, because at the turn of the twentieth century Podin moved in all these circles. In the Pashkovite context he was awakened to his ministry of compassion. In 1905, while staying at the palace of Countess Natalie Lieven in St Petersburg during one of his evangelistic tours, he met a high-ranking and influential tsarist government official who challenged him three times, almost like Jesus challenged Peter at the Lake of Galilee, 'Are you ready to work among prisoners?' The answer was 'Yes, but … it is extremely complicated to get access to convicts.' Then a miracle happened: Podin was provided with documents that opened all Russian prison doors for his missionary ministry.[20] Earlier, in the 1880s and the 1890s, other pan-evangelical figures such as Friedrich Baedeker and Johann Kargel, had similar access to Russian prisons.[21]

Referring to the beginning of his prison ministry in Russia, Podin wrote,

> Suddenly, in front of me there was a field for work that extended from my small homeland on the Baltic shores to where the powerful waves of the Pacific Ocean wash the eastern coasts of Siberia [sic!], a field that reached from the Black Sea and the Caspian Sea up to the Arctic Ocean. Almost half a million prisoners were in destitution in numerous locations. Yet, they all had an immortal soul, though this was perhaps a little more soiled with sins than in other people. But this was my consolation, that the power of Christ's suffering is able to set them free.[22]

In the personal archive of Tõnu Karu, some permits granting access to prisoners have survived, showing – in almost identical language – that Adam Karlovich Podin was allowed to 'visit prisoners, to distribute books of Holy Scriptures and conduct

---

[19] Sharyl Corrado, 'The Gospel in Society: Pashkovite Social Outreach in Late Imperial Russia', in Sharyl Corrado and Toivo Pilli (eds), *Eastern European Baptist History: New Perspectives* (Prague: IBTS, 2007), 54-66.

[20] Kaups, *50 aastat apostlite radadel*, 190.

[21] *Istorija Evangel'skih Hristian-Baptistov v SSR* (Moskva: VSEHB, 1989), 110; Nichols, *Development of Spirituality*, 162-66.

[22] Quoted in Kaups, *50 aastat apostlite radadel*, 190.

conversations of a moral-religious character with incarcerated persons'.[23] When the tsarist government fell in Russia and was replaced by Soviet powers, and Estonia became an independent country in 1918, this ministry was narrowed to Estonian prisons, yet Podin continued it with significant persistence and energy.

In the evangelical spirit of his day, Podin distributed New Testaments and other parts of the Bible to the prisoners. In 1922 he said, 'By the way, I can confirm that by the grace of God I have distributed more books of the Bible than the whole Estonian Bible Society during its 100 years of existence.'[24] In 1934, the historical survey published for the fiftieth anniversary of the Estonian Baptists stated that during his twenty-eight years of ministry Podin had distributed 200,000 to 300,000 copies of the Bible or New Testaments. Funds for this ministry were provided by Podin's personal friends in Britain and other countries, as well as by the Evangelical Alliance. During tsarist times, the Mennonites of Southern Russia, some of them persons with considerable wealth, also supported this work. The British and Foreign Bible Society offered significant (50% or 75%) discounts for these orders.[25]

Podin conducted pastoral counselling with prisoners, sometimes with criminals facing capital punishment. When preaching, he was able to ignite a spark of interest even in an indifferent and hostile audience. Ain Kalmus (alias Evald Mänd) witnessed such a situation. In his memoirs Kalmus, himself an outstanding Baptist preacher, recalls Podin's preaching in a prison: 'During my long life I have seen and heard a number of preachers with international fame, but seldom have I witnessed a more influential preaching.'[26]

Another characteristic element of Podin's prison ministry was his ecumenical spirit. In tsarist Russia he sometimes conducted worship services for prisoners in Orthodox premises. Later, in Estonia, he worked with representatives of other churches. For example, the wife of the Lutheran pastor and minister of education, Jaan Lattik, on several occasions accompanied him in visiting prisoners.[27] Podin's pan-evangelical spirituality is expressed in one of his reports: 'My wish has not been to proclaim the doctrines of one denomination ... but to bring the living Saviour through his Word close to them [prisoners].'[28]

Intensive work, travelling, and multiple responsibilities – all these had their drawbacks too. It has already been noted that there were long periods of time when

---

[23] Permit of the Vice-Governor of the Province of Estonia no. 944 (7 March 1909), Permit of the Superintendent of Prisons of Jaroslavl Province no. 6894 (4 June 1909), Permit of the Superintendent of Prisons of Tomsk Province (1 November 1911). Tõnu Karu's personal archive.

[24] Eesti Baptisti koguduste aruanne 1922.

[25] Kaups, *50 aastat apostlite radadel*, 191. See Adam Podin's correspondence with Evangelical Alliance General Secretary H.M. Gooch, 24 January 1930 and 29 October 1931. Tõnu Karu's personal archive.

[26] Ain Kalmus, *Kadunud saar* (Lund: Eesti Kirjanike Kooperatiiv, 1972), 158.

[27] Kaups, *50 aastat apostlite radadel*, 190-91; Eesti Baptisti Usuühingute Liidu (Koguduste Ühenduse) aruanne 1926.

[28] Eesti Baptisti koguduste aruanne 1922.

his pastoral work was practically in his co-workers' hands. Referring to the time before the First World War, Podin mentioned that one year he was at home only thirty-eight days out of 365. One need not be a prophet to tell that his family also had to pay the cost. 'The hardest moment was when I came home and wanted to hug my children, as I had dreamed during the whole journey, but when I arrived they did not recognise their "papa" and thought I was a stranger, because I had been away for so long.'[29] Even in the 1920s and 1930s, when his ministry was limited mainly to Estonia, it was a time and energy consuming enterprise. Podin reported that in 1934 he visited all Estonian prisons, except one, and conducted altogether thirty-eight worship services – in different languages – for prisoners.[30]

Podin was certainly not the only Estonian evangelical pastor who worked in prisons but he was no doubt the only one whose ministry was extraordinarily wide, systematic and intensive, and who modelled for others the idea of evangelical compassion work. However, prison ministry was only one half of Podin's social service, the other half being ministry in Estonian lepers' homes, which he undertook with similar zeal and devotion.

A Ministry of Compassion among Lepers

Today it is almost forgotten that before the Second World War there were four lepers' homes in Estonia, one of which – in Kuuda – continued to operate until 1977. In 1920 there were 316 lepers in the country and in 1940 there were 113.[31] Adam Podin practically knew all these patients, as he regularly visited the lepers' homes, preached, conducted worship services, baptised, shared the Lord's Supper, encouraged, but sometimes also buried the patients. About 1923 he wrote that the Estonian government and the doctors did their best to bring relief to the patients' lives and into their illness, 'nevertheless, there is enough to do for a compassionate heart'.[32]

Podin experienced a heartfelt calling for lepers' ministry in 1904 or 1905, shortly before he became involved in prison work. He was shocked by the loneliness and social isolation that accompanied the disease. It must be underlined that his help was not only pastoral but also practical. Here, again, he applied his international links and pan-evangelical vision. There were burning everyday practical needs in the lepers' homes. During the First World War and in its aftermath the patients were in need of commodities, food and clothes. Podin provided basic goods in this time of deepest desperation.[33] Through the years of his ministry Podin, in cooperation with doctors, also helped patients with a medicine that he was able to acquire from abroad

---

[29] Eesti Baptisti koguduste aruanne 1922.

[30] Eesti Baptisti Usuühingute Liidu aruanne 1934.

[31] Ken Kalling, 'Dermatoveneroloogia institutsionaliseerimine Eestis enne 1940. aastat', *Eesti Arst* 89.5 (2010), 340.

[32] Eesti Baptisti koguduste aruanne 1923.

[33] Former Tarvastu lepers' home patients and Marie Reimann to Adam Podin, 17 March 1940. Tõnu Karu's personal archive.

for Estonian patients. In 1927 he reported that in his work he had spent 103,000 Estonian marks for lepers' medicine; this money came largely from abroad through his personal contacts and fundraising efforts in the USA and Britain. 'From Estonia I have received only a couple of hundred marks, and one patient gave five golden roubles as a gift.'[34] The effective and expensive medicine that Podin was able to provide, helped, over the years, at least twenty patients to recover fully, and the condition of many others improved.[35] A grant for Podin from the funds of the Evangelical Alliance substantially helped his work among lepers.

Podin, led by empathy and compassion, saw his ministry also from a missional perspective: preaching, Bible study, distribution of New Testaments and praying with patients were essential elements of his work. Some patients converted to evangelical faith and became members of Keila Baptist Church.[36] A letter from 1940, written by some leper patients on the occasion of the thirty-fifth anniversary of Podin's social ministry, stated,

> We greatly rejoice that we can come and thank you with this letter for the work that – with God's help – you have done among us during these 35 years, consoling us with the Word of God, encouraging us and leading us to Jesus. Through your proclamation of the Word God has done his work of grace in the heart of many. Of those who have become believers, 17 have become members of Baptist church, while many who through your proclamation have come to Jesus have remained outside Baptist church membership, and a number of them have gone to the Heavenly Father's home – in strong faith and rejoicing in hope.[37]

This social and missional ministry responded to the existential and spiritual needs of the lepers, but it also helped to raise their quality of life by meeting the practical needs of patients. In caring for these patients, Podin did not spare his energy. For example, in 1934 he visited all four lepers' homes, and some of these he visited three or four times per year.[38] In 1931 he was awarded a Red Cross medal for his social work.[39]

In his social ministry, Podin's relations with the Estonian Baptist leadership were ambiguous. He expected that his colleagues in ministry would offer more help and resources, and would show a clear interest in social work. The Estonian Baptists, however, appreciated Podin's work in this field but they did not have the resources, skills or motivation to be more directly involved. Their logic was: Podin is a Baptist, so this is a Baptist work that is appreciated, but at the same time it is his private

---

[34] Eesti Baptisti koguduste aruanne 1927.
[35] Kuuda lepers' home patients to Adam Podin, 19 March 1940. Tõnu Karu's personal archive.
[36] Kaups, *50 aastat apostlite radadel*, 59.
[37] Kuuda lepers' home patients to Adam Podin, 19 March 1940. Tõnu Karu's personal archive.
[38] Eesti Baptisti koguduste aruanne 1934.
[39] See www.president.ee/et/vabariik/teenetemargid/kavalerid.php?id=8954), accessed 17 August 2012.

effort, as most of the support is channelled into this ministry through his own contacts.

Podin realised that to make this work sustainable, he needed committed younger followers. He wrote in 1922,

> It would be very commendable that the continuity of this work would not depend only on me, but that the union of our churches would join in and experience what a joy it is when we can console those in misery and when we can alleviate their pain.[40]

However, in 1930 the Union had not found a tangibly defined way to be part of either the prison or the lepers' ministry. Their report stated, 'For the most part this has been a work of individuals and has not found a direct link to the Union.'[41] The reasons for this lack in cooperation can only be guessed. It is possible that Podin himself lacked motivation to involve others in his plans, planning and projects. It is also possible that the leaders of the Baptist Union, focusing on strengthening their denominational identity, especially in the 1930s, were cautious about getting too closely related to wider evangelical efforts.

Although receiving less support than he expected from his fellow Baptists, Podin set a model for holistic social ministry, both for the churches and for the wider society. Even today his ministry is an example and source of inspiration.

Director of the Preachers' Seminary

Each of the areas of ministry described so far could be a full-time job and a life's mission in itself, yet Podin still found energy to undertake another task: from 1922 to 1938 he was director of the Estonian Baptist Preachers' Seminary, later re-named the Baptist Theological Seminary. The role of the seminary, and Podin's contribution to its development, cannot be underestimated, as a number of the seminary graduates worked in ministerial roles during the later communist years. They drew theological balance and the necessary knowledge and skills from the training they had received at this theological institution.

The seminary was established within the wider context of decisions made after the First World War. In 1920, Baptist delegates from Britain, North America, Australia and continental Europe met for the so called 'London Conference of 1920'. Besides other strategic decisions, this meeting took the important step forward of founding Baptist seminaries in Europe and providing funds for these institutions. New theological schools were started in Spain, Hungary, Romania, Latvia and other places, including Estonia.[42] Podin was present at the London conference and vividly explained the needs of the Estonian Baptists in the aftermath of the First World War. Estonian Baptist popular sources have tended to exaggerate Podin's role in this

---

[40] Eesti Baptisti koguduse aruanne 1922.
[41] Eesti Baptisti koguduste aruanne 1930.
[42] 'London Conference of 1920', in William H. Brackney, *Historical Dictionary of the Baptists* (Lanham, MD: The Scarecrow Press, 1999).

situation, but there is no doubt that he was a charismatic personality and there is probably a grain of truth in the story that after Podin's speech the English Baptist Dr John Clifford, who chaired the meeting, stood up and exclaimed, 'Everything Podin has asked, he must get!'[43] What Podin asked for was not humanitarian aid for those in need, but first and foremost theological education for future Estonian Baptist pastors. The timing of this plea, which emotionally and convincingly emphasised the ideas that were already in the air at the London conference, was perfect.

After a period of preparations, the seminary was festively opened in 5 March 1922, with Adam Podin as its director. The school started in Podin's private house in Keila.[44] Funding relied mostly on American and British donations. James H. Rushbrooke from Britain and Walter O. Lewis from the USA coordinated the Baptist support for the seminary. Both visited Estonia and the seminary on several occasions, and Podin was well acquainted with both of these international key-figures.[45] Podin also used the resources he had generously, not sparing even his personal means. In addition, his Europe-wide fame, his personality and evangelical zeal offered a certain guarantee for the seminary 'project' on an international scale. The seminary moved into a new building in Tallinn in 1931. The funds were raised in the USA thanks to Walter O. Lewis' contacts[46] and once again it was Adam Podin who coordinated the whole project on the Estonian end.

Podin gave some lectures and classes to students, but his practical modelling of Christian mission was more impressive than his lectures. Ain Kalmus, who studied at the seminary, evaluated Podin's educational ministry as follows:

> The seminary director Adam Podin was a better administrator than teacher. Obviously he was himself aware of this, as his teaching was limited only to a couple courses on exegetical subjects. He especially loved the apostle Paul and was able to interpret the Epistles in a practical way.

Kalmus also tells that Podin's son Samuel taught English to the students; Samuel had lived in England and America.[47] Being academically less impressive than some other teachers, Podin had a special gift that he shared with students. He involved students in ministry, supervising them in 'workplace-based' practical training. In the Tartu Theological Seminary archive there is a photo from 1928 which shows seminary students lined up in front of Podin's home: they are ready to go on a visit to a prison, some have bags with gifts in their hand, some have guitars. Podin's role in mentoring and supervising, in addition to his administrative and organisational skills at the seminary, was significant.

---

[43] Kaups, *50 aastat apostlite radadel*, 180.

[44] Minutes, no. 9 (22 February 1922), Eesti Baptisti Usuteaduse Seminari Protokolliraamat 1920–[1940], EEKBLA; Kaups, *50 aastat apostlite radadel*, 181-82.

[45] See, e.g., the Minute Book of the Estonian Baptist Theological Seminary which on several occasions refers to visits by Rushbrooke and Lewis or to correspondence with them.

[46] Kaups, *50 aastat apostlite radadel*, 184.

[47] Kalmus, *Kadunud saar*, 153-54.

In 1938 Podin handed the job of seminary director over to Osvald Tärk who had studied at Newton Theological Institute, near Boston, and had received his master's degree from Union Theological Seminary, New York, in 1925–29. Podin's role in sending Tärk and some other talented students to study abroad had been crucial. His recommendations helped to open doors for young pastors and theologians for their further development.[48] The openness and willingness of Podin to use his connections for the benefit of a younger generation of ministers, renders him as a man of a broad vision, a vision expanding beyond his personal and present horizons.

A Pan-Evangelical Liaison in Estonia

International and pan-evangelical dimensions were like glue that held together the numerous ministries and projects that Adam Podin undertook. Some further light must be shed on his role as a liaison for the Evangelical Alliance and other international organisations. In the 1920s and 1930s Podin was an Evangelical Alliance contact in Estonia, though obviously his links with this organisation had started earlier. At the same time, he helped to represent the story of Estonian Baptists in the Anglo-American evangelical world. Evangelical leaders also sought his opinions regarding political and anti-religious developments in communist Russia.

The personal archive of Tõnu Karu contains letters that help to acquire an insight into Adam Podin's correspondence with the Evangelical Alliance (EA) headquarters in London.[49] The letters are from the years 1927 to 1932, but there is no doubt the correspondence was more extensive and covered a much longer period. The messages confirm that the EA supported Podin's social ministry. There are also reports published in *Evangelical Christendom* which give surveys of Podin's travels, prison-visits and other social-missional activities. In 1923 *Evangelical Christendom* assured its readers that the editors were willing to give more information to a wider audience about Podin's work.[50] In 1930, the EA helped Podin with funds for a car for his mission work, providing £145, which included some private donations, and which enabled Podin to buy the vehicle.[51] The EA put a considerable amount of effort into supporting Podin. In 1929, Henry M. Gooch even wrote a letter to Henry Ford in Detroit in order to get some support for this 'car-project', but the appeal was rejected. Gooch commented to Podin, 'You can see ... what they think there in Detroit.'[52] The correspondence shows that Podin and Gooch had a friendlier relationship than one of just formal partners in ministry – they must have known

---

[48] Ruudi Leinus (comp and ed.), *Osvald Tärk: Uskuge Jumalase* (Tallinn: Eesti EKB Liit, 1999), 15.

[49] I express my gratitude to Tõnu Karu who graciously introduced me to the documents that are held in his private ownership and provided me with copies of the documents.

[50] *Evangelical Christendom* (March–April 1923), 39.

[51] H.M. Gooch to Adam Podin, 28 February 1930. Tõnu Karu's personal archive.

[52] H.M. Gooch to Adam Podin, 3 January 1929. Tõnu Karu's personal archive.

each other well. Gooch visited Estonia, probably on several occasions.[53] The EA regularly helped to cover Podin's travelling costs and literature expenses. In 1930 the quarterly support for Podin was £37 10s,[54] a considerable sum of money. Some – though probably not regular – help was also offered to a small orphanage that Emilie Podin ran in Keila.[55] The EA's support of Podin certainly had other reasons than just personal links: the combination of evangelism and social activism, which Podin embodied *par excellence*, fitted well with the pan-evangelical vision. In addition, the EA was interested in supporting mission in continental Europe as it helped to bring 'Continental Brethren' on the radar of British evangelicals, and to unite evangelicals in Europe.[56] In turn, Podin's ministry told a catching story that helped to promote the work of the EA.

Podin had other international links, both with Baptists and other evangelicals. The archival sources available in Estonia show that he was a liaison between the Estonian Sunday School Union, a pan-evangelical organisation established in 1928,[57] and the World's Sunday School Association. Due to Podin's influence Estonia was received into membership of the World's Sunday School Association. He corresponded with the Association's office in Glasgow and with its honorary secretary, James Kelly. The British office of the association provided some funds for the Estonian organisation for promoting Sunday school work.[58] In 1930 Kelly visited Estonia in order to learn more about the situation. The trip was coordinated by Tabea Korjus, but Podin was provided with copies of the correspondence and the travel schedule. In 1930 Kelly wrote to Korjus,

> I should therefore be glad if, in conference with Mr. Podin, you would decide when the meeting of the Sunday School Committee will be held, as I am very anxious to have a good conference to discuss the whole Sunday School situation in Estonia, and I am anxious to know, if possible, what views Mr. Podin and others have concerning the present religious situation in Russia.[59]

Living out his pan-evangelical convictions, and being a trusted person and liaison both for British and American Baptists, as well as for the EA and the World's

---

[53] Kaups, *50 aastat apostlite radadel*, 58; Ian M. Randall and David Hilborn, *One Body in Christ: The History and Significance of the Evangelical Alliance* (Carlisle: Paternoster Press, 2001), 171.

[54] H.M. Gooch to Adam Podin, 28 March 1930, 8 July 1930, 17 December 1930. Tõnu Karu's personal archive.

[55] H.M. Gooch to Adam Podin, 6 December 1929. Tõnu Karu's personal archive.

[56] Randall and Hilborn, *One Body in Christ*, 170-72, 176.

[57] Riho Altnurme (ed.), *History of Estonian Ecumenism* (Tartu and Tallinn: University of Tartu and Estonian Council of Churches, 2009), 100.

[58] Adam Podin to James Kelly, 28 November 1928, handwritten draft; World's Sunday School Association British branch to Adam Podin, 25 July 1929 and 17 March 1930. Tõnu Karu's personal archive.

[59] James Kelly to Adam Podin, 26 February 1930; James Kelly to Tabea Korjus, 26 February 1930. Tõnu Karu's personal archive.

Sunday School Association, Podin helped to promote unity among evangelicals. Already in the early years of his pastoral ministry – in the first decade of the twentieth century – he participated in Allianz Bible courses that conveyed German Blankenburg and British Keswick theology and spirituality. Over the years such courses were organised in Laitse, in Baron Woldemar von Üxküll's manor, as well as in Keila, where Podin pastored the church. Speakers at these conferences represented a wide spectrum on the evangelical-holiness-alliance scale: Friedrich Baedeker, Ernst Ströter, Johann Kargel, Baron Paul Nicolay, Henry M. Gooch and others.[60] In addition, Adam Podin helped to introduce EA prayer weeks in Estonia. In 1923 he reported that the prayer week was an enormous blessing everywhere and that he authorised 2000 programmes to be printed in Estonian, which were distributed all over the country.[61] Through these and other activities, as well as his ability to speak Russian, Latvian, Estonian, German and English, Podin built contacts across the borders: both geographically and denominationally, both on personal and organisational levels.

Summary and Conclusion

In many ways, Adam Podin's life demonstrates the wider horizons of the Estonian evangelical landscape in the first half of the twentieth century. He was born in northern Latvia, but after years of travelling and working internationally for the Seamen's Mission, he chose an Estonian wife, Emilie. He accepted a pastoral ministry in Keila (Kegel) Baptist Church in Estonia, but he represented an evangelical spirituality that reached beyond denominational and geographical borders. His conversion in 1884 in London took place in a pan-evangelical setting, even if detailed information about this event is lacking. His personal acquaintances, friends and co-workers included persons with broad evangelical convictions, whom he also involved in his ministry. The unifying element in all this was redemption in Christ, and the Christian activism that followed from this central theological truth. Adam Podin was influenced by Blankenburg and Keswick holiness spirituality. As a Baptist pastor in Estonia, involved in local Baptist structures, he continued to live out his broader pan-evangelical beliefs, thus helping to broaden the Estonian Baptists' understanding of mission and social ministry. Unfortunately, not much about his theological views survives in firsthand written form; many conclusions in this paper are based on his work reports, biographical data and the memoirs of contemporaries, as well as on secondary sources.

All through his years of spiritual service Podin combined – in tune with the theology and practice of the Evangelical Alliance – evangelism by means of preaching, social ministry and international vision. He also believed in the need of theological education and he had a central role in establishing the Estonian Baptist Seminary in 1922, helping to shape its curriculum and faculty, and securing its

---

[60] Kaups, *50 aastat apostlite radadel*, 58, 176.
[61] *Evangelical Christendom* (March–April 1923), 39.

financial basis. As far as the historical sources allow us to see, he was impressive in preaching, charismatic in human relationships, energetic in action and compassionate when meeting fellow humans in need. He supported the development of his younger co-workers and in some cases acted as a mentor. He was also an excellent fundraiser and many of the opportunities for ministry that Estonian evangelicals in general, and Baptists in particular, had in the 1920s and 1930s were due to Podin's contacts, public relations work and recommendations. In addition, he used a considerable amount of financial support for buying and distributing the Scriptures as well as for humanitarian help for those in need.

Adam Podin's spiritual heritage is wider than Estonia. He belongs to European evangelical history, as a liaison for the Evangelical Alliance and other organisations, such as the World's Sunday School Association. He helped Estonian Baptists to develop links with British and American fellow Baptists as well as other evangelicals. One should also remember that Podin was part of a pan-evangelical movement in tsarist Russia as before 1918 he worked in social ministry and evangelism in this vast area. He was acquainted with Pashkovite and other evangelical key figures in the country. As to Podin's multifaceted areas of ministry, one can only admire his energy and persistence. He helped to build – both literally and figuratively – the Keila Baptist church, even if this, because of his travels and other responsibilities, required heavy reliance on his co-workers.

Perhaps his most outstanding contribution was his social and missionary ministry, both in Russia and Estonia. He became involved in prison work in Russia in 1905 or 1906, and after 1918 he focused on Estonian prisons. Adam Podin's compassion-work with lepers, which he started in 1905, is part not only of Estonian church history, but it belongs also to the social, medical and cultural history of this country. He not only addressed the patients' spiritual needs but also helped to improve their quality of life. Both these social ministries – visiting prisons and lepers' homes – he conducted until the later years of his life. Podin also has a large place in the story of the Estonian Baptist Theological Seminary as its first director. He played a key role in establishing, leading and developing the seminary. In a way this was the most long-term investment of his skills and energy, as a number of students served in ministry later, during the Soviet years, offering hope and leadership in the midst of atheistic pressures. The results of this work Podin was unable to see himself because he passed away on 24 November 1941 in Keila.

CHAPTER 8

Sarah Terrett, Katherine Robinson and Edith Pearce: Three Nonconformist Women and Public Life in Bristol, 1870–1910

Linda Wilson

In June 1909, the Lady Mayoress, Katherine Robinson, taking the place of her husband who was unwell, presided at a Sunday school anniversary meeting at Old King Street Baptist Church, Bristol, with the understanding that she would not need to give a speech. However, when the moment came and she saw 'the great number of scholars' she felt 'constrained to say a few words', telling her listeners that

> she thought, after all, she had a better right to be there than the Lord Mayor, because it was in Old King Street Sunday School she gave her heart to the Saviour, and she considered that all the good that had come to her in life was due to the early influences she received in the Sunday School. She concluded her address by urging all the scholars to give their hearts to the Lord whilst they were young.[1]

This account demonstrates how the Lady Mayoress, a prominent Baptist woman, responded to an opportunity to speak. It also indicates the role played by evangelical Nonconformists in the life of Bristol at this time, as well as the personal faith at the heart of such church and public involvement. Less prominent women, too, found opportunities for activity both within and beyond the church in Bristol during this period. This chapter will focus on three evangelical women in Bristol during the period 1870–1910, exploring their roles in the life of the city. Katherine Robinson is one: the two others, Sarah Terrett and Edith Pearce, provide an interesting contrast to each other and to Katherine.

Sarah and Edith were both instrumental in the local temperance movement, illustrating the hold that the drink issue had over evangelicals during this period.[2]

---

[1] B.J. Gibbon, *A Child A Hundred Years Old: Centenary Memorial of Old King St Baptist Sunday School, Bristol* (Bristol: Ranking Bros, 1909), 62.

[2] F. Knight, 'Recreation or Renunciation?: Episcopal Interventions in the Drink Question in the 1890s', in S.J. Brown, J. Morgan-Guy and F. Knight (eds), *Religion, Identity and Conflict in Britain* (Farnham: Ashgate, forthcoming 2013). Also, see B. Harrison, *Drink and the Victorians* (London: Faber & Faber, 1971), still the standard work on the subject. Although the period covered is only up to 1872, many of the issues are the same.

Sarah, a Bible Christian, launched an independent temperance movement, the White Ribbon Army, in 1878, based in Bedminster, south Bristol, and oversaw its rapid expansion for eleven years before her sudden death in November 1889. Edith, the wife of a Primitive Methodist minister, chose to start a branch of an existing organisation, the National British Women's Temperance Association. She led this group in east Bristol for just over two years, from 1906 to July 1908, before moving away from the city. Katherine Robinson was the daughter of the Principal of Bristol Baptist College, the Rev. Frederick Gotch, and married to Edward, a high-profile Bristol manufacturer and magistrate. Her high public and church profile (her name frequently appeared in the local papers) was largely due to these family connections. These three reflect a little of the variety of women involved in evangelical Nonconformity in Bristol, representing two of the four major Nonconformist streams, Baptist and Primitive Methodist, and one of the minor ones, the Bible Christians.[3] Whilst excellent work has been done by Madge Dresser,[4] June Hannam[5] and others into the lives and role of women in other Nonconformist groups, Bristol women who worshipped in these more conventional, predominantly evangelical denominations have yet to receive similar attention. This research is a contribution to filling that gap.

Women were active in Bristol life. June Hannam has noted that Bristol was 'one of a small number of cities at the forefront of the development of feminist politics' between 1860 and 1914, and that initially women from Nonconformist professional and business families, especially Quakers and Unitarians, played a significant role in this.[6] She argued, however, that evangelicals were less likely to challenge the status quo of gender relations. More recently, Sue Morgan and Jacqueline de Vries have commented on the 'paradoxical relationship between feminism and religion', which they believe is still 'strikingly under-researched'.[7] Their work indicates that the situation is more complex than Hannam suggested. This 'paradoxical relationship' provides the backdrop to any consideration of women and religion in this period.

Evangelicalism, it has been suggested, both restricted women and gave them new opportunities. For instance, Leonora Davidoff and Catherine Hall have argued that evangelicalism was an integral part of the development of separate spheres, the idea

---

[3] Clyde Binfield, *So Down to Prayers* (London: Dent & Sons, 1977), 7, has noted that the four mainstream Nonconformist denominations were Wesleyan Methodists, Primitive Methodists, Baptists and Congregationalists.

[4] See, for instance, M. Dresser, 'Women in the Bristol Moravian Church in the Eighteenth Century', in J. Bettey (ed.), *Historic Churches and Church Life in Bristol* (Bristol: Bristol and Gloucestershire Archaeological Society, 2001), 134-47.

[5] June Hannam has written about the role of Unitarians and Quakers in late nineteenth-century Bristol politics in '"An Enlarged Sphere of Usefulness": The Bristol Women's Movement, c.1860–1914', in M. Dresser and P. Ollerenshaw (eds), *The Making of Modern Bristol* (Tiverton: Redcliffe Press, 1996), 184-209 (184-85).

[6] Hannam, '"Enlarged Sphere"', 184-85.

[7] S. Morgan and J. de Vries (eds), *Women, Gender and Religious Cultures in Britain, 1800–1940* (London: Routledge, 2010), 7.

that the Victorian middle classes regarded the home as the women's sphere of activity and interest, and the public world as belonging to men, but also provided them with a sense of community.[8] Whilst this theory has not gone unchallenged and is now accepted as needing to be more nuanced,[9] the basic concept remains a useful one. I have argued elsewhere that in the mid-nineteenth century churches frequently provided a 'third sphere' for women.[10] Those whose opportunities for engagement in the public world were limited could develop skills and experience an outlet for their abilities within a church context, through such activities as teaching Sunday school classes, visiting the poor, helping to organise societies, and praying or singing solos in meetings or services or, in some limited situations, preaching. These activities developed skills which, once learnt, could be transferred to the public sphere.[11] One of the questions this chapter will consider is whether the 'third sphere' was still relevant to women in this slightly later period.

Two of the women under discussion were connected to business interests in Bristol. Katherine's husband, Edward, and his brother, Arthur, headed up a prosperous paper bag and stationery firm, E.S. & A. Robinson. By 1911 there were 2,500 employees in several factories covering an area of ten and a half acres,[12] and the Robinsons lived in The Towers, Sneyd Park, one of the most exclusive areas of Bristol. By contrast, William and Sarah Terrett lived near their butcher's business in the less attractive area of Bedminster, although the fact that they owned a sizeable house and that in 1882 William was returned as a councillor, indicates they were better off than many of their fellow shopkeepers. Both of these businesses were part of the 'sedate, though always persistent'[13] growth that Bristol, 'the unofficial regional capital of the south west',[14] was experiencing during this period. Part of the city's strength was the variety of enterprises that emerged as it developed into an industrial city, especially after 1880.[15] Between 1881 and 1911 the population grew by over 70% as new workers were drawn to Bristol.[16] Much of this growth occurred beyond the city limits, necessitating a series of boundary changes to incorporate the

---

[8] L. Davidoff and C. Hall, *Family Fortunes* (London: Routledge, 1987), for instance 115-18, 450; for community, see 103.

[9] See S. Williams, 'Gender, Religion and Family Culture', in Morgan and de Vries (eds), *Women, Gender and Religious Cultures*, 11-31 (15), for a brief overview.

[10] L. Wilson, *Constrained by Zeal: Female Spirituality amongst Nonconformists, 1824–75* (Carlisle: Paternoster, 2000), 210-11.

[11] Wilson, *Constrained by Zeal*, 210-211.

[12] D. Bateman, 'The Growth of the Printing and Packaging Industry in Bristol, 1800–1914', in C. Harvey and J. Press (eds), *Studies in the Business History of Bristol* (Bristol: Bristol Academic Press, 1988), 83-107 (99).

[13] Bateman, 'Printing and Packaging', 99.

[14] P. Ollerenshaw and P. Wardley, 'Economic Growth and the Business Community in Bristol since 1840', in Dresser and Ollerenshaw (eds), *Modern Bristol*, 124-55 (124).

[15] J. Lynch, *A Tale of Three Cities* (Basingstoke: Macmillan, 1988), 19.

[16] Lynch, *Three Cities*, 19.

new areas into the city.[17] Several of the key manufacturing firms contributing to this growth were owned by Nonconformists, including W.D. & H.O. Wills, tobacco manufacturers,[18] and J.S. Fry & Sons, chocolate and cocoa producers, as well as the Robinsons. There were also smaller businesses, such as that owned by the Terretts. Men and women from these families, usually Liberals, played significant parts in the life of the city.[19] The Wills family, for instance, were responsible for providing buildings for the new University College in 1876. The existence of this Nonconformist 'aristocracy' is evident in a newspaper advertisement for a meeting of the NSPCC, with an evening reception to follow. Those named as being part of the reception committee for the event included Mr and Mrs Edward Robinson, his brother Alfred and his wife, and members of the Wills and Fry families.[20] Our three women lived in the context of an increasing public profile of Bristol Nonconformists and Katherine belonged to the local Nonconformist 'aristocracy'.[21]

Sarah Terrett: General of the White Ribbon Army

Sarah Terrett came from a humbler background: her father ran a butcher's shop. She and her husband William belonged to the Bible Christian Chapel in Bedminster, south Bristol, one of several Methodist connexions in the area. Its heartland was in rural Devon, the area where Sarah had grown up, and it generally drew its members from the poorer sections of society.[22] She was active in the chapel, teaching in the Sunday school, fundraising and occasionally preaching. The connexion had maintained its early theology which allowed women to preach,[23] and although as the century progressed the number of female ministers declined steeply,[24] Sarah's involvement is a confirmation that there were still women on the preaching plans. As well as this church involvement, she helped with the family business (her husband's and father's butchers' businesses were amalgamated, becoming Babbage & Terrett), into which, according to her biographer, 'she entered heart and soul'.[25] She also brought up three children (six more died in infancy) and ran a busy home, frequently

---

[17] H.E. Meller, *Leisure and the Changing City, 1870–1914* (London: Routledge & Kegan Paul, 1976), 21.

[18] The Wills family was originally Congregationalist although by the late nineteenth century several of them had become Anglican.

[19] For instance, the establishment of a University College in Bristol, in 1877, was partly due to the generosity of the Wills family.

[20] *Bristol Mercury and Daily Post*, 19 October 1896.

[21] Meller, *Leisure*, 93, mentions the Robinsons in the context of a chapter called 'Bristol's Leading Citizens – A Governing Elite?'

[22] J.M. Lloyd, *Women and the Shaping of British Methodism: Persistent Preachers, 1807–1907* (Manchester: Manchester University Press, 2009), 73.

[23] Lloyd, *Women and British Methodism*, 91-92, 105-107.

[24] Lloyd, *Women and British Methodism*, 111-13.

[25] F.W. Bourne, *Ready in Life and Death: Brief Memorials of Mrs S.M. Terrett* (London: Bible Christian Book Room, 1893), 30.

offering hospitality to visitors,[26] including for occasional connexional finance meetings[27] and holding an annual butchers' festival in her garden.[28] Sarah's life was thus already full before she embarked on the temperance enterprise. She was the epitome of a Bible Christian activist, as is also demonstrated by the fact that her rather hagiographical biography was written by the Bible Christian historian F.W. Bourne.

Sarah's own narrative, which forms a substantial part of Bourne's memorials, includes a description of the origins of the White Ribbon Army. She recalled how, one Sunday evening in November 1878, she visited a woman in the slums in Bedminster and was shocked by the sight of women and children 'half fed, dirty, clothed in rags, shoeless and stockingless, going with broken vessels, into the pothouses to fetch intoxicating drinks'.[29] Her response to this experience was to invite selected people to a meeting at her house to discuss the problem. At this gathering, on 28 November 1878, the White Ribbon Army was formed. After this small beginning, despite the presence of a multiplicity of other temperance organisations in the city,[30] the Bedminster White Ribbon Army grew steadily, especially after Sarah took over the old Bible Christian Chapel in Bedminster, opening it as a Mission Hall and base for the movement in January 1881.[31] By the time she became known as the 'General', in June of the same year, 3,700 people had apparently taken the White Ribbon pledge.[32] Later that year, 'invitations came pouring in from all parts of Bristol and neighbourhoods for battalions to be opened'.[33] The Army spread outside Bristol to various places including Bath, Exmouth, Taunton and Plymouth, Dawley in Shropshire and even one outpost in London. It continued to expand until, by time of her death in November 1888, there were fifty-five battalions.[34]

As a result of the establishment of so many new centres, Sarah found herself travelling widely and speaking frequently in the cause of temperance.[35] She was skilled at handling disruption: on one occasion, she was interrupted by two drunken men when speaking to a crowded meeting in the Countess of Huntingdon's Chapel in Weston-super-Mare. James Shergold, leader of the local battalion, recalled that she handled the disturbance skilfully: 'In her winning, loving way, Sarah answered the questions and eventually got these two men on to the platform, and both of them signed the pledge and left donning the white ribbon.'[36] She appears to have thrived

---

[26] Bourne, *Brief Memorials*, 29-30.
[27] Bourne, *Brief Memorials*, 152.
[28] *Bristol Mercury*, 5 July 1881.
[29] Bourne, *Brief Memorials*, 48.
[30] Meller, *Leisure*, 164.
[31] Bourne, *Brief Memorials*, 54.
[32] Bourne, *Brief Memorials*, 63-64.
[33] Bourne, *Brief Memorials*, 68.
[34] Bourne, *Brief Memorials*, 111.
[35] Bourne, *Brief Memorials*, 124.
[36] Bourne, *Brief Memorials*, 113.

as a public speaker and campaigner, not being intimidated by the demands involved. One friend, the Rev. W. Higman, recalled how, after dealing all day with 'pressing' family and business matters, Sarah Terrett would take a train 'for Taunton, Bridgewater or Plymouth, conduct a crowded meeting, sometimes addressing thousands, and when possible, returning by the night mail to be in her place in the home and business the next morning'.[37] He was full of admiration for this busy lifestyle, not thinking it might have been the cause of her early death. Bourne also applauded her energetic development of the White Ribbon Movement, although he was eager to point out that she made domestic concerns a priority, stating at the end of his biography that 'The best praise of her public work is, that it did not spoil her beautiful home life.'[38] Perhaps Bourne was careful to stress her home life because of her unusual degree of public involvement and presence. In 1893, when the memoir was published, it seems that a well-run home was still regarded as a necessary validation for a woman's successful public life.

Sarah's husband William was her chief supporter and second-in-command. She became the General whilst he was the Lieutenant-General. He coped with a disrupted life due to her involvement in the campaign and with decisions made without consulting him. For instance, she committed her organisation to buy the old Bible Christian chapel in Bedminster to use as a Mission Hall for her temperance movement without consulting him,[39] and once the hall was opened she gave away a good suit of his to the doorman without asking William, a move which seemed to amuse more than annoy him.[40] At the anniversary meetings held from 1882 onwards in the Colston Hall,[41] a sizeable Bristol concert hall, she presided whilst he had the role of reading a report on the previous year's activities and developments.[42] She also seems to have had the final word on whether to give some of their income to church work.[43] Yet he was not an insignificant man in his own right, running businesses which were at times quite successful and becoming a city councillor.[44] In their marriage Sarah appears to have been the stronger character.

Although Sarah had often suffered from ill health, her death at the age of fifty-three, during a meeting of the White Ribbon Army, was unexpected. The organisation depended heavily on her as an individual and after her death it seriously declined. In the only hint of criticism in his entire book, Bourne commented that if it had been better organised, the work might have better survived her death.[45] Her

---

[37] Bourne, *Brief Memorials*, 124.
[38] Bourne, *Brief Memorials*, for instance 151.
[39] Bourne, *Brief Memorials*, 54.
[40] Bourne, *Brief Memorials*, 59.
[41] Bourne, *Brief Memorials*, 78-79.
[42] For example, *Bristol Mercury*, 28 November 1882.
[43] Bourne, *Brief Memorials*, 153.
[44] M.J. Crossley Evans, 'Christian Missionary Work among the Seamen and Dock workers of Bristol, 1820–1914,' in Bettey (ed.), *Church Life in Bristol*, 162-95 (178), and *Bristol Mercury*, 2 November 1882.
[45] Bourne, *Brief Memorials*, 99.

name lived on for some years in the shape of the Terrett Memorial Hall, built in 1893/4 to commemorate her work.[46]

Jennifer Lloyd has suggested that Sarah Terrett was one of many middle-class women who 'took advantage of the greater leisure available to them in city life and driven by their religious faith', became involved in philanthropy and often ended up speaking in public.[47] Sarah is not a good example of this trajectory, however, as she was already preaching and giving speeches before she became involved in the temperance movement: her biography contains a substantial speech given at the time the foundation stones of the new Bible Christian Chapel in Bedminster were laid, in 1877, and she was evidently preaching long before that. She also had little leisure to fill, as she was already involved in helping with her husband's business. Lloyd also argued that Sarah was one of many women 'bridging the divide between public and private in ways that did not overtly challenge acceptable gender roles', suggesting that 'her public presence and eloquent oratory while certainly not typical, were not unusual'.[48] It is certainly true that, in the condolence letters after her death, several writers commented on her hospitality and her well-organised home, a very feminine virtue,[49] but I would contend that speaking at such a large venue as the Colston Hall, and frequently travelling and speaking in a variety of other towns, moved Sarah beyond a normal female role even for the 1880s.

Although Sarah was never closely involved with feminist campaigns, she was active in the Bristol Women's Liberal Association. Established in 1881, this was the first such organisation in the country,[50] and all three of the women considered in this article had some connection with it. As early as 1883 Sarah and her husband both signed a letter in support of extending the franchise to women,[51] and in 1888 she allowed the Mission Hall to be used for a meeting of the Women's Liberal Association to discuss the issue. The meeting was chaired by the Rev. Brokenshire, the minister of her local chapel, whom she would have known well and who was evidently a strong supporter of votes for women.[52] Sarah was not unaware of the wider issues concerning women's rights, although, perhaps because of her busy life and passion for the gospel temperance cause, she never got closely involved in either the Women's Liberal Association or the issue of suffrage. What is clear is that she was an example of a woman who developed her skills in the third sphere of the church but then demonstrated her ability in a very public role.

Sarah was also a good example of the paradoxical relationship between feminism and gender referred to by Morgan and de Vries. She believed strongly in the home and in the importance of raising girls who would be good wives and mothers.[53]

---

[46] Crossley Evans, 'Christian Missionary Work', 179.

[47] Lloyd, *Women and British Methodism*, 132.

[48] Lloyd, *Women and British Methodism*, 134.

[49] Bourne, *Brief Memorials*, 124, 127.

[50] Hannam, '"Enlarged Sphere"', 195.

[51] *Bristol Mercury*, 20 November 1883.

[52] *Bristol Mercury*, 22 February 1888.

[53] Bourne, *Brief Memorials*, 36.

However, her husband was certainly not subservient: in many ways he seemed to be the dominant partner. More significantly, although her home life was clearly important to her, she spent much of her time either working with her husband's butcher's business, or promoting the White Ribbon Army and the cause of temperance. Her faith, capacity for hard work and passion for those in need, drove her into the wider sphere of public life. Despite appearing to have little awareness of gender issues, her motivation being conversion and temperance, in practice Sarah was a pioneer of women's public involvement.

Katherine Robinson

Katherine Robinson's background was very different from Sarah's and the work she did was also different, but she also had a significant public role. When Katherine spoke to the Sunday school children at Old King Street Baptist in 1909, urging them to 'give their hearts to the Lord whilst they were young',[54] she was already a seasoned campaigner in a wide range of church and charitable work in the city. Martin Gorsky has shown that women played a large part in philanthropy in Bristol in the nineteenth century and Katherine was one of those who continued this into the next century.[55] From the late 1880s, brief accounts of events in which she had been involved started to appear regularly in the local papers. She judged a competition for children including Band of Hope members in April 1890,[56] and later that same year helped to cook a Christmas Eve dinner for poor children at Lodge Street Congregational Chapel.[57] Three years later, in July 1893, she participated in a stone-laying ceremony for East Street Baptist Chapel, presumably having been asked because of the Robinson involvement in the area.[58] She opened church bazaars and sales in Baptist churches as far apart as Victoria Street, central Bristol (April 1888), Keynsham, slightly south of Bristol (October 1898) and Uley in Dursley, Gloucestershire, in March 1899.[59] The interweaving of the spheres of church and public life through newspaper accounts of these events meant that these kinds of occasions were no longer 'third sphere' events but genuinely public. Katherine was known as a public figure well before her husband Edward became Mayor.

Katherine was also involved in charities and activities beyond the church. In 1890 she organised a concert in aid of a Working Girls' Club of which she was President, at which she presented the future professional singer Clara Butt with a gift, on the occasion of Clara leaving Bristol to study at the Royal College of Music.[60] Katherine

---

[54] Gibbon, *A Child A Hundred Years Old*, 62.

[55] M. Gorsky, *Patterns of Philanthropy: Charity and Society in Nineteenth-Century Bristol* (London/Woodbridge: Royal Historical Society/Boydell Press, 1999), 162-77.

[56] *Bristol Mercury*, 17 April 1890.

[57] *Bristol Mercury*, 27 December 1890.

[58] *Bristol Mercury*, 4 July 1893.

[59] *Bristol Mercury*, 12 April 1888; *Bristol Mercury*, 27 October 1898; *Bristol Mercury*, 3 March 1899.

[60] *Bristol Mercury*, 26 April 1890.

clearly had a gift for planning such events: 1896 saw her organising theatricals in aid of the Bristol District Nurses Society.[61] She also participated in various social occasions: at a YWCA party on New Year's Eve, 1891, Katherine sang two solos and then a duet with her husband Edward.[62] The Robinsons fulfilled a role similar to a country squire and his lady in a previous century, holding garden parties at The Towers and gracing social events with their presence;[63] her attendance at weddings and funerals was often noted by the local papers.[64] In December 1895, the local press reported on the wedding of Katherine's younger sister Mary Gotch, with the immediate family named (there were over 200 guests in total), making special mention of the fact that Mary was married from The Towers.[65] These events were about portraying aspects of the lives of Nonconformist 'aristocracy' for the interest of Bristol readers.

With her husband, Katherine attended Tyndale Baptist Church, the building of which had been largely financed by the Robinson family.[66] Dr Richard Glover was the minister during this period, known amongst other things for his support of the 'missionary enterprise'.[67] Katherine also had a keen interest in missions, presumably partly fostered by Dr Glover's influence. For several years she was the secretary of the Zenana branch of the local section of the Baptist Missionary Society, which aimed to reach secluded women in India and China with the Christian message.[68] By 1909 she was also the president of the national Baptist Zenana Mission. In her capacity as local secretary, which until 1908 was combined with the role of treasurer, she presented annual reports to the Bristol branch of the Baptist Missionary Society. The branch gave generously when the mission got into financial difficulties towards the end of 1908, a generosity which the Sheriff of Bristol, S.H. Babcock, hinted was due 'to the presence of Mrs Robinson'.[69] The fact that she continued with these responsibilities during a year when she must have been more than usually busy demonstrates her strong commitment to the cause. Katherine's interests ranged beyond the Baptist denomination, however. She was a strong believer in ecumenical enterprises and on at least one occasion chaired and spoke at a meeting of the Anglican Bristol Missionary Society, 'remarking that they were all working for one aim ... She spoke of the importance of the women's work as a department of

---

[61] *Bristol Mercury*, 16 January 1896.

[62] *Bristol Mercury*, 7 January 1891.

[63] *Bristol Mercury*, 17 September 1898.

[64] *Bristol Mercury*, 8 November 1890. In an account of the funeral of the Rev. Dr Trestail, Mrs Robinson was the only non-family member mentioned by name.

[65] *Bristol Mercury*, 5 December 1895.

[66] http://www.digitalbristol.org/members/tyndaleb/history.html, accessed 27 July 2012. This building was bombed during the Second World War and the existing church is a replacement.

[67] R. Glover, *Tyndale Echoes* (Bristol: J.W. Arrowsmith, 1954), 5.

[68] *Bristol Mercury*, 16 May 1888; *Bristol Mercury*, 17 September 1898.

[69] *Western Daily Press*, report of Bristol meeting of the Baptist Missionary Society, 12 May 1909.

missionary effort.'[70] Her typically evangelical interest in mission was specifically focused towards the lives of women.

In common with many of the leading Nonconformists in this period, the Robinsons were supporters of the Liberal Party. Katherine was for some time one of several vice-presidents of the Bristol Women's Liberal Association and was thus active in politics on her own account.[71] Although Katherine was absent from a meeting in April 1899, when a resolution was passed in favour of the vote for women,[72] the organisation had been strongly supportive of women's suffrage for many years and she would not have been in the position of vice-president had she been an opponent of this agenda. This is not to suggest that her support was militant in any way but just to note that there was a strong correlation between Nonconformity, Liberal women and votes for women. In this respect the relationship between evangelicalism and feminism, although still not straightforward, was closer in this period than before the 1880s. More open-minded Nonconformists, such as those who wrote for the *Christian World*, a popular weekly Christian paper, or who were comfortable with new forms of theology, tended to be openly in support of women's rights, even suffrage, in the 1880s and beyond.[73]

Katherine took advantage of her position as Lady Mayoress to launch the Social Service League in 1908, a linking of local mission work with the increasing emphasis within missions on welfare. It was mainly concerned with housing problems but also encouraged youth organisations. By 1910 it had been amalgamated with the Bristol Charity Organisation Society.[74] She was active in the public sphere, giving her support to a wide range of charitable works. Katherine's public role and position in the Nonconformist elite were a result of a combination of two factors: her parentage and her marriage. However, she must also have had an inclination for the role, as Mrs (later Lady) Monica Wills, from the even more prosperous Wills family, who potentially could have had a similar public profile, preferred to work more quietly, whilst Katherine was active publicly in Bristol over a wide spread of years, by the nature of her involvement personifying the Nonconformist conscience.

Katherine Robinson died in 1930, having lived in Sneyd Park all the intervening years. Her husband, who had frequently been ill during their marriage, did not die until five years later. She made the most of her position of influence, was active in many areas of public life of Bristol and had a particular interest in the place of women.

---

[70] *Bristol Mercury*, 23 September 1893.
[71] *Bristol Mercury*, 26 April 1899.
[72] *Bristol Mercury*, 26 April 1899.
[73] See for instance L. Wilson, *Marianne Farningham: A Plain Woman Worker* (Milton Keynes: Paternoster, 2007), 89-91. Marianne, a Baptist writer, became more openly supportive of the issue towards the end of the nineteenth century.
[74] Meller, *Leisure*, 204.

Edith Pearce: Minister's Wife and Political Campaigner

Whilst Sarah Terrett was involved in a public role for over ten years and Katherine Robinson for more than twice that time, Edith Pearce was only visible in the life of Bristol for a brief period, from the founding of a local east Bristol branch of the National British Women's Temperance Association in 1906 until she left Bristol in July 1908. Her husband, Joseph, was a Primitive Methodist minister and as such was regularly transferred from circuit to circuit. Whilst Edith does not appear to have had a preaching ministry like Sarah Terrett, she appears to have been comfortable addressing small public meetings and it was her drive and enthusiasm that led to the formation of a new branch of this temperance organisation in Eastville, east Bristol.

Her involvement began when, on Tuesday 16 January 1906, a public meeting, presumably arranged on her initiative, was held in a church in Eastville at which she spoke about the work of the National British Women's Temperance Association.[75] Thirty women gave her their names to indicate that they were willing to join the Association. At a follow up meeting a week later, Edith stated that 'she now had much pleasure in moving that a Branch be formed to be called the "Eastville Branch"'. She was appointed president and other officers were selected.[76] The group decided to ask the ministers' wives of the district to become vice-presidents, an indication of their status in the local Christian communities, but it is also possible that the women believed it would be easier to recruit members of the various congregations if their ministers' wives were already involved. Mrs Hall, wife of the minister of Gladstone Street Bible Christian Church, had already expressed her willingness to take on the role and was unanimously elected a vice-president.

Having launched this local branch, the committee, led by Edith, put considerable energy into establishing it and increasing its influence. It met regularly at the Primitive Methodist manse and organised public meetings during the following months in a variety of Primitive Methodist and Bible Christian chapels in east Bristol. There were usually a handful of new members each time, unless bad weather prevented a significant turnout. Unlike those of Sarah Terrett's organisation, these meetings were aimed at eliciting participation from women already involved in churches, rather than drawing into the meetings people who were habitual abusers of drink. Talks informing the listeners about the evils of drink were a central part of the proceedings, sandwiched between hymns and musical offerings. On one occasion, interestingly, Edith urged people to take the 'white ribbon book' and read about the issues of drink for themselves.[77] Presumably this was a book that had been produced by Sarah Terrett some years earlier.

Talks were on topics such as 'The duties of Christians in relation to the sale and use of intoxicants', 'Some things Women should know' (described as 'both amusing and beneficial') and 'Women's enterprise and its result for God and home and every

---

[75] Minutes of the Eastville Primitive Methodist Branch of the British Women's Temperance Association, 9 April 1906 (Bristol Record Office, 39361/122).

[76] Minutes of Eastville Branch, 9 April 1906.

[77] Minutes of Eastville Branch, 3 September 1907.

land',[78] the latter an interesting combination of domesticity and mission. A typical evening on 9 April at Bourne Hall consisted of speeches and business followed by 'coffee and tea, the partaking of which brought a homely feeling into the meeting'. There was then a recitation. 'The meeting broke up at about 10 o/c, all feeling that a very enjoyable evening had been spent. 10 new members received.' These busy evenings clearly served a social as well as a serious function: there were always refreshments such as coffee and buns, and at least a brief opportunity for conversation. On 16 January 1907, for instance, the minutes noted that 'Light refreshments were served and the last half hour spent in social intercourse.'[79] One wonders whether the members signed up because they were convinced about temperance or to enjoy a sociable evening with their friends, with the added attraction of coffee and buns.

However, there was a serious aspect to the gatherings. It was at this same meeting in April which was described as having a 'homely feeling' that political activism was first discussed. Only a few months earlier a Liberal government had been voted in with a substantial majority. With the strong connection between Nonconformity and Liberalism, chapel-goers were likely to feel there was a sympathetic ear in the government and were hopeful of new legislation on issues which concerned them. On this occasion, Edith read out a letter which had been sent to the local MPs, Charles Hobhouse and the Hon. Augustine Birrell, on behalf of the members, stating that they 'respectfully but earnestly request Mr H' to support a parliamentary resolution the following day aimed at reducing the drink trade. Hobhouse had replied saying 'he was pleased to be able to support Mr Leif Jones'.[80] Other political lobbying followed related to temperance, with letters being written urging the government to pass a licensing bill.

Support was also given at an early stage for women's suffrage: the Eastville Branch was one of the signatories to a document presented to the Prime Minister, the Rt Hon. Sir Henry Campbell-Bannerman, from women's societies in Bristol, when he visited the city. The document was read out at a public meeting on 19 November 1907. Participation appears to have been a committee decision and there was an expectation that everyone else would happily support such a document without being asked first.[81] It was believed that if women had the vote, useful legislation such as

---

[78] Minutes of Eastville Branch, 16 January 1907, 3 September 1907 and 12 December 1907.
[79] Minutes of the Eastville Branch, 16 January 1907.
[80] Minutes of Eastville Branch, 9 April 1906.
[81] The document read:
'We, the representatives of women's societies in Bristol take the opportunity of your visit to this city to assure you of our gratitude for the personal sympathy which you have given to the principle of the political enfranchisement of women. We believe that our claim is just and urgent.
Because women who are taxed and rated equally with men should have equal control over national expenditure.

temperance measures was more likely to be passed in Parliament. Edith also read out the Prime Minister's reply, which was extremely sympathetic and stated that 'he is in hearty sympathy with the claims advanced'. However, he had already indicated to a suffrage deputation that because of divisions within the party, he was unable to translate his sympathy into law. It was to be another twenty-one years before full female suffrage was achieved.[82]

This political activism did not survive the departure of the founder; indeed, the heyday of this society, which started out with lots of enthusiasm, public meetings and extra members being gained, only lasted until Edith and her husband left Bristol. After her departure, the branch quickly became rather small and struggling. The next minister's wife, Mrs Wilkinson, was clearly uninterested, despite the best efforts of the committee to engage her as their next president. Although the group continued to meet intermittently until September 1942, it never regained the numbers it had in the early months, nor is there any evidence from the minutes that the leaders or members engaged in political lobbying. This demonstrates the importance of a woman with motivation, understanding of politics and an ability to inspire others, in leading such an organisation. In this there is a parallel with the other, local temperance organisation headed up by Sarah Terrett, which steadily declined following her sudden death. It also indicates the danger of an organisation being too dependent on one person.

This group, including Edith Pearce's activity, was well within acceptable boundaries for women at this time, as just speaking in public was by now no longer controversial. The group engaged in some gentle political lobbying, both for temperance bills and women's suffrage, but this too was by now an acceptable and common occurrence and everything was kept within the bounds of propriety. And although the meetings were public, they were much quieter than those led by Sarah Terrett: they were only for women and probably drew women from the congregations of similar churches in the local area of east Bristol. Edith was following in the footsteps of many women in the previous century who had pioneered involvement in charitable organisations and temperance campaigns. Yet her eagerness to support women's suffrage, even if increasing support in Parliament for drink laws seems to have been her main motivation, indicates that she was ready to challenge the status quo of gender relations.

Because social legislation being so much on the increase women are more and more affected by laws made without reference to their opinion.
Because large and increasing numbers of women are engaged in so many sphere's [sic] of work, and especially in the industrial world, that it is of vital importance to them to have some share in making the laws which regulate their labour.
We therefore earnestly desire that this reform should be included in the |King's Speech and respectfully urge you to make it a government measure before the end of this Parliament.'

[82] M. Phillips, *The Ascent of Woman* (London: Abacus, 2004), 179.

Conclusions

Drawing together the stories of these three women, what final comments can be made? For each of them, we can make some connection between personal spirituality and their public lives, although in Edith Pearce's case this can only be tentative as we have little extraneous information about her life, including her spiritual experience. Presumably as the wife of a Primitive Methodist preacher she had a strong personal faith, but the available sources give us no clear evidence.

More can be said about Katherine Robinson, despite the lack of personal sources. Her spontaneous response to the Sunday school children, in which she spoke of her personal faith, is a rare moment of disclosure, demonstrating that she was happy to talk about her faith in personal, recognisably evangelical terms. Similarly, her keen involvement in missionary enterprises indicates that the spread of the Christian faith remained close to her heart, whilst the charities she was involved with indicate that she also had a concern for the poor. She and her husband also maintained a strong loyalty to the Baptist denomination, again indicating clear evangelical allegiance, although they also shared a wider sympathy with other Christian churches. Although we know little of her theology, an assumption that she was at the more liberal end of the evangelical spectrum would probably be fairly accurate, as she was clearly comfortable with bazaars, concerts and amateur dramatics. Katherine clearly maintained a personal faith.

We know most about Sarah Terrett's belief and spirituality, as the *Brief Memorials* include one of her sermons and fragments of other addresses, a discussion of her belief in healing and an account written by herself. Sarah's faith seems to have been true to her Bible Christian allegiance, with a strong belief in personal conversion and the possibility of transformation, a focus on Scripture, and the need for Christians to be active in their faith, clearly demonstrating three out of the four markers of evangelicalism identified by David Bebbington.[83] The personal spirituality of all these women, especially of Katherine and Sarah, informed and inspired their public activity.

Turning to the significance of the 'third sphere' of the church, it can be seen that for all three women it was potentially a useful training ground. This was most clearly the case for Sarah Terrett, who taught in the Sunday school and preached in Bible Christian churches before she moved on to the larger, more public stage afforded by her temperance movement. However, it was probably also a factor for Katherine Robinson, who had taught Sunday school when she was younger; presumably this had started to give her the confidence for the public role her marriage later thrust upon her. Whilst we know little of Edith Pearce's background, her willingness to take hold of the opportunities afforded her as a minister's wife indicates that she, too, may already have developed skills within the third sphere of the church. More than that, it is difficult to say, except to note that from the 1890s and beyond there seems not to have been the same need to defend a woman's public role with rhetoric

---

[83] D.W. Bebbington, *Evangelicalism in Modern Britain: A History from the 1730s to the 1980s* (London: Unwin Hyman, 1989), 2-17.

about her domestic dedication and efficiency. A change was taking place in the expectations women had to work with and the barriers they had to overcome to operate in the public sphere.

Indeed, by the last quarter of the century Nonconformist women were increasingly venturing into public space, and these three are examples of that change. Whilst Katherine Robinson had the most prominent public profile, especially as Lady Mayoress, all three were to some extent active in the public sphere and appear to have been comfortable with public speaking. Katherine gave speeches at meetings of various kinds, such as meetings of missionary societies, Sarah Terrett frequently preached and spoke about temperance and Edith Pearce addressed small public meetings. Between them they supported charities, preached sermons, spoke at missionary meetings and contributed in several different ways, and in different degrees, to the public life of Bristol.

In doing this, there was a mixture of conventional behaviour and challenge to the status quo in their lives. Sarah Terrett, not from a middle-class background, was involved in her husband's business but also appears to have been the dominant partner in at least some aspects of their marriage. Perhaps she could be said to have been challenging gender roles. However, although she was extremely active in working out her faith, her behaviour, even the preaching, was not unusual for a woman in the Bible Christians. Katherine Robinson, whilst to some extent playing the public role that Bristol society assigned to someone who was part of the Nonconformist elite, chose charities and organisations which reflected her personal interest. Despite her connection with the Women's Liberal Association, she does not appear to have been closely associated with the developing suffrage movement: one can assume sympathy but there is no evidence of engagement. Edith Pearce, on the other hand, although keeping within the bounds of propriety in her behaviour, was clearly a supporter of women's suffrage, although her main reason for this appears to have been that this would further the cause of temperance and restrictive licensing laws.

From a distinctly evangelical base, these Nonconformist women made contributions to the public life of the city in various ways. Their behaviour was usually within accepted conventions of gender roles but at times they were close to challenging these: Sarah and Edith's support of suffrage, the nature of Sarah's marriage, and her lifestyle including business and preaching engagements, were examples of these. Even Katherine, although conventional in all she was doing, was raising the public profile of women by being so active in the public life of Bristol churches and society. The 'paradoxical relationship between feminism and religion' was to some extent played out in the lives of these three remarkable women.[84]

---

[84] Morgan and de Vries (eds), *Women, Gender and Religious Cultures*, 7.

CHAPTER 9

Baptists from East and West at the World Missionary Conference in Edinburgh, 1910[1]

Brian Stanley

William Carey's 'pleasing dream' Fulfilled?

William Carey's famous proposal in his *An Enquiry Into the Obligations of Christians to Use Means for the Conversion of the Heathens* for the formation of missionary societies to take the gospel to the non-Christian world, although addressed in the first instance to his own Particular Baptist denomination, was in principle intended to evoke a response 'by every one who loves our Lord Jesus Christ in sincerity'.[2] Baptist by conviction though he was, Carey always maintained spiritual horizons which were broader than his own Baptist family – and the same has been true of the life and numerous writings of Ian Randall. Almost as well known as the *Enquiry* itself is Carey's letter of 1806 to Andrew Fuller, the first secretary of the Baptist Missionary Society (BMS), making the suggestion that 'a general association of all denominations of Christians' should meet every ten years or so at the Cape of Good Hope, commencing in 1810, to share experiences and wisdom relative to the common missionary enterprise. This notion Fuller famously dismissed as 'one of bro[r] Carey's pleasing dreams'.[3] It appeared to Fuller as a fanciful notion, far removed from the reality of a Christian scene in which even

---

[1] Earlier versions of this article were delivered to the Scottish Baptist History Project in April 2010 and at Hong Kong Baptist Seminary in March 2012. The article draws on my book-length study, *The World Missionary Conference, Edinburgh 1910* (Grand Rapids, MI: Eerdmans, 2009). Unless otherwise specified, all sources cited may be referenced from my book.

[2] William Carey, *An Enquiry into the Obligations of Christians to Use Means for the Conversion of the Heathens* (1792), facsimile edition (London: Carey Kingsgate Press, 1961), 84.

[3] Ruth Rouse, 'William Carey's "pleasing dream"', *International Review of Missions* 38.150 (April, 1949), 181-92; Norman Goodall, *The Ecumenical Movement* (London: Oxford University Press, 2nd edn, 1964), 4-5, 8; Kenneth S. Latourette, 'Ecumenical bearings of the missionary movement and the International Missionary Council', in Ruth Rouse and Stephen C. Neill (ed.), *A History of the Ecumenical Movement 1517–1948* (London: SPCK, 1954), 355; Hugh Martin, *Beginning at Edinburgh: A Jubilee Assessment of the World Missionary Conference 1910* (London: Edinburgh House Press, 1960), 3-4; Ernest A. Payne, *The Growth of the World Church* (London: Edinburgh House Press and Macmillan, 1955), 140-41.

evangelical Christians were frequently to be found arguing with each other. Nothing came of Carey's proposal. In 1806 it seemed inevitable that the task of winning the world for Christ was to be attempted by a loose coalition of western denominational agencies, each dedicated to planting their own denominational brand of Christianity in a particular segment of non-western territory.

A century later, however, a conference took place in Edinburgh that some have seen as a belated fulfilment of Carey's 'pleasing dream'. The World Missionary Conference held in June 1910 in the Assembly Hall of what was then the United Free Church of Scotland (now the Church of Scotland) was not in fact 'a general association of all denominations of Christians'. Its delegates were drawn from all the main Protestant churches of the day, and (unprecedentedly) from both the Evangelical and High Church wings of the Anglican communion, but not from the Roman Catholic Church nor from the Orthodox family of churches. Neither were there present any of the first Pentecostals, even though what we now know as Pentecostalism had first surfaced in the western world at Azusa Street in Los Angeles in 1906. Moreover, the participants were representatives, not of churches but of voluntary missionary societies or denominational mission boards. Nevertheless, the Edinburgh conference was an event whose aim was substantially the same as that envisaged by Carey in 1806: it was to be a forum in which Protestants from different national and denominational backgrounds could share their vision and their wisdom with a view to co-operating more effectively in the cause of the evangelisation of the world.

World Baptist Leaders in Edinburgh, June 1910

In this article I wish to focus attention on some of the Baptist participants in the conference, both those from the missionary sending nations of the western world and those from the so-called 'younger churches'. As we shall see, however, that conventional distinction was subverted by the presence at the Edinburgh conference of a Baptist who was an overseas missionary sent from one of the 'younger' churches.

Just before 1.00 p.m. on Tuesday 14 June 1910, an international group of Baptist leaders could be seen making their way from St Giles' Church, the mother church of the Church of Scotland, up the Royal Mile to Edinburgh Castle. They had just attended a service in St Giles' where they had heard the minister, the Revd Dr Andrew Wallace Williamson, preach from Matthew 13:38, 'The field is the world'. On arrival at the castle, they were entertained for lunch by Mr David Lockhart, a leading civic figure in Edinburgh and a member of Dublin Street Baptist Church in the city.[4] They came from a variety of countries, including Britain, the United States, Canada, China and Japan. After a word of welcome by the host, addresses were given on behalf of British Baptists by Sir George W. Macalpine, the newly knighted

---

[4] I owe this information about Lockhart to Dr Derek B. Murray.

first chairman of the BMS and in that year also president of the Baptist Union,[5] and on behalf of Baptists from the United States by the Revd Dr Thomas Barbour, Foreign Secretary of the American Baptist Foreign Missionary Society. On either side of the chairman sat the venerable figures of Dr Timothy Richard, the veteran Welsh missionary from Shanghai who was secretary of the Christian Literature Society for China, and Dr Richard Glover, minister of Tyndale Baptist Church in Bristol, who had visited China in 1890-91 on behalf of the BMS. One person present stood out from the others on account of his Chinese dress; of him we shall hear more presently. At 8 o'clock that evening these same Baptist leaders gathered in the Assembly Hall of the United Free Church of Scotland for the opening session of the World Missionary Conference.

The Edinburgh conference was not the first international missionary conference ever assembled, nor was it the largest: in terms of numbers of participants it was significantly smaller than the 'Ecumenical Missionary Conference' held ten years earlier in New York. But it was without doubt by far the most important missionary conference held to date, indeed it was probably the most important that has *ever* been held. Historians of the modern ecumenical movement are virtually unanimous in tracing the descent of the principal organs of the twentieth-century ecumenical movement, including most notably the formation of the World Council of Churches in 1948, from the Edinburgh conference. But the conference was also the high-water mark of an era in the history of Christian world mission which came to an end in the 1960s: an era in which the denominational missionary societies of Anglo-American Protestantism saw themselves as primarily responsible for the evangelisation of the world.

The conference had a serious and ambitious intent. Its goal was to unite all Protestant Christians in a concerted and systematic endeavour to achieve the goal of 'the evangelization of the world in this generation'. That was a rousing slogan adopted by eager young Evangelicals in the universities of Britain and America in the 1890s and taken up to some extent by the missionary movement as a whole. The Americans loved it, as it was a stirring call to urgent evangelistic action; the Germans hated it because it seemed to them trite and theologically presumptuous. (Surely we humans cannot dictate to God when the world will be converted?) The British were, as always, somewhere in the middle, caught between American zeal and German reflectiveness: they just couldn't make up their minds about it.

By 1910 the slogan itself had lost something of its allure in the face of German criticism – notably by Gustav Warneck, the father of Protestant missiology – and it was in fact rarely cited at the conference. Nonetheless, realising the goal that lay behind the slogan was what Edinburgh was all about. The conference organisers believed that by the application of systematic scientific method and exhaustive statistical enquiry the missionary problems of the day could be accurately diagnosed, and that by the assembling together of representatives of Protestant mission agencies

---

[5] Until 1903, when Macalpine first assumed the chairmanship of the Society, the treasurer presided over meetings of the BMS Committee. Macalpine was an Accrington industrialist.

from the whole globe a common strategy could be adopted that would lead under God to the overcoming of those problems. What caught the mood at Edinburgh in June 1910 was the vision of a world remarkably and comprehensively transformed – within the lifetime of those present – by the evangelistic efforts of Christian missionaries.

The Delegates to the Conference

The 1,215 official delegates were overwhelmingly white, male and western: 1,008 were men and 207 women – perhaps more than one might have expected. Only twenty came from what were then termed the 'younger' churches of the non-western world[6] and even they were there not as delegates of their own churches but only as guests of western missionary societies or the organising committee. Seats in the conference hall were in fact allocated to missionary societies on the basis of the size of their annual income: the more financial muscle you could exert in the cause of world evangelisation, the more delegates you were allowed. Almost everybody else apart from the twenty came from Europe or North America: 509 were British, 490 were North American, 169 originated from continental Europe, twenty-seven came from the white colonies of South Africa and Australasia. Of the twenty non-western participants, there were nine Indians, four Japanese, three Chinese, one Korean, one Burmese, one Turk and one black African from the Gold Coast (Ghana), of whom I shall say more later.

Most, though not all, of those involved in Edinburgh 1910 regarded the conference as a gathering of mission executives and missionaries; indigenous Christians were a dubious luxury whose presence was not integral to the character of the event. The conference secretary, J.H. Oldham, referred in later years to the role of the American chairman, John R. Mott, in overriding this prejudice: 'it was Mott above all others who insisted in the face of a good deal of conservative opposition that the younger Churches should be represented at the Edinburgh Conference in 1910'.[7] Thanks to Mott, twelve of the non-western delegates spoke to the conference, either by giving invited main addresses or by being chosen to contribute to the debates or in both capacities: six of them addressed the conference on more than one occasion. Mott's biographer confirms that the prominence of the Asians on the Edinburgh platform was no accident: 'As Chairman, Mott recognized the few Orientals for whose presence he had labored, perhaps disproportionately.'[8] As chairman of the conference, Mott had sole responsibility for selecting a few speakers from the large number of those who made application to contribute to the open

---

[6] Only nineteen are mentioned in my book. Professor Dana Robert of Boston University has subsequently identified a twentieth – Grace Stephens, an Eurasian Methodist from Madras.

[7] J.H. Oldham, 'John R. Mott', *Ecumenical Review* 7 (1955), 258.

[8] C.H. Hopkins, *John R. Mott 1865–1955: A Biography* (Grand Rapids, MI: Eerdmans, 1979), 357.

debates. He undoubtedly exercised positive discrimination in favour of the Asian delegates, and the East Asians in particular.

The international committee responsible for preparations for the conference had suggested as early as July 1908 that missionary societies should be asked to include in their delegations 'if practicable, one or two natives from mission lands'. Most missions, however, failed to fulfil even this modest injunction. The BMS, as also the Wesleyan Methodist Missionary Society and the Foreign Mission Committees of both the Church of Scotland and the United Free Church of Scotland, was unable to muster a single delegate from its mission churches. A comment made in February 1910 by Ralph Wardlaw Thompson, foreign secretary of one of the largest British societies, the London Missionary Society (LMS), is instructive in illuminating the prevailing attitudes that lay behind this failure: 'I do not think the time is ripe for the inclusion of delegates appointed by the Churches in non-Christian lands in any great Conference such as ours. Ten years hence I hope there may be such a development of independent Church life as will make it necessary to have representation from various parts of the world.'[9]

Size and Composition of the Baptist Delegation

The remainder of this article will be devoted to the Baptist representation at Edinburgh. It is not possible to know with total accuracy how many of the delegates were Baptists because some of the mission agencies represented at Edinburgh were interdenominational in character, and the denominational affiliation of their delegates is frequently not known. These included the British and Foreign Bible Society, the Scottish and American Bible Societies, the YMCA, and the new 'faith missions', though most of the latter were still too small to merit more than a few delegates each: the China Inland Mission (CIM), founded by James Hudson Taylor in 1865, was much the largest, with seventeen delegates (fourteen from Britain and three from the North American branch). The useful list of Scottish Baptist foreign missionaries serving with all societies in 1926 compiled by George Yuille in his *History of the Baptists in Scotland* does not contain any obvious matches with the names of CIM or other delegates of non-denominational agencies in 1910, though the list is not retrospective.[10] We do know, however, that there were ninety-four delegates of specifically Baptist mission agencies at the Edinburgh conference. The numbers of delegates reflect the comparative size of the different Baptist missions at that time; what may surprise us is how relatively small in 1910 was the Foreign Mission Board of the Southern Baptist Convention, the body which would in the

---

[9] School of Oriental and African Studies, Council for World Mission archives, box 2, LMS Home Office Outward Letters, Thompson to Oldham, 7 February 1910.

[10] George Yuille (ed.), *History of the Baptists in Scotland: From Pre-Reformation Times* (Glasgow: Baptist Union Publications Committee, n.d. [1926]), 290-95. No such list exists for English or Welsh Baptist missionaries.

course of the twentieth century grow into probably the largest Protestant mission agency in the world.

In addition, there were three Baptist delegates who were specially invited guests of the British executive committee, either for reasons of their eminence or on account of roles they had taken in the preparatory commissions for the conference: Timothy Richard was one; Sir George W. Macalpine was another, in his capacity as vice-chairman of one of the eight preparatory study commissions, Commission VI on 'The Home Base of Missions'; a third, lesser known figure, was J.R.M. Stephens, a BMS missionary with extensive experience of both the upper and the lower Congo, who served as secretary of the (Baptist) Bible Translation Society from 1907 to 1910.[11]

One other Baptist participant from West Africa, however, deserves particular notice. It appears that African Christians were generally regarded as too primitive and uneducated to merit an invitation to the conference. Indeed, for most of the ten years that I spent working on my history of the conference I was under the impression that there were no black African delegates at all, and I published statements to this effect. However, about a month before I sent the manuscript off, and just in time, I discovered one, and was delighted to find that he was a Baptist.

Baptist Mission Agency	Number of delegates
American Baptist Foreign Missionary Society	43
Baptist Missionary Society	22
Foreign Mission Board of the Southern Baptist Convention	8
Baptist Zenana Mission	4
Foreign Mission Board of the General Conference of Free Baptists	3
Baptist Foreign Mission Board of Canada[12]	3
United Baptist Foreign Mission Board of Canada	2
Foreign Mission Board of the [black] National Baptist Convention [of the USA]	2
German Baptist Foreign Mission	2
Missionary Society of the Seventh Day Baptists	1
Victorian Baptist Foreign Mission [Australia]	1
Special guests of the British executive committee	3
Total (excluding Baptist delegates of interdenominational missions)	94

Delegates of Baptist Mission Agencies at the World Missionary Conference, Edinburgh 1910[13]

---

[11] *BMS Annual Report*, 1937–1938, 95.

[12] A united national Canadian Baptist Foreign Mission Board was not formed till 1912. The first of these two Canadian Mission Boards represented the Baptist churches of Ontario and Quebec; the United Board represented the Maritime or Atlantic Provinces.

The Sole Black African Delegate

Dr Mark Christian Hayford was born in 1864 into a Fante-Euro family on the Gold Coast (modern Ghana). His father, Joseph de Graft Hayford, was a leading Methodist minister, but in 1898 Mark Christian Hayford was baptised as an adult believer by Dr Mojola Agbebi, founder of the Native Baptist Church in Lagos, one of the earliest African Independent or Initiated Churches. Hayford went on to become a principal founder of the Baptist communities in both Ghana and the Ivory Coast.[14] He was a rather Europeanised African, an inhabitant of two cultures, who spent much of his time in Britain and the United States, attempting to raise funds for his Baptist churches in West Africa. Hayford was a last-minute addition to the delegate list at Edinburgh and is mentioned as an additional delegate only in the final issue of the conference daily newspaper.[15] He was possibly a special guest of a member of the organising committee; he was certainly not a delegate of the BMS, though he had close links to Baptist worthies in Britain such as F.B. Meyer (who later chaired his English support committee) and Herbert Marnham, the stockbroker and treasurer of the Baptist Union.

Hayford published two works. In 1903 appeared his *West Africa and Christianity*, which was a lecture delivered at Rochester Theological Seminary, New York, then under the presidency of Augustus H. Strong. It included an eloquent exposition of the case that black Africa, far from being barbaric, had an ancient and noble civilisation:

> Before England was a Monarchy ... there existed in the northern parts of the Sudan [or Country of the Blacks] several large and fairly well ordered native Negro States, which had developed indigenously a comparatively high condition of civilisation.[16]

Hayford dedicated this work to Herbert Marnham, 'as a Humble Acknowledgment of HIS LIBERAL SPIRIT AND CHRISTIAN GENEROSITY by which The Cause of Christ in Africa has been Materially Served'.[17] Marnham had evidently given generously towards the Baptist cause in West Africa.

Later, in 1913, Hayford published a paper read at an international conference on the Negro, held in April 1912 at the pioneering institution of black higher education

---

[13] These figures are based on the delegate lists contained in World Missionary Conference, 1910, *The History and Records of the Conference Together with Addresses Delivered at the Evening Meetings* (Edinburgh and London: Oliphant, Anderson & Ferrier; and New York, Chicago, and Toronto: Fleming H. Revell, n.d. [1910]), 41-71.

[14] See Jacques Blocher, 'The Early Days of the French Bible Mission in the Ivory Coast, 1927–1945', in Ian M. Randall and Anthony R. Cross (eds), *Baptists and Mission: Papers from the Fourth International Conference on Baptist Studies* (Milton Keynes: Paternoster, 2007), 277-88 (281-86).

[15] *Conference Daily Paper* 9 (23 June 1910), 171.

[16] Mark C. Hayford, *West Africa and Christianity* (London: Baptist Tract and Book Society, n.d. [1903]), 6-8.

[17] Hayford, *West Africa and Christianity*, ii.

in Alabama, the Tuskegee Institute: *Educational Conditions on the Gold Coast of West Africa; or, The Negro: His Great Past and Hopeful Future*. It was a further trenchant defence of African intellectual and moral capacity, and paid particular tribute to American Baptists for their contribution to the evangelisation of West Africa.[18]

Mark Hayford had a much more famous brother, J.E. Casely Hayford, one of the pioneers of West African nationalism and author of a seminal political novel expounding the place of African identity and consciousness. *Ethiopia Unbound: Studies in Race Emancipation* was published just a year after the World Missionary Conference.[19] Mark Hayford is rather less distinguished than his brother, as is suggested by the unkind title of the one scholarly article devoted to him, by Gordon Haliburton – 'Mark Christian Hayford: A Non-Success Story'.[20] Nonetheless, he deserves to be remembered on various counts, among them his pioneering, if in the long run rather mixed, record in Baptist church planting in the Gold and Ivory Coasts.[21] In the person of Hayford, black Africa was therefore represented at Edinburgh 1910, but only at the most minimal level, and there is no record that Hayford spoke in any of the conference sessions. Hayford lived in Liverpool for two years after the conference and did not return to West Africa until 1913.

Taking Hayford into account, plus some Baptist representation among the interdenominational agencies, we may estimate that in aggregate there were approximately 100 Baptists among the 1,215 official delegates. As may be expected, they included many of the most notable figures in Baptist denominational life at the time: in addition to those already mentioned there were others who were well known in Baptist circles in their day, though they are not so widely remembered today. From the American Baptist (or Northern Baptist) community, Dr Thomas S. Barbour, foreign secretary of the American Baptist Foreign Missionary Society, played a major role in planning the conference as a member of the Business Committee and of the American Executive Committee. Charles Edward Wilson, former Serampore missionary and the general (later foreign) secretary of the BMS, was the only Baptist member of the British executive committee. The BMS delegation also included the society's home secretary, William Young Fullerton. Fullerton came from Northern Ireland, trained for the Baptist ministry under C.H. Spurgeon and wrote a fine biography of Spurgeon.[22] He is remembered today above

---

[18] Mark C. Hayford, *Educational Conditions on the Gold Coast of West Africa; or, The Negro: His Great Past and Hopeful Future. A Paper read at the International Conference on the Negro, at the Tuskegee Institute, Ala., USA, April 17th, 1912* (London: Lovejoy, 1913), 13.

[19] J.E. Casely Hayford, *Ethiopia Unbound: Studies in Race Emancipation* (London: Frank Cass, new edn, 1969, 1st edn 1911).

[20] G.M. Haliburton, 'Mark Christian Hayford: A Non-Success Story', *Journal of Religion in Africa* 12.1 (1981), 20-37.

[21] On Hayford's later poor reputation, see Blocher, 'Early Days of the French Bible Mission', 283-84.

[22] W.Y. Fullerton, *C.H. Spurgeon: A Biography* (London: Williams and Norgate, 1920).

all for his moving missionary hymn, 'I cannot tell why He whom angels worship', sung to the Londonderry Air of his native Ulster. It is almost the only missionary hymn written in the high imperial age which has a sufficiently objective and non-imperial theology to ensure that it is still regularly sung today. Other members of the BMS delegation included Dr Archibald McCaig, principal of Spurgeon's College, and Dr R. Fletcher Moorshead, secretary of the BMS medical auxiliary. Australian Baptists were represented by the sole delegate of the Victorian Baptist Foreign Mission, who was in fact British: he was the renowned denominational historian, Dr W.T. Whitley (1861–1947).[23] Whitley had been first principal of the Baptist College of Victoria from 1891 to 1901 and had evidently been asked by the Mission to be its representative at the conference. At the time Whitley was minister of Fishergate Baptist Church in Preston.[24]

There were also Baptist women delegates: the Baptist Zenana Mission (the British women's mission that worked among the high-caste Hindu women secluded in the zenanas of North India) included in its delegation the two notable daughters of Dr Joseph Angus, one-time secretary of the BMS and in 1910 principal of Regent's Park College (which at that time was located in London): Amelia, who was foreign secretary of the Baptist Zenana Mission, and Isabel, who was its India general secretary, based in Calcutta.[25]

In the course of the conference all 100 or so of the Baptist delegates were invited to take 'tea and refreshments' at the city's largest Baptist church, Charlotte Baptist Chapel, by the pastor, Joseph Kemp.[26] Kemp was a vigorous supporter of the conference, subsequently claiming that 'not since the Apostolic Council at Jerusalem has there been held a conference more spiritual, or more significant or far-reaching in importance and influence'.[27] That Kemp, who was a stalwart opponent of modernism, should exhibit such unqualified enthusiasm for the conference is a reminder that the more polarised theological scenario of the 1920s should not be read back into the 1910 conference, which attracted strong support from the most conservative of Evangelicals.

It is worth noting that the American Baptist Foreign Mission Society had in its delegation of forty-three persons five indigenous Christians, more in both aggregate and proportion than any other mission agency. These five Asian Baptists will occupy

---

[23] World Missionary Conference, 1910, *The History and Records of the Conference*, 71.

[24] See Ian Sellers, 'W.T. Whitley: A Commemorative Essay', and K.R. Manley, '"The Right Man in the Right Place": W.T. Whitley in Australia (1891–1901)', *Baptist Quarterly* 37.4 (October, 1997) 159-73 and 174-92.

[25] Brian Stanley, *The History of the Baptist Missionary Society 1792–1992* (Edinburgh: T.&T. Clark, 1992), 232. Ian Randall has written about Angus's life-long passion for mission in his *'Conscientious Conviction': Joseph Angus (1816–1902) and Nineteenth-Century Baptist Life* (Oxford: Regent's Park College, 2010), 19-24.

[26] *Missions* 1 (1910), 574.

[27] Ian L.S. Balfour, *Revival in Rose Street: Charlotte Baptist Chapel, Edinburgh, 1808–2008* (Edinburgh: Rutherford House, 2007), 128.

our attention for the remainder of this article. The first of the five is one of three official delegates from the Chinese churches.[28]

Five Asian Baptist Leaders

Dong Jingan (c. 1872–1944) was a professor from the Shanghai Baptist Theological Seminary. He was the only one of the three Chinese delegates to appear in national dress throughout the conference, resplendent in his skull-cap and pigtail, flowing grey skirt and 'stuffed, quilted jacket of richest peacock-blue silk'. He was converted as a young man; his parents were members of the Baptist church at Ningbo, the oldest American Baptist church in China.[29] Dong Jingan was one of three founding members of faculty of the Shanghai seminary from its inception in 1906 to 1919, and its vice-president from 1915.[30] His two colleagues were R.T. Bryan, a Southern Baptist, and F.J. White, a Northern Baptist. The seminary was a co-operative enterprise between Northern and Southern Baptists that was conceived in 1900 in the wake of the Boxer Movement, which brought Northern and Southern Baptist missionaries together in the relative security of Shanghai – one of a number of examples of how anti-Christian movements in twentieth-century China threw different missionary groups into close proximity and thus had the effect of promoting ecumenical co-operation. The seminary joined with the neighbouring union college in 1912 to form the Shanghai Baptist College and Seminary. This joint institution was renamed Shanghai College in 1918, and in 1931 evolved into what is now the University of Shanghai for Science and Technology. Dong attended Edinburgh 1910 as a delegate of the American Baptist Foreign Missionary Society. He is almost certainly the 'Chinese pastor in his quaint native costume' who is described by one female observer as having presided 'with much dignity and most acceptably' at one of the half-hour mid-day prayer meetings in the parallel conference for home supporters of missions held in the Synod Hall.[31]

Thang Khan Sangma was a Baptist evangelist from Tura in the remote Garo Hills of Assam in north-east India, who had studied at the Newton Theological Institution (now Andover Newton Seminary) in Massachusetts. He must have been one of the very first Assamese to have followed a course of higher education outside India.[32]

The Revd Chiba Yugoro from Japan was born in Sendai and adopted into a family of 'high rank'.[33] He was converted in about 1887 as a result of attending evening

---

[28] The other two were Cheng Jingyi (London Missionary Society, Beijing), and Mr Tsang Ding Tong (Board of Foreign Missions, Presbyterian Church in the USA).

[29] *Missions* 1 (1910), 190.

[30] For information on Dong Jingan and the history of the Shanghai Baptist institutions I am indebted to Dr Thomas G. Oey.

[31] *Women's Missionary Magazine of the United Presbyterian Church* 24.2 (September, 1910), 43.

[32] On Thang Khan Sangma see *Missions* 1 (1910), 189.

[33] On Chiba, see *Missions* 1 (1910), 190; F.C. Parker, *The Southern Baptist Mission in Japan, 1889–1989* (Lanham, MD: University Press of America, 1991), 19, 64, 72, 78-80,

classes run by American Baptist missionaries. After graduating from the Methodist Aoyama Gakuin school in Tokyo, Chiba went to the USA, to study first at Colby College in Maine from 1893 to 1895 and then from 1895 to 1898 at Rochester Theological Seminary. In 1910 he was president of the Southern Baptist Theological Seminary at Fukuoka, Japan, and dean-elect of the new Japan Baptist Seminary in Tokyo, another co-operative venture between American Baptists and Southern Baptists, something that would sadly not be possible today. At Edinburgh he participated in the debate on the Commission I report, pointing out that the Japanese church was still largely an urban phenomenon, with very little work having been done among farmers and the labouring classes. Chiba later became chairman of the National Christian Council of Japan and the most prominent leader in twentieth-century Japanese Baptist life.

Then there was Professor L.T. Ah Sou from the small Baptist community in Burma that traces its history back to the American missionary, Adoniram Judson, a contemporary of William Carey. His father was Chinese and his mother Talain. He had spent two terms studying at the Moody Bible Institute in Chicago and in 1910 was a member of the faculty of Rangoon Baptist College.[34] Like Chiba, he was part of the new Asian Protestant intelligentsia who had had the rare privilege of higher education in the United States.

John Rangiah, Indian Baptist Missionary

The fifth, and perhaps the most interesting, representative of the American Baptists was John Rangiah (sometimes called Rungiah; 1866–1915) from south India, who was accompanied to Edinburgh by his wife.[35] Rangiah's father was one of the first indigenous evangelists in the American Baptist churches in the Godaveri district of Madras presidency, churches which had witnessed one of the most remarkable mass movements of conversion among the depressed castes in late nineteenth-century India. In 1882 the American Baptist church at Ongole had an aggregate membership of 20,865, almost certainly the largest Baptist church in the world at the time. Baptists from this region formed part of the growing movement of Indian emigration to Natal for work in the sugar plantations as indentured labourers. Some of them made an appeal to the Telegu Baptist Home Missionary Society in Madras to send a missionary to minister to them in Natal.

155-56, 169; Kathleen Lodwick (comp.), *Chinese Recorder Index: A Guide to Christian Missions in Asia, 1867–1941* (2 vols; Wilmington, DE: Scholarly Resources, 1986), I, 85.

[34] On Ah Sou, see *Missions* 1 (1910), 189.

[35] On Rangiah, see *Missions* 1 (1910), 189-90, 452-53, 661-62; J.B. Brain, *Christian Indians in Natal 1860–1911: An Historical And Statistical Study* (Cape Town: Oxford University Press, 1983), 222-24; A.W. Wardin (ed.), *Baptists around the World: A Comprehensive Handbook* (Nashville, TN: Broadman & Holman, 1995), 57; S. Hudson-Reed (ed.), *Together for a Century: The History of the Baptist Union of South Africa 1877–1977* (Pietermaritzburg: South African Baptist Historical Society, n.d. [1977]), 86.

John Rangiah, who was headmaster of a large mission girls' school in Nellore, heard of the appeal from Natal and spent a year hunting for a suitable candidate for this mission, until, like Carey in 1792, he came to the eventual conclusion that he must volunteer himself. He left India in 1903 as not simply the first missionary sent by the Telegu Baptist Home Missionary Society to Natal, but also the first overseas missionary sent out by any of the mission churches of the American Baptists. Although technically a 'home missionary' charged with ministering to those of the indentured labourers who were already Baptists, he is thus an early example of what would now be called 'south-to-south' mission. A wealthy Christian tea and sugar planter and philanthropist, Sir James Liege Hulett, invited Rangiah to settle on his estate at Kearsney, near Durban, where a sizeable Baptist community of indentured labourers already existed.[36] Hulett provided Rangiah with a house, and later with land for the erection of the first Baptist chapel. The first Telegu Baptist church in Natal was formed at Kearsney in December 1903 by Rangiah, his wife and sixty-two members. Rangiah devoted himself to ministry on horseback, visiting neighbouring estates and going down to the docks in Durban to minister to those arriving off the ships. He also began prison visiting. His first convert was a convicted murderer who was baptised in the prison bath before his execution. By 1910 Rangiah had been instrumental in planting ten Baptist churches in the Durban and Pietermaritzburg areas, with an aggregate membership of 218, and all of them financially self-supporting. It is interesting to speculate whether Rangiah ever met 'the Mahatma', Mohandas Gandhi, whose years among the Indian population of Natal were, of course, the source of his anti-colonial political vision.

Rangiah appears not to have made any public contribution to the conference. Nevertheless, he counted his participation in the World Missionary Conference as a great honour. Rangiah kept diaries in Telegu which survive to this day in family hands in Natal. Sadly they have not yet been translated. However, the American Baptist missionary magazine, *Missions*, records his enthusiastic impressions of his visit to Britain: 'I often had a wish to visit and see the Christian countries of the West, and now I have had that wish realized and have seen something of the country of Great Britain. While here I have learned and seen much that will be of great benefit to me in my future service for my Master.' Rangiah was impressed, we might say rather too impressed, with the outward appearance of a confessedly Christian country:

> This visit enables me to compare the condition of this country with that of my own. The towns and villages of this land look so neat and clean, and the people seem to be so active and full of life, and God has wonderfully favored and blessed the nations of the West. We do not see this cleanness and activity when we pass through our own country. Here we see no idols and idol worship, but there idols and idol worship and

---

[36] On Hulett (1838–1928), see www.sahistory.org.za/dated-event/sa-sugar-magnate-sir-hulett-born (accessed 7 July 2012); and *Dictionary of South African Biography* (5 vols; Pretoria: National Council for Social Research and Human Sciences Research Council, 1968–87), I, 394-95.

the practice of the heathen on all sides. ... I came to the Conference with a question in my mind. In spite of all our preaching and Christian work I had wondered whether the world was coming nearer to Christ or not. But I was fully made to realize that the world is coming so.[37]

Rangiah reminds us that the rhetorical conjunction of Christianity and civilisation that was so marked a feature of the western missionary movement was not without its appeal to some early Christian converts in countries such as India where the fabric of society was so untouched by Christian influence. It was not just western Christians in 1910 who believed that God had singularly favoured the Christian nations of Europe and North America.

No doubt Rangiah was naïve in his initial impressions of the Christian West and its apparent lack of the idolatry with which he was so familiar from the popular Hinduism of rural south India. In fact his ecclesiastical career in Natal was marked by an unhappy schism in the Natal Baptist community in 1914 that endures to this day. Rangiah and his supporters severed their links with the ABFMS, and formed a separate Natal Telegu Baptist Association, leaving the Indian Baptist Mission in connection with the missionary society. One of the causes of the schism appears to have been Rangiah's too close identification with the economic interests of his planter patron, Sir Liege Hulett. Nevertheless, Rangiah deserves to be remembered as the founder of the Indian Baptist community in South Africa, and his family remains involved in Baptist church life there today. Rangiah testifies to having left Edinburgh with a new confidence in 'the power and love of Christ in the preaching of the gospel', and a widened vision of its global progress.[38]

A century later, one wonders how he would have reacted to the collapse of the western Christendom that he so admired or to the advance of Islam in Natal or to the sobering fact that the percentage of the world's population that is estimated as being Christian is actually slightly lower now, at 33.2 per cent, than it was in 1910, at an estimated 34.8 per cent.[39] But no doubt he would have rejoiced to see the advance of the gospel in the continent which he had made his adopted home, on a scale that nobody who attended the World Missionary Conference in 1910 was able to envisage. Furthermore, we can be sure he would have been glad to see the vastly increased scale of mission movements from the non-western world in comparison with his own day. What Rangiah anticipated and embodied in 1910 has now become reality: international Christian mission is no longer a movement that flows in one direction only from west to east. The World Missionary Conference was a turning point in a number of respects. It marked the point at which some Christians in the West first began to realise in response to voices from India and China that their cherished denominational identities might not be quite as central to the ongoing story of the world church as they had previously supposed. But perhaps more significant

---

[37] *Missions* 1 (1910), 661-62.
[38] *Missions* 1 (1910), 662.
[39] Todd M. Johnson and Kenneth R. Ross (eds), *Atlas of Global Christianity* (Edinburgh: Edinburgh University Press, 2009), 7.

still was the fact that at Edinburgh delegates such as Dong Jingan, Mark Hayford and John Rangiah began to open the eyes of the Church in the West to the truth that Christians from Asia and Africa would in the future no longer be simply the recipients, but also initiators and leaders of Christian mission. Today missionaries are more likely to be Chinese, Korean, Nigerian or Brazilian then they are European, and almost as likely as they are to be North American. What began in 1910 has gathered pace and is transforming the face of world Christianity today.

CHAPTER 10

Dynamics versus Mechanics:
Baptists and the Welsh and Lowestoft Revivals

Timothy B. Welch

Given that the historiography of early twentieth-century revivals has predominantly been interpreted through the prism of Keswick teaching and influence, this paper focuses explicitly upon British Baptist engagement with revival, in three main respects:

1. Baptist promotion of revival: we will identify a strand of Baptist influences whose voices significantly advocated revival aspirations and expectations.
2. Baptist involvement in revival: the narratives of the 1904–05 Welsh revival and the 1921 Lowestoft revival will be explored to ascertain the degree of Baptist participation and leadership in these movements.
3. Baptist interpretation of revival: notions of 'revival' generate a range of concepts such as outpourings of the Spirit, increased gospel enthusiasm, notable success in evangelism with significantly more conversions, and awakenings. Acknowledging the chicken and egg aspect of revival and revivalism, this paper employs the paradigms of **mechanics** (or the human laws of revival) and the **dynamics** of divine power with its inherent spontaneity, utilising the title from a sermon preached by Harold Turner, a Baptist minister, in 1921.[1]

Rather than dealing with these three facets individually, they are incorporated in a chronological and biographical framework, exposing some of the key Baptist 'voices' which were prominent before, during and after periods of intense revival. Ian Randall has helpfully elucidated the dynamics of revival with his apposite motif *Rhythms of Revival* which, he states, are to be regarded rather like 'seasons' or 'musical notes' while 'never suggesting that there is any formula that can produce a movement of the Spirit. God's work is not subject to human control'.[2] Continuing

---

[1] H.H. Turner, 'Dynamics v. Mechanics; or, The Essence and Laws of Revival', *Baptist Times and Freeman* 18 March 1921, 166-67.
[2] Ian M. Randall, *Rhythms of Revival: The Spiritual Awakening of 1857–1863* (Milton Keynes: Paternoster, 2010), 5.

this theme, it is therefore an immense privilege to offer my contribution to Ian, in deep appreciation of the vast groundwork he has already established with his meticulous research and writing covering many significant revivals.

Early Twentieth-Century Calls for Revival

In his Baptist Union Presidential address of 1900, William Cuff, minister of Shoreditch Baptist Tabernacle, spoke of 'the one great want of the hour – [being] a primitive and real faith in the abiding presence and power of the Spirit in the modern church'.[3] Cuff interwove both dynamic and mechanic components with a 'Back to Pentecost' message which reminded the audience that the 'Holy Ghost is not exhausted or impoverished or impotent' but is the 'life and power of our institutions'.[4] Anticipating criticism, Cuff continued,

> Of course I know not a few will say, 'This is poor commonplace stuff to come from the Chair of the Baptist Union.' ... This subject may be commonplace, and only very poorly handled; but I am deeply convinced that a ministry charged and saturated with the Holy Ghost, and a Church baptised into, and filled with, the Holy Ghost is the most pressing urgent need of England to-day.[5]

The emphasis on being 'saturated with the Holy Ghost' continued through Cuff's presidential year, alongside other Baptist voices such as Dr T.R. Glover who addressed the Autumn Assembly on 'The Elements of the Revival we Require',[6] raising more questions about the need for attention to revival. Interestingly, both speakers drew upon the positive revivals in church history while making applications to their contemporary context, such as the Twentieth Century Fund which was recognised for triggering 'a real spiritual blessing to the churches where it has been adopted' by 'rousing ... holy impulses ... [which have] become *intensely spiritual*'.[7] A deepening spirituality was inevitably earthed in organisational responses, based around gospel efforts and prayer, in attempts to evoke potential revival.

> Our Wesleyan friends will raise their million guineas, and our Congregational friends will raise their half-million; so [with the Baptist Twentieth Century Fund] there will be a million and three-quarters of money laid on God's altar.[8]

---

[3] W. Cuff, 'President's Address', *Supplement to the Baptist Times and Freeman* 27 April 1900, iv.

[4] Cuff, 'President's Address', v; see also W. Cuff, 'Three Great Movements', *Supplement to the Baptist Times and Freeman* 5 October 1900, v.

[5] Cuff, 'President's Address', v.

[6] T.R. Glover, 'The Elements of the Revival we Require', *Supplement to the Baptist Times and Freeman* 5 October 1900, xi.

[7] Cuff, 'Three Great Movements', vii.

[8] Cuff, 'Three Great Movements', viii.

Indeed, it is possible to trace a steady flow of similar Baptist interest in revival, with sermons stressing pneumatological themes printed in *The Baptist Times and Freeman*. Yet revival rhetoric required divine power. In 1903, the catalytic mix of felt personal need and desperation for the power of the Holy Spirit brought F.B. Meyer together with a number of Welsh ministers via the Keswick convention in Llandrindod Wells. Ian Randall, among others, has written comprehensively on this aspect of Keswick and Meyer's influence on the emerging Welsh revival.[9]

At the 1904 Baptist Assembly in Bristol, J.H. Jowett preached a sermon based on Acts 19:1-3, entitled: 'Communion with "IT" or with "HIM"?', in which he reckoned that 'judged experimentally, by our daily life and practice, much of the mental attitude and spiritual pose of the modern church is pre-Pentecostal'.[10] Furthermore, a cursory trawl through *The Baptist Times and Freeman* editions of 1904 reveals further articles which plot positive signs of revival, such as,

> Churches are feeling that they must have the help of God, and have a fresh sense of His communion in the strife against sin. The holy discontent of the Church is rediscovering the great truth of the personality and the availability of the power of the Holy Spirit. Our sense of helplessness makes us lean hard on the Holy Ghost.[11]

It was in the same week that this article was published that accounts of the emerging revival in Wales were first being reported in *The Times*.[12]

The Welsh Revival Fire Spreads

Thomas Phillips, minister of St Mary's Baptist Church, Norwich, responded immediately to this news. He left East Anglia after his Thursday evening meeting ended and travelled to Wales overnight in order to be able to experience the revival first-hand by attending the services through the Friday. Phillips' record of this visit is contained in the first of a series of regular *Baptist Times and Freeman* features entitled 'Impressions of the Welsh Revival'.[13] Phillips was concerned that 'through the smoke English Christians may fail to see the fire', as other commentators highlighted only the 'extravagant and fanatical'.[14] His advocacy and verdict after just one day's meetings was unequivocal, 'There is only one conclusion possible – this is

---

[9] Ian M. Randall, *Spirituality and Social Change: The Contribution of F.B. Meyer (1847–1929)* (Milton Keynes: Paternoster, 2003), 99-102.

[10] J.H. Jowett, 'Communion with "IT" or with "HIM"?', *Baptist Times and Freeman* 7 October 1904, 731.

[11] G.R. Hern, 'The Signs of a Coming Revival', *Baptist Times and Freeman* 11 November 1904, 831.

[12] N. Gibbard, *On the Wings of the Dove: The International Effects of the 1904–05 Revival* (Bridgend: Brynterion, 2002), 19.

[13] T. Phillips, 'Impressions of the Welsh Revival', *Baptist Times and Freeman* 2 December 1904, 881.

[14] Phillips, 'Impressions of the Welsh Revival', 899.

the power of the Holy Ghost; God is in the midst of these people.'[15] The impression which especially caught Phillips' attention was the spontaneity of the movement. He describes how the revival is 'not engineered or arranged by a committee ... There was no one to guide the proceedings; there was no regular beginning and no proper conclusion.'[16] Testimonies from old men and young people were interspersed by rousing singing which 'stirred and subdued me as no sermon ever did'.[17]

Having attended various meetings during that Friday, Phillips returned to his church in Norwich and proceeded to recount the scenes he had witnessed in Wales two days previously, even abandoning the sermons he had prepared for that Sunday in favour of describing the revival.[18] Phillips was also struck by the 'Rediscovery of the Central Truths of the Gospel', specifically 'Christ upon the cross and a vivid consciousness of his nearness', which translated into ethical consequences in respect of temperance, breaking down the sectarian divisions of denominations, and inclusion of young people converted and participating. 'There was', he noted, 'little or no theology', rather 'a movement in harmony with the genius of the people, and, therefore, largely musical.'[19]

Further impressions followed over coming weeks. Phillips was invited by Thomas Spurgeon to visit the Metropolitan Tabernacle in London to tell 1,200 people about his experiences the previous week. He prefaced his account with the reading of Scriptures 'bearing upon the Holy Spirit' and then cited what he believed to be some of the characteristics of the revival: (a) prayerfulness, (b) a vivid realisation of the spiritual world, (c) the sovereignty of the Holy Ghost, (d) the effect upon character, and (e) joyousness.[20] Thomas Spurgeon then 'threw the meeting open for prayer', pleading for revival to come to England.

The national and the Christian press also played a daily part in updating Christians around the country about the events in Wales. On the final day of 1904, a devotional conference was arranged in London. Meyer presided and time was given for testimonies from those who had visited Wales (including Thomas Phillips) and for prayer. It was noted that many of the Free Church leaders sitting on the platform had 'not co-operated in any strictly religious work for many years'.[21] As a consequence of this prayer time in London, and of numerous leaders visiting Wales themselves, churches around the country started meeting for united prayer for spiritual revival.[22] Here are just a few quotes by way of illustration.

---

[15] Phillips, 'Impressions of the Welsh Revival', 881.
[16] Phillips, 'Impressions of the Welsh Revival', 881.
[17] Phillips, 'Impressions of the Welsh Revival', 881.
[18] 'Table Talk', *Baptist Times and Freeman* 2 December 1904, 882.
[19] 'Table Talk', 882.
[20] T. Phillips, 'The Welsh Revival', *Baptist Times and Freeman* 23 December 1904, 939.
[21] 'The Revival Movement', *Supplement to the Baptist Times and Freeman* 6 January 1905, vi.
[22] 'The Great Religious Awakening', *Baptist Times and Freeman* 13 January 1905, 21.

1) Cardiff: 'The meetings begin, proceed and end, guided by some mysterious impulse. They are chaotic without confusion, and decent though disorderly. No one can say what the audience will do next'. There was an acute desire not to quench the Holy Spirit.[23]

2) South Woodford: Without advertising or organisation, meetings have gone on night after night with much blessing. Drunks have been converted after midnight. 'The congregation wept, broken prayers were offered, and five souls asked for help.' The end of the meeting was one of intense joy.[24]

3) Torrington, Devon: 'Some of the episodes in this revival are too sacred to publish. ... Nearly 100 persons above fifteen years of age have within twelve or thirteen days openly confessed Christ.'[25]

4) Leicestershire: 'During the past thirteen days revival and evangelistic meetings have been held in the church at Hinckley. Up to the present there have been 47 decisions for Christ, and there are many under deep impression.'[26]

5) Queensberry Street, Old Basford, Nottingham: '[the pastor] gave opportunities at each service for the congregation to take any share in the services they felt prompted by the Spirit to do. Immediately prayers were offered, hymns were sung, choruses repeated again and again; several testified, and, before the day was over, Christ was confessed by thirteen young people ... From the beginning the work has been spontaneous, unorganised, informal ... Our Sunday services are as spontaneous as the week-days. I [the minister] speak when I get the opportunity.'[27]

Similar accounts from churches all around Britain were reported in the *Baptist Times and Freeman* weekly. The common denominators of surprise, expectation, devotion to earnest prayer, and personal testimony proved to be powerfully transferable. The accompanying questions appear to have been part of that dynamic in progress, such as, 'Will it [the revival] come to England?'; 'Will it last?'; 'how has the revival affected you?'; and attempts to discern whether 'the Spirit is really present?' Such questions fuelled further revival interest and debate, and perhaps even shaped the paradigms of expectation. Although countless anecdotes may be reported to add evidence to the ferocity of revival fires spreading from Wales throughout Britain and internationally, this paper now shifts to examine Baptist participation in a different movement, the revival of 1921.

The Lowestoft Revival of 1921

Douglas Brown, a Baptist pastor, was booked to speak at a four day mission in Lowestoft, starting on 7 March 1921,[28] for the benefit of young people in the town.[29]

---

[23] 'The Great Religious Awakening', 21.
[24] 'The Revival in England', *Baptist Times and Freeman* 3 February 1905, 87.
[25] 'The Revival in England', 87.
[26] 'The Revival in England', 87.
[27] 'The Revival at Queensbury Street', *Baptist Times and Freeman* 17 January 1905, 65. In the text above the original *BT&F*'s 'Queensbury' has been amended to the correct spelling 'Queensberry'.
[28] 'A Great Revival at Lowestoft', *Baptist Times and Freeman* 15 April 1921, 235.

However, this visit developed into a four week mission, in spite of Brown just recovering from influenza when he began the meetings.[30] The gatherings every morning at the London Road Baptist Church were primarily for prayer and intercession, with the 'power of the Spirit being very perceptible'.[31] Afternoon meetings were arranged, primarily for Christians, including teaching on the theme of the second coming, followed by evening meetings which, by the end of the first week, were attracting crowds of nearly 2,000. In the early weeks of revival over 500 'signed decisions have been taken ... backsliders have been reclaimed, and the spiritual life in the whole district has been awakened'.[32] By April 1921, the impact of the revival was spreading across the region and as far as London, as information about God at work was communicated through the *Baptist Times and Freeman* and other Christian papers. Interestingly, at first 'the daily and weekly Press in East Anglia ... left the revival severely alone' and 'no sensational advertising was adopted' and there 'were no parades or newspaper boosting'.[33]

The background to Douglas Brown's involvement at Lowestoft provides good insight into the mesh of mechanics and dynamics at work in this (or any) revival. Brown was pastor of the Ramsden Road Baptist Church in Balham, South London, which by all accounts had enjoyed the blessing of God in 'a record year' with membership additions and giving to outside causes.[34] Yet God was evidently dealing with Douglas Brown privately, as a pivotal personal crisis ensued. In his own words,

> God laid hold of me in the midst of a Sunday evening service, and He nearly broke my heart while I was preaching. I went back to my vestry and locked the door, and threw myself down on the hearthrug in front of the vestry fireplace broken-hearted. Why? I do not know. My church was filled. I loved my people, and I believe my people loved me ... I was as happy there as I could be. I had never known a Sunday there for fifteen years without conversions.
>
> That night I went home and went straight to my study. My wife came to tell me that supper was ready and waiting. 'You must not wait for supper for me', I said. 'What is the matter?' she asked. 'I have got a broken heart' was my reply. It was worth having a broken heart for Jesus to mend it. I had no supper that night. Christ laid his hand on a proud minister, and told him that he had not gone far enough, that there were reservations in his surrender, and He wanted him to do a piece of work that he had been trying to evade. I knew what He meant. All November that struggle went on, but I would not give way ... It was in February 1921, after four months of struggle that there came this crisis ... On the Saturday night I wrote out my resignation to my church and it was marked by my own tears. I loved the church, but I felt that if I could not be holy I

---

[29] 'The Revival in Suffolk: Interviews with Local Clergymen', *Baptist Times and Freeman* 3 June 1921, 345.

[30] 'A Great Revival at Lowestoft', 235.

[31] 'A Great Revival at Lowestoft', 235.

[32] 'A Great Revival at Lowestoft', 235.

[33] 'The Revival in Suffolk', 345.

[34] 'Baptist Times Table Talk', *Baptist Times and Freeman* 4 March 1921, 134.

would be honest; I felt that I could not go on preaching while I had a contention with God. That night the resignation lay on my blotter and I went to bed but not to sleep ...

Then something happened. I found myself in the loving embrace of Christ forever and ever; and all power and joy and all blessedness rolled in like a deluge ... That was two o'clock in the morning. God had waited four months for a man like me; and I said: 'Lord Jesus, I know what you want; you want me to go into mission work. I love Thee more than I dislike that.'[35]

The timing of Brown's private battle with God and the invitation to speak at the mission in Lowestoft are not insignificant factors in this or any revival. Divine preparation coupled with human factors of health and diary planning coalesced in the months that followed. Having spoken all week in Lowestoft, Brown returned to London for 'pulpit ministry' on Sundays, before travelling back to East Anglia for more revival meetings.[36] Working twenty hours out of every twenty-four, he expressed that this was the hardest experience of his life, in 'so glorious a movement and one so manifestly under the impulse and control of the Holy Spirit'.[37] The following three facets of the 1921–22 revival are each worth itemising, because they again demonstrate the defining factors of every true revival.

The Preparation of Prayer

Well before the mission meetings commenced in March 1921, it is notable that 'the outstanding feature in the life of the London Road Baptist Church prior to the revival was the weekly prayer meeting' on a Monday evening, when around ninety people were 'seeking God for a great manifestation of His power'.[38] In addition to the Lowestoft church, Brown also had the prayer back up of his home church in Balham. As with every such movement, intense prayer does not occur in a vacuum but rather in response to the prevailing issues – normally bad and challenging. Such was the setting at the start of the 1920s, particularly following the First World War, with escalating unemployment, gloom and depression. In addition, Evangelicalism in the 1920s 'became so sharply divided that some members of one party [conservatives or liberals] did not recognise the other as Evangelical – or even, sometimes, as Christian'.[39]

Prayer was an essential and integral response to any declension, and obviously struck a nerve when the matter became a feature in regular *Baptist Times and Freeman* sermons and letters pages. In one printed sermon, Harold Turner

---

[35] S.C. Griffin, *A Forgotten Revival: East Anglia and NE Scotland – 1921* (Bromley: Day One, 1992), 17-18.

[36] 'Baptist Times – Table Talk', *Baptist Times and Freeman* 22 April 1921, 248.

[37] 'Baptist Times – Table Talk', 22 April 1921, 248.

[38] Griffin, *Forgotten Revival*, 14.

[39] David W. Bebbington, *Evangelicalism in Modern Britain: A History from the 1730s to the 1980s* (London: Unwin Hyman, 1989), 181.

referenced the pattern of prayer and revival through history, and the establishment of the Prayer Call of 1784, asking,

> has not the time arrived for another great prayer union? Worship is formal, the Church dead, conversions rare ... Today we have better facilities, better advantages, more perfect machinery, but we have not the power.[40]

The sermon prompted various letters of approval, encouraging more sermons to be preached on the great revivals of history, and this succinct assessment that

> Wherever and whenever Christians have banded themselves together, 'Mechanics' have given way to 'Dynamics', and such revivals have not been the result of mere emotion, but ... simple obedience to spiritual laws.[41]

One article asked the question, 'Can we save the Prayer Meeting?' It was generally felt that the state of the prayer gathering in Baptist churches was in 'a bad way'.[42] Views expressed thereafter seem similar to contemporaneous opinions: wrong methods, monotony, lack of attraction for young people, etc.[43] However, the accounts of revival prayer meetings emanating from the Lowestoft area – and before long from many other towns and cities also – were a practical retort to this question. Prayer meetings were 'going on all day long ... with no organisation, no evangelistic engineering, it was a movement comparable only to the free winds of heaven ... or the original miracle at Pentecost'.[44] Numerous petitions for prayer were read out, one by one, at the prayer services led by Brown and other ministers, a correspondent noting how 'quiet and undemonstrative' the methods were.[45]

By the first anniversary of the Lowestoft revival, the number of prayer groups around the country had been rising steadily and powerfully. At Bloomsbury Baptist Church, for example, their minister Thomas Phillips (mentioned above in connection with the Welsh revival), commented how crowds from all over London had been praying for a revival for a long time.

> When it was announced that the leader of the East Anglian Revival was to hold services at Bloomsbury, Anglicans and Quakers, Presbyterians and Primitive Methodists, Salvationists and Brethren gathered. All the material was smouldering and Mr Douglas Brown came like a torch and set it all on fire.[46]

---

[40] Turner, 'Dynamics v. Mechanics', 166-67.

[41] 'Correspondence', *Baptist Times and Freeman* 25 March 1921, 185.

[42] 'Can we save the Prayer Meeting?', *Baptist Times and Freeman* 26 August 1921, 519.

[43] 'Correspondence', *Baptist Times and Freeman* 2 September 1921, 535.

[44] 'Baptist Union Assembly: The Rev. A. Douglas Brown', *Baptist Times and Freeman* 6 May 1921, 281.

[45] 'The Revival in Suffolk', 345.

[46] 'The Rev. Douglas Brown at Bloomsbury', *Baptist Times and Freeman* 24 February 1922, 116.

Plans were then put in place for sixty-two prayer hubs to be established 'to surround London with a belt of prayer meetings for revival', with a weekly joint prayer gathering at Bloomsbury every Thursday lunchtime.[47]

To gain a sharper perspective on Baptist prayer for revival, three brief reflections posited in this period are worth mentioning. Firstly, desperate prayer ought not to be confused with compulsion towards God, as if somehow we are twisting God's arm to do something he does not wish. God wants to revive his Church and to save people, so there is no need to ask inappropriately.[48] Secondly, Brown emphasised that the prerequisite of revival is always a revival of prayer 'not so much for the well-being of the local Baptist Church as for the conversion of the community'.[49] Similarly, Frederic Spurr noted that when prayer is revived, people seek God 'not only singly, but in social groups. They recognize once more their solidarity, and seek a boon, not simply for the individual, but for the society to which they belong.'[50] Thirdly, the expectation of prayer was, as it always is in revival, an integral feature of the meetings.

The Experience of God's Presence

The dramatic phenomena which accompanied this revival are constantly remarked upon by eyewitness records: the sheer size of the expectant crowds attending meetings; the emotionally charged atmosphere in meetings; the power of the preached word; the numbers of all ages responding at the end of meetings; testimonies resonating; these were obviously occasions 'not to be forgotten'.[51] Perhaps surprisingly, the account of early meetings at Great Yarmouth highlights the fact that 'as a whole the services were reverent and worshipful'.[52] On several occasions, during early and later days of revival, Brown was appreciated for not adopting the 'force' methods of some evangelists and he came to be described as 'the Apostle of sane missions' for deploying methods which gave 'room for the operations of the Holy Spirit'.[53]

There are countless recorded anecdotes of these revival meetings across the country, with this account of the first meetings in Ipswich typifying the overwhelming sense of God's presence experienced by those gathered.

> The very first meeting on Monday evening was one never to be forgotten. Mr Brown gave a plain, straight talk on revival, and what it means, the need for it and its urgency. Everyone felt that the message struck the right note, emphasising the need for getting

---

[47] 'The Rev. Douglas Brown at Bloomsbury', 116.
[48] 'The Coming Revival', *Baptist Times and Freeman* 17 March 1922, 166.
[49] 'The Rev. A. Douglas Brown', *Baptist Times and Freeman* 6 May 1921, 281.
[50] F.C. Spurr, 'Religious Revivals in the Light of their History', *Baptist Quarterly* 1.1 (1922), 8.
[51] 'The Revival in East Anglia', *Baptist Times and Freeman* 17 June 1921, 375.
[52] 'The Revival in East Anglia', 375.
[53] 'Rev. Douglas Brown at Harborne', *Baptist Times and Freeman* 30 June 1922, 421.

back to primitive methods and fundamental truths such as made the Church mighty in the days of the Apostles. Two hundred and fifty Christians rose at the close on the appeal of God's servant pledging themselves to stand with him in a new dedication to God and to seek with him God's blessing on the town.

The spirit of expectancy and determined prayer was aroused, and it soon became manifest that this was not simply a mission but a movement of the Holy Spirit. People came from all the district around; ... people were converted, and blessed from districts all around. From the very first the local clergy and ministers began to show their sympathy and co-operation ...

Nevertheless, Ipswich was not easy to move, and although night after night the spacious chapel, seating 1,000, was filled, and every night there were those who yielded to the Saviour ... the presence and power of the Holy Spirit, however, was very marked at all the services, and the breaking down came on the last night.

[After that service individuals began to return from the enquiry room.] Starting with a young girl, one after another quite spontaneously came straight for the platform, and facing the audience cried, 'I want to tell you I *do* love Jesus now', or 'I have been a backslider and now have come right out for Jesus Christ.' Some were completely overcome and burst into tears before they could find utterance.[54]

Douglas Brown was invited to speak at the Spring Assembly of the Baptist Union in 1921. News about the Lowestoft revival was already being widely circulated, so interest was inevitable and various critiques of Brown and the revival were forthcoming.

The Interpretation of Revival

Brown began his Assembly address by immediately identifying that his anticipations were the same as 'Dr. Clifford and Rev. Thomas Phillips'.[55] Together they shared the 'expectation that before long there would be in this country a great religious awakening ... That hour was on the point of arrival if only the Churches were willing.'[56] The delegates at Bloomsbury then listened to Brown recount his narrative of the revival events in East Anglia in a talk which was described as 'pure volcanic energy'.[57] It seems that Brown was 'carried away' with 'ecstasies' which a year or two previously would have been totally misunderstood in Bloomsbury Chapel but which were now considered in light of his words.

---

[54] 'The Revival in East Anglia', 375.

[55] 'Baptist Union Assembly: The Rev. A. Douglas Brown', 281; and Griffin, *Forgotten Revival*, 12.

[56] 'Baptist Union Assembly: The Rev. A. Douglas Brown', 281.

[57] 'Baptist Times Table Talk', *Baptist Times and Freeman* 6 May 1921, 279.

Today the need of revival in many of our churches is so acute, the desire for it so eager, that we are ready to sit at the feet of anyone who has reached the springs from whence come those impulses which can alone save the Church and the world.[58]

Brown then set out two lessons which he promoted as instructive for the wider church, namely:

a) Unity: 'the spiritual forces of the evangelical Churches of a town should be induced to unite for prayer and effort'.
b) Preaching: 'in preaching reversion must be made to the elementary simplicity of the evangel, the Cross of Christ made central, the Blood of Christ as the one fountain for the cleansing of sin and on the part of the hearers repentance and faith'.[59]

The evaluation of the 1921 London Assembly was reported as 'the most notably significant of the past twenty-five years',[60] although for some Brown's account of revival, albeit 'impressive', actually 'gave rise to conflicting conclusions'.[61] One lead article noted that Brown's address was probably the most discussed session of the Assembly, with delegates asking one another the question, 'What does it [the revival] mean?'[62] While suggesting that time should be taken for a proper evaluation of this movement, an anonymous critic revealed more caution and suspicion with a proposal that Douglas Brown, 'if he is wise, he will at an early date, cut himself loose from the work he is doing and play golf every day for a fortnight'.[63] There was also a call for any such revival to have 'an ethical edge', fearing 'there is a type of evangelism which looks somewhat coldly upon the work of the Borough Councils, Boards of Guardians, Trade Unions, Chambers of Commerce, Rotary Clubs, and Social Reform agencies'.[64]

Not surprisingly, such views drew sharp criticism from respondents via the letters page who complained that 'golf recommendations' and 'wait and see' conclusions did nothing to support the work and ministry of Brown and others in revival. The point was also made that evangelism and social concern are not incompatible, rather 'is it not better to have a clean heart and a pure spirit first, and then will not the love from within pour out to cleanse our citizen life?'[65] A wary voice was that of the Baptist Union President, J.C. Carlile, who had been chairing the Assembly session when Brown spoke.

---

[58] 'Baptist Union Assembly: The Rev. A. Douglas Brown', 281.
[59] 'Baptist Union Assembly: Fourth Session', *Baptist Times and Freeman* 6 May 1921, 282.
[60] 'With One Accord in Many Places', *Baptist Times and Freeman* 27 May 1921, 326.
[61] 'Ethics and Evangelism', *Baptist Times and Freeman* 6 May 1921, 275.
[62] 'Ethics and Evangelism', 275.
[63] 'Ethics and Evangelism', 275.
[64] 'Ethics and Evangelism', 275.
[65] 'The Lowestoft Revival', *Baptist Times and Freeman* 20 May 1921, 313.

> Listening to my beloved friend, the Rev. A. Douglas Brown, my heart was thrilled with thankfulness for the story he had to tell; but – and it was a terrific but – while it was a great thing to hear the report of the revival which is moving, yet the emotional wave gives the psychologist pause for serious thought ...[66]

The charge and suspicions of emotionalism which accompany revivals were debated in the public domain. In a joint letter of response from across the denominations, the Lowestoft ministers argued that the methods employed by Brown and others in the revival were identical to those Carlile was actually propounding. With no attempt at 'hypnotic' preaching or 'playing somewhat skilfully' upon the feelings of 'neurotic' and 'narcotic' audiences, the Lowestoft ministers were satisfied that the results were of 'the most tangible and convincing kind, and must carry conviction to the most sceptical observer'.[67] Their call for prayer instead of 'interjecting' a human 'but' led to this conclusion:

> Revivals in the past, it is true, have sometimes been followed by coldness, barrenness and sterility. It is no less true, however, that revival seasons have been the most fruitful and pregnant periods in the history of the Church.[68]

Further support from participants of the revival ensued, most notably this call from another Baptist minister in Lowestoft, the Rev. F.J.H. Humphrey, who challenged the Baptist denomination to respond to the East Anglia revival by witnessing the visitation of God's Spirit first hand.

> Here is the happening for which we longed and prayed. Here is the new evangelical revival in our midst. If we ignore it we are in danger of grieving or quenching the Holy Spirit ... Before our Denomination to-day a great door and effectual is open. It is an answer to our prayers, it is the sequel we desired to the Sustention Fund.[69]

Humphrey's call for the Union's Spiritual Welfare Committee to address the challenge of the religious awakening in East Anglia was endorsed by others outside 'the circle of revival'.[70] Ridley Chesterton desired a 'sympathetic lead' from the Baptist Union, fully

> aware of the danger that lies in any attempt to legislate for the spread of any such movement ... The reluctance to intrude with our poor human machinery upon a work marked so manifestly by that freedom of the Spirit 'that bloweth where it listeth' is altogether a worthy one.[71]

---

[66] 'Correspondence', *Baptist Times and Freeman* 27 May 1921, 328.
[67] 'Correspondence', 328.
[68] 'Correspondence', 328.
[69] 'A Challenge to the Denomination', *Baptist Times and Freeman* 8 July 1921, 423.
[70] 'The Revival in East Anglia', *Baptist Times and Freeman* 15 July 1921, 441.
[71] 'The Revival in East Anglia', *Baptist Times and Freeman* 26 August 1921, 523.

A telegram sent by Dr J.H. Shakespeare to Douglas Brown in July 1921 simply read, 'Deeply interested in your wonderful work. This is the way to unite the Church and save the world.'[72]

By September 1921, Dr Carlile had responded with a longer paper on 'The Dangers and Delights of Revival'.[73] Emphasising a Christ-centred approach to revival, he elaborated upon the dangers of emotionalism, citing the Welsh revival experience as illustrative of 'no clear demarcation between the psychic and the spiritual' and 'we know so little of the psychic and the spiritual that no one is competent to differentiate'.[74] Carlile also argued for a 'joy of revival' which is more than 'mere emotion' but retains the intelligent perception of a changed life by the Spirit's power.

Amid the revival awakenings of 1921, Douglas Brown's diary was full for months ahead, with 600 applications for him to visit towns and cities around Britain.[75] Some challenged whether it was right for Brown to be the pivotal figure in revival or whether the belief in God the Holy Spirit being with each church and each individual who believes should rather live out the Baptist Union's 'declaration of principle', 'That it is the duty of every disciple to bear personal witness to the Gospel of Christ, and to take part in the evangelization of the world'.[76] The secular press questioned to what extent the East Anglian religious movement would have any effect in Central London.[77] Others, while focusing on forthcoming revival meetings, debated the merits of revivalist methods per se.[78] It was considered a 'bold venture' when Thomas Phillips and Bloomsbury Baptist Church inaugurated 'revivalist services in Central London' led by Douglas Brown.[79] On the Monday night, 'over 200 persons took cards of re-dedication or allegiance ... The afternoon services were an astonishment so far as numbers were concerned, and the morning prayer meetings a revelation of what might happen.'[80] Even as the Bloomsbury meetings opened, Thomas Phillips proclaimed, 'The revival is not coming; it has come', as 'a large number' of individuals responded to the appeal.[81] As the revival meetings continued they 'crammed the chapel, the institute, the school room and the French Church next door. The people would not go away. Five hundred of them blocked Shaftesbury Avenue with an open-air meeting'. Phillips' reflections as a participant and one who had witnessed the Welsh Revival first hand are insightful. The 'crowning mercy', he

---

[72] 'The Revival in East Anglia', *Baptist Times and Freeman* 15 July 1921, 441.

[73] 'The Dangers and Delights of Revival', *Baptist Times and Freeman* 16 September 1921, 556.

[74] 'The Dangers and Delights of Revival', 556.

[75] 'Mr Humphrey's Challenge – and Another', *Baptist Times and Freeman* 15 July 1921, 440.

[76] 'Mr Humphrey's Challenge – and Another', 440.

[77] 'Revival in Central London', *Baptist Times and Freeman* 17 February 1922, 100.

[78] 'The Church and Revival', *Baptist Times and Freeman* 10 February 1922, 89.

[79] 'Revival in Central London', 100.

[80] 'Revival in Central London', 100.

[81] 'Revival in Central London', 100.

felt, was that the chapel was equally full whether Douglas Brown was present or not, countering any hints that the revival was intrinsically bound up with 'the magnetism and prestige of the revivalist ... Call it whatever you like – revival or Pentecost – it has come to London.'[82]

By March 1922, the first anniversary marked 1,000 meetings led by Douglas Brown, and an appropriate time for some reflections on the revival movement. Some thought the revival had 'developed' with a sharper vision for personal evangelism.[83] Rather than being regarded as a 'mission', Brown was advocating a 'movement towards the Cross and the radical fundamental experiences of the soul' which had stood the test at Norwich and Bloomsbury among other places. Other methods had also shifted.

> The 'Enquiry Room'... has been supplemented with the better method of 'the Room of Quiet'. Into this room ... people with whom the Spirit of God is striving are invited to go, they are not in any way interfered with; if they wish they may sign a card registering decision or rededication; but the matter is regarded as being between God and the individual soul, and there is no intrusion unless it is desired.[84]

F.J.H. Humphrey also noted that to an increased extent Brown's revival message was blending the 'evangelical and the ethical' with the 'implications of the Gospel in personal and social life'. At the closing meeting of his Southampton campaign in December 1922, Brown proposed taking an offering for 'the Mayor's Fund for the Unemployed, of whom there are a large number in the town'.[85] Although it is difficult to analyse the nuances of the methods deployed by Brown in revival meetings, these few examples do corroborate what one eyewitness observed.

> The wise restraint and the human sympathy of this beloved Campaign leader captured the confidence of all. His methods under the guidance of the Holy Spirit were varied. One night the address was followed simply by a brief prayer, the Benediction and dismissal. On other evenings the value of the Room of Quiet was brought home, and in this way many on their knees met with God.[86]

The import of Brown's personal traits resulted in both an appreciation and a critique among Baptists that revival was the urgent need, as well as the emerging experience of the 1920s. Frederic Spurr argued on the basis of history for a revival of religion as the 'main factor in spiritual and social progress', whether from a 'great pulpit' or a

---

[82] 'The Rev. Douglas Brown at Bloomsbury', 116.

[83] 'Some Reflections on the Revival Movement', *Baptist Times and Freeman* 17 March 1922, 173.

[84] 'Some Reflections on the Revival Movement', 173.

[85] 'The Rev. A. Douglas Brown at Southampton', *Baptist Times and Freeman* 15 December 1922, 822. The thank offering reached 'nearly £20'.

[86] 'The Rev. A. Douglas Brown at Southampton', 822.

'spontaneous movement'.[87] However, by late 1922 there were other voices questioning whether the 'after meetings' had a detrimental impact upon young people attending the services. Using Spurgeon's stance on after-meetings to corroborate his own position, Thomas Phillips commented,

> I am convinced he [Brown] would make a wider appeal if he discarded after-meetings, and I am sure that he deeply influenced hundreds who did not enter the quiet room at all. That is why I call the after-meetings skittish.[88]

During the third year of revival meetings, there was a call for the ministry of Douglas Brown to be developed within the Baptist denomination, with J.E. Roberts writing,

> I want to urge the value of Douglas Brown to our denomination. Cannot we retain his services for more intensive work? It will repay us a hundredfold … What a fine Commissioner of Evangelism he would make if the Denomination could secure at least his part time services.[89]

Conclusion

The paradoxical nature of revival, felt by many, was summarized by Thomas Phillips in 1922:

> I sympathise with the men that are distrustful of all such [revival] movements … I know the extravagances that are bound to come. Not will only the saints be glad, but the cranks will be boisterous. Not only will there be ethical but magical results. But the winter of our discontent is so bleak that I would welcome the summer and risk its weeds – welcome Pentecost and risk its tongues.[90]

He then elucidated some of the dangers warned by psychologists, including excess of emotionalism, fear of hypnotism, and the riot of the herd-instincts. 'Two years ago I should have written revive the old prayer-meetings, to-day I write change them from top to bottom and learn the tremendous significance of New Testament intercession.'[91]

After a prolonged period of itinerant ministry accompanied by abundant harvesting, frequent health battles through 1924 inferred that the revival role for

---

[87] F.C. Spurr, 'Religious Revivals in the Light of their History', *Baptist Quarterly* 1.1 (1922), 14-15.

[88] 'Mr Douglas Brown's Second Visit to Bloomsbury', *Baptist Times and Freeman* 13 October 1922, 658; see also T. Phillips, 'Some Thoughts on the Psychology of Revivals', *Baptist Quarterly* 2.1 (1924), 6.

[89] J.E. Roberts, 'The Rev. Douglas Brown in South Manchester', *Baptist Times and Freeman* 28 September 1923, 680.

[90] Phillips, 'Psychology of Revivals', 6.

[91] Phillips, 'Psychology of Revivals', 8.

Douglas Brown was decreasing by necessity, with other protagonists sharing the call and prayer for revival. In the shifts of these years, in spite of the dissipating revival, various voices within the Baptist denomination continued to focus on the person and work of the Holy Spirit, both at meetings and in the writing of various strategic Baptist thinkers. Wheeler Robinson, for example, developed theological considerations about the work of the Spirit particularly with regard to baptism, but also concerning revivalism, where he was far more cautious, with these blunt assertions:

> Through intensive emotion, we get the incidents of a religious 'revival'; every revivalist knows how one confession stimulates another ... There is the thrill of leadership and of the response of a group to it, which may so easily be regarded as a proof of special inspiration, yet is found in every social grouping, from the animal world upwards. The co-operative emotion of a religious assembly, listening to an eloquent speaker, may be paralleled at a political meeting.[92]

Discussion at the 1926 Assembly revolved around 'a new baptism of the Spirit' with J.H. Rushbrooke's call for Baptist 'self-dedication'.[93] The presidential address of May 1928 was entitled 'Preparing for Revival' and given by Mr A.R. Doggart,[94] who noted that although apparently previous 'remarkable results' have in time revealed shallowness of much that passed for being genuine, 'revival is the will of God for the Church and we ought diligently to seek it'.[95] By 1929, Douglas Brown was President of the Baptist Union and used his presidential address to speak on 'The Lordship of Christ in individual Life', an address which combined personal testimony of God's work of revival experience with the dire need of the Baptist denomination given their recent decline.[96] In the next decade, such calls and prayers for revival were to be repeated with yet more organisation, including the formation of the Baptist Revival Fellowship in 1938.

Baptist involvement in the revivals in Wales and Lowestoft confirms that while there is no guaranteed formula for revival, a heightened pneumatology can and does transform individuals as well as a denomination, although the longevity of renewal is far more difficult to maintain. The merger of need, anticipation and hope can grow faith and prayer and deepen spirituality. Douglas Brown's advice is surely a message for every generation, as he encouraged all ministers and churches 'to put the Holy

---

[92] H.W. Robinson, *The Christian Experience of the Holy Spirit* (London: Fontana, 1962 [1928]), 126.

[93] A.R. Cross, *Baptism and the Baptists: Theology and Practice in Twentieth-Century Britain* (Carlisle: Paternoster, 2000), 108.

[94] 'Preparing for Revival: Presidential Address', *The Baptist Times* 3 May 1928, 311.

[95] 'Preparing for Revival: Presidential Address', 311.

[96] A.D. Brown, 'The Lordship of Christ in Individual Life', *The Baptist Times* 9 May 1929, 353.

Spirit in the Presidential Chair' to bring about the further revival so desperately needed.[97]

---

[97] Brown, 'Lordship of Christ, 354.

CHAPTER 11

Jews in the Mindset of German Evangelicals

Erich Geldbach

Who are German Evangelicals?

This essay must begin by asking how one can identify German Evangelicals. This is a linguistic question as far as the meaning of the term 'evangelical' is concerned. The English word was originally used to translate the German adjective *evangelisch* which is derived from the noun *Evangelium*, the German word for gospel. To this day *evangelisch* is translated into English as 'evangelical'. The official website of the *Evangelische Kirche in Deutschland* (*EKD*), which is the umbrella organisation of twenty regional churches of Lutheran, Reformed or United backgrounds, renders its name in English as 'Evangelical Church in Germany',[1] just as the *Oxford Dictionary of the Christian Church*[2] does.[3] The word, thus, suggests that the *EKD* and its affiliated regional churches are rooted in the gospel as it was proclaimed anew by representatives of the Reformation period. *Evangelisch*, therefore, not only means 'according to the gospel' but also 'not Roman Catholic'. A further clue as to its meaning can be obtained by looking at the Community of Protestant Churches in Europe, formerly known as the Leuenberg Church Fellowship. Whereas the English name uses the word 'Protestant', the German says *Gemeinschaft Evangelischer Kirchen in Europa*. The word 'Protestant' underlines that the churches which make up the community trace their origins back to the Reformation, whereas the word *evangelisch* reflects more the gospel content. In both cases, however, it means 'not Catholic' and it does not mean 'evangelical' as defined by the Bebbington quadrilateral conversionism, activism, biblicism, and crucicentrism.[4]

Since the mid-1960s, however, the neologism *evangelikal* came up in the German language to translate the English word 'evangelical' in the sense in which it is used in the Anglo-Saxon world (in the USA, e.g., the National Association of Evangelicals) and as defined by David Bebbington. A case in point is the

---

[1] See <www.ekd.de/english/index.htlm>.

[2] Frank L. Cross (ed.), *Oxford Dictionary of the Christian Church* (London: Oxford University Press, 2nd edn, 1974), 486.

[3] My late friend Franklin H. Littell rendered *Evangelische Akademie* as 'Evangelical Academy', in Franklin H. Littell, *The Church and the Body Politic* (New York, NY: The Seabury Press, 1969), 81.

[4] David W. Bebbington, *Evangelicalism in Modern Britain: A History from the 1730s to the 1980s* (London: Unwin Hyman, 1989), 2-17.

Evangelical Alliance, which ever since its inception in 1846 was referred to in German as *Evangelischer Bund*, or, somewhat later, as *Evangelische Allianz*, although nowadays its supporters seem to wish it were translated as *Evangelikale Allianz*. The main source and the main advocate of such usage is the religious news service *informationsdienst der evangelischen allianz* (*idea*) which popularised the term *evangelikal* as a party name within German Protestantism.

As the term *evangelikal* was introduced into the German language only in the mid-1960s, the question arises if the subject of this essay should be limited to the period from the mid-1960s to the present. There seems to be little that can be said in favour of such an approach other than the linguistic peculiarity. The persons, movements, church organisations and church parties which are gathered under the term *evangelikal* did not begin in the mid-1960s. To be sure, some did and some have begun to operate since then, but most had a history long before the 1960s, and most would look back to their past and claim that there is an unbroken continuity in their experience and theology which goes back at least two centuries. The conclusion, therefore, is that it is not only legitimate, but necessary to include in an essay on German evangelicals such movements and organisations for whom the term 'evangelikal' had not been used prior to the mid-1960s.

A clue to this understanding may also be found when one considers that the term evangelical is often used interchangeably with 'pietistic', deriving from 'pietism'. The idea is thus conveyed that the present-day evangelicals have, as their antecedents, the pietists of the eighteenth century. Present-day evangelicals consider themselves (rightly or wrongly) to be legitimate heirs to men like Philipp Jacob Spener (1635–1705), August Hermann Francke (1663–1727), Nikolaus Ludwig Count Zinzendorf (1700–60), Johann Albrecht Bengel (1687–1752), Friedrich Christoph Oetinger (1702–82), Gerhard Tersteegen (1697–1769), and others. The links between then and now are to be found in the 'Awakening Movement' (*Erweckungsbewegung*) of the nineteenth century which eventually emerged as the 'Fellowship Movement' (*Gemeinschaftsbewegung*) during the latter part of the nineteenth century.

The Fellowship Movement with its many organisations and sub-organisations has always been part of the established regional churches (*Landeskirchen*). In its efforts to evangelise the country and to bring people together for prayer and fellowship beyond denominational boundaries, the movement has more or less cooperated with the so-called Free Churches, notably the Baptists, the Methodists and the Federation of Free Evangelical Congregations, through the Evangelical Alliance. It appears, therefore, that the Evangelical Alliance is a loose umbrella organisation for both the Fellowship Movement as the conservative wing of the regional churches and the Free Churches. It comprises basically that which may be referred to as the evangelical movement in Germany.

The Free Churches, however, have sometimes voiced opposition to being classified as *evangelikal*. It is true that the evangelicals are a party within the Free Churches just as they are a faction within the regional churches. Some Free Churches, notably the Federation of Free Evangelical Congregations, are closer to, others, particularly the United Methodist Church (*Evangelisch-methodistische Kirche*), are further removed from the evangelical centre. It is true, however, that in the German context even the Free Churches consider Pietism as an antecedent to their own movements. The present survey will, therefore, begin during the baroque period and run to the year 2000.

Spener as an Example of Early Pietism

Philipp Jacob Spener has often been referred to as the father of pietism. His book *Pia Desideria*[5] of 1675 was originally a preface to a collection of sermons by Johann Arndt (1555–1621), but was then published separately in both German and Latin. It is widely regarded as the starting point of Pietism. Spener's contention is that God had promised 'better times' for his church, a better state of affairs than exists today; therefore it is attainable. The first point in his programme to improve the church is Spener's belief in the 'homecoming' of all of Israel to God and to his Son Jesus Christ.[6] For this statement he relies on Romans 11:25-26:

> I do not want you to be ignorant of this mystery, brothers and sisters, so that you may not be conceited: Israel has experienced a hardening in part until the full number of the Gentiles has come in, and in this way all Israel will be saved. As it is written: 'The deliverer will come from Zion; he will turn godlessness away from Jacob.'

He also refers to passages by the church fathers. Thus Spener rejected the notion of the Protestant orthodoxy of the sixteenth and seventeenth centuries that the mission of the Church towards the Jewish people had been fulfilled by the apostles and that mission is no longer the task of the present-day Church. His approach is radically different: not only does he support the notion that the Church has an on-going mission to the Jews as well as to the world, he also thinks that the conversion of the Jews will invigorate the Church tremendously.

Spener worked in the free imperial city of Frankfurt for twenty years (1666–86). Here he had daily encounters with Jews as about one sixth of the population was Jewish. His personal contacts were certainly important, but equally important was his theological concept. When he was asked whether a German midwife could also help Jewish expectant mothers, he answered in the affirmative. The Jews were, for him, the 'noblest' people in the world as they derive from the seeds of the holy patriarchs. Even though they are presently under the wrath of God, this 'extraction' from the patriarchs Abraham, Isaac and Jacob demands that they should be loved above all other people. An additional reason for loving the Jewish people is the fact that the

---

[5] *Pia Desideria* or Earnest Desire for a God-pleasing Betterment of the True Evangelical Church.

[6] For the following and for more details, see Martin Schmidt, 'Judentum und Christentum im Pietismus des 17. und 18. Jahrhunderts', in Karl Heinrich Rengstorf and Siegfried von Kortzfleisch (eds), *Kirche und Synagoge. Handbuch zur Geschichte von Christen und Juden. Darstellung mit Quellen*, Volume 2 (Stuttgart: Klett Verlag, 1970), 90-128.

Saviour is their kinsman according to the flesh. Spener follows Paul's line of thinking as expressed in Romans 11:20, 'they [the Jews] were broken off because of unbelief, and you stand by faith. Do not be arrogant, but tremble.'

Spener advocated the Church's mission to the Jews (*Judenmission*) but he was very cautious as far as conversion was concerned. The homecoming of the Jews is God's own task, not a human endeavour. Above all, the application of force must be avoided. Only spiritual weapons should be applied, that is the preaching of the Word of God and prayer. The Kingdom of Christ is not of this world and hence the means used in the conversion of the Jews must be in accordance with the spiritual aim. Nothing may be done which is contrary to the conscience of the Jews. He demands that the freedom of conscience be respected vis-à-vis the Jewish people.

Spener also supported the view that the Jews – being dispersed throughout the world – should be given decent homes and such surroundings that they could exercise their religion. He also thought that the Jews should be admitted to all sections of society so that they would not have to rely on money-lending for their livelihood and therefore appear to be materialistic. Spener knew that the ill-treatment of the Jews and their standing in society were caused by the Christians and that this Christian behaviour was wrong.

In a way, Spener supports the notion of what later came to be known as assimilation on the basis of human rights. He also supports the Church's mission but he wants this to take place in accordance with the freedom of conscience and not by coercive means. Although Spener believes that God's final aim is the homecoming of all Jews, he is realistic in his assessment that at present only individual conversions will be the result of the missionary efforts. The conversion of a Jew, the re-birth, became, for him, the paradigm of all pietistic efforts at converting people: a deep inner experience of turning around and becoming a different person, accompanied by a proper instruction and baptism as necessary ingredients of the re-birth experience.

Even though Jews do not like the term *Judenmission*, it must be stressed that Spener's approach was a radical break with the teaching of contempt for the Jewish people which had been so deeply engrained in the Christian tradition. Spener sees the Jews as God's beloved people. Although he agrees with the commonly held Christian belief that the Jews are now suffering under God's wrath and are, therefore, deprived of their homeland and dispersed throughout the world, he does not think that the Church or the so-called Christian nations should make the fate of the Jews even more unbearable. His idea of *Judenmission* is derived from the notion that God had promised better times for both the Church and the Jews and that the conversion of the latter will invigorate the Church so that it be better prepared to face the return of Christ.

Spener followed the mystical approach of Christian Hoburg (1607–75) who had in 1644 written a book entitled *German-Evangelical Jewry* in which he constructs a parallel development of Christianity and Judaism. Luther had written about *The Babylonian Captivity of the Church* (1520). This means that medieval Catholicism resembles the Jewish exile in Babylon, the Reformation correlates with the return of the Jews from exile, and the post-Reformation era, especially the Thirty Years' War, is as much a time of decline as the post-exile period. Spener and Hoburg agree that an improvement can be expected from God in the here and now.

Consequences of Spener's Approach

In 1728 Spener's ideas led to the establishment of an Institutum Judaicum at the University of Halle, founded by Johann Heinrich Callenberg (1694–1760),[7] a friend of August Hermann Francke. It had a printing press with Hebrew, Yiddish and Arabic letters. During the nineteenth century several other such institutions came into being. Their main purpose was to make the necessary preparations for missionary efforts among the Jewish population. *Judenmission* was carried out by the Berlin Society for the Promotion of Christianity among the Jews (founded 1822), the Basel-based Association of the Friends of Israel (founded 1830 as part of the 'Spittler empire' of organisations[8] to promote awakenings, with support coming chiefly from southern Germany), the Rhinish-Westphalian Association for Israel, and the umbrella organisation Evangelical-Lutheran Central Association for Mission among Israel (founded 1871 in Leipzig). The latter became famous as its main promoter was the biblical scholar, Professor Franz Delitzsch (1813–90), who believed that only a solid theological education would qualify a person to work as a missionary among the Jews.[9] His translation of the New Testament into Hebrew was used for 100 years between 1877 and 1977 by the British and Foreign Bible Society.

These organisations and persons, not all of them in the tradition of Pietism, but at least closely related to it, did much to enhance the knowledge of the Hebrew language, Jewish religion, philosophies, traditions and customs. Although they made use of the Jews to reach a Christian aim, they nevertheless became instruments to disseminate knowledge of the Jewish culture and religion.

---

[7] Cf. Christoph Rymatzki, *Hallischer Pietismus und Judenmission. Johann Heinrich Callenbergs Institutum Judaicum und dessen Freundenkreis (1728–1736)* (Tübingen: Verlag der Franckeschen Stiftungen Halle im Max Niemeyer Verlag, 2004 = Hallesche Forschungen, vol. 11).

[8] Some details as to the Holy Land are given in my article 'The German Protestant Network in the Holy Land', in Moshe Davis and Yehoshua Ben-Arieh (eds), *With Eyes Toward Zion III: Western Societies and the Holy Land* (New York, NY: Praeger Publishers, 1991), 150-69.

[9] See the paper which he delivered in Berlin on 28 April 1870 and which was printed the same year: Franz Delitzsch, *Welche Anforderungen stellt die Gegenwart an die Missions-Arbeit unter den Juden?* (Erlangen: Deichert, 1870). For interesting contributions from a Lutheran perspective, see Folker Siegert (ed.), *Kirche und Synagoge. Ein lutherisches Votum* (Göttingen: Vandenhoeck & Ruprecht, 2012). This collection of essays deals with problems of historical as well as present-day significance.

Evangelical Christians and *Judenmission*

It goes without saying that the movement called 'German Christians' (*Deutsche Christen, D.C.*) condemned the *Judenmission*: 'In missionary effort to the Jews we see a grave danger for our national existence. It is the access of alien blood into our people-body [*Volkskörper*] ... Holy Scripture knows also of holy wrath and love that does not give in. In particular, all marriages between Germans and Jews are to be outlawed' (No. 9 of the guidelines of the D.C. of 26 May 1932).

Evangelical Christians in Germany had always advocated mission to the Jews. Two examples of recent German history may illustrate this assertion. In 1999 at the *Kirchentag* (national assembly of the church) in Stuttgart the Working-Group of Jews and Christians (*Arbeitsgemeinschaft Juden und Christen beim Deutschen Evangelischen Kirchentag*) issued a statement which was endorsed by about 700 people who had attended the dedicated session. The headline of the statement reads '*Nein zur Judenmission!*' and the declaration says that it is not necessary for the salvation of the Jews to have Jesus proclaimed as their Messiah. 'We reject any endeavours of Christians, either directly or indirectly, to support the conversion of Jews.' It is the contention of the *Arbeitsgemeinschaft* that the Great Commission directs Christians to the nations of the world but not to the Jews. When one looks at the history of the Church, its application of force against Jews and its claim to be the 'true Israel', one must realise that proclamation of the gospel to Jews lacks credibility. Therefore, any attempt at *Judenmission* must be rejected.

One day later, at the same *Kirchentag*, about 900 people gathered in a 'Workshop Pietism'. They took issue with the statement by the *Arbeitsgemeinschaft* and instead passed a resolution in which they affirmed that 'Jesus, the Son of God, first came for Israel, that he also died on the cross for Israel and rose on the third day. Jesus is the Saviour of the nations and the Messiah of Israel.' This biblical line of thinking must not be obscured, the pietist statement continued. It also says that the term *Judenmission* is open to misunderstanding, which is why its supporters instead prefer to speak of 'Christian witness'. That witness, the resolution declared, is extremely imperilled by the cruelties committed by Germans in the twentieth century, and one must question whether it is the specific task of Germans to invite Jews to Jesus, the Messiah, while the Holocaust generation is still alive. But these considerations do not alter the fact that it is the task of the Church to obey the New Testament. Thus the 'Workshop Pietism' emphatically rejected the statement by the *Arbeitsgemeinschaft*. In other words, they said 'yes' to missionary efforts towards the Jews, and even though it may not be the task of the present generation of Germans to be involved in this endeavour, it may be 'business as usual' once the Holocaust generation has died out.

More than two decades earlier, the same debate had been held. It had been caused by the broadcasting of the Hollywood television series 'Holocaust' in 1976 and the ensuing, widespread popular debate about the meaning of the Holocaust and its implications. Some theologians and churches began to call into question missionary effort towards the Jews as a consequence of that watershed event.[10] However, the evangelically-minded *Theologischer Konvent Bekennender Gemeinschaften* in 1980 insisted that the Great Commission applied to all people, including the Jews. 'Not to bring Christ to the Jews would be an offence against the king of Israel and his people' (No. 1). A complete rejection of any missionary efforts towards the Jews is going astray theologically (No. 9). 'The church must not water down the gospel to a mere dialogue. Rather, its confession of the messiahship and God's sonship of Jesus (Mt. 16:16), of the expiatory sacrifice on the cross, of his resurrection, ascension and return, as well as of the Trinity of God must not be given up for the sake of an agreement. It would lead to an *ex post facto* theological justification of the rejection and condemnation of Christ by the then leaders of Israel, and it would lead to an anti-Christian concept of Jesus (2 Cor. 11:3-4).'

Several key theological terms that are characteristic of evangelical theology occur in the statements of 1980 and 1999: the cross, atonement, resurrection and the return of Christ as salvific facts, and the Trinity. These declarations and their support for mission among the Jews may serve as examples of how the historical situation can render the self-same concept meaningful or counter-productive and self-deceptive. Whereas Spener's call to *Judenmission* is an example of liberating the Church and its theology from an age-old tradition of teaching of contempt, the support for *Judenmission* by a conservative confessional group or by a 'Workshop Pietism' in the post-Holocaust era is enslaving the Church in propositional language which amounts to nothing less than a new and subtle way of the teaching of contempt.

Evangelicals during the Third Reich

It must be remembered that the confessional group which drafted the 1980 statement was under the theological guidance of Professor Walter Künneth (1901–97), formerly of Erlangen University, and Professor Peter Beyerhaus (b.1929), formerly of Tübingen University. In 1936 Künneth published a book against Alfred Rosenberg's *The Myth of the Twentieth Century*; he was heavily involved in an apologetic effort by the church to confront Nazism. Yet early in April 1933 he had also written about 'The Jewish Problem and the Church'.[11] He maintained that the new state and the uniqueness of German nationhood would necessarily raise the issue to regulate the Jewish problem in a new way. Too many Jews, in his opinion, had in the immediate past been in highly visible positions, which was why the new regulations must be seen as protective measures to secure the future of the German people. In the church, Künneth continued, things are different as membership there is not acquired by racial descent – race being qualified as one of God's creation-orders – but by participating in the sacraments. The ministers of the church cannot be selected on racial or political grounds. However, as the church has a mission to the

---

[10] Franklin H. Littell used that term in many of his publications and addresses.

[11] In Walter Künneth and Helmuth Schreiner (eds), *Die Nation vor Gott. Zur Botschaft der Kirche im Dritten Reich* (Berlin: Wichern Verlag, 1933), 90-105.

German people, it follows that its *judenchristliche Elemente* should not be too conspicuous in the *Volkskirche*, the church of the German people.

On the other hand, in a time of crisis and public boycott the Church has a special responsibility. It must, first of all, display Christian charity toward *Judenchristen* (Jewish Christians) in need. Secondly – and the two realms are neatly separated according to the Lutheran two-kingdom-theory – 'It is the church's task that the exclusion of the Jews as an alien element in the life of the people (*Volksleben*) must not take place in a way which violates the Christian ethos.' The right of the State to apply new measures is not questioned; Christians must obey those in authority. The Church need only watch that the new measures are applied in accordance with the Christian ethos. Furthermore, Christian charity, so it seems, is not to be extended to all Jews, but only to those who had converted to Christianity. Even they should not be in leadership positions as the Church deals with Germans, not with those of alien blood. A minister of Jewish descent would cause consternation among the Germans.

Künneth was not the only voice in the evangelical camp to argue along these lines. None other than Walter Michaelis (1866–1953), who from 1906 to 1911 and again from 1919 down to his death served as chairman of one of the main evangelical organisations, the *Gnadauer Verband*,[12] echoed the same sentiments when in May 1933 he wrote that the repression of the Jews in public life must be conducted 'humanely' (*menschlich*). Long before he had heard of fascism or national-socialism, he had been convinced 'that the nations had falsely interpreted the will of God' with regard to the Jews when they had granted them full citizenship (*volles bürgerliches Heimatrecht*). In hindsight Michaelis discovered that he had always been a theological anti-Semite; the new political order gave him a new language code in which he found his theology rightfully expressed. Michaelis described this as a 'discovery': he had thus far been unaware of the compatibility of political and theological anti-Jewish language, but found to his astonishment that the political situation re-enforced his religious tradition.

According to Michaelis' insights, the dispersion of Israel among the nations is God's judgmental wrath upon the Jews. For him a solution would be the return of the Jews to Palestine. Until the Jewish people are again gathered in Palestine, however, it is their 'legitimate fate' to be in the diaspora. 'To give them full citizenship is against God's clear will. If a people distinguishes the Israelites as Israelites legally from the Germans, we have no objections from the biblical point of view. Rather, this is in accordance with the thoughts of God concerning these people.' The negative influences of the Jews were, for Michaelis, a 'moral and national danger', especially when it concerns the 'faithless Jewry without principles' (*das glaubens- und grundsatzlose Judentum*) which shows its strength 'in the press, high finance, economy, motion picture and theatre'.[13] The leadership of the evangelical youth organisation Christian Endeavour (E.C.) wrote a letter to its sister organisations throughout Europe to protest against what it perceived to be an anti-German smear

---

[12] The name of the Fellowship Movement within the regional churches.
[13] W. Michaelis, *Licht und Leben* 25 (1933), 392ff.

campaign after the Nazis had organized a boycott of Jewish businesses as early as 1 April 1933. That boycott, said the E.C. leaders, had been 'humane' in every respect.[14]

Hitler's rise to power caught the evangelical community, including the Free Churches, politically and theologically unprepared. They had looked at themselves as the 'unpolitical' 'quiet of the land', yet most of them had doubts about democracy and the democratic process in the Weimar Republic (1918–33). Many were 'monarchists' at heart. Even though they had always taught that the Jews had a special place in God's plan and that they were the 'apple of God's eye' (Dt. 32:10), evangelicals were also susceptible to all kinds of conspiracy theories that would conform to their reading of the 'signs of the time'.

Nazi propaganda proved to be very deceptive for evangelicals. They applauded the Nazis' promise to build a future society that was 'clean' and in which the young people were brought up in decent order. They also believed that in many cases the Jews, notably the secular or anti-religious Jews, were the leading cause of the turmoil they experienced in society. Jewish bankers and businessmen, Jewish owners of houses of prostitution, Jewish filmmakers, Jewish theatre directors and Jewish writers were all seen in a kind of conspiracy against German society. Even if evangelical leaders professed not to follow the racial anti-Semitism, they nevertheless said that Jews who had rejected the Messiah were now the corrupting elements in the life of nations and were causing revolutions, notably the Soviet revolution in Russia. Fear of communism had been part of the evangelical community ever since word of heavy persecution of 'brethren' in Russia had been widely spread in the 1920s. Evangelicals, therefore, were open to the Nazi propaganda concerning 'world Jewry' and its secret impact on the lives of nations. They believed the myth that it was Jewish money, Jewish intellectual ability, Jewish political influence, and Jewish cultural impact that were at work to change Germany for the worse. It became imperative for all Germans to unite in order to build a dam against the flood.

That world Jewry and the Free Masons were combining their forces and that the Bolshevist revolution in Russia was intellectually spearheaded by Jews and that all of these evil forces together threatened not only world peace, but especially the well-being of Germany, were some of the myths that circulated among evangelicals. Some leaders approvingly referred to the Prussian court preacher and vigorous head of the Berlin City Mission, Adolf Stoecker (1835–1909), a notorious anti-socialist, anti-liberal and anti-Semite, who had promoted the elimination of all Jews from the legal and educational professions in order to curb Jewish influence. Stoecker may well have been the most influential man to shape the evangelicals' perception of the Jews and make them forget their 'pietist fathers'.

---

[14] *Auf der Warte* 22 (1933), 261.

The End-Time Theory

Evangelical leaders looked at the Jewish people from the point of view of a special reading of history. History is viewed as 'salvation history' with special emphasis upon eschatology. The quote from Michaelis above can be taken as a clue. At present the Jewish people are suffering under the wrath of God, but they will again be gathered in Palestine as history goes on and as God will show that he is the prime mover of human history. When the Zionist movement advocated a Jewish state and when Jews were beginning to leave Germany for Palestine, evangelical commentators were encouraged and reassured by this move that God was at work.[15] Evangelicals referred to passages from Holy Scripture to support their contention that the end-time was close at hand. The most frequently quoted scriptural citation is Jesus' reference to the fig tree. Evangelical Christians have always taken this as their favourite text to read the 'signs of the time'. When the branches of the fig tree become green and tender, one can know that the summer is near (Mk 13:28-31). This passage is most often interpreted to mean that the Jewish people will again be placed (or have in the meantime been placed) in such a position that they can play a major role in salvation history. The first green shoots are coming out so that whoever has eyes to see will know that the end-time is imminent. When the state of Israel was established in 1948, evangelical Christians began to interpret this passage to mean that Israel was being restored and that history would soon come to its dramatic end.

The group which had a great influence upon evangelical Christians when it came to interpreting eschatology and the role of Jews in the end-time is the Christian Brethren, the followers of John Nelson Darby (1800–82). Darby's dispensationalist reading of Scripture, the translation and use of the Scofield Reference Bible and, in the last fifty years, the translation and publication of a number of books by fundamentalist American writers, have contributed to outlining eschatological events and timetables for the end-time among evangelical Christians in Germany.[16] To be sure, not all German evangelicals have followed Darby's teaching, especially not the leaders who had been trained in theology in the universities, but Darby's system has had great influence through Bible conferences and independent Bible schools both before and especially after the Second World War.

The key for a dispensational reading of Scripture is 'rightly dividing the word of truth'.[17] The word of Scripture appears as a unity only if it is first rightly divided.

---

[15] For a thorough investigation of one of the journals of the evangelical movement, *Evangelisches Allianzblatt*, see Nicholas Railton, *The German Evangelical Alliance and the Third Reich: An Analysis of the ‚Evangelisches Allianzblatt'* (Bern: Peter Lang, 1998), especially ch. 7, 'The Jewish Question', 171-89.

[16] Recently, Tim LaHaye's *Left Behind* series of books was also marketed in Germany, but with little success as compared to the English-speaking world. According to the publisher only about 80,000 books were sold in the country, most of them to 'evangelikale' groups. See my article 'Das apokalyptische Fieber. Die Buch-Serie *Left Behind*', in Michael Klöcker und Udo Tworuschka (eds), *Handbuch der Religionen* (München: Olzog Verlag, 2012), 1-24.

[17] William Kelly (ed.), *The Collected Writings of J.N. Darby* (34 vols; Kingston-on-Thames: Stow Hill Bible and Tract Depot, n.d.), XIII, 367.

The divisions will make it possible to treat different biblical texts differently as every text was designed by God for a certain dispensation. The underlying idea here is that salvation history unfolds in a succession of different dispensations. Each dispensation rests upon some conditions which God sets humankind. In every instance, however, humankind failed to meet that condition because of its disobedience, and the dispensation was a failure in principle. Now the point is to correlate biblical texts to the various dispensations; each text applies only to one dispensation, and it is the task of the interpreter to find out which text goes with which dispensation. This is what is meant by 'rightly dividing the word of truth'. However, the various dispensations did not develop gradually in history. There is what may be called a succession of 'dispensational leaps', with each dispensation operating on a different condition, each having nothing to do with the preceding one and each ending in complete failure shortly after its inception. The 'rightly dividing' of the word of truth amounts to the allocation of biblical texts to presupposed dispensations, and thus biblical exposition is extremely arbitrary. The method is totally unhistorical or, at best, ahistorical.

The present dispensation began at Pentecost with the outpouring of the Holy Spirit and will end with the so-called secret rapture of the saints. Like all preceding dispensations the Church dispensation was also destroyed in principle shortly after it began. The Church dispensation or the 'dispensation of the Spirit' is, however, different from all preceding ones in that it is placed like a parenthesis into the Jewish dispensation. The prophets did not see it as they related their prophecies to history: 'Prophecy applies itself properly to the earth; its object is not heaven. It was about things that were to happen on the earth; and not seeing this has misled the church.'[18] But during the parenthetical dispensation of the Spirit this history is suspended. It will again be in effect as soon as the parenthesis is closed. When the Church, that is the true believers, the saints only, is secretly raptured to its heavenly place, the pre-Church Jewish dispensation will resume. Or, to put it in yet another way, when the Church dispensation will have come to an end by the saints having been taken away, Israel will again be the sole object of God's favour, and all prophecies with regard to Israel will be fulfilled. The instrument of God's dispensational dealings with the world after the Church has been 'raptured' is Israel as a kind of redeemer nation.

This concept of history serves two purposes. On the one hand, the end for the Church must be expected at any moment. The rapture will come as a surprise, and it may happen at any time, like a thief comes in the night: 'When is the Christian to expect the Lord? I answer, Always. It is his right spiritual character.'[19] On the other hand, there are signs of the times which one is expected to read and prophetic utterances which take more time in history to be fulfilled. These things are to wait until the time after the rapture. The 'dividing of the word of truth' serves both ends well. It also ensures that the Church is a spiritual entity which looks for 'spiritual' – heavenly – ends, whereas the Jewish nation is earthly and looks for 'earthly'

---

[18] Darby, *Collected Writings*, II, 376.
[19] Darby, *Collected Writings*, XI, 156, cf. also 117.

blessings. The Jews await the formal completion of the covenant. Their hope, then, is directed toward the historical fulfilment of prophecy, whereas the hope of the Church is directed entirely to the heavenly things with Christ.

This particular hermeneutical principle, developed by Darby and later popularised in the Scofield Bible, appealed to many evangelical leaders in the latter part of the nineteenth century in western countries[20] and has ever since been a guiding principle for reading Scripture in many evangelical circles. This dispensational-premillennial vision reinforced an escapist mentality in those countries where the pious had traditionally been the 'quiet of the land', such as in Germany. That this hermeneutical system has greatly influenced evangelical groups is surprising when one considers that the immediate followers of Darby have remained a small group, greatly divided over points of minor importance. Darby's dispensationalist hermeneutics, however, greatly appealed to many. One can only speculate why this is so. The most notable reason, it seems, is the fact that the system which can be constructed on the basis of a dispensationalist reading of Scripture gives people a sense of security amidst change. It also creates a sense of belonging to the same salvation history together with Jews even though Jews and Christians do not belong to the same dispensation but have different expectations. With regard to both the evangelical community and the Jews, the God of history is in command, and he will enact that which is in accordance with his will. An eschatological timetable can be constructed because some people who are considered 'teachers of the church' claim to have access to the key that opens the pages of prophecy. For evangelical Christians this approach resulted in a deep love for the Jews and for the state of Israel. This can be documented by the many groups of tourists under the leadership of evangelical pastors which visit Israel. These groups also passionately support the messianic Jews. It should be critically noted that within this system Jews are instrumentalised to serve the highly speculative purposes of eschatologically-minded Christian dispensationalists.

In view of these developments, it is possible to understand to some extent why the evangelical community in Germany in the 1930s so easily became supporters of the NSDAP, its *Führer* and the anti-Jewish political agenda. Even if some leaders did not follow the dispensationalist approach, all evangelicals believed in salvation history and in the fact that the Jews at present were under the wrath of God. They also maintained that the fate of the Jews had not yet reached its climax. The worst was still to come when the great tribulation would set in of which the Lord himself had predicted that it will be the worst since the beginning of the world. Prophecy was being fulfilled, therefore, when Jews were evicted from Germany and were escaping to Palestine, for it would be in their 'homeland' that the facts of the end-time history would occur.

It seems that this particular concept of 'salvation history' acted as a blindfold for German evangelicals. This type of 'salvation history' presupposes that within the

---

[20] Cf. Yaakov Ariel, *On Behalf of Israel: American Fundamentalist Attitudes Toward Jews, Judaism, and Zionism, 1865–1945* (Brooklyn, NY: Carlson Publishing, 1991).

historical process a meta-historical concept, a divine plan for world history, can be detected. The reading of the 'signs of the time' serves to explain the ongoing stream of historical events and to bring the different pieces together in such a way that history resembles the divine plan. This can be done on the basis that God had sent prophets who under the guidance of God's Spirit foretold future events. The reading of prophetic parts of Scripture and the reading of the signs of the time go hand in glove. The application of scriptural references to historical-political events was the central idea of many editorials in the evangelical press, not only in 1933 and beyond, but even before.

Three facts are especially revealing.

1. The religious or pseudo-religious rhetoric used by the Nazi propaganda and by Adolf Hitler himself appealed to evangelicals. They found it attractive that the new Chancellor publicly confessed for himself and for the German people his faith in the living God and asked for his blessing. They eagerly scattered the news that Hitler had a well-read New Testament on the table beside his bed, that he neither smoked nor drank, and that he lived a sexually abstinent life. Evangelical Christians joined hands with the right-wingers on moral issues. In the evangelical community smoking, heavy drinking, loose sexual behaviour, homosexuality, prostitution, but also issues of disobedience of children towards their parents or of workers towards management demanded clear answers. When Hitler spoke of God, evangelicals did not notice that he meant a nebulous 'providence' (*Vorsehung*) and that the religious connotations which they heard were absolutely not intended.

2. Evangelicals had been told to look for a 'new era', for the ushering in of the Kingdom of God. Now they felt that they were eye-witnesses of this almost cosmic event. Providence, or the God of history, was at work, and the national awakening (*Deutschland erwache!*) was similar to what awakened Christians attributed to their faith experience (*Erweckung*).

3. In this context the Jews played a significant role in the mindset of the evangelicals. In the present dispensation they were not God's favourite children, but under his wrath. God would use political leaders to lead them back to Palestine so that salvation history would come to its fulfilment.

These points clearly underline the danger of this concept of salvation history. It is, first of all, based on a false conception of the prophetic literature in the Hebrew Bible and the New Testament. Prophets are not 'foretellers' of the future, but people who proclaim here and now what God wants his people to do. Prophecy cannot be used to construct a meta-historical divine plan on the basis of prophetic 'predictions'.

Secondly, why would evangelicals assume that Jews had to undergo a time of tribulation while they were part of a political awakening at the same time and by the same mover of history? And why would the political awakening be the prime factor, the catalyst, in bringing about the tribulation?

Finally, this salvation history is constructed in order to give coherence to and make sense of human history. It is supposed to 'explain' the myriads of historical events. In the mindset of German evangelicals the Jews play three different roles in salvation history:

1. Before the Holocaust the Jews were under the wrath of God, therefore second-class citizens. Evangelicals felt that they were not responsible for what happened to Jews as this was God's business: he apparently used the state to reach his end with his erstwhile chosen people.

2. After the Holocaust and especially after the founding of the State of Israel, the Jews are respected as a people with whom God is directly dealing as they are again enjoying a homeland of their own. To support them and their State becomes a major religious duty.

3. Jews are nevertheless targets of missionary efforts. This is not only true of evangelicals in Germany but of the international evangelical community as well. In 1989 the most representative gathering of world-wide evangelicals took place in Manila. The 'Manila Manifesto' rejected the notion that the Jews had their own covenant which would make faith in Christ unnecessary. Christ, the Manifesto affirmed, is God's unique way to salvation, and no religion, including the Jewish religion, is an alternative to the gospel.

Salvation history, which is meant to be a coherent method to explain the integrity or the perfect wholeness of history as God had intended it, is open to many interpretations and misreadings. Walter Michaelis may serve as an example once more. He had after some manoeuvring been able to commit the Executive Committee of the evangelical organisation *Gnadauer Verband* against the 'Faith Movement *Deutsche Christen*' even though some associate members[21] left the fellowship and voluntarily recognised *Reichsbischof Müller*. In other words, Michaelis, similar to Künneth, was able to discern and make the correct decision. The same man, however, felt no unease when he wrote that the Nazi treatment of the Jews was in accord with the biblical tradition. The concept of salvation history made him a prisoner of the traditional interpretation when he discovered that the 'wrath-of-God' symbol was in agreement with the Nazi policy of eliminating 'Jewish elements' from German culture. It seems that the critical reading of history is more important than the pious reading of salvation history, even though one must also concede that, perhaps, both are not mutually exclusive but can support each other. The question remains as to the criteria. When in 1933 Michaelis and the youth organisation Christian Endeavour both thought that the boycott of Jewish businesses had been humane (*menschlich*), the question becomes so much more acute: which criteria will open our eyes so that we may see and act?

A Personal Story

It is my hope that Ian Randall, to whom this essay is dedicated in friendship, will appreciate particularly my concluding personal remarks. It is a story about my maternal grandfather, Wilhelm Deuster, who passed away three years before I was

---

[21] Notably the strong *Deutscher Gemeinschafts-Diakonie Verband*.

born so that I never knew him. But people still talked about him in the small town where I grew up so that on several occasions I was confronted with my grandfather. In 1950 a census was being taken and some kids from the local school were chosen to help folks fill out the forms. A friend and I were assigned a special street in town where people of low income lived who, in some cases, could neither read nor write. In one home a man told me that he had heard my grandfather say in the early 1930s that the Jewish people were going to return to their homeland to set up a state. 'Your grandfather was right', he concluded, 'look at the state of Israel.' As an eleven year old kid I was greatly impressed that this man still knew my grandfather and that my grandfather had made a prediction which had apparently been fulfilled.

Later I learned, too, that he had made other remarks which were astounding. As early as 1933 when my father, who had been trained to be an elementary school teacher, was thinking about joining the Nazi party in order to get a job, my grandfather advised his future son-in-law not to do so because he considered Hitler to be the Antichrist. A sales representative of a chemical company told me in the 1960s that, as a young businessman, he and my grandfather – who ran a drugstore – had often held conversations about the fate of the Jewish people and that my grandfather had always told him that no nation can touch God's eyeball without invoking the wrath of God.

When in 1936 a Jewish neighbour by the name of Karl Marx died, there was much consternation in the neighbourhood. In those days it was customary in that little town that the coffin with the body was placed in the home and that a procession was held from the home to the cemetery. Relatives, friends and neighbours would follow the coffin which would be placed on a horse-drawn carriage. In 1936, of course, the question for the neighbours was whether the authorities would react negatively when a so-called Aryan person would pay his last respect to a Jew. The neighbour right above was the publisher of the local newspaper. He came to my grandfather and said: '*Wilhelm, was tun wir?* – what are we going to do?' My grandfather replied: '*Franz, wir gehen* – we are going.' The two men were the only persons who had the courage to accompany their neighbour Karl Marx on his last journey from his home to the Jewish cemetery. Only a few months later my grandfather passed away himself.

In early January 1999, when I was in Jerusalem, I visited a lady in her early 90s in a nursing home, who was originally from my home town. After 1 April 1933, Klara Stern and her husband had decided to pack up and leave for Palestine. She could still remember my grandfather, called him a friend who had always talked to her and her family when they would walk by his store, and related to me that they would often hold conversations on religious topics. When he learned that she was to leave, he said, 'Klara, send me a picture postcard from the holy land.'

Why do I relate these stories? My grandfather, who had been a heavy drinker but was converted to the Christian Assembly in Wuppertal before moving to my home town just before the outbreak of the First World War in 1914, had apparently made the correct Christian response to a demonic system of government only weeks after it had been installed. He had resorted to traditional Christian language and called

Hitler the Antichrist. His criterion was the way the Nazis talked about and treated the Jews. He again resorted to biblical language when he identified the Jewish people as God's eyeball and argued that any provocative touching of that eyeball must have very serious consequences for the perpetrator. This example may demonstrate that an unsophisticated theology as that of my 'Darbyite' grandfather may nevertheless lead people to a correct response in a crisis situation, whereas a sophisticated and highly learned theology like that of Lutheran theologians Künneth and Michaelis may prove to be a total failure in real life situations. Having said this, I must hasten to add that the response of my grandfather was not enough. It lacked the political consequences that needed to be drawn in order to meet the demands of a crisis situation which came about through total political mismanagement and failure. Evangelicals still have to learn political lessons from their past.

CHAPTER 12

A Moment of Transformation: The European Baptist Federation and the Collapse of the Soviet Union and its European and Central Asian Empire, 1989–92

Keith G. Jones

Introduction

Historians may argue that it is still far too soon to come to definitive conclusions about the transformation of the 'countries of the peninsula'[1] at the end of the twentieth century. Nevertheless, Baptists in Europe, in common with many others, experienced the years 1989–92 as a pivotal period of political and economic change with many consequences which are still being worked out. Already, familiar terms of the 1980s are being forgotten or unknown to a generation born at the end of the twentieth century. I therefore take the trouble in footnotes to remind readers of some of the commonplace terms and realities we grew up with in post-war Europe, but which have already faded in the memory as we celebrate over twenty years of post-communist Europe. I try to indicate changes of names of cities and whilst using titles of countries pre- and post-1989 I seek to explain the changes as, with every passing year, people forget the order which existed from 1945 to 1989.

In the aftermath of the Second World War, Sir Winston Churchill, the British wartime premier, made a speech at Westminster College, Fulton, Missouri, in which he prophetically exclaimed,

> From Stettin on the Baltic to Trieste on the Adriatic, an Iron Curtain has descended on the continent. Behind that line, lie all the capitals of the ancient states of central and eastern Europe –Warsaw, Berlin, Prague, Budapest, Belgrade, Bucharest and Sofia ... This is certainly not the liberated Europe we sought to build up.[2]

Churchill may have omitted the historic Baltic nations of Estonia, Latvia and Lithuania[3] from his litany, but his overall judgement was correct. The Union of

---

[1] Norman Davies, *Europe: A History* (London: Pimlico, 1997), 46-59, expounds the idea of what today we call 'Europe' as basically a peninsula of Asia.

[2] Winston S. Churchill, address at Westminster College, Fulton Missouri, 5 March 1946.

[3] Countries which had their own history before being absorbed into the Russian Empire; on Lithuania, see Norman Davies, *Forgotten Kingdoms* (London: Allen Lane, 2011), ch. 5, 229-308.

Soviet Socialist Republics (USSR), wartime member of the Allied powers in the fight against fascism, was given a sphere of influence over central and eastern Europe, drawn up at a meeting between the Allied leaders, Stalin,[4] Roosevelt and Churchill in Yalta, Crimea, during a crucial summit in World War II. There they sought to plot the rebuilding of Europe after the defeat of the Axis powers (Germany, Italy and their allies). After the capitulation of the German Third Reich, the communist leaders Stalin, Khrushchev and their successors rigorously imposed a political model on the Baltic states, central and eastern Europe which turned out not to be supportive of the freedom of religion and in many instances regarded Baptists as particularly insidious communities which had to be suppressed.[5] Contact between Baptists in western and northern Europe[6] and the Baptists of central and eastern Europe was severely limited. Baptist pastors were imprisoned, churches closed, and activities restricted in lands under the control of the communists.

Despite these restrictions, the European Baptist Federation (EBF)[7] sought to hold together Baptist communities throughout east, central, south and west Europe. Successive presidents and general secretaries of the EBF sought to maintain contact and were able to make visits to Baptist leaders in the communist states from time to time.[8] However, it is fair to state that contact with churches and their leaders outside of the main cities was limited and that there were great difficulties supplying Christian literature to many communities.[9] The EBF, led by people such as British Baptist leaders Ernest A. Payne[10] and David S. Russell,[11] made regular visits behind

---

[4] On Stalin, see Helen Rappaport, *Joseph Stalin: A Biographical Companion* (Santa Barbara, CA: ABC-Clio, 1999).

[5] From 1945 until 1990 it was not generally possible to record and report on these communities. With the collapse of communism, archives and records have become available and a young generation of Baptist scholars nurtured by Ian M. Randall are now researching and recounting the story of these years. See, for instance, Keith G. Jones and Ian M. Randall (eds) *Counter-Cultural Communities: Baptistic Life in Twentieth-Century Europe* (Milton Keynes: Paternoster, 2008).

[6] In order to avoid complications of language I will generally use the term western Europe hereafter, by which I mean the Scandinavian and Nordic countries, the isles (Ireland and Great Britain), France, West Germany and West Berlin, the Benelux countries, the Iberian peninsula, Austria, and Italy.

[7] The European Baptist Federation (EBF) was formed in 1949; see Keith G. Jones, *The European Baptist Federation: A Case Study in European Baptist Interdependency 1950–2006* (Milton Keynes: Paternoster, 2009).

[8] For ease I shall refer to 'communist states' and 'communist countries', by which I mean the USSR and the nations in Europe within its sphere of influence from 1945 to 1990.

[9] For a partial account of one family from Lithuania, see Keith G. Jones, 'Baptists and Anabaptists Revisited', in Anthony R. Cross and Nicholas J. Wood (eds.), *Exploring Baptist Origins* (Oxford: Regent's Park College, 2009), 139-55.

[10] On Payne, see W.M.S. West, *To Be a Pilgrim: A Memoir of Ernest A. Payne* (Guildford: Lutterworth Press, 1983).

[11] David S. Russell, *In Journeyings Often* (London: n.p. [but Baptist Union of Great Britain and Northern Ireland], 1981).

the 'Iron Curtain'[12] and sought to meet government officials to secure alleviation of some of the worst circumstances of oppression.

Within the EBF a programme was developed to provide written materials in various Slavic languages. This 'Eurolit'[13] initiative was spearheaded in practical action by the British Baptist minister, Alec Gilmore.[14] The minutes of the EBF Executive Committee regularly recorded aid projects focused on books and translations for Baptist communities in communist countries. So, for instance, the 1985[15] list included a proposal of 40,000 West German Deutschmark (hereafter DM) for specific books and translations, a photocopy machine for Czechoslovakia[16] costing DM5,000 and Bibles for the Baptists in the USSR at DM10,000.[17] At the same meeting it was agreed that David Russell, as chairman of the Books and Translations Committee, would travel with two seminary lecturers, Theo van der Laan (Netherlands) and Christian Wolf (East Germany), and make a tour of countries in eastern Europe to discover what other needs there were.[18]

Despite many efforts, opportunities for western leaders to visit the east of Europe were few, while those who could come from communist countries to meetings or for education in western Europe were severely limited.[19] Occasionally, the communist authorities would agree an unexpected action, so the EBF Executive was delighted to

---

[12] The phrase 'Iron Curtain' became commonplace to describe the countries in the Soviet Union sphere of influence between 1945 and 1989.

[13] On 'Eurolit', see J.H.Y. Briggs (ed.), *A Dictionary of European Baptist Life and Thought* (Milton Keynes: Paternoster, 2009), 177.

[14] Alec Gilmore remains actively involved in developing theological expertise in central and eastern Europe. He is a Senior Research Fellow of the International Baptist Theological Seminary (IBTS), Prague, and archivist to the EBF.

[15] EBF Executive Minutes, 31 July 1984, Hamburg, 2. EBF Archive Collection B Box 808. The archives are currently held in the IBTS Archive, Jenerálka, Prague 6, Czech Republic.

[16] The country of Czechoslovakia came into being as a result of the collapse of the Austro-Hungarian Empire at the end of World War I. It consisted of Bohemia, Moravia, a part of Silesia and Slovakia. It came to an end in 1992 when the Slovakians decided to create their own free and democratic Slovakia, thus leaving Bohemia, Moravia and part of Silesia, the remaining constituent parts of Czechoslovakia, to form the Czech Republic. The famous dissident and playwright, Vaclav Havel, was first President of post-communist Czechoslovakia and then first President of the Czech Republic.

[17] The West German Deutschmark existed from the partition of Germany at the end of the Second World War until the introduction of the European Union currency, the Euro, in 2002. The Euro is currently used by seventeen countries within the European Union. At the reunification of Germany in 1990 the Deutschmark replaced the Ostmark as the currency of the former East Germany (GDR).

[18] EBF Executive Minutes, 31 July 1984, Hamburg, 5.

[19] Some students from Yugoslavia, Poland and the Czech Republic were allowed to study at the Baptist Theological Seminary (BTS), Rüschlikon, in neutral Switzerland. See the forthcoming history of BTS/IBTS by Carol Woodfin. A small number of Russian students were allowed to study at Spurgeon's College, London, and at Bristol Baptist College.

learn in May 1985 that the USSR authorities in Estonia had agreed that 2,000 hymn books in Estonian could be imported.[20]

Glasnost

In the end-of-year (1988) Christmas message to 'Christians all over the world', the leadership of the All-Union Council of Evangelical Christians-Baptists (AUECB) in the USSR referred to this thaw in attitudes of the communist authorities, noting the celebration of 1,000 years of Christianity in Russia,[21] together with numerous gifts of Bibles from the Baptist World Alliance (BWA). The message continued that AUECB leaders could 'see that the Lord is opening new doors in order that sinners may accept [the Lord] ... as their personal saviour'.[22] Another dramatic move occurred in 1989 when the government of the USSR permitted the printing of a new 'authorised' Russian translation of the Bible in an initial print run of 500,000, to be sold through state bookshops. It was the first new translation of the Bible to be published in the USSR since 1917.[23]

Just as remarkable to the AUECB leadership was that the Soviet authorities allowed women members of Baptist churches to engage in social service, and seventy women from Moscow Central Baptist Church were serving in hospitals bringing comfort to those who were ill.[24] The work focused on the Kashinko Mental Hospital, Moscow, and the atheist hospital director commented, 'You have brought us a new climate' as he praised the women for their work. This initiative was followed by developments at other hospitals in Moscow and in St Petersburg.[25] Within a year the AUECB was reporting that five churches were engaged in hospital work and seven working in orphanages. In the previous year twelve new churches had been established and sixteen churches had opened new 'prayer houses'. April 1989 saw the Leningrad authorities release an 'Old Believers' building, not used for Christian worship since the 1920s, for Baptists to establish a church there which they called the 'Temple of the Gospel'. The building style was Orthodox with onion-shaped domes. Sergei Nikolaev, the Regional Baptist Superintendent, confidently predicted that a congregation of between 500 and 700 people would soon meet there. He estimated the cost of restoration of the building at one million roubles.[26] The year 1988 saw 2,300 baptisms in churches belonging to the AUECB.[27]

---

[20] EBF Executive Minutes, May 1985, Lisbon, 2.

[21] This refers to the tsarist Empire, encompassing what today are separate countries such as Russia, Belarus and Ukraine.

[22] AUECB Christmas Message, 25 December 1988. Copy in EBF Archive Section D Box 12.

[23] European Baptist Press Service (EBPS) 89:055. EBF Archive Section D Box 12.

[24] EBPS 88:169. EBF Archive Section D Box 11.

[25] In communist times St Petersburg was called Leningrad. It reverted to the original name after the collapse of communism in Russia.

[26] EBPS 89:98. EBF Archive Section D Box 12.

[27] AUECB News Release. EBF Archive Box 91.

It also proved possible, under freedoms being offered to the AUECB, to contemplate that pastors from the USSR could attend the Summer Institute of Theological Education (SITE) which was held each year at the Baptist Seminary in Rüschlikon. SITE Director, Dr Harry Moore, commented, 'this will be the first time that SITE has enrolled a group of students from the USSR'.[28] At that time the only theological training available for Baptist pastors in the USSR was a correspondence course organised out of the AUECB headquarters in Moscow.

An element of the new '*glasnost*' (openness) policy of the USSR leadership, which would have repercussions for the next twenty years, was the granting of exit visas to Russians of Germanic extraction. Two hundred years previously the tsars had appealed for foreign help and many Germans had answered the appeal. In the 1840s Johann Gerhard Oncken and his colleagues had participated in a spiritual awakening in this group and churches had been formed. Others of German extraction had been caught in the Soviet sphere of influence after the defeat of the Nazis and had been forcibly moved east at the end of the Second World War. Large numbers of them had been moved to eastern Russia, but now many, including Mennonites and Baptists, were given permission to leave the USSR. This became a significant issue for West German Baptists. By June 1989 the flow of people was estimated to be 1,000 per week. Günter Wieske, Director of Immigrant work for the German Baptist Union, commented, 'our Government calculates that this year (1989) over 350,000 will enter the FRG [West Germany] ... the magnificent opportunity we German Baptists face is that as many as 15 to 25% of these "*Aussiedler*" (late immigrants)[29] are Baptists. During this year alone about 15,000 Baptist immigrants will enter our country to live. This is a staggering figure, representing undoubtedly the greatest European Baptist migration of all times'.[30] He posited that by 1992 there would be more Russian-German Baptists in West Germany than German Baptists. The immigrants were to form their own Baptist churches, establish a seminary and present continuing challenges of integration into German Baptist life for many years to come, having a different church culture and emphasising different theological opinions to the Germany Baptist community.

In other communist countries the iron grip on Baptists was also being relaxed. Leaders in Poland and Czechoslovakia were allowed to travel to the west, which they had not been able to do for many years.[31] The Polish delegation included Konstanty Wiazowski, who would be prominent in EBF affairs in the 1990s, and Zygmunt Karel, who would later found and serve as first Rector of the Evangelical Seminary

---

[28] EBPS 89:051. EBF Archive Section D Box 12.

[29] The Federal Republic of Germany (West Germany) in its constitution, paragraph 116, allowed anyone who 'has been admitted to the territory of the German Reich within the boundaries of December 31 1937' the right of return. Nine million people were involved from central and eastern Europe and a further nine million from East Germany whom Stalin moved. Issues of compensation continue to be discussed.

[30] EBPS 89:122. EBF Archive Section D Box 12.

[31] EBPS 89:03. EBF Archive Section D Box 12.

in Wroclaw,[32] Poland. In Katowice, Jerzy Rogaczeswki[33] created a Christian music group and the authorities allowed the group to go into the local prison and perform gospel concerts.

At the same EBF meeting, planning[34] began for the 1989 Congress with the bold decision to look for a venue 'behind the Iron Curtain' in either Hungary or Yugoslavia.[35] Eventually, the decision was made to hold the 1989 Congress in the Sportstadium, Budapest, as Baptist Unions in communist countries judged that the authorities would be more likely to permit travel to Hungary than Yugoslavia.[36] The movement of currency from eastern European countries to pay for the delegates to the Congress would also be easier as Hungary was in the Warsaw Pact[37] and Yugoslavia was not. So the scene was set for the EBF 1989 Congress which was to be held in what turned out to be the pivotal year in the reconstruction of post-war Europe into post-communist Europe.

Despite many efforts, opportunities for western leaders to visit the east of Europe were still few and those who could come from communist countries to meetings of the EBF or for education in western Europe were severely limited.[38] However, in his report as General Secretary to the EBF Executive in April 1987, Knud Wümpelmann[39] wrote,

> The breakthrough of new hope which has caused the greatest interest all over the world is the democratization process going on in the Soviet Union. This process is felt also in

---

[32] For details of the seminary, see <http://www.ewst.pl/en/>, accessed 18 July 2012. The seminary was founded in 1990 and is now recognised by the Polish government and is a European Union Erasmus institution.

[33] Jerzy Rogaczewski went to McMaster Divinity College in Canada for theological formation. He has succeeded his father as pastor in Katowice, is a regional minister in Poland and has served two terms on the IBTS Board of Trustees. He continues to use a guitar in his music ministry.

[34] EBF Executive Minutes, May 1985, 10.

[35] In the transition to post communist politics in Europe the communist state of Yugoslavia, after a time of civil war, divided into the republics of Bosnia and Herzegovina, Croatia, Macedonia (see n. 93 below), Montenegro, Serbia and Slovenia, together with the United Nations/European Union specially administered area of Kosovo.

[36] EBF Executive Minutes, October 1985, Prague, 2.

[37] The Warsaw Pact was an organisation drawing together the USSR, Bulgaria, Romania, Czechoslovakia, Poland and East Germany in a defence alliance over against the North Atlantic Treaty Organisation (NATO) of western Europe, Canada and the USA. The Warsaw Pact effectively imploded post 1990.

[38] Some students from Yugoslavia, Poland and the Czech Republic were allowed to study at BTS in neutral Switzerland. See the forthcoming history of BTS/IBTS by Carol Woodfin. A small number of Russian students were allowed to study at Spurgeon's College and Bristol Baptist College.

[39] On the Dane Knud Wümpelmann, see Bent Hylleberg, 'Knud Wümpelmann: General Secretary of the European Baptist Federation and President of the Baptist World Alliance', *Journal of European Baptist Studies* 2.3 (May, 2002), 5-20.

the churches. The USSR has opened up for more basic Christian literature, imprisoned leaders ... have been released... 'glasnost' has become a new internationally known word.[40]

Wümpelmann expressed this hope, but perhaps no one saw the extent of the change which would come over the succeeding five years.

Change was occurring throughout central and eastern Europe, sweeping aside communism and opening up the possibility of social democracy. In January 1989, János Papp,[41] then a student at the Baptist Seminary in Budapest, commented, 'so many doors are opening in Hungary we can hardly keep up with them'.[42] It was reported to the EBF that on 7 January 1989, forty-five Hungarian Baptists met in Budapest to establish a Sunday School Board. Later that day seventeen young people from all over Hungary organised a Hungarian National Baptist Youth Committee in Budapest. Work amongst children and young people by Baptists had been forbidden in communist countries, but now it proved possible to create national organisations in the climate of the communist authorities either relaxing existing laws or, as was the case in Hungary, introducing new laws[43] which made such things possible.[44] János Viczián, the President of the Hungarian Baptists, commented, 'the new laws of association and assembly allow us to move forward in new directions'.[45] Amazingly, as a Baptist leader, Viczián had been elected to the communist Hungarian Parliament. To the astonishment of many in the EBF, on 15 January 1989, Hungarian state television broadcast a short segment of worship from the Jozsef Street Baptist Church in Budapest in a service commemorating Martin Luther King, Jr.[46] This was judged to be a first for Baptists in communist eastern Europe.[47]

---

[40] Report of Knud Wümpelmann to the EBF Executive, April 1987. EBF Archive Section B Box 808.

[41] Papp was elected President of the Hungarian Baptists in 2012.

[42] Reported in EBPS 02:89. EBF Archive Section D Box 12.

[43] It is salutary to note that in 2012 the Hungarian government is being criticised within the European Union for the introduction of more restrictive laws on religious liberty. Perhaps 1988–2011 has been a golden period for religious freedom in Hungary?

[44] EBPS 02:89. EBF Archive Section D Box 12.

[45] EBPS 02:89. EBF Archive Section D Box 12.

[46] Dr M.L. King, Jr, was an African American Baptist preacher who led the US Civil Rights Movement in the 1960s and was assassinated in 1968. 15 January is a state holiday in the USA in his honour.

[47] EBPS 02:89. EBF Archive Section D Box 12.

The 1989 Budapest Congress

As has been noted, the EBF Executive took the key decision to hold its five-yearly[48] conference of member bodies in July 1989 to the east of the 'Iron Curtain'. Even though the EBF General Secretary could address the Executive in a hopeful spirit, nevertheless it was unclear quite how this bold experiment would turn out. Would it be possible for people in neighbouring communist states to attend? Would ordinary Baptists from western Europe be willing to obtain visas and pass through this significant wall of ideology and travel restrictions erected across Europe? The member bodies of the EBF at that time were Austria, Belgium, Bulgaria, Czechoslovakia,[49] Denmark, European Baptist Convention,[50] Finland (Swedish speaking), Finland (Finnish speaking), France, West Germany, East Germany, Great Britain,[51] Hungary, Italy, the Netherlands, Norway, Poland, Portugal, Romania, Scotland, Spain, Sweden, Switzerland, USSR, Wales and Yugoslavia; twenty-seven in total,[52] and all previous conferences had been held in western Europe.[53] Nevertheless, the EBF Executive stepped forward in faith and decided to hold this event behind the so-called 'Iron Curtain'; a bold decision which turned out to herald a moment of transformation for the EBF,[54] occurring on the back of momentous changes in Europe. It was agreed there would be a special encouragement to the

---

[48] EBF Congresses occurred every five years until the 1994 Congress in Lillehammer, Norway. This was a marvellous occasion in terms of attendance, but a financial disaster. The EBF Council could not contemplate a further event, despite an attempt to plan one in Bratislava, and later in Wroclaw, referred to as 'the Congress that never was'. The last major EBF event was Amsterdam 400 in 2009 when 400 years of Baptist life and witness was celebrated. This was a significantly smaller scale event which required funding from the EBF reserves.

[49] Czechoslovakia was to throw off its communist government in the 'Velvet Revolution' of October 1989. By 1992 the post-First World War construct of Czechoslovakia had become two independent sovereign states, cf. n. 16 above.

[50] A group of English language churches often founded by US service personnel principally in West Germany and Austria in 1957. Since the end of communism the number of member churches has grown rapidly and expanded throughout Europe and the Middle East. In 2003 the Convention was renamed the International Baptist Convention; see <www.ibc-churches.org/>, accessed 23 July 2012.

[51] The Baptist Union covering churches in England and parts of Wales was called the Baptist Union of Great Britain and Ireland, though Scotland, Ireland and Wales all had their own Unions. The Union is today called the Baptist Union of Great Britain and is a member of the Fellowship of Baptists in Britain and Ireland as well as the EBF.

[52] Details in EBF Directory, December 1988; copy in possession of the author.

[53] Recent conferences had been Brighton, England, in 1981 and Hamburg, Germany, in 1985.

[54] Until the 1990s the EBF consisted of the Baptist Unions in west and central Europe and the All-Union Council of Evangelical Christian Baptists; cf. n. 7 above.

Unions in eastern Europe to send young people[55] to this Congress and, as it turned out, this was an important development.

As the event drew near, Hungarian Baptists, who had not been allowed to attend the previous congresses in the West, became apprehensive about the challenge they had taken on. Sandor Gereszenyi, editor of their newspaper 'The Peace Messenger', commented that 'in the past we have always been on the receiving end of anything which was done by Baptists in the west. This time it is different: we must organize and we must give, and that is new for some of us and was frightening when we began.'[56]

The Congress theme, 'Come and See What God has Done' was based on Psalm 66 and chosen under the direction of retiring EBF General Secretary, Knud Wümpelmann.[57] A special hymn was composed using the text of the Psalm. The Congress programme was planned by a committee headed by Dr David Lagergen and with a local arrangements committee formed with Emil Kiss as chair. As this local committee worked at the organisation of the Congress, it struggled with inflation in Hungary which increased to 120% in 1988.[58]

By January 1989 the local arrangements committee reported that choirs and soloists from several countries had already signed up to participate. Pal Beharka was appointed musical director for the Congress and announced the booking of choirs from Czechoslovakia, with 100 members, together with choirs from East Germany, Romania and the USSR. The Hungarians themselves had a fine musical tradition and their national Baptist choir and a Baptist brass band also participated.[59]

The enthusiasm for a Congress 'behind the Iron Curtain' was noted at this time, with the AUCECB in the USSR promising to contribute 50,000 roubles, a significant sum which, they assured the EBF, would easily be transferred to Congress funds in Hungary.[60]

The event, held from 26 to 30 July 1989, was a great success. On arrival the delegates were greeted by the Hungarian Baptist brass band and people dressed in national costumes. Though the small Hungarian Baptist Union had faced challenges in staffing the Congress and with registration software, Gábor Viczian, in charge of the computer registration system, was able to confirm that forty-seven countries had been represented and that the number of delegates had been the highest ever. It proved possible for Baptists from Bulgaria (over forty attended, which was seen as

---

[55] The designation of a young person in Baptist life is difficult, but the age group has been assumed to be 16–30.

[56] EBPS: 09:89, 16. EBF Archive Section D Box 12.

[57] Hylleberg, 'Knud Wümpelmann'.

[58] Report of the local committee chair, Emil Kiss, to the EBF Executive in Rüschlikon, April 1988, 6; EBF Archive Section B Box 808.

[59] EBPS 01:89, 3. EBF Archive Section D Box 12.

[60] This was perhaps a high point of the ability of AUCECB and its successor, the Euro-Asiatic Federation (EAF) to contribute funds to an EBF venture. Since the collapse of communism, EAF and its member Unions have struggled to contribute to EBF general funding and special events, such as Amsterdam 400 in 2009.

amazing given the high level of repression by the communist authorities in that country), Czechoslovakia, the German Democratic Republic (East Germany), Poland, Romania,[61] the USSR and Yugoslavia to attend. Western European Baptists also attended in their usual numbers.

At the opening session astonished delegates heard Mátyás Szűrös, President of the communist Hungarian National Assembly, praising Baptist churches for their democratic system of government, suggesting they might become models for the creation of necessary structures of a new society. He went on to say that Baptists were spokespeople of Christian love and forgiveness, tolerance and justice.[62]

For European Baptists, being in Budapest in that critical summer of 1989 was transformative. The Congress passed a resolution calling upon all Baptist churches 'to contribute creatively and constructively toward building the "House of Europe" [the phrase "our common European home" had been used by Gorbachev, the then President of the USSR] in which the different cultural and religious traditions may reside in an atmosphere of justice and peace'.[63] The opportunity for so many musicians to be present was exceptional; the Hungarian Baptist brass band was reported to have over 150 instrumentalists. A Baptist choir from Moscow, which had recently had the privilege of performing in the Bolshoi Theatre, participated in Budapest under the leadership of Evgenii Goncharenko.[64]

Peter Barber, who became EBF President at the close of the Congress, summed up some of the key features of the Budapest Congress in a circular letter of 14 August 1989:

> The numbers attending far exceeded all that had gone before. In Brighton (1979) there were 2,200 delegates; in Hamburg (1984) 2,300. In Budapest the total soared to 5,212.[65] Added to this it was the most widely-representative Congress we have had with two-thirds of the delegates from Eastern Europe and Bulgaria represented amongst us for the first time.[66]

The whole event had concluded with a Billy Graham evangelistic rally in the open air sports stadium adjacent to the Conference Centre, where an estimated 90,000 people had participated from all Christian traditions in Hungary.[67]

---

[61] Romania, sometimes known as Rumania. The Kingdom of Romania emerged in 1859. It has a Latin-type language, unlike its Slav language neighbours.

[62] Taken from notes of the author made at the time. Personal papers.

[63] Taken from notes of the author made at the time. Personal papers.

[64] EBPS 89:143. EBF Archive Section D Box 12.

[65] On the EBF Congress at Lillehammer in 1994, see above n. 48. The deficit was later removed from the EBF accounts by taking money out of the IBTS reserves as a gift to the EBF.

[66] Letter of Peter Barber, EBF President, to member Unions, 14 August 1989. EBF Archive Box 809.

[67] Document on the EBF Congress 1989, EBF Archive Section B Box 809.

Throughout their time in Budapest, delegates were constantly aware that rapid changes were taking place in the majority of regimes in eastern Europe. No-one could fail to observe the atmosphere and expectation of change which were in the air, referred to in conversations and prayed about in small groups. Yet the fact that in the next four months so much was to happen was beyond the wildest imaginings of the delegates.

The Re-Shaping of Europe (September–December 1989)

The Congress delegates dispersed from Budapest into events which then moved very rapidly. No sooner had the Congress finished than the Polish communist government invited the reformist Solidarity[68] movement to form a government under their own continuing communist constitutional and state presidency. A devout Roman Catholic, Tadeusz Mazowiecki, became premier and attended meetings of the Warsaw Pact.[69] At the same time Hungarian political life was being reconstructed and the Protestant churches in East Germany were campaigning for political change. Signs of decay of the '*ancien* communist regimes' were everywhere.

On 23 October, the 33rd anniversary of the Hungarian uprising,[70] the communist Hungarian People's Republic was abolished. On 9 November, East German border guards stood to one side as East and West Berliners began to demolish the hated Berlin Wall. The East German communist government had, effectively, caved in. On 17 November, great crowds of students gathered in Wenceslas Square, Prague, to demonstrate against the ruling regime. A student was killed by the police but within a week the dissident playwright, Vaclav Havel,[71] and the former premier, Alexander Dubček, a communist liberaliser and author of the 1968 'Prague Spring', stood together on a veranda in the square as students exclaimed 'Havel for the *Hrad* [Prague Castle]'. The Prague 'Velvet Revolution' had happened. Timothy Garton Ash, a noted historian, commented that 'In Poland it took ten years (Solidarity), in Hungary ten months, in East Germany ten weeks, in Czechoslovakia ten days.'[72]

The change that was in the air at the Congress in Budapest had largely come to pass in key states by Christmas 1989. At their annual Conference in October, the Czechoslovak Baptists drew up a series of 'reminders' to those in the nation working on a new constitution. These 'reminders' included guaranteeing the equal rights of all churches, abolition of discrimination against Baptist children in public schools,

---

[68] *Solidarność* (Solidarity) was created by workers in the Gdansk shipyard in 1980. It was the first non-communist trade union in eastern Europe. Led by Lech Wałęsa it spearheaded the move towards a non-communist Poland.

[69] On the Warsaw Pact, see n. 37 above.

[70] For this sequence of events I have drawn on Norman Davies, *Europe: A History* (Oxford: Oxford University Press, 1996), 1123.

[71] For the European vision of Havel, see his collected speeches, *Towards a Civil Society* (Prague: Lidové Novine, 1994).

[72] Timothy G. Ash, *We the People: Revolutions of 1989 witnessed in Warsaw, Budapest, Berlin and Prague* (Cambridge: Cambridge University Press, 1990), 78.

abolition of capital punishment and permission for Baptists to train as teachers.[73] The East German government formally opened the borders to the west on 9 November, and on 12 November Baptist churches in West Berlin hosted their neighbours from East Berlin. At Charlottenburg, Baptist church people turned up from East Berlin and there was much emotion 'and tears, lots of tears'.[74]

There was violence in Bulgaria and Romania, but the communist regimes disintegrated there as well. It was more difficult in the old USSR but the Baltic States rose up against communist USSR oppression and essentially, by non-violent protest, overthrew the Soviet oppressor. A chain of free Baltic people, perhaps as many as two million, was formed from Tallinn to the Polish border. Ancient states claimed their liberty and the Soviet oppressor stood to one side. The Latvian Supreme Soviet adopted a Declaration of Independence in May 1990, but this was disregarded by Moscow. In March 1991 a popular referendum effectively declared independence. The so-called 'Singing Revolution' led to a formal declaration of Estonian statehood in August 1991. Lithuania suffered the death of citizens from the Soviet oppressors, but by 17 September 1991 it had been accepted into the United Nations as an independent state. The Baltic States were joined by Armenia, Georgia, Azerbaijan, Ukraine, Belarus, Kazakhstan, Kyrgystan, Uzbekistan, Turkmenistan and Tajikistan. By October 1991 the old communist empire was no more. There may have been some political alliances, as between Russia, Ukraine and Belarus, but the central Asian states were carving out their own future, and the Baltic States and the *Vysegrad* states[75] had applied to join NATO and then the European Union.[76]

A Change of General Secretary

The Council of the EBF had chosen Karl Heinz Walter, a West German[77] pastor, as successor to Knud Wümpelmann who was about to retire from the post and to assume the Presidency of the Baptist World Alliance.[78] Walter could hardly have

---

[73] Minutes of the Czechoslovak Annual Baptist Conference, 13–14 October 1989. Copy in possession of the author.

[74] Report from the Rev. Jim Smith who was a CBF Missionary in Berlin and a member of the church at that time.

[75] Czech Republic, Slovakia, Hungary and Poland.

[76] The European Union admitted the Czech Republic, Estonia, Hungary, Latvia, Lithuania, Poland, Slovakia and Slovenia in 2004. Croatia is due to become part of the EU. Armenia, Macedonia, Serbia and Ukraine all seek membership.

[77] As part of the Yalta agreement, the Allied Powers had divided Germany into two with East Germany under Soviet influence and West Germany as a democratic republic, but initially with zones under the control of the allied powers USA, Great Britain and France. Gradually West Germany was allowed to run its own affairs, though armies from the allied powers remained to protect the country. The capital city, Berlin, was likewise divided into zones under the control of the four allied powers.

[78] A.W. Wardin, Jr, and R.V. Pierard, 'The New World, 1988–95', in R. Pierard (ed.), *Baptists Together in Christ, 1905–2005: A Hundred-Year History of the Baptist World*

imagined the pressures he would face from the moment he acceded to office with the rapid changes in the situation of central and eastern Europe. Suddenly liberated from the long oppression of communist atheistic regimes, the Baptists were presented with profound challenges and opportunities. Religious freedom was suddenly available but the collapse of controlled economies led to very difficult winters in 1989 and 1990 for countries such as Bulgaria and Romania. Humanitarian relief on a scale never before attempted by the EBF had to be mobilised. On 15 November 1989 BWA General Secretary, Denton Lotz, expressed the excitement and the challenges of the moment in a letter to Walter.

> The historic and unbelievable events in East Berlin and East Germany must bring much joy to your heart and that of all German people. Who could have believed that such things could have happened in so short a time! And to think that even in Bulgaria the old leader has been toppled ... I believe it is important now to go to Bulgaria to encourage our brethren and to tell the government that we cannot endure any longer having non-Baptists put in as pastors of our churches and the time is ripe for a convention.[79]

The converse side of this was that some of the smaller Baptist Unions in the south of Europe felt neglected and ignored, leading to tension within the EBF. So the President of the Italian Baptists, Paulo Spanu, wrote to Karl Heinz Walter in May 1990 expressing a concern that he and Italian Baptists were experiencing 'progressive marginalization'[80] as events unfolded.

Baptist Response-Europe

From the EBF Congress in Budapest until December 1989, communist governments in central Europe collapsed at an amazing speed and it was apparent to the EBF leadership that impressive opportunities and possible great needs were presented from Berlin to Kiev, from Tallinn to Dubrovnik. As a result, it was agreed to hold an 'East Europe consultation' at the conference centre in Dorfweil, West Germany, in January 1990, which led to the founding of Baptist Response-Europe (BR-E). Working out how to do this was not easy. Denton Lotz, the BWA General Secretary, wrote to out-going EBF General Secretary, Knud Wümpelmann, on 17 October 1989, in answer to a letter from the EBF of 3 October 1989, expressing support for the proposal that

---

Alliance World Alliance – a Global History 1905–2005 (Falls Church, VA: Baptist World Alliance, 2005), esp. 235-274.

[79] Letter from Denton Lotz to Karl Heinz Walter, 15 November 1989. EBF Archive Section B Box 809.

[80] Letter of Paulo Spanu to Karl Heinz Walter, 22 May 1990. EBF Archive Section B Box 809.

> There should be a meeting of Baptist agencies concerned about coordinating efforts for the Soviet Union. You are exactly right concerning overlapping of requests etc. On our recent trip there we saw the problem with a rush of para-church organizations coming in and with no co-ordination.[81]

At Dorfweil, Baptist leaders from Bulgaria, Czechoslovakia, the German Democratic Republic, Hungary, Poland, Romania and the Soviet Union met with representatives from Baptist 'contributing organizations'.[82] Speaking at the meeting, Denton Lotz noted that a conference had been convened in London after the First World War to plan European Relief and he hoped that this meeting would have a similar broad vision.[83] A coordination committee was established consisting of Archie Goldie, soon to be succeeded by Paul Montacute (Director of Baptist World Aid), G. Keith Parker (Southern Baptist Convention-International Mission Board [SBC-IMB]) to represent mission agencies working in Europe and Karl Heinz Walter (EBF General Secretary). The immediate list of requests for help amounted to over $6 million!

As a result of the collapse of the communist economic structures, great concern developed about the ability of people in Romania, parts of Russia, the new Baltic States, Bulgaria and Poland to survive the winter with a severe lack of basic food and fuel.[84] Karl Heinz Walter reported to the EBF Council in Varna, Bulgaria, in September 1991:

> When we had visited Romania and Bulgaria at the end of August and beginning of September (1990), we clearly noticed what was coming up and started to plan for this programme. We are very happy, although this has become a very heavy extra burden for the office, that meanwhile ten thousands of parcels [of food and clothing] could be sent and many more will be sent in the coming months.[85]

In the period January–September 1990 over DM1 million was spent on food parcels, clothing and other essential aids. Walter expressed the fear that as events unfolded in the USSR it might also be necessary to address issues of food distribution in that very large and unravelling territory. The Romanian leadership wrote a special letter of appreciation to the EBF Council in Varna.

> In the name of all our Baptist churches and families that received food parcels we thank you from the bottom of our hearts ... We appreciate the spiritual way the Federation

---

[81] Letter from Denton Lotz to Knud Wümpelmann, 17 October 1989. EBF Archive Section B Box 809.

[82] EBPS 01:90. EBF Archive Section D Box 12.

[83] EBPS 90:003. EBF Archive Section D Box 12.

[84] Baptist Response – Europe (BR-E) Report to EBF Council, De Bron, Dalfsen, Netherlands, document 3, September 1990 (Hamburg: EBF, 1990).

[85] BR-E report to the EBF Council, Varna, Bulgaria, document 3, September 1991 (Hamburg: EBF, 1991).

acted toward the Eastern European countries, and we are looking forward to a greater future cooperation with you.[86]

By the time of the EBF Council in High Leigh, England, in September 1992, the situation had developed to such a point that Walter acknowledged it was now impossible to know the full extent of the partnerships between the USA, Canada, western Europe and the former communist zone. He commented that

> some of the Scandinavian countries have done an immense programme of providing food for the Baltic countries, and for some other countries at the beginning of the year, and we know that the Hungarian Baptist Union had an intensive programme first for the Romanians and then, especially with the beginning of the war in Yugoslavia, for refugees crossing over from Yugoslavia to Hungary.[87]

János Viczián reported in 1991 that over 15,000 people had already crossed from Yugoslavia to Hungary and that pastors in eastern Hungary were looking for help to support refugees.[88]

The EBF Council was very concerned about the way civil war was unfolding in Yugoslavia, and Sime Orcic was invited to address the Council on this topic. He reported that thirty-two churches were in conflict zones and that many had mixed ethnicity, which made them feel very vulnerable.[89]

The Hungarian Baptists were to continue their commitment to humanitarian work which was later to develop into Hungarian Baptist Aid, with specialist teams and a rapid response group able to get to disasters across the world within twenty-four hours.[90]

In Varna, Bulgaria, the emergence of the state of Moldova was discussed. Representatives from Romania asked the Baptist Unions in western Europe to urge their governments to recognise this new state which wished for ties with Romania rather than the former Soviet Union countries. Yet Wiard Popkes[91] expressed anxiety in making a hasty decision at this time and asked for further reflection on the complex issues involved. Moldova joined the Council of Europe and looked, later, towards membership of the European Union. It was to become an interesting

---

[86] The letter was signed by Vasile A. Talos, Nic Gheorgita, Vasile Talpos, Beniamin Poplacean and Iosif Stefanuti. A change in the Romanian presidency under Paul Negrut some years later led to Romania pulling back from involvement with the EBF. This situation was reversed in the mid-2000s with the election of Professor Otniel Bunaciu to the presidency of the Union.

[87] BR-E Report to the EBF Council, High Leigh, Hertfordshire, England, document 3, September 1992.

[88] EBF Council Minutes, Varna, 1991, contained in the EBF Report Book, 1992.

[89] EBF Council Minutes, Varna, 1991.

[90] The development of Hungarian Baptist Aid out of this period is, in itself, a fascinating story still waiting to be fully documented and written up.

[91] Wiard Popkes was Professor of New Testament at Hamburg and chaired the EBF Nominations Committee at this time.

example of a former Soviet State where Baptists were prepared to engage in politics. In later years, the Moldovan Baptist President, Valeriu Ghiletchi,[92] was to become President of the EBF, to serve in the parliament of Moldova and as one of the country's representatives in the Council of Europe.

New Unions and Free Churches in Former Communist States

New Baptist Unions emerged as the former Soviet Union and the former Yugoslavia disintegrated; new or reformed independent republics were established in the Baltic States, Belarus, Ukraine, Armenia, Azerbaijan, Georgia, Kazakhstan, Kyrgystan, Uzbekistan, Tajikistan, Croatia, Bosnia and Herzegovina, Slovenia, Serbia, Montenegro and Macedonia.[93]

At the 1991 Council in Varna, the following were received into membership: the new single Union for Germany, the Hungarian speaking Union in Romania, Estonia, Latvia and Georgia; Lebanon was also accepted into full membership.[94] The next EBF Council at High Leigh, in Hertfordshire, in September 1992, faced a further pile of applications for membership: Croatia, Byelorussia,[95] Moldova, Ukraine, Russia and Lithuania. The Council recognised that the Baptist Union of Yugoslavia had ceased to exist and so it was removed from the list of members.

Whilst the collapsing USSR had passed a useful law on religious freedom, as the new states asserted independence their governments did not always carry forward appropriate legislation. It became a key task of the EBF to work with others to assist Baptists in these countries to secure appropriate legislation for religious freedom. In 1990 and 1991 Karl Heinz Walter was especially concerned about developments in Georgia[96] and in the countries of central Asia where there is a Muslim majority culture.

In these crucial years, Christian churches which were the majority church in these former communist countries sought to establish or re-establish positions as national or state churches. They had enjoyed privileged situations in the pre-communist era and though leaders might have willingly co-operated with Baptist leaders in the years of communist persecution, there was now a breakdown in relations as they sought to establish special positions and rights in the newly re-formed nations. On 31 January 1990, the Czechoslovak Office for Religious Affairs was closed and parliament approved a new law, having taken advice from the various Christian traditions in the country. Commenting on the proposed sections regarding state aid to churches, Baptist General Secretary, Jan Pospišil, commented, 'Baptists will never request the

---

[92] President of the EBF 2009–11.
[93] Because of objections from the Greek government, Macedonia is normally referred to in political circles as the 'Former Yugoslav Republic of Macedonia'. I will not follow that governmental convention in this article. As Baptists we simply use the title Baptist Union of Macedonia.
[94] EBF Council Minutes, Varna, 1991.
[95] In the west, this country and union soon became known as Belarus.
[96] Karl Heinz Walter, Report to the EBF Council, Varna, September 1991, 3.

state to pay salaries.'⁹⁷ Recompense by the Czech Republic to the churches for land and assets which were seized under communism continues to be an issue before parliament and, in fact, some Czech Baptist churches in the 2000s have taken state money to pay salaries, but this has created tension and disagreement within the Union until the present time.

In Bulgaria, the Baptists met with other evangelicals to make demands to the politicians which included a new law on religious freedom in which all restrictions on working with children and young people should be removed. As compensation for all Christian literature seized by the communist authorities, it was proposed that the state should give permission for the import of 10,000 Bibles and 10,000 hymnals and that Christmas and Easter be celebrated in Bulgaria as official holidays.⁹⁸

Meanwhile, the AUECB was restructuring itself in the light of the reforms in the USSR under the leadership of Michael Gorbachev.⁹⁹ The 44ᵗʰ AUECB Congress abolished the office of General Secretary and created a new and more powerful presidency, with much greater executive power. The AUECB changed its name at the Congress to 'The Union of Evangelicals Christian Baptists' (UECB). The Congress went on to elect forty-four year-old Gregory Ivanovich Komendant,¹⁰⁰ at that time Deputy Superintendent in the Ukraine, as the new President. Komendant would prove to be a pivotal figure in creating the Euro Asiatic Federation when the AUECB came to an end. He was later to be elected President of the EBF and eventually returned from Moscow to Kiev¹⁰¹ to be President of the Baptist Union of the Ukraine. A further development was the appointment of a Vice President for mission and evangelism, signalling the new possibilities that the changes in the USSR permitted.¹⁰²

Theological Education

Under the communist regimes it had been virtually impossible for Baptists to have centres for theological education and ministerial formation in central and eastern Europe. There was a seminary at Novi Sad in Yugoslavia, a restored seminary in Bucharest, which had commenced work in 1988 with Vasile Talpos as President,¹⁰³ a

---

⁹⁷ EBPS 90:008, EBF Archive Section D Box 12.

⁹⁸ Resolution of the Initiative Committee for Contact between Evangelical Christians in Bulgaria, 24 December 1989. EBF Archive Section B Box 809.

⁹⁹ Mikhail Sergeyevich Gorbachev was General Secretary of the USSR Communist Party from 1985 until 1991. He was the only leader of the USSR to have been born under communist rule.

¹⁰⁰ Komendant's father and grandfather had been pastors. He studied in Hamburg 1973–75 and was therefore fluent in German, which was to prove an advantage working with EBF General Secretary, Karl Heinz Walter.

¹⁰¹ Kyiv. I use the western spelling here for the capital city of Ukraine.

¹⁰² EBPS 03:90. EBF Archive Section D Box 12.

¹⁰³ Bucharest has proved a rare example of a Baptist institution gaining state recognition. There is now a Faculty of Baptist Theology in the State University and a Baptist Theological

seminary in Budapest, some work conducted in the offices of the Polish Union, and a correspondence course run by the AUECB from Moscow. Some Baptists in eastern Europe, especially from Yugoslavia and Poland, had been allowed to study at the Baptist Theological Seminary in Rüschlikon, Switzerland, which had been founded in 1949 by the Southern Baptist Foreign Mission Board. Interestingly, on 28 May 1989, the key of Rüschlikon had been handed over by the Foreign Mission Board to European Baptist leaders. Receiving the key from Dr R. Keith Parks, SBC-IMB President, Knud Wümpelmann commented,

> This historic moment for Rüschlikon and for European Baptists ... gratitude is the dominating feeling [which we have] but also a kind of trembling in our hearts. This historical moment fills us with great expectation. The future is ours ... All over Europe Baptist leaders, many of them former students of this seminary want to cooperate in building the future of this institution.[104]

The seminary relocated to Prague in the Czech Republic in 1997.[105] Whilst it continued to form many European leaders and seminary teachers through the next twenty-five years, Europeans never rose to the challenge of funding the work, and with the economic downturn of 2008 the EBF had to establish a special group to look at the future of this EBF institution.[106]

As events unfolded in 1989 one desperate need was for the development of contextual theological education in the new emerging Baptist Unions. The BWA established a Theological Assistance Group (TAG) headed by Dr Andrew McRae, a Scottish Baptist serving as President of the Acadia Divinity School in Wolfsville, Nova Scotia, Canada. Very soon the EBF established a regional TAG headed up by Paul Fiddes of Regent's Park College, Oxford. At the EBF Council in 1992 Fiddes set out some of the pressing concerns. These were a need to expand membership of the group to secure participation from eastern and southern Europe, an information base to be related to the German Baptist Seminary in Hamburg,[107] the development of a catalogue of Baptist institutes for Theological Education and the recognition that new Bible Schools have needs and things to teach one another as they begin new ventures.[108]

Institute with an accredited bachelor's degree. The Romanian government has also recognised a more recent post-communist development of Emmanuel Baptist University in Oradea.

[104] IBTS Archive, Prague, Section A, Box 01.

[105] On the hand over and defunding, see Jones, *European Baptist Federation*, ch. 4; cf. also the forthcoming history of BTS and IBTS by Carol Woodfin, an *alumnist* of BTS.

[106] After this chapter was written, the EBF decided to move the Seminary to Amsterdam [editors].

[107] The Hamburg Seminary moved to Elstal, Berlin, in the mid-1990s following the re-unification of Germany and the desire of German Baptists to establish a centre on which to focus their national, theological education and mission work.

[108] Minutes of the EBF Council, High Leigh, England, 28 September 1992. EBF Archive Box 809.

In February 1989 the AUECB was given permission by state authorities to establish a seminary; it had taken ten years of negotiations by the AUECB and pressure from Baptists in the BWA, EBF and western Baptist Unions. The AUECB leadership wanted to establish an institution in Moscow and Alexei Bichkov, the General Secretary, suggested another centre in the Ukraine. Odes[s]a,[109] Ukraine, soon became the first institution to serve 'all Russia' in an institution using money for building work originally intended for a seminary in Moscow. It started in Odesa Baptist Church in June 1989 with thirty students and six lecturers. Thanks to the energy of the Director, church historian Sergey Sannikov, Odesa outstripped other fledgling institutions in the USSR, and a building programme commenced. Institutions in Moscow, Kiev and Minsk began to develop and Alexei Bichkov[110] was elected Vice President of UECB with responsibility for theological education. The Moscow institution was to struggle both in recruiting students and in developing resources; for several years it occupied offices in the AUECB, then Russian Baptist Union offices, before opening dedicated premises. This was only possible thanks to the fund raising efforts of Ian Chapman after he retired as President of the Northern Baptist Seminary, Chicago, USA.

The Estonian Baptists[111] had previously had a seminary until 1957 when state authorities closed it down. On 16 October 1989, classes began in a church, with plans to create a seminary complex at a new campus in Tartu, an important university city. Polish Baptists had some educational work in their offices in Warsaw but they started fundraising to build a seminary and conference facilities at Radosc, their Baptist camp site, near Warsaw. Knud Wümpelmann placed a brass cylinder in the first building to be erected on the campus at a ceremony on 22 May 1989. The Moldovans were developing an institute in Kishinev and the Romanians in Bucharest. Armenian Baptists had plans to begin work in Ashkarat, near Yerevan, and the Latvians had started a modest institute in the Matheus Baptist Church in Riga with a group of fifteen young men meeting for two weekends each month to study, led by Janis Tervits,[112] the Latvian Baptist leader. Like the Estonians, they had previously had a seminary, which the Soviet authorities had closed in the 1950s. Plans were afoot for St Petersburg Christian University and a similar institution in Donetsk.

These were later followed by seminaries in Moscow, Kiev, North Caucasus, and the fascinating development of the Non-Residential Bible School in Lithuania which achieved, at one stage, the enrolment of about 10% of the Lithuanian Baptist Christians within its programme.

---

[109] The spelling of Odesa varies in transliteration from the Slavic. Odesa is now generally accepted as correct when transliterated from Ukrainian as opposed to Russian.

[110] Former General Secretary of the AUECB.

[111] For the history of Estonian Baptists, see Toivo Pilli, *Dance or Die: The Shaping of Estonian Baptist Identity under Communism* (Milton Keynes: Paternoster, 2008).

[112] From the moment of separation from AUECB, Latvians, Moldovans and Georgians use the title 'bishop' for what other Unions call 'president'. Later Georgia was to have more than one bishop and the senior was titled 'archbishop'.

In the early years building programmes were supported enthusiastically by Baptists in Scandinavia, western Europe and the USA, but some of the grander buildings faced challenges after the first decade as funding for operational costs from outside the country declined.[113]

The International Baptist Lay Academy

The pivotal period of 1989 through to 1990 saw the development of another initiative by the EBF. This was the proposal from the BTS Rüschlikon Board to establish a lay training academy. This would be a 'satellite' agency relating to the Rüschlikon Seminary, working essentially with lay leaders to offer studies in English language and theology. The first Director of what was called The International Baptist Lay Academy (IBLA) was Laszlo Gerzsenyi, a professor at the Budapest Seminary. He commented, 'we hope that Baptists in all of the socialist countries will profit from the fruits of IBLA'.[114] He was succeeded by Dr O. Errol Simmons, a Southern Baptist Missionary, who directed the work until his retirement in 2001. The course was then turned from an eight week summer theology course with a year-round English language programme into a nine months Certificate in Theology, Baptist Identity and English. It was moved from Hungary to Prague, where it was operated by the faculty of IBTS until 2013 as the Certificate of Applied Theology (CAT); in this way, over 200 students graduated.

Difficult Issues between East and West

We saw that in the communist era contact between the western Unions in membership with the EBF and the Unions in the east was very limited. Representation from the east at EBF Council meetings was severely proscribed. With the collapse of communism it was possible for representatives of all Baptist Unions to meet together and soon tensions began to be noticed in various theological and ecclesial issues within the EBF community. As an example, in May 1991 the EBF Nominations Committee discussed who might be proposed for the Presidency of the EBF. The name of Birgit Karlsson, an ordained woman serving as General Secretary of the Swedish Baptists, had been mentioned. Several western Unions (Great Britain, Germany, Denmark, Italy and Sweden) ordained women pastors, but most Unions in the east did not. Peter Barber, chairing the Committee, specifically asked those from eastern Europe on the Nominations Committee if they would give their candid reactions. All three, Julia Gero, János Viczián and Vasile Talpos agreed that Birgit Karlsson should be nominated and the Committee was unanimous that Peter Barber should write to Birgit Karlsson[115] to seek her consent.

---

[113] The heating and maintenance of buildings erected in the flush of enthusiasm of the early 1990s are now major problems for Baptist Unions in central and east Europe.

[114] IBLA Archive, IBTS Archive C Box 11.

[115] Letter from Peter Barber to Birgit Karlsson, 3 May 1991. EBF Archive Box 91.

The report of the Nominations Committee was received by the EBF Council in Varna in September 1991 and Birgit Karlsson was duly elected as Vice President. Perhaps all present did not see the consequences of this. The pattern of the EBF was that the Vice President normally acceded to the Presidency two years later. The Council in 1993 took place in Kishinev, Moldova, and Karlsson was to assume the presidency. But prior to the meeting it became clear that officers in several Unions in eastern Europe were concerned about the development, even though they had voted for her appointment as Vice President two years earlier. The Council of the Baptist Union of Romania met on 16 June 1993 and declared that the ordination of women was unbiblical. This was viewed as strange by many in the EBF as Romania had been represented in the Nominations Committee and in the 1991 Council which had elected her as Vice President. In the event, BWA and EBF officers overcame the hesitancy of some unions and Birgit Karlsson was duly elected in what the minutes describe as a 'moving occasion'.[116]

This election marked a turning point in the relationships between east and west as they emerged from the split world which they had inhabited since the EBF had been founded in 1949. Though disagreements over theological, ecclesial and ethical issues continued to arise and were debated in the Council, from this moment on debate and discussion became possible in an atmosphere of pastoral concern for one another.

The Middle East and the EBF

Simultaneous with the opening up of central and eastern Europe for renewed Baptist life after the collapse of the Soviet Empire, Baptist groups in the Middle East expressed the need to belong to a regional Baptist grouping and one-by-one they chose the EBF as the appropriate community in which to belong. They were hardly strong enough to form a regional body of their own and recognised their vulnerability as support from the Southern Baptist Convention began to fall away. First, the Association of Baptists in Israel was accepted into the EBF at the 1989 Council; then the Lebanese Baptist Convention applied to join and was accepted. People from Lebanon were present at the Budapest Congress, but unlike member bodies did not have a sign with their Convention name on it during the formal roll-call. This issue had to be explained to the Lebanese leadership after the event. By 2012, Egypt, Israel, Jordan, Lebanon and Syria were members of the EBF, together with Baptist churches in Bahrain, Iraq and Turkey.[117]

Conclusion

The period from the EBF Congress in July 1989 through until January 1992, when the USSR finally collapsed with the creation of Republics in Kazakhstan, Kyrgyzstan, Uzbekistan and Tajikistan, marks a period of profound political and

---

[116] Minutes of the EBF Council, Kishinev, Moldova, 1993. EBF Archive Box 811.
[117] EBF Directory 2012.

economic change in terms of the short-time scale and geographical spread for Baptist Christians in Europe, unparalleled since the first Baptist communities of 1609. The EBF grew from twenty-seven member bodies in 1989 to fifty-two with three associated bodies in 2012.

Future historians will be better placed to make sense of all that happened in a momentous period. Here, I have simply sought to record some aspects of four important events, the 1989 EBF Congress, the establishment of Baptist Response-Europe, the transfer of the seminary at Rüschlikon from the SBC-IMB to the EBF, and the development of theological education within the orbit of the Theological Assistance Group.

To have lived through such events and to rejoice in so many of the outcomes has been very special. Ian M. Randall did so and has helped to ensure that much of what happened has been evaluated critically and recorded for posterity.

CHAPTER 13

Mainstream: 'far greater ambitions' – An Evaluation of Mainstream's Contribution to the Renewal of Denominational Life, 1979–1994

Derek Tidball

The *Baptist Times*' editorial of 16 January 1986 was headed 'Mainstream comes of age'.[1] It declared that Mainstream, which at the time was just seven years old, 'holds a unique position as a potential contributor to unity within the denomination'. The 'ginger group' had just attracted 400 persons to its annual conference, with a further 100 on the waiting list, making it 'the largest national gathering of Baptists after the denominational assembly'. Yet, the editorial continued, 'a respected organisation must be prepared to face hard questions from other members of the same family'. It queried the lack of involvement of women and non-ministerial Baptists, the lack of balance in some of its *Newsletter* 'stereotype "success" stories', and asked why many adherents were on the 'fringe' of Baptist association life.[2]

This paper seeks to re-evaluate the contribution Mainstream made to the renewal of the denomination, with the advantage over the *Baptist Times* editorial of the perspective greater distance brings. It argues that Mainstream's existence was vital in bringing very diverse evangelicals together, maintaining their otherwise uncertain commitment to the denomination, and contributing positively to the denomination's renewal.[3]

Origins

Mainstream was born at a meeting on 8 February 1978 between Dr Raymond Brown, then principal of Spurgeon's College, Dr Paul Beasley-Murray, senior minister of

---

[1] It is a pleasure to contribute to a volume in honour of Ian Randall, whose personal friendship, historical scholarship and evangelical commitment I have enjoyed over many years, beginning with a shared love of F.B. Meyer. The title of this paper comes from a letter from Dr Raymond Brown to the author, 23 September 2011, on which see below.

[2] *Baptist Times,* 16 January 1986, 2.

[3] The author was a member of the Advisory Group from its early days, joined the Mainstream Executive in 1989 and was briefly its Chairman, a post he relinquished on becoming Secretary for Mission and Evangelism at the Baptist Union of Great Britain in 1991.

Altrincham Baptist Church, and Douglas McBain, the minister of Lewin Road Baptist Church, Streatham. The meeting followed the 1977 Nottingham Assembly at which Douglas McBain had expressed concerns about the denomination's continued decline. During the 1978 Baptist Assembly a wider group met together, and this was followed by a planning meeting that September which was attended by eighteen people. This was held at Gorsley Baptist Church, which was to become Mainstream's 'spiritual home'.[4] Patrick Goodland, minister at Gorsley, was to become Mainstream's first chairman.[5] By January 1979 Sir Cyril Black had donated £1,250 to its formation and arranged for his solicitor to register Mainstream as a charitable company.[6] Raymond Brown reported that he had contacted the Baptist Revival Fellowship to avoid any sense of competition between them and also 'spent some time explaining MAINSTREAM to Dr David Russell, Secretary of the Baptist Union of Great Britain and Ireland who received the idea warmly and applauded our aims'.[7] The planning meeting rejected the idea of subscribing to the Lausanne Covenant as its basis, choosing instead to align itself 'wholeheartedly' with the Baptist Union's 'Declaration of Principle'.[8] Plans for the public launch and the first conference were agreed.[9]

Prior to the launch, the Mainstream committee issued a press release, since 'there [had] ... already been so many enquiries that a statement [was] now necessary'.[10] Confident that the denomination was on 'the verge of one of the most exciting periods of its life', the press release announced that Mainstream was committed to 'the life and work of the denomination' and was 'determined to encourage, co-ordinate, publicise and support every venture that will lead to further life and growth'.[11]

A remarkable 700 people attended Mainstream's public launch on 24 April 1979 at a late night fringe meeting of the Baptist Assembly.[12] The theme of the event was 'Life and Growth' and it included interviews about growing churches, music, dance, and a visual talk on church growth, as well as an introduction to the vision of

---

[4] Letter from David Coffey to Mainstream Executive, 16 March 1982. Barrie White papers.

[5] Douglas McBain, *Fire Over the Waters: Renewal Among Baptists and Others from the 1960s to the 1990s* (London: Darton, Longman and Todd, 1997), 83.

[6] Item 2, Memorandum of Planning Session at Gorsley, 9-10 January 1979, Paul Beasley-Murray papers. The Minutes of the Mainstream Executive, 16 September 1982, speak of Sir Cyril having donated £2,250 for its launch. It could be that one note contains a typographical error, or more likely that Sir Cyril donated more than the initial donation of £1,250. The minutes show that by 1981 Mainstream was just about breaking even in its trading operation.

[7] Item 2, Memorandum of Planning Session, 9-10 January 1979.

[8] Item 3, Memorandum of Planning Session, 9-10 January 1979.

[9] Items 11 and 12, Memorandum of Planning Session, 9-10 January 1979.

[10] Press Release, 15 October 1978, Paul Beasley-Murray Mainstream File.

[11] This wording also appeared in *Mainstream Newsletter* 1 (March, 1979), 1.

[12] *Baptist Times*, 3 May 1979, 4; the *Newsletter* 2 (August, 1979), 1, more modestly reports '600-700 people'.

Mainstream. The evening was characterised by vitality and breathed an air of optimism.[13] The initial momentum was carried through to the first Mainstream Conference held at Swanwick, 28-30 January 1980.

The initial executive consisted of Raymond Brown (president), Patrick Goodland (chairman), Clifford Roseweir (briefly secretary until he resigned because of ill-health and was replaced by David Coffey), Peter Grange (treasurer), Douglas McBain, and Paul Beasley-Murray (who became editor of the *Newsletter*). They were supported by a wider advisory committee. Although self-formed, the response demonstrates the respect and trust in which they were held and indicates that they were in tune with the mood of the time.

Objective and Motivation

The objective of Mainstream was to give expression to the evangelical life and growth that was believed to be characteristic of many churches but which often did not find expression through the official organs or in the public face of the Baptist Union (BU). Its founders self-consciously chose the title Mainstream because, as Raymond Brown put it later, they were 'deeply aware ... that the vast majority of our people throughout the country were basically "evangelical" in their theological allegiance though many of them had an aversion to labels. But at the same time, denominational leadership, both regionally and centrally did not necessarily reflect the convictions of the constituency, and we wanted that to change.'[14]

Mainstream set itself against any separatist tendencies and pledged its loyalty to the BU. The first *Mainstream Newsletter*, as well as the introductory leaflet, spoke of its purpose as 'to give wholehearted commitment to the gospel as expressed in the Union's Declaration of Principle and also to the life and work of the denomination'.[15] 'It is', the *Newsletter* declared, 'not a protest, but a progressive group.'[16] Given the recent track record of evangelicals within the denomination, some of whom had recently grown impatient with it and withdrawn from the Union (see further below), this was a necessary and unprecedented pledge of commitment.[17] While a decade later some charismatic, evangelical Baptists were attracted to join New Frontiers,[18] or at least to be dually aligned, the existence of Mainstream served

---

[13] *Baptist Times*, 3 May 1979, 4.

[14] Letter from Dr Raymond Brown to the author, 23 September 2011.

[15] *Newsletter* 1 (March, 1979), 1.

[16] *Newsletter* 1 (March, 1979), 1.

[17] The present author, as one who had known evangelical commitments, was directly asked at his Association Ministerial Recognition Committee in 1971 whether he would envisage a situation where he would encourage his church to withdraw from the Union.

[18] Craig Millward, '"Chalk and Cheese?": An account of the impact of restorationist ecclesiology and charismatic renewal upon the Baptist Union – with particular reference to those churches in joint fellowship with the Baptist Union of Great Britain and New Frontiers International' (unpublished PhD thesis, Brunel University, 2003).

the great purpose of keeping others not only within the Union from which otherwise they felt disenfranchised but also actively involved.

Mainstream set out to be an inclusive evangelical body, an objective in which it largely succeeded, though not without difficulty. Its inclusiveness was noted from the beginning. The *Baptist Times* commented on its desire to be 'an antidote to the curse of evangelicalism: fragmentation',[19] while John Capon noted in *Crusade* that it had adopted 'an unashamed non-sectarian evangelical stance ... [and] seemed to symbolize a long overdue cessation of hostilities between those who for want of a better label are called Charismatics, and the rest of us'.[20] Douglas McBain saw it as a significant alliance of three main streams of evangelical: traditional, younger progressive, and charismatic.[21] With the appointment of Barrie White, principal of Regent's Park College, Oxford, to its executive, Mainstream sought to embrace those who would be regarded as central evangelicals by the Union.

Mainstream sought unashamedly to influence the Union. An early document said that 'its very *existence* keeps evangelical leaders *constantly aware* of the *strength* of evangelical presence in the Union'.[22] The same document spoke of a desire to meet with the new General Secretary of the BU, strategies for engaging with Area Superintendents and checking that evangelicals were represented on the BU Council and committees. Mainstream developed a monitoring role on BU appointments and constantly put forward, often unsuccessfully, nominees for the various vacant posts.[23] By 1982 David Coffey already felt the evangelical wing was 'being taken more seriously' in the denomination.[24]

Context

The formation of Mainstream did not take place in a vacuum and several contextual factors self-evidently contributed to its inception.

The Baptist Revival Fellowship

Mainstream came into being as much due to the failure of the existing body that had provided a meeting place for Baptist evangelicals as to any issues faced within the Union itself. The Baptist Revival Fellowship (BRF) had been formed in 1938 by a

---

[19] McBain, *Fire*, 84.

[20] John Capon, 'Charismatic cease-fire', *Crusade*, June 1979, 5. It is interesting in the light of subsequent developments that Capon says 'it was definitely not a "charismatic" function' but that it was entirely natural that people raised hands in worship and he placed it in the tradition of the nineteenth-century 'higher life' movement.

[21] McBain, *Fire*, 108-109.

[22] Mainstream Questionnaire Response, Paul Beasley-Murray papers. Not dated but its content suggests Spring 1981. Emphasis in original.

[23] E.g., Minutes of Executive Committee, 17 November 1984, 19 November 1985, 21-22 March 1988.

[24] Minutes of Executive Committee, 22-23 March 1982.

group of influential ministers 'who were burdened by the low level of spiritual life in the churches'.[25] As convinced Keswick-style pietists and premillennialists they represented the central evangelical stream of their day, but ironically were never going to be in a position to embrace adherents of the later charismatic movement. From the beginning, the group's relationship with the Union was insecure, although periodically it participated constructively, with one of their number, the Rev. Hugh Butt, being elected as the West Midlands Area Superintendent.

Under the Rev. Theo Bamber, long the most influential figure in the BRF, it became more aggressively opposed to the ecumenical stance of the Union, increasing liberal theology and centralisation being advocated by the new Baptist Union General Secretary, Dr Ernest Payne.[26] Dr Martyn Lloyd-Jones' call at the Evangelical Alliance Assembly in 1966 for evangelicals to withdraw from theologically mixed denominations and to form a new association of churches resulted in divided opinions and relationships in the BRF.[27] But, exacerbated by the Union's ecumenical agenda, the BRF became increasingly separatist in stance. The 1969 BRF annual conference officially adopted a policy of secession, to the great regret of some, including the Rev. Geoffrey King, who had been among its founding members. Discussions between the BRF and the Union that might have prevented this demonstrated intransigence on both sides. It was 'a dialogue of the deaf'. Philip Hill's considered verdict is that both sides bear the responsibility for what happened, but that the Union was 'frankly dismissive' of the BRF 'beyond giving its representative a polite hearing', even though in the mid-60s a quarter of ministers had belonged to it.[28] The result was unsurprising: 'growing conservative alienation and marginalization'.[29]

When, then, the christological controversy of 1971 erupted, not only did it confirm the frustration of evangelicals within the BU concerning its doctrinal laxity, but the BRF's course had left them without a ready-made channel to organise and express their views.

The Christological Controversy of 1971 and Beyond

The christological controversy of 1971, which has recently been examined by Ian Randall and others,[30] left evangelicals feeling deeply uneasy about their relationship

---

[25] Baptist Revival Fellowship Constitution and Rules (adopted in 1964), cited by Philip Hill, 'The Baptist Revival Fellowship (1938–1972). A study in Baptist conservative evangelicalism' (unpublished MPhil thesis, University of Wales, 2011), 18 and 95.
[26] For details see Hill, 'Baptist Revival Fellowship', 50-74.
[27] Hill, 'Baptist Revival Fellowship', 85-124.
[28] Hill, 'Baptist Revival Fellowship', 91.
[29] Hill, 'Baptist Revival Fellowship', 124.
[30] See Ian M. Randall, *The English Baptists of the Twentieth Century* (A History of English Baptists, 4; Didcot: Baptist Historical Society, 2005), 365-82; Hill, 'Baptist Revival Fellowship', 125-62; Nigel G. Wright, 'Sustaining Evangelical Identity: Faithfulness and

with the BU. Michael's Taylor's address at that year's Baptist Assembly, entitled 'The Incarnate Presence – how much of a man was Jesus Christ?', argued that 'however remarkable this life [of Jesus], I think I must stop short of saying categorically: Jesus is God, and I understand the New Testament probably stops short of it as well ... Jesus is a man. I do not say that Jesus is God, but I do say with the New Testament that God was in Christ or that I encounter God in Jesus.'[31] Such a statement by the principal of one of the denomination's colleges[32] was bound to cause controversy. The failure of the Union's leadership and Council to resolve the issue promptly, or even to recognise the seriousness of the concerns evangelicals expressed, caused disaffection. The matter was belatedly resolved when an unequivocal statement was overwhelmingly agreed at the following Assembly, but not before much damage had been done to relationships. Dr George Beasley-Murray, at that time the principal of Spurgeon's College,[33] resigned as chair of the Baptist Union Council, and forty-eight conservative evangelical ministers resigned from the Union altogether, some of them taking their churches with them.[34]

The significance of the controversy goes beyond the controversy itself. To many evangelicals it was a symptom of the marginalisation of evangelicals in the Union and proved again that their voice went unheard. Whether legitimate or not, that impression was long-standing and ammunition was frequently provided for those who felt it. In March 1979, Sir Cyril Black put a motion to the BU Council expressing regret about 'certain statements' in an article in the *Baptist Times* of 12 October 1978 called 'Putting the pieces together'. The article had declared the Billy Graham Crusades to be 'as phony as the other great deception of the 60s, the pop culture', suggested that '"Evangelical Christians" are less zealous in their secular employments than other workers' and that 'all Puritans, whether religious or political, are to be mistrusted'.[35] The Council was asked to judge these statements as 'uncharitable and unchristian' and in the case of the reference to the Billy Graham Crusade 'probably defamatory'. But the Council did no more than 'take note of Sir

---

Freedom in Denomination Life' (The Dr G.R. Beasley-Murray Memorial Lecture 2010, delivered at the Baptist Assembly 4 May 2012).

[31] Typescript of the address, 3.

[32] Michael Taylor was principal of Northern Baptist College, 1969–85.

[33] On the significant role played by George Beasley Murray, see Paul Beasley-Murray, *Fearless for the Truth: A Personal Portrait of the Life of George Beasley-Murray* (Carlisle: Paternoster, 2002), 145-65.

[34] Patrick Goodland gives this figure in 'Mainstream Reflections the First Decade', *Mainstream Magazine* 63 (September, 1998), 16. Hill, 'Baptist Revival Fellowship', 184, cites John Capon in the *British Weekly*, 21 April 1971, 11, as stating that forty ministers had resigned and a new Association of Evangelical Baptist Churches formed.

[35] The article was written by Fred Sedgwick from his own experience as one who went forward at a Billy Graham rally but then became disenchanted with its 'massive sentimentalism' and the failure of his evangelical upbringing to produce a grown-up faith that prepared people for 'the real world'.

Cyril's objection to the article'.[36] Such a complacent response was further evidence that the Council was not representative of the evangelical commitment and vitality to be found in the majority of Baptist churches and was symptomatic of what provoked the formation of Mainstream.

Signs of Hope

The environment in which Mainstream was born was not all negative. Douglas McBain's intervention at the 1977 Nottingham Assembly challenged the annual report's comments on state of the denomination. His comments led to the setting up of an inquiry group, chaired by John H.Y. Briggs, into 'the causes for the numerical and spiritual decline in our denomination', which published a report called *Signs of Hope* two years later. The initial response of the BU's General Purposes and Finance Committee demonstrated some defensiveness about such an inquiry but set out the task to be undertaken 'if the Council considers that a Commission or Special Committee would be advisable and helpful'. It recommended that it should consist of ten members 'with the officers given the right to attend'; thus, perhaps, somewhat influencing the direction the inquiry would take.[37]

The report charted 'a staggering loss of members'. Whereas there had been 205,013 members in 2,109 churches in 1952, there were now 147,200 in 1,745 churches. Though it carefully qualified the picture, it could do little else than conclude that there had been a 21.7% decline during the period.[38] It reviewed 'Factors impinging upon the size and health of our churches'[39] before devoting a chapter to outlining the perspective of the Church Growth Movement that was making its influence felt from the USA.[40] The report concluded by making fourteen recommendations, some addressed to the churches, such as that they should periodically assess their goals, and others addressed to the Union's departments, colleges and associations.[41]

Mainstream was anxious to capitalise on *Signs of Hope*. Barrie White commended it in the *Newsletter* and encouraged readers to respond to it. White commented on the Church Growth Movement that 'however "American" its idiom and jargon may sometimes seem, it has much to say to us'.[42] Reports of four British church growth situations followed. The next *Newsletter* published the response of 'The [Baptist] Church Growth Working Group' to *Signs of Hope,* signed by Arthur Thompson, who two years later became General Superintendent of the Metropolitan Area.[43] This

---

[36] Minutes, Baptist Union Council, 14 March 1979.
[37] Minutes, Baptist Union Council, 13-14 November 1979.
[38] *Signs of Hope: Report of the Denominational Enquiry Group* (London: Baptist Union of Great Britain and Ireland, 1979), 8-9.
[39] *Signs of Hope*, 24-36.
[40] *Signs of Hope*, 37-42.
[41] *Signs of Hope*, 45-48.
[42] *Newsletter* 2 (August, 1979), 3.
[43] *Newsletter* 3 (December, 1979), 2-4.

response advocated stronger 'spiritual and evangelistic leadership' by the Union and Superintendents, giving priority to evangelism without neglecting social concern. It further urged the colleges to train people for the current missionary situation in the UK, and that ecumenism should be seen more widely with links to the Evangelical Alliance and other interdenominational agencies celebrated openly. The following *Newsletter* took up the 'challenge and optimism' of *Signs of Hope* and welcomed the Union's response to it, under the title 'Call to Commitment'[44] suggesting that deacons should arrange day conferences to study it.[45] The 1981 Mainstream conference pursued this agenda of 'Call to Commitment'.

The Resurgence of Evangelicalism within other Free Church Denominations

From the mid-1970s there had been a growing resurgence of confidence among evangelicals within mainline denominations. Several factors aligned to produce it, especially the charismatic movement. But charismatic renewal was not the sole cause of evangelical resurgence, which included the legacy of the Billy Graham crusades, the leadership of John Stott,[46] the impact of evangelical biblical scholarship and the new approach offered by the American Church Growth School.[47] In May 1977, prior to the formation of Mainstream, a conference entitled 'Let My People Grow', influenced by but not limited to thinking from the Church Growth Movement, was held at Pilgrim Hall, Uckfield. Sponsored by David Pawson, Patrick Goodland and Douglas McBain, it brought together many who were subsequently to be involved in Mainstream. Goodland and McBain were both plenary speakers and I, at the last minute, stood in for David Pawson, who was present but unwell, to speak on 'Structures for Church Growth'.

The most immediate parallel to the formation of Mainstream is found in the formation of Conservative Evangelicals in Methodism in 1971, following an initiative of the Rev. Donald English.[48] According to the Methodist historian, Martin Wellings, Methodism in the 1960s and 1970s had shown 'a growing endorsement and an acceptance of difference' which presented Methodist evangelicals both with

---

[44] 'A Call to Commitment', adopted by the Baptist Union Council in April 1980, and published as *A Call to Commitment: Baptist Christians through the 80s* (London: Baptist Union of Great Britain and Ireland, 1980).

[45] David Taylor, *Newsletter* (April, 1980), 3-4

[46] At the public launch of Mainstream, Raymond Brown stated that they hoped 'to contribute to the Baptist cause what the evangelicals have done for Anglicans and others', *Baptist Times*, 3 May 1979, 4.

[47] Rob Warner, *Reinventing English Evangelicalism 1966–2001: A Theological and Sociological Study* (Studies in Evangelical History and Thought; Milton Keynes: Paternoster, 2007), gives some insight, albeit selective, into this.

[48] Brian Hoare and Ian M. Randall, *More than a Methodist: The Life and Ministry of Donald English* (Carlisle: Paternoster, 2003), 98-102.

'a problem and an opportunity'.[49] Some perceived the problematic element as uppermost and, as with their Baptist counterparts in the BRF, chose to leave the Methodist Church.[50] Others decided to seize the opportunity to found the Methodist Revival Fellowship, which chose only to concentrate on prayer for revival and shunned involvement in wider denominational affairs; an inadequate vehicle.[51] At the 1978 CEIM Annual Conference, Howard Belben, formerly principal of Cliff College, delivered an extensive and carefully crafted apologia for staying within the denomination, insisting that although they would be uncompromising about key evangelical tenets, they were not spoiling for a fight, but were 'ready for partnership'.[52] A similar development was taking place in the United Reformed Church with the formation of *GEAR,* the Group for Evangelism and Renewal, in 1974. While no history of *GEAR* is yet available, it is clear that Mainstream openly followed their pattern of organisation with regard to membership.[53]

Many evangelicals, therefore, felt confident enough not only to reject Martyn Lloyd-Jones' call to separate but to take a more confident theological stance within their respective denominational structures. This was expressed in the publication of *Include us in,* in which Paul Beasley-Murray and Maurice Markham joined with like-minded representatives from other denominations. They reviewed the nature of the church, discussed the nature of church discipline and some other practical issues. They concluded that 'It cannot be right to stay in "at any price"', but that separation was only legitimate on 'a matter of absolutely fundamental importance'. There was 'more to be gained by staying than leaving', and since Christ had not forsaken the church for all its weaknesses and 'in his mercy continues to use' it, so we should not abandon the church either.[54]

The Contribution of Mainstream

Mainstream had no official standing and its authority derived from the respect in which its leaders were held as the mature pastors of growing churches or college

---

[49] Martin Wellings, 'Evangelicalism in Twentieth-Century Methodism', in Mark Smith (ed.), *British Evangelical Identities Past and Present:* Volume 1. *Aspects of the History and Sociology of Evangelicalism in Britain and Ireland* (Studies in Evangelical History and Thought; Milton Keynes: Paternoster, 2008), 58-59.

[50] '"Secession is an Ugly Thing": The Emergence and Development of Free Methodism in Late Twentieth Century England', *Wesley and Methodist Studies* 3 (Manchester: Didsbury Press, 2011), 55-79.

[51] Hoare and Randall, *More than a Methodist,* 99; Martin Wellings, 'The Methodist Revival Fellowship 1952-87', *Proceedings of the Wesley Historical Society* 57.3 (October, 2009), 89-107. The MRF merged with CEIM in 1987 to form Headway and is now known as Methodist Evangelicals Together.

[52] Howard Belben, *The Evangelical Methodist* (n.pl.: Conservative Evangelicals In Methodism, 1978), 35.

[53] Item 5, Memorandum of Planning Session, 9-10 January 1979.

[54] *Include us in* (London: Evangelical Alliance, 1980), n.p..

principals. Initially some in the Union's committees spoke disparagingly of it. Lewis Misselbrook, who was working in the BU's Mission Department, reported a comment in a Union meeting in which someone sought to dismiss Mainstream by saying, 'that is only a little group of six people and only half of them have any kind of following in the denomination', a comment which he said seemed to have been 'generally accepted'. The principal of Bristol Baptist College and, at the time, President of the Union, Morris West, spoke up for it, however, saying Mainstream was 'likely to be an important development and you cannot possibly ignore it'.[55] Time proved it could not be dismissed as the vehicle for eccentric views or power-hungry radicals who spoke from the margins. Mainstream pursued its objectives through four channels: conferences, both large and small; the *Newsletter*; other publications; and meetings with denominational leaders.

Keeping Evangelicals Together

Mainstream, as stated, aimed to represent a wide range of evangelicals who strove to work together for the renewal of church life without fragmentation. It was a tough call and the conferences, correspondence and publications often demonstrate that Mainstream became the lightning rod for tensions.

The first conference in 1980 on 'Spiritual and Church Growth' was thought to be an 'outstanding first'.[56] It embraced several divergent perspectives on the theme of spiritual and church growth and was addressed by Raymond Brown, Barrie White, Lewis Misselbrook, and Tom Houston. Barrie White's address, *Opening Our Doors to God*, in which he spoke of personal prayer and corporate worship with a rare combination of theological depth and practical application, was to become Mainstream's first publication.[57]

The plenary sessions in 1981 conference were on the theme of 'Commitment' with Jim Graham, a leading charismatic minister, speaking on 'Worship' and Graham Ashworth speaking on 'Learning'. Practical seminars on music, drama and changing patterns of worship provided a more participatory element to the programme. People appreciated Jim Graham's considered address, but Peter Hetherington wrote to the *Newsletter* to complain that 'when it came to the workshop on worship the "careful" approach disappeared' and charismatic worship was claimed to be superior to others. Nonetheless, while openly addressing a number of divisions, he urged the avoidance of splitting and an embracing of 'each theory on worship'.[58]

---

[55] Letter from Lewis Misslebrook to David Coffey, 11 January 1980. Patrick Goodland papers. Morris West had previously written to Patrick Goodland on 4 April 1979, saying, 'So far as I read the purposes of the "movement" I have great sympathy with them...' Patrick Goodland papers.

[56] Minutes of Mainstream Executive, 17-18 March 1980, Mainstream Box, Barrie White papers.

[57] B.R. White, *Opening Our Doors to God* (Ilkeston: Mainstream, 1980).

[58] *Newsletter* 7 (April, 1981), 3-5. *Contra* Millward, 'Chalk and Cheese', 105.

In 1982 the conference was a mixed bag producing diverse reactions and served to bring tensions regarding the variety of groups that coalesced in Mainstream to the surface at the Mainstream executive that followed. The theme, 'The Caring Church', was addressed by Bernard Green, incoming General Secretary of the Baptist Union, Bill Hancock and Michael Eastman. Several criticised it as not sufficiently adventurous. One unknown respondent said the programme and speakers were 'safe', another that it was like any 'Superintendent's annual conference', another wanted it to be more prophetic. Others wanted more time for worship, more consideration to be given to the laity and for the focus to be practical with one commenting, the 'BU can organise theory conferences'. One wrote, 'whereas I felt last year it really was a Mainstream Conference, this year it was more like a glorified B.U. Assembly. I don't think the Mainstream Committee should be afraid to give positive leadership and themselves tackle issues which concern us all at this time.'[59]

Yet, Douglas McBain's conduct of the final communion service was anything but 'safe' and led to 'two months of ferment' before the Mainstream executive met in March. McBain was about to leave pastoral ministry to engage in an itinerant 'apostolic' ministry with Manna Ministries caring for isolated and hungry ministers, something which was a contributory factor in provoking the reaction that occurred.[60] A leading charismatic minister and radical thinker, his views were already well known. He thought the Union's response to *Signs of Hope* 'went nowhere near far enough, since it concentrated its appeal to great responsiveness on churches and ministers, but showed little awareness of the need for changes within the structured life of the Union'.[61]

McBain's radical views had been published by Mainstream in its third publication entitled, *No Gentle Breeze*. Speaking of 'the breath of the Spirit moving through a considerable number of Baptist Churches in Britain' and of a 'welcome new surge of life' it set out distinctive Baptist principles before reviewing pressures to change which included a significant section concerned with charismatic renewal. This section ended with a trenchant paragraph calling for change. Consistent with Mainstream's aims, he wrote,

> Let it be said as explicitly as possible that we have the denomination we deserve. It is to our shame if we have been swifter with our condemnations about our shared life than our positive contributions to it. This is particularly true of those who come as I do from

---

[59] 'Swanwick Conference Post Bag 1982', Barrie White papers.

[60] McBain 'explained his new venture' to the Executive Committee 21-22 March 1983. It was reported in *Newsletter* 10, April 1982, 11. See also McBain, *Fire,* 115-19. This move to wider ministry was controversial and many were nervous as to how it would be viewed in relationship to the established General Superintendency. On Manna Ministries, see McBain, *Fire,* 115-19.

[61] McBain, *Fire,* 111.

a background in which it has almost been the touchstone of orthodoxy to be critical of the Union.[62]

Dismissing those who constantly re-played the Downgrade Controversy, McBain continues,

> Those days were long ago even if they seem but yesterday. Now it is vital that our Council, its Executive and its Committees become more of a catalyst for change than a talkshop about history. To change from being a brake and become an accelerator they must identify God's activity in our midst, then epitomise and cultivate it throughout the denomination. The fundamental question which they must face is whether it is possible for the present institution to move reformingly with sufficient speed and conviction to keep a hold upon the new life which is emerging, whilst not losing touch with the continuum of our tradition. I am forced to one conclusion regarding the prospects for Baptist life in Britain. It is that whatever timetable for change God may have adopted for other Christians, His time for us is now. If we do not take it then we sign the death warrant for our institutions. It will be executed in the name of financial economics.[63]

The communion service that caused the stormy reaction began fairly traditionally, but McBain's address, about Caleb, was taken by some as 'a swingeing attack on the Union and its structures'.[64] Some welcomed it, fearing that unless positive leadership took the churches forward they would be lost in the desert for a generation. One commented that with this address 'the pace accelerated in terms of radical confrontation on the part of some'. Another noted that people seemed 'less happy to live side by side and live together' than previously, suggesting that 'we have spent so long fighting a rearguard action in the ghetto that we don't know how to cope with the resurgence of evangelicalism'. Yet another expressed great concern about 'the overt impatience among the charismatic brethren' about the liaison with the Union.[65]

While presented as the result of a theological tension between a conservative and a charismatic evangelicalism, the tension was as much about strategy and personality as theology. The more conservative in outlook feared that McBain's comments would undermine the very relationships they were seeking to build with the Union's leadership, while the more adventurous thought such conservatism would never produce change. The Mainstream executive had 'frank discussions' about the reaction to the conference, and at least rejoiced there had been a reaction. Douglas McBain represents the episode as a 'crisis'[66] and refers to Raymond Brown circulating an article to the Mainstream executive by Tom Smail, a respected

---

[62] Douglas McBain, *No Gentle Breeze: Baptist Churchmanship and the Winds of Change* (Ilkeston: Mainstream, 1981), 17. Significantly, this part of the paragraph is highlighted in the margin in George Beasley-Murray's copy, held at Spurgeon's College.

[63] McBain, *No Gentle Breeze*, 17, cited by McBain himself, *Fire*, 109-10.

[64] McBain, *Fire*, p. 112.

[65] These comments come from 'Swanwick Conference Post Bag, 1982'. Barrie White papers.

[66] McBain, *Fire*, p. 110.

Anglican charismatic leader, cautioning against an exclusivist charismatic spirituality. While McBain seemed to consider this as somehow underhand, it was a quite responsible way of exploring differences between members of Mainstream and taking the discussion further. The executive recorded it needed to be clearer about its basic aim of 'seeking to express the breath and variety of evangelical life within the denomination'.[67] Later, McBain confessed that 'the wisdom of a more guarded approach' had been justified.[68]

Although publicly the Mainstream conference was 'back on course'[69] the following year, tensions were to be part of the DNA of Mainstream. Typically, on the one hand Alan Pain felt the ministry time at the 1986 conference 'was a tremendous step forward' and urged that more time be given to it in future (the *Baptist Times* considered it 'too emotional').[70] On the other hand, Humphrey Vellacott wrote a strong letter to Alistair Campbell protesting that 'Apparently we are going charismatic without so much as a protest raised' and setting out his vigorous reservations about the movement. He asked for 'a clear declaration that we do really stand in the "Mainstream" of orthodox theology and are not going to be swept into the shallow waters of passing enthusiasms'.[71]

The differences were undoubtedly deeply felt, but the genius of Mainstream was that it continued, albeit sometimes uneasily, to resist the fragmentation to which evangelicalism perennially succumbs. Its leaders continued to strive to work together for a greater cause. In personal correspondence, Raymond Brown, agreeing that he took John Stott's line on baptism in the Spirit but was not 'stridently anti-charismatic', writes that the essential point for Mainstream was that 'These issues were matters we could freely and happily discuss and they did not remotely divide us, if only because we all had *far greater ambitions* than the pursuit of a particular theological line on the precise natures of our spiritual resources. We were all committed evangelicals ...'[72]

Given its openness to the charismatic movement, many wondered if Mainstream was actually a charismatic movement. Paul Beasley-Murray asked in the *Newsletter* in April 1981 if Mainstream was 'the Fountain Trust in another guise'. His reply was 'no' and he pointed to the membership of the Mainstream executive as proof. But, he pleaded, 'we do need to recognize that charismatics too are in the mainstream'.[73] This is underlined by the statement of the executive published in the tenth *Newsletter* asserting that Mainstream was emphatically evangelical and Baptist but not 'to be seen only in "charismatic terms"'. Mainstream served rather as 'a forum where evangelicals can share together what they see God doing and what they themselves

---

[67] Minutes of the Mainstream Executive, 22-23 March 1982.
[68] McBain, *Fire*, p. 122.
[69] McBain, *Fire*, p. 121.
[70] Letters, 6 March 1986, Barrie White Papers.
[71] Letter from Humphrey Vellacott to Alistair Campbell, 18 April 1985. Patrick Goodland papers.
[72] Letter from Raymond Brown to the author, 23 September 2011. Emphasis original.
[73] *Newsletter* 7 (April, 1981), 1.

are doing in the name of renewal, church growth, or whatever, and where the truth and wholesomeness of our claims can be tested in love'.[74]

Looking back on this period Patrick Goodland bears this out in commenting,

> One of the strengths of the movement in the 1980s was a willingness to listen to each other and to absorb the tensions which variety creates. The Executive meetings were not safe havens. We were lobbied, criticised and affirmed ... [O]ne of my cherished memories of those early days, is of the quality of creative discussion, sometimes impassioned, often deeply affecting, which was the hallmark of our two-day conferencing as an executive twice a year. Bonds of fellowship were created in worship and prayer as we sought God's will and direction for this unique movement, its conferences and the right choice of speakers.[75]

There was great rejoicing in Mainstream when David Coffey, its former secretary, was elected President of the BU in 1986 and a long interview with him was included in the *Newsletter* exploring his passion for unity without compromise to his evangelical convictions. He saw the rising level of confidence among evangelicals but pleaded that this should not lead to narrow fragmentation. He argued that 'just as people cause conflicts, people can also solve conflicts' and he pointed out 'the many good things' he had seen done at Baptist Church House while serving as Vice-President.[76] Typically, the article was followed by one pleading for variety rather than partisanship in worship music by David Peacock, his colleague at Upton Vale, Torquay.[77]

Abreast of the Current Agenda

In subsequent years, Mainstream continued to tackle the issues of the moment both in its conferences and the *Newsletter*. The 1983 conference tackled head-on the question of authority and especially the then much spoken-about issues of eldership and apostleship.[78] When in 1984 the topic chosen was holiness, the programme would have broken new ground for many evangelicals in including the Mennonite Alan Kreider speaking on 'Social Holiness' alongside Stanley Voke on 'Personal Holiness' and Bob Roxborough on 'Corporate Holiness'. In 1985 under the wider theme of 'Mission Still Matters', Alan Pain and the Methodist Donald English both tackled from different perspectives the topic of 'Evangelism and Signs Following'. The following year, Douglas McBain addressed the conference's opening session on

---

[74] *Newsletter* 10 (April, 1982), 1.
[75] Patrick Goodland, 'Mainstream Reflections. The First Decade', *Mainstream Magazine* 63 (September, 1998), 17.
[76] *Newsletter* 22 (April, 1986), 8-10.
[77] *Newsletter* 22 (April, 1986), 10-12.
[78] Interestingly, these were topics at the first Ministers' Conferences arranged by New Frontiers in 1985 and 1986. See Millward, 'Chalk and Cheese', 196. Of course, they would have been addressed differently.

the question 'Where is the Breeze Blowing today?', whilst the main speaker was the American writer on spirituality, Richard Foster, a member of the Society of Friends. In 1987, the conference addressed specific issues of the broken world. Mainstream's council had suggested in 1985 that future topics of discussion should include women in the church, divorce and remarriage, and sexual ethics – topics that may have been discussed *ad nauseam* since but were not as common then.

Alistair Campbell succeeded Paul Beasley-Murray as editor of the *Newsletter* in 1982. Then minister of Broadmead, Northampton (subsequently New Testament tutor at Spurgeon's College), Campbell continued to give the *Newsletter* an edge, not least through his own tackling of controversial topics such as eldership and prophecy.[79] The same practical edge was maintained when Terry Griffith assumed the editorship in 1986. Woven into a succession of articles about the practice of ministry and the nature of mission were articles on church membership,[80] church meetings,[81] church discipline,[82] the nature of covenanting,[83] and church planting (tackled initially by a non-Baptist author).[84] There was an article entitled 'When is a Baptist Church not a Baptist Church?',[85] others dealing with signs and wonders, the third wave and John Wimber,[86] and various reviews of books on charismatic renewal. Despite his own trenchant writing, Campbell's irenic spirit was manifest in his early open letter to Paul Fiddes following his publication of a booklet on *Charismatic Renewal*. He spoke of the booklet as stimulating and in parts 'wise' and 'excellent' and pointed out sections with which he had 'nothing but agreement'. He believed it could help the church to move 'forward from the impasse of some current debates'. Even so, he felt that Fiddes had not 'heard fully what the charismatic movement was saying' in its call to radical obedience and mutual submission.[87] Subsequently he positively reviewed J.I. Packer's book *Keep in Step with the Spirit*, calling it 'a great book' and encouraging that its strictures of the charismatic movement be taken seriously.[88]

---

[79] *Newsletter* 10 (September, 1982), 2-4; 11 (January, 1983), 2-7; 12 (January, 1983), 2-9; 17 (September, 1984), 1-2; 21 (January, 1986), 6-8.

[80] *Newsletter* 20 (September, 1985), 5-7; 44 (May, 1992), 4-8.

[81] *Newsletter* 16 (April, 1984), 2-10; 18 (January, 1985), 6-9; 26 (September, 1987), 5-7.

[82] *Newsletter* 15 (January, 1984), 1-2 and 4-9.

[83] *Newsletter* 13 (April, 1983), 2-4.

[84] *Newsletter* 16 (April, 1984), 10-11; 17 (September, 1984), 2-5; 30 (October, 1988), 3-8; 39 (January, 1991), 3-4; 44 (May, 1992), 1-4; 45 (August, 1992), 4-5; 47 (March, 1993), 9.

[85] *Newsletter* 20 (September, 1985), 7-10.

[86] *Newsletter* 19 (April, 1985), *passim*; 26 (September, 1987), 8-11.

[87] *Newsletter* 6 (January, 1981), 3-5. See Paul S. Fiddes, *Charismatic Renewal: A Baptist View* (London: Baptist Publications, 1980).

[88] *Newsletter* 18 (January, 1985), 1-3.

Contribution to the Denomination

The *Baptist Times* editorial quoted at the start of this chapter asserted that many of Mainstream's supporters were only on the fringe of sssociation life. That was contradicted by my own experience in the Devon and Cornwall Association and by my many visits to associations and ministers' conferences at the time. It was an easy accusation to make, but I wonder what evidence lay behind it.

While hard evidence is not available, my own judgement and experience strongly suggests that the existence of Mainstream kept a number of evangelical and charismatic ministers within the BU who might otherwise have drifted into other networks.[89] Running parallel to the development of Mainstream was the emergence of Coastlands, later to be known as New Frontiers International. By the late 1970s, Terry Virgo, its founder, was lending leadership support to between twenty and thirty churches.[90] Craig Millward has identified twenty-one Baptist churches which in the early 1980s identified with Virgo of which, significantly, only eight were led by accredited Baptist ministers.[91] It was a time of ferment during which many more could have left the Union. The evangelical and missional commitment of Mainstream's leadership, its incorporation of the charismatic wing, its statesmanlike leadership, and its encouragement of younger leaders, all within a commitment to the Union, prevented a greater leakage, even if it did not plug the leak completely.[92]

The hard work done to ensure Mainstream made a positive contribution to the denomination did not always attract public attention. One of its first acts was to call a covenanting study conference that was held in Bristol on 15 September 1981. It was addressed by Roger Nunn and Morris West and set out to explore new proposals for ecumenical relations with those who were not known for their enthusiasm about the issue. On 10 November 1981 the executive met with the Superintendents' Board. As a result they sought to ensure that some of the superintendents were invited to the Mainstream conference each year and endeavoured to communicate regularly and openly with both the superintendents and the Union's staff at Baptist Church House. Douglas McBain's role in openly advocating participation in the new ecumenical instruments by his seconding of a resolution that went to the 1989 Assembly in Leicester was crucial for many.[93]

In 1987 Mainstream sought to make a constructive contribution to the discussion on Baptist identity, which had been re-ignited by addresses given by Bryan Haymes and published by the Yorkshire Baptist Association.[94] It was a tribute to Brian

---

[89] See a related comment by Peter Grange, 'Mainstream Reflections. The First Decade', *Mainstream Magazine* 63 (September, 1998), 20.

[90] Millward, 'Chalk and Cheese', 227.

[91] Millward, 'Chalk and Cheese', 231.

[92] In addition to New Frontiers, a few, like Stephen Thomas and Mike Beaumont, chose to join the 'Salt and Light' Stream, rather than remain within the Baptist Union.

[93] Randall, *English Baptists*, 447.

[94] Brian Haymes, *A Question of Identity: Reflections on Baptist Principles and Practices* (Leeds: Yorkshire Baptist Association, 1986).

Haymes, then principal of the Northern Baptist College, and an indication of the seriousness of the desire of Mainstream to participate in a crucial debate, that they called a consultation and then published its papers by way of a response in *A Perspective on Baptist Identity* in 1987. The contributions ranged from a general and appreciative critique of Haymes' addresses to specific discussions of association life, ecclesiology, ministry, worship, and confessing our identity. The contributors were not lightweight and included pastors and theological educators.[95] They were convinced that the papers represented 'the views of many Christians who worship in local Baptist Churches' whilst freely admitting the papers were not speaking for all.[96] It was disappointing how little subsequent discussion and literature wanted to engage with their work.

Of course, Mainstream did not always get it right. Barbara Askew, on the staff of Baptist Church House, wrote to object to *Mainstream Newsletter's* 'disparaging remarks about the Baptist Assembly in Nottingham' in 1983. Alastair Campbell had written that the event 'lacked passion'.[97] In commenting on Campbell's remarks in a letter to David Coffey, Barrie White, whose commitment to the Union and integral role within it could not be questioned, wrote, 'The difficulty is I have a great deal of sympathy with the thrust of Alistair's letter.' Nonetheless he urged that Mainstream leaders 'do all in their power to support the new leadership at Baptist Church House by making criticisms in private and by avoiding hurting those who get enough kicks all round already …'[98] It was important for Mainstream to learn what battles to fight, which it did by experience and honest discussion among themselves.[99]

Promoting Individuals

Mainstream self-consciously sought to give a platform to emerging leaders and made recommendations for appointments to positions that fell vacant at the Union, at first without success.[100] Given that David Coffey was elected BU President in 1986, appointed Secretary for Mission and Evangelism in 1988 and then elected General Secretary of the Union in 1991, it might be judged more successful in this from the

---

[95] The contributors, in order, were Derek Tidball, Barrie White, Alastair Campbell, Nigel Wright, Michael Nicholls, Stephen Ibbotson and George Beasley-Murray. See further Randall, *English Baptists*, 466-49.

[96] David Slater (ed.), *A Perspective on Baptist Identity* (Kingsbridge: Mainstream, 1987), 5.

[97] Letter from Barbara Askew, 29 April 1983. Barrie White papers.

[98] Letter from Barrie White to David Coffey, 10 May, 1983. Barrie White papers.

[99] Unhappiness was expressed over articles written by Michael Taylor for the *Baptist Times* in 1983, but caution prevailed and rather than protest there was recognition of how circumstances had changed since 1971. Evangelicals no longer needed to feel they were 'standing on the last barracades' (sic) and the way forward was to supply decent copy for the *Baptist Times*. Letter from Barrie White to David Coffey, 16 March 1983, Barrie White papers.

[100] Minutes of Executive Committee, 18 November 1986, and 17 November 1984.

mid-1980s onwards. Douglas McBain, after his sojourn with Manna Ministries, was appointed to be Metropolitan Area Superintendent in 1989, in succession to Arthur Thompson, another 'Mainstreamer'. Peter Grange, its treasurer, was to serve as East Midlands Superintendent and then as Regional Minister (team leader) from 1994 to 2007, and Iain Collins, David Taylor and Brian Nicholls, all committed to Mainstream, became area superintendents in 1995. Spurgeon's College looked to Paul Beasley-Murray as principal in succession to Raymond Brown when the latter stepped down, exhausted and facing some health issues with the conviction that he had given it all that he could and it needed a younger man at the helm.[101] Except for Mainstream, I am sure I would not have been elected President of the Union in 1990 or become Secretary of Mission and Evangelism in succession to David Coffey. Others made vital contributions, if not always so publically. Patrick Goodland, for example, was on the committee that produced the new hymnbook. As McBain rightly said in 1997, 'Mainstream has served as a nursery in which leaders have received valuable early training for their new roles within the Baptist Union.'[102]

After those who had been given a platform by Mainstream assumed positions of leadership in the Union, the Mainstream executive did not immediately relax in its efforts to keep the Mainstream agenda before them. The executive minutes of 12 December 1992 record a meeting with the BU's relatively new secretariat which was composed of David Coffey, Keith Jones, Derek Tidball and Malcolm Goodspeed.[103] It commented that major points were made but there was a need to ensure they present 'OUR views and vision of the Union to the Secretariat, not just responding to what they want of us'.[104] Nigel Wright, then chairman of Mainstream, set out 'An Agenda for Baptist Christians' in the *Mainstream Newsletter* in January 1990, calling on the Union to be 'unambiguously and self-consciously evangelical', to 'cultivate a spirit of warmth and personal affirmation', 'reform its structures', 'see itself more clearly as a resource agency' enhancing 'the life of the churches and the associations', and produce 'high quality publications'; also, that an enquiry should be set up to see how the Union should be 'reformed and reshaped to meet the challenge of the new millennium'.[105] Much of this bore fruit under David Coffey's secretaryship of the Union, not least as a result of the denominational consultation that was called in September 1996.[106]

---

[101] McBain, *Fire*, 123, is misleading at this point. Letter from Raymond Brown, 23 September 2011.

[102] McBain, *Fire*, 124-25.

[103] These are the names listed in the minutes but it would also have included David Nixon, then Treasurer of the Baptist Union.

[104] Minutes of the Mainstream Executive, 12 December 1992. Upper case theirs.

[105] *Newsletter* 35 (January, 1990), 2-4. Nigel Wright addressed the agenda more fully in *Challenge to Change* (Eastbourne: Kingsway, 1991).

[106] Randall, *English Baptists*, 517-20.

The Irish Dimension

A further contribution of Mainstream, which has so far been under-appreciated, was the relationships which were forged with Irish Baptists. This took place at a time when such relationships between the respective official bodies were nonexistent. A group of Irish Baptist leaders, both ministers and lay, had hoped to attend the Mainstream conference in 1986, but their first visit did not actually take place until 1987 when eight attended and were warmly welcomed. In 1988 Maurice Kinkeard spoke at the conference about the work of The Bridge in Belfast. By 1989 a regular contingent were attending from Ireland and two years later members of the delegation preaching at the Baptist churches in Poynton and Rossendale before attending the conference itself. At the 1993 gathering Roy Searle led a spontaneous time of prayer for Ireland. In fact, Stephen Adams, one of the regular attendees from Ireland, comments that 'we never left home without being prayed for'. Through 'our troubled years', he says, 'we found many folk with a praying heart for Ireland'.[107] Lasting friendships were formed which have remained to this day and many Mainstreamers have visited Ireland as a result. Adams continues, '[Mainstream] gave us a fresh ability to get perspective on our local situation in the safety of others who loved God and did it differently!'

Adams, who with David McMillan later formed the Irish Baptist Network so as to maintain relationships with Baptists outside of Ireland, records several supportive conversations between them and existing or incoming officers of the Union. He writes that 'during this 12–14 year period we circulated news to interested friends in Ireland – hoping it might help in a better understanding of the mission heart of BUGB friends'.[108] Mainstream was probably the only forum in which Baptists from Ireland could meet British Baptists at the time.

Mainstream: Victim of its own Success?

Was Mainstream to become a victim of its own success? David Neil wrote to the Mainstream executive on 15 October 1985 from the Northern Baptist Association to say that the Association 'is now increasingly evangelical in outlook', that all but one minister would identify with Mainstream's stance, but that this meant that 'all kinds of thrusts that Mainstream would encourage are in fact becoming normal features of Association life', and that they did not really need an 'umbrella' to coordinate them. He was not questioning 'the value of Mainstream', but was not sure of its local relevance.[109]

Less than two years later, David Harper, General Superintendent of the Eastern Area, wrote to Jack Ramsbottom, following the conference, to query whether it had

---

[107] Email from Stephen Adams, 4 July 2012. The information in this paragraph comes from his files.

[108] Email from Stephen Adams, 4 July 2012.

[109] Letter from David Neil to Mainstream Executive, 15 October 1985. Barrie White papers.

served its purpose and should be disbanded, although, he added, there might still be a need for a conference like the one he had just attended. His reasoning was,

> I have no doubt that Mainstream has made a contribution to the life and witness of our denomination. It came into being at a time when the emphasis on growth and life that the organisation brings, was much needed in our churches. However, I believe that the situation has changed, I believe the denomination as a whole has taken up the emphasis that Mainstream has espoused and that what it represents is more than ever before the main stream of our denomination's life. Some of the early founding fathers of the group are now to be seen as among the establishment figures of our denomination.[110]

Mainstream was not unaware of these challenges. The executive discussed the role of the movement at length at its meeting in November 1985 and restated its aim as not only reflecting and representing its constituency but of instigating 'new initiatives'. The executive agreed that there was still 'a need to raise up people who will fill posts at national level', adding, 'there is a dearth of evangelicals committed to the denomination who would be likely to gain election to posts of influence in the denomination'.[111] Further discussion about the continuation of Mainstream took place in 1988, and, having decided its continuance was necessary 'for the time being', it was decided to revamp the executive, David Coffey and Douglas McBain having resigned because they were appointed to significant denominational posts. A new statement of purpose was drawn up and put to the conference in 1990, which stressed Mainstream's commitment to 'the renewal and deepening of evangelical faith and life among Baptist churches', the quest for 'a distinctive Baptist identity', the 'advocacy of reform', the 'appointment of men and women to positions of denominational responsibility' and 'the fostering of healthy-life giving relationships among Baptist Christians.[112]

During the 1990s, Mainstream evolved into new forms. First a younger leaders' forum was set up and then greater emphasis was put on regional networks. From 1994 it metamorphosed into a 'Word and Spirit Network' which, according to David Slater, long-time secretary of Mainstream in succession to David Coffey, 'was a significant shift of emphasis towards involvement in renewal [which] reflected the same kind of shift within the life of the churches'.[113] In doing so, however, it lost any real sense of wanting to encourage evangelicals of all stripes to play significant roles in the Union, perhaps in the mistaken belief that this could now be taken for granted, and Mainstream became a movement more committed to an internal agenda and nurturing spiritual experience.

---

[110] Letter from David Harper to Jack Ramsbottom, 16 January 1987. Barrie White papers.
[111] Minutes of Mainstream Executive, 18-19 November 1985.
[112] Statement of the Vision of Mainstream 1990, Barrie White papers.
[113] David Slater, 'Mainstream Reflections. The First Decade', *Mainstream Magazine* 63 (September, 1998), 27.

Conclusion

How far did Mainstream achieve its 'far greater ambitions' of uniting evangelicals of all kinds so as to become a positive influence in the Union's life? The answer must be to a considerable degree, but not wholly. Relationships between evangelical groups within Mainstream were sometimes uncomfortable but held together during crucial years of change. Attitudes to the Union were changed and evangelicals played a much greater role within the structures than in any previous twentieth-century generation, many rising to positions of influence and leadership in the Union. And it is not unreasonable to argue that many, especially charismatically-renewed Baptists, would have slipped out from under the Union's umbrella but for Mainstream. Throughout the early years it shunned membership, held to light structures and sought to preserve its nature as a movement rather than an organisation. In becoming the Word and Spirit Network it maintained part of its original vision but lost something of its reforming agenda within the denomination and focused more on spiritual refreshment for those who attended its conferences. Only subsequent generations will be able to tell whether the changes stimulated by Mainstream in 1980s have fundamentally affected the nature of the Baptist Union of Great Britain or merely affected them for a time. The inherent tendency of even a fellowship of churches like the Union, aided by the social context of our age, is towards bureaucratic centralisation and regulation. Each generation, therefore, has to fight its own battles against such trends and to ensure that the centre is truly reflective of the continuing evangelical life and vitality of the 'mainstream' of local churches, which remain evangelical and missional at their heart.

CHAPTER 14

What is truth?:[1] Evangelicalism, Foundationalism and a Hermeneutic of Witness

John E. Colwell

I guess that those of us who write academic articles and books, for the most part, have to live with the humbling frustration that our work will be read and engaged by a relatively small circle of the interested and remains highly unlikely to prompt popular interest or response. It is now almost fourteen years since Harriet Harris published her Oxford doctoral dissertation identifying fundamentalism as an evangelical form of foundationalism:[2] it is a fine and carefully argued academic treatise, it was well received within its own field of interest but, predictably (as far as I am aware), it created barely a ripple in the stream even of thoughtful Evangelicalism – which is to be greatly regretted since the thesis poses a challenge, not merely to the fundamentalism that it targets, but to Evangelicalism as a whole. Perhaps a couple of definitions would not be out of place since both 'foundationalism' and 'Evangelicalism' are slippery and contested terms.

'Foundationalism' is a term – usually employed dismissively – that occurs within post-modern criticisms of modernism and refers to any system of belief or knowledge that claims to ground that belief or knowledge on a rational or experiential foundation, a foundation that can be assumed *a priori*. 'Foundationalism' holds that the truth of a claim can be verified by reason or by experimentation. 'Foundationalism' seeks to demonstrate the truth of a claim by means of the assumed truth of another claim. 'Foundationalism' holds certain ways of knowing to be properly basic, *a priori*, beyond dispute, 'foundational'. 'Foundationalism', therefore, is predisposed to deal with certainties.

Calvin

Thus understood it would be difficult to sustain the charge of 'foundationalism', or at least 'biblical foundationalism', against the sixteenth-century Protestant reformers: I would not doubt for a moment that Luther and Zwingli, Bucer and Calvin, assumed a confidence in their reasoning and in the perception of their senses – a confidence

---

[1] John 18.38.
[2] Harriet Anne Harris, *Fundamentalism and Evangelicals* (Oxford: Clarendon Press, 1998).

that only recently has been called into such serious doubt – but they resisted the temptation of appealing to such assumed foundations in their affirmations of the truthfulness of Holy Scripture. For John Calvin in particular Holy Scripture is 'self-authenticating':

> ... those whom the Holy Spirit has inwardly taught truly rest upon Scripture, and that Scripture indeed is self-authenticated; hence it is not right to subject it to proof and reasoning.[3]

Notwithstanding the clumsy translation of the Latin *probationes* and *argumenta* with the English word 'proofs',[4] Calvin insists that the truthfulness of Scripture is confirmed through the inner testimony of the Holy Spirit and that supporting testimonies (*secundaria adminicula*) ought never to displace this primary (and inherently non-foundational) witness:

> ... Scripture will ultimately suffice for a saving knowledge of God only when its certainty is founded upon the inward persuasion of the Holy Spirit. Indeed, these human testimonies which exist to confirm it will not be in vain if, as secondary aids to our feebleness, they follow that chief and highest testimony. But those who wish to prove to unbelievers that Scripture is the Word of God are acting foolishly, for only by faith can this be known.[5]

While Calvin speaks of certainty (*certitudo*) here it is explicitly not that form of certainty attained through rational proofs or repeatable empirical experimentation: it is a certainty impressed upon us by the Spirit; it is not at our disposal; it is not subject to our manipulation; it is irreducibly 'gift'. The very next chapter of the *Institutes* with its rebuttal of those Calvin deems 'fanatics' clarifies that the 'inward persuasion of the Holy Spirit' of which he speaks is no mere indeterminate felt experience independent of Holy Scripture,[6] it is rather the dynamic of the Spirit speaking through Scripture – a dynamic that is promised to us but which never becomes our possession or right.

The charge that Evangelicalism tends towards Foundationalism – if this charge can be sustained – would therefore challenge those who seem to assume a seamless progression from the Reformation, through Puritanism, to the Evangelicalism of the eighteenth century and beyond. This, of course, is not at all to deny any continuity between these movements – the Reformation's insistence on the *sola Scriptura* principle (a principle often misconstrued and misappropriated) remains a touchstone of evangelical conviction – but it is to deny that the transition is seamless. All such trends of thought and practice merge into one another but, inasmuch as it is possible

---

[3] John Calvin, *Institutes of the Christian Religion* (ed. J.T. McNeill, trans. F.L. Battles; Philadelphia, PA: Westminster Press, 1960), I vii 5.

[4] Calvin, *Institutes*, I viii, and I viii 4.

[5] Calvin, *Institutes*, I viii 13.

[6] Calvin, *Institutes*, I ix 1-3.

to date the beginnings of the Enlightenment to the latter part of the seventeenth century, its beginnings coincide with the close of the Puritan age and give shape to a significantly different and distinct context of thought for the development of the Evangelicalism we have inherited.

Though again not undisputed, the promotion of Calvin's supporting testimonies (*secundaria adminicula*) to primary witnesses is well rehearsed:[7] rational arguments and demonstrations of the truthfulness of Scripture come to be pressed into service as confirmations of Scripture's inspiration – here understood not so much in terms of an inner witness of the Spirit to the reader or hearer as the process through which Scripture comes to be written in the first place. Or, to express the matter more blandly, the truthfulness of Scripture comes to be assumed as rationally demonstrable. Moreover, a context of thought that assumes rational objectivity and coherence encourages the reduction of Scripture's witness to a particular form of systematisation in which it is assumed that truth can be adequately expressed propositionally. Consequently, the narratives of Scripture fade from view, diminished to provide merely the dramatic background for dogmatic confessions. It is hardly surprising, therefore, that a particular stream of contemporary Evangelicalism defines orthodoxy through a series of shibboleths: creationism, virgin birth and penal substitution, or (more recently and even more disturbingly) headship, hell and homosexuality. Rather than issues of humble biblical and doctrinal enquiry, partisan and assumed interpretative affirmations are imposed as criteria for ecclesial exclusion. One is tempted to suggest Hermeneutics, an alternative word beginning with the letter 'H', as offering the possibility of a more basic, constructive and biblically faithful approach to truthfulness.

But one of the reasons Evangelicalism proves hard to define is that it derives from diverse roots and thereby issues in diverse expressions. If the scriptural focus of Puritanism transmogrifies in a rationalistic context into propositional reductionism so also late seventeenth-century German Pietism transmogrifies in an empiricist context into a similarly disturbing and damaging focus on felt experience. Principally through the influence of the Wesley brothers, German Pietism constitutes a separate and distinct source for contemporary British and North American Evangelicalism, a source every bit as constrained by philosophical empiricism as some aspects of British Puritanism became constrained by philosophical rationalism (though late Puritanism also has not been immune to empiricist tendencies). Here humble assurance morphs into a tangible insurance as, *in lieu* of trustfulness, certainty is sought in felt experience. And here, similarly, particular forms of felt experience are promoted as criteria for ecclesial inclusion or exclusion.

---

[7] See, for instance, George M. Marsden, *Fundamentalism and American Culture: The Shaping of Twentieth-Century Evangelicalism, 1870–1925* (New York, NY: Oxford University Press, 1982); Mark A. Noll (ed.), *The Princeton Theology, 1812–1921: Scripture, Science, and the Theological Method from Archibald Alexander to Benjamin Breckinridge Warfield* (Grand Rapids, MI: Baker, 1983); and my own *Living the Christian Story: The Distinctiveness of Christian Ethics* (Edinburgh: T&T Clark, 2001), 69-87.

The common denominator between these (admittedly simplified) streams of Evangelicalism is a quest for certainty, the assumption that faith can be confirmed, whether rationally or empirically, by criteria distinct from the subject of faith itself. In this respect one could claim that Evangelicalism is inherently apologetic (using the term in its Enlightenment rather than its patristic or medieval sense): it seeks to establish the truth of its claims by appeal to supposed universal criteria. Whether appeal is made to claimed healings, ecstatic charismatic phenomena or a transformed life; whether appeal is made to the 'scientific' evidence for creationism, the reasonableness of the empty tomb or (more modestly) the general reliability of the Gospels, the validity and persuasiveness of rational and empirical verification is presumed; the truth of faith is established by appeal to something other than the subject of faith, by appeal to supposedly objective criteria.[8] And in these respects at least, not withstanding its roots in the Reformation and in Puritanism, Evangelicalism (as a distinct historical and ecclesial movement) is an Enlightenment phenomenon and, as such, is innately Foundationalist.

I would be surprised if, by now, some readers were not responding with a 'so what': what is so wrong with Foundationalism? Do we not take for granted the validity of rational and empirical verification every time we boil a kettle, turn on a light or board an aircraft? What is so fatally wrong in seeking to confirm the truthfulness of Christianity rationally and empirically? As has often been noted, post-modernism is neither the opposite nor the end of modernism: as with most terms prefixed by 'post-', post-modernism is parasitic on continuing modernism; at its best it is a criticism of modernism; a humbling of modernism. It is not that rational and empirical criteria are invalid; it is rather that they fall short as guarantors of certainty. Pure objectivity is delusory and unobtainable: there can be no knowledge without a knowing subject, a knowing subject inhabiting a context, a community, a tradition; the observer is part of the experiment or, in hermeneutical terms, every reading is itself an act of interpretation. This is not necessarily to deny the distinct reality of the object known (though some would seem to go that far), it is merely a recognition of the limitations of our access to the object known. Any quest for certainty, even in the most rigorously scientific context, is over-ambitious.

The humbling implications of all this on biblical studies and preaching should be immediately apparent: no longer ought the scholar ever to boast of the assured conclusions of historical criticism; no more should the preacher pontificate concerning an author's intentions; discussions of significance should dethrone discussions of meaning; assumed implications should give way to admitted inferences. All this is well rehearsed and I have discussed it more carefully, at

---

[8] 'A postmodern (or post-liberal) theology ... must reject two forms of "foundationalism". First, it has to refuse the idea that faith is grounded in a series of propositions about "objects" available to our rational gaze: God, eternity, the soul, or incarnate divinity, "proven" by miraculous events and fulfilments of prophecies. Secondly, it has to refuse equally the idea that Christian beliefs are somehow "expressions" of experiences entirely preceding those beliefs.' John Milbank, *Theology and Social Theory* (Oxford: Blackwell, 1990), 382.

greater length, in other places, and on other occasions.⁹ My concern here is with something more basic: there is something far more foundationally wrong with Foundationalism with respect to Christian faith; the more profound issue is not that of the certainty or otherwise of our access to truth but, far more radically, of the nature of truth itself. The assumption that the truth with which Scripture is concerned can be verified rationally or empirically is seriously to mistake the nature of that truth, to misconstrue truth itself.

> What, then, is wrong with foundationalism? It is not that it seeks a common basis for rationality, but that it seeks the wrong one and in the wrong way. It seeks the wrong basis, because it seeks one that is merely secular: something inherent within human reason and experience. It thus expects human reason to ground itself. It seeks it in the wrong way, because it believes that it can find what it wants apart from revelation. Another way of putting the matter would be to say that it is intellectually Pelagian.¹⁰

All of which brings us to the central question of this essay, the question which is perhaps more searching and disturbing than any other question, the question posed (perhaps cynically) by Pilate, the question 'what is truth?'.

Truth in John's Gospel

The common sermonic response to Pilate's question is that truth is a someone, not a something; truth is personal; truth is Jesus himself. Does not Jesus himself, earlier in this Gospel, precisely identify himself as the truth (John 14:6)? Well, perhaps not, or at least perhaps not as straightforwardly as we sometimes assume. It is not that I want to deny that Jesus is himself the truth, truly divine and truly human, the truth about God and the truth about humanity – I am a Christian after all and, I trust, a thoroughly orthodox Christian. It is rather that, hesitantly, I want to question the way in which, popularly at least, we perhaps jump rather too quickly to an assumed christological answer to Pilate's question.

In the first place, the common translation of John 14:6 – 'Jesus answered, "I am the way and the truth and the life ..."' – though (in this case) 'literal', is perhaps too literal: the Greek conjunction καὶ is not always most appropriately translated by a simple 'and' but can be translated as 'even' or even as 'that is to say', rendering the second two terms, 'truth' and 'life' as expansions and explanations of the first term

---

⁹ See ch. 4 of *Promise and Presence: An Exploration of Sacramental Theology* (Eugene, OR: Wipf and Stock, 2011; first published by Milton Keynes: Paternoster, 2005); or the first four chapters of *Living the Christian Story: The Distinctiveness of Christian Ethics* (Edinburgh: T & T Clark, 2001); and, more recently, 'The word of his grace: what's so distinctive about Scripture?', in Helen Dare and Simon Woodman (eds), *The "Plainly Revealed" Word of God?: Baptist Hermeneutics in Theory and Practice* (Macon, GA: Mercer University Press, 2011), 191-210.

¹⁰ Colin E. Gunton, *A Brief Theology of Revelation: The 1993 Warfield Lectures* (Edinburgh: T&T Clark, 1995), 50.

'way'. Indeed these second two terms could be translated adjectively: 'I am the true and living way' (or 'I am the way – the true one and the living one').[11] Not only would such a translation accord better with the remainder of the sentence where the focus clearly is on Jesus as the way to the Father, it would similarly accord better with the other 'I am ...' sayings in the Gospel by focusing on a single metaphor. Succinctly, I am suggesting that Jesus is the truth in this passage deferentially: he is the truth inasmuch as he is the true and living way to the Father.

Similar could perhaps be claimed for Jesus' response to the Samaritan woman's theological question in John 4:23-24. I have never thought it likely that the text could be reduced to a commendation of sincerity: whatever else may be said of this Samaritan woman – as sinful, as unfortunate or as abused – there is nothing to suggest that her question or her worship were insincere. Rather her question concerns the proper location for worship, Samaria or Jerusalem, and, for all its apparent awkwardness, Jesus' response is better understood as specifically a response to the question of location: the Father is properly worshipped *in* the one who is the Spirit and *in* the one who is the Truth. If such a translation of the text commends itself then Jesus here is identified as the one who himself is the truth – but once again deferringly so, as the one who, with the Spirit, is the location point of access to the Father.

Moreover, in the Prologue to the Gospel, just as the Word 'became' (ἐγένετο) flesh so also grace and truth 'came' (ἐγένετο) through Jesus Christ (Jn 1:14, 17); it is not simply that Jesus Christ is himself truth but that truth, like grace, is accessed through him. Throughout this Gospel's upper room discourse the Spirit is referred to as the Spirit of truth – but does such reference identify the Spirit as being the truth or as characterised by the truth or pointing to the truth? It is not, then, that Jesus Christ is not the truth, but that he is the truth specifically inasmuch as he, with the Spirit, gives access to the Father. Indeed, Jesus' declaration that gives occasion to Pilate's question (Jn 18:37) falls short of a self-identification as the truth, speaking rather of being a witness to the truth. When, within this Gospel, Jesus claims to be speaking truly it is a claim supported by the corresponding claim that he knows what he is talking about (Jn 3:11), he is the one who has come from heaven (Jn 3:13), he witnesses only to 'what he has seen and heard' (Jn 3:32). This same dynamic of personal witness is claimed by the author of 1 John.

> That ... which we have heard, which we have seen with our eyes, which we have looked at and our hands have touched – this we proclaim concerning the Word of life. (1 Jn 1:1)

The point that I am attempting to establish is that truth, at least as it is expressed within this Fourth Gospel, does not admit to simple identification, whether personal or otherwise; it can only be witnessed to, indicated, mediated. Through Christ and by

---

[11] 'Both words are inserted here as explanatory of ὁδός.' C.K. Barrett, *The Gospel according to St. John: An Introduction with Commentary and Notes on the Greek Text* (London: SPCK, 2nd edn, 1978), 458.

the Spirit we can know the truth, and that truth has the power to liberate us (Jn 8:32), we can 'do' the truth (Jn 3:21), we can be 'of' the truth (Jn 18:37), we can even walk 'in' the truth (3 Jn 4). Yet the truth (as it is expressed here) never becomes our property or possession, never falls subject to simple identification. Even the Word made flesh is but a witness to truth rather than a simple and direct embodiment of truth. And it is this notion of truth as that which can be witnessed to but never possessed that fatally undermines foundationalism and also Evangelicalism inasmuch as it takes foundationalist form: we can witness to this truth but we cannot encapsulate this truth propositionally, establish this truth rationally or demonstrate this truth empirically.

Pannenberg

In an essay first presented in 1961 Wolfhart Pannenberg poses Pilate's question again and, having first compared Hebrew and Greek notions of truth, concludes in response to G.W.F. Hegel that truth must be eschatological, ultimately known in its unity only at the end of history but proleptically anticipated in the revelation of God in Jesus Christ.[12] This present essay does not afford sufficient space to explore Pannenberg's proleptic account of Christ, the manner in which this is developed in his later work, and the degree to which he too could be interpreted as conceding too much to historical positivism. This early (and in many ways programmatic) essay is mentioned here merely for its commonsensical affirmation that truth is historical and that, consequently, truth in its unity can only be encountered at the end of history – it can be and has been anticipated in Christ, witnessed in Christ and by Christ, but it can only now be encountered by way of anticipation, it can be witnessed but it cannot be possessed.[13]

As hinted above, the historical nature of truth as that which occurs through time and space – one could perhaps say that it 'becomes' (ἐγένετο) in time and space – may lead Pannenberg to give rather too much weight (in a foundationalist manner) to a positivistic approach to historical science. Yet, far more promisingly, here and in his subsequent work, it also leads Pannenberg to focus on the 'destiny' of Jesus: the proleptic anticipation of the final unity of truth is something that 'happens' in his life, death and (especially) his resurrection.[14] I am not suggesting that Jesus' witness to truth was exclusive of his teaching and proclamation but, following Pannenberg (and the entire Christian tradition), I am asserting that truth is witnessed in Christ's

---

[12] Wolfhart Pannenberg, 'What is Truth?', in *Basic Questions in Theology*: Volume 2 (trans. George H. Kehm; London: SCM Press, 1971), 1-27.

[13] '[T]he eschatological revelation of God is present in Christ's person and work only proleptically, and with the Not Yet of the Christian life this implies a brokenness of the knowledge of revelation in the context of ongoing debatability and of the power of doubt that constantly assails believers.' Wolfhart Pannenberg, *Systematic Theology*: Volume 1 (trans. Geoffrey W. Bromiley; Grand Rapids, MI: Eerdmans, 1991), 250.

[14] This is at the very least the sub-theme of Pannenberg's *Jesus-God and Man* (trans. Lewis L. Wilkins and Duane A. Priebe; London: SCM Press, 1968).

person and history at least as fundamentally as in his words. The incarnate one witnesses to truth as he who is simultaneously in his single person truly God and truly human – but what it means for him to be truly God and truly human is narrated in the gospel story, the story of his birth, his ministry, his passion and his resurrection and ascension. The truth witnessed in Christ, the truth of his deity and humanity, cannot be propositionally reduced as a static abstraction – it is a history, it is gospel, it is a story, it is narrated.

Scripture

And it is *narrated*. Since the history itself is witness to truth rather than simply encapsulation of truth or even embodiment of truth the narration of that story most definitely cannot pretend to a directness or identity other than that of witness. As witness to the one who in himself is witness to truth, Holy Scripture, of course, is not a merely human re-telling – Holy Scripture is inspired; it is a means of grace; it is read and heard with the promise and expectation that the Holy Spirit will render present the one who is the Word through these human words – but Holy Scripture is nonetheless a human re-telling and, as such, in its genuine humanity its words are read and heard under all the limitations and qualifications common to human texts. In the first (or perhaps last) place the narrative of Scripture is read and heard, read and heard by human readers and hearers who inhabit communities and traditions that bring shape and assumption to the text. This is not to imply that texts do not have the power to challenge those assumptions and to resist interpretative shaping, and in the power of the Spirit this is most certainly the case, but it is great folly to minimise or to ignore the potential of such shapings and assumptions. Moreover, commonly the text that is read and heard is read and heard in translation and, just as every reading is interpretative, so every fresh translation is certainly such. But primarily, the narrative of Scripture itself (if we can speak meaningfully of an original text) is still but text, human words that can never be wholly adequate even to merely human concepts (cf. Jn 3:12), human words that can never fully and unambiguously express an author's intentions. If it is the nature of all texts to be a deferring of meaning then as a narration of the one who is himself the witness to truth there can only be a deferring of truth in any reading or hearing of Holy Scripture.

To any who may find such conclusions disturbingly negative and overly hesitant I can only respond that I have come to find them refreshingly liberating. James Alison comments on the pressure within Protestant Evangelicalism to be 'right' and the contrasting 'freedom to be wrong' that he came to experience as a Catholic.[15] When

---

[15] 'I was brought up in a conservative middle-class English evangelical Protestant environment. The gift of Catholic faith, which I received at the age of eighteen, was never a movement towards the exotic, the liturgical, the aesthetic. It was, and is, the gift of enabling me to be wrong, and not to worry about it, of letting go of being right so as to receive being loved.' James Alison, *Faith beyond Resentment: Fragments Catholic and Gay* (London: Darton, Longman and Todd, 2001), xi.

I first read this it puzzled me: holding to a typically Protestant caricature, I had always assumed that the Magisterium represented a demand for doctrinal conformity. But maybe this central (and hierarchical) authority serves to alleviate an otherwise individualistic responsibility for doctrinal correctness. The degree to which Evangelicalism as we know it is an Enlightenment phenomenon is the degree to which it represents the expectation for correctness – generally an experiential correctness or a doctrinal correctness propositionally expressed. Buying in to the Enlightenment myth of pure objectivity (a manifest nonsense), Evangelicalism is suspicious of the subjective and dismissive of anything that whiffs of relativism. But there can be no knowledge whatsoever without a knowing subject, no hearing without a hearer, no reading without a reader. And, more pertinently for this present discussion, there can be no propositional dogmatic certainty if ultimate truth is narratively witnessed and eschatologically deferred.

It may be less than apparent thus far but the simple purpose of this short paper is to call Evangelicalism back to the Bible – a call which may sound surprising but to which there surely can be no principled objection. But it is a call back to the Bible as the book that it is as distinct from the book that it isn't; not to the Bible as an infallibly accessible repository of detached or detachable propositional truths and context-free rules and regulations but to the Bible as a 'book full of stories',[16] to the Bible with a narratival rendering of the Word made flesh as the witness to the truth at its centre, to the Bible as God's Word being given to us in the power of the Spirit, to the Bible as heard and read within the connected community of the Church in all its frailty and with all its historically rooted misconceptions and distortions. There can be no claim to infallibility here: we are but frail human hearers of a human word, albeit a human word being given again and again to us as a means of God's grace. But, more especially, there can be no claim to infallibility here since it is the nature of truth – or at least the nature of the truth with which Scripture is concerned – to be witnessed rather than encapsulated propositionally. Similarly, there can be no arrogance here: there can and should be sincere conviction but such conviction can only be held humbly and in continuing critical conversation within the community of the Church. (The Anabaptist tradition of a community hermeneutic has particular pertinence here.)

The Church

Moreover, and more positively, since it is the nature of truth to be witnessed and since Scripture primarily witnesses to this truth narratively, might it not be the case that the Church's witness to truth ought similarly to be primarily narratival rather than propositional or even proclamatory? I am not, of course, pretending that the Church has nothing to say – Jesus taught the multitude many things (Mt. 9:36) and the Church has much validly to say. But Jesus is at least as much the witness to truth

---

[16] The quotation comes from the hymn by Maria Penstone (1859–1910), *The Baptist Hymn Book* (London: Psalms and Hymns Trust, 1962), number 740.

in his person and destiny as in his teaching and the Church, if it is rightly to witness to truth, must do so through the connected narrative of its life as much as in its proclamation. And here again it is not just a matter of the inadequacy of the Church's proclamation (though it can never be other than frail and fallible) but rather of the nature of the truth to which the Church is called to bear witness.

> It is not dry manuals (full as these may be of unquestionable truths) that express with plausibility for the world the truth of Christ's Gospel; it is the existence of the saints who have been grasped by Christ's Holy Spirit. And Christ himself foresaw no other kind of apologetics ...[17]

It surely is ironic that the question of practical holiness, or rather the question of the validity of an expectation for practical holiness, has been an issue of doctrinal division within Evangelicalism. (I have argued elsewhere that John Wesley's account of perfect love is a restatement of a catholic tradition rather than an easily dismissed personal idiosyncrasy.[18]) How predictably and foolishly we evade the challenge to a coherent narratival witness through doctrinal dispute. The question, surely, ought not to be whether the Church witnesses to the truth in the narrative of its life but, more pressingly, the kind of narrative life that validly witnesses to this truth.

Jesus stands before Pilate as witness to truth, as the king whose kingdom 'is not of this world' (Jn 18:36), as one who refuses to defend himself or to be defended. Pilate can no more comprehend the truth to which Jesus witnesses than he can comprehend the manner in which Jesus is a king.

> Jesus' disavowal of the kingship of this world does not mean that he is not a king. Rather his dialogue with Pilate reveals that he is not the kind of king that Pilates are capable of recognizing. For Pilates are people who have disavowed truth, and in particular, a truth that comes in the form of a suffering servant.[19]

For the Church authentically to witness to truth, then, is for the Church to narrate over and again the story of Jesus and to echo that narrated story in its own narrative life. It is for the Church to proclaim the suffering servant and to be the suffering servant within the world. It is for the Church to proclaim the Cross and itself to walk the way of the Cross. It is for the Church to proclaim the resurrection and itself to face suffering, persecution, sickness and death confidently and peacefully in the light

---

[17] Hans Urs von Balthasar, *The Glory of the Lord: A Theological Aesthetics*: Volume 1. *Seeing the Form* (trans. Erasmo Leiva-Merikakis, ed. Joseph Fessio S.J. and John Riches; Edinburgh: T&T Clark, 1982), 494.

[18] John E. Colwell, 'Offending in Many Things: A comparison of John Wesley and Thomas Aquinas on the nature of sin in the believer', in Paul Taylor (ed.), *Wesley Papers: Papers presented to The Wesley Fellowship Conference in 2000* (Ilkeston: The Wesley Fellowship, 2002), 3-14.

[19] Stanley Hauerwas, *After Christendom?: How the Church Is to Behave If Freedom, Justice, and a Christian Nation Are Bad Ideas* (Nashville, TN: Abingdon Press, 1991), 91-92.

of that resurrection. It is for the Church to proclaim the faith and to live faithfully, hopefully and lovingly. It is for the Church to witness to the truth and to live truthfully.

> Here is my servant, whom I uphold,
> my chosen one in whom I delight;
> I will put my Spirit on him
> and he will bring justice to the nations.
> He will not shout or cry out,
> or raise his voice in the streets.
> A bruised reed he will not break,
> and a smouldering wick he will not snuff out.
> In faithfulness he will bring forth justice;
> he will not falter or be discouraged
> till he establishes justice on earth.
> In his law the islands will put their hope. (Isa. 42:1-4)

As the true servant Jesus stands before Pilate, not raising his voice, nor even dismissing the flawed grasp of his identity and mission that Pilate represents, but quietly, even in this extremis, bearing witness to truth. Without prejudice to valid but ultimately futile discussions of the identity of the 'servant' in the mind of the original author, surely we can accept this dramatic depiction as descriptive of God's true servant in every age and context and, thereby, as archetypically represented in Christ. God's true servant brings justice to the nations not by haranguing or aggression, nor by breaking the bruised or extinguishing the faint and flickering; God's true servant proclaims truth truly by truthful manner as much as by truthful content. The arrogant and hectoring are incongruous in the service of the true God because such are a denial of his nature and person; they are precisely a denial of the very truth they seek to declare. The gospel narratives witness to one who witnesses to truth by bearing with most unlikely and unpromising disciples, by repudiating the miraculous as too simple confirmation of his message and person, and by submitting to a torturous death as the ultimate witness to truth. And he calls us to follow him, to bear witness to truth in the manner that he bears witness to truth, and thereby to be 'of the truth', to 'walk in the truth', to be means of the truth, to be those in and through whom the truth 'becomes' in the world. To be other than thus, sadly, is to be denying of the very truth to which we are seeking to witness.

And, sadly, an all too common experience of contemporary Evangelicalism bears little resemblance to the humble and affirming servant: here all too often one is accosted by aggressive and strident affirmation; by an eagerness to quench that which is deemed insufficiently aflame; by encounters that are bruising and self-confidently dismissive. My argument in this paper is that this embodied distortion of truthfulness is inevitable inasmuch as Evangelicalism is an Enlightenment phenomenon, inasmuch as Evangelicalism is inherently foundationalist. If, at its best, post-modernism can be understood as a humbling of modernism, then perhaps post-

Evangelicalism can be affirmed and welcomed, not as a rejection of the proper characteristics of Evangelicalism – a focus on Scripture, on the Cross, on spiritual transformation and responsive action – but as a humbling of the manner in which those characteristics are expressed, as a rejection of the presumptions of foundationalism, as an embracing of the more modest responsibility of witness.

That Evangelicalism is undergoing some form of identity crisis at present is the unavoidable consequence of its Enlightenment heritage. Regrettably, the predictable response of some to this crisis of identity has been an entrenching within the very foundationalist supposed certainties that initiated the crisis in the first place and that are unsustainable in their foundationalist form. The call, then, is not just for a humbling for humbling's sake, nor merely for an abandoning of foundationalism for the sake of philosophical development and fashion, but for a renewed appreciation of the nature of the truth to which the gospel is witness and a renewed commitment to witness to that truth in a manner that is truly truthful.

CHAPTER 15

Sapientia Experimentalis: 'Knowledge by experience' – Aspects of a Baptist Baptismal Spirituality

Anthony R. Cross

Introduction

Baptists are not known for their spirituality and, arguably, have not provided the church with any of its 'spiritual giants'.[1] Brian Graves suggests this is because Baptists 'generally remain unclear about what "spirituality" means and how it relates to Baptists'.[2] But this is common across the Christian spectrum as there are so many understandings – not all of them complementary – of what spirituality is.[3] This applies to Evangelicals more widely[4] and Baptists in particular.[5] The result of this is summed up well by Glenn Hinson: 'Baptists have approached spirituality much as they have approached virtually every other concept or practice – with a great deal of diversity.'[6] All this said, however, is not to suggest that Baptists lack a spirituality, even if it is a diverse one. Rather, spirituality is an often neglected yet vital part of the Baptist tradition,[7] so much so that Ian Randall has explored the myth of the

---

[1] At least five British Baptists, however, suggest themselves: John Bunyan, Anne Dutton, Anne Steele, Charles Haddon Spurgeon, and F.B. Meyer.

[2] Brian C. Graves, 'Centered Hearts, Circled Hands: Biographical Explorations of Baptist Spirituality', *Perspectives in Religious Studies* 36.1 (Spring, 2009), 77-100 (77).

[3] On which, see, e.g., the useful introduction with survey by Karen E. Smith, *Christian Spirituality* (SCM Core Text; London: SCM Press, 2007), 1-20.

[4] The relevance of evangelical spirituality for this study lies in Baptists being the most overtly evangelical of the mainstream denominations.

[5] E.g., Ian M. Randall, '"Look to Jesus Christ": English Baptists and Evangelical Spirituality', *American Baptist Quarterly* 25.1 (Spring, 2006), 8-26; Paul Fiddes and Stephen Finamore, 'Baptists and Spirituality: A Rule of Life', in Paul S. Fiddes (ed.), *Under the Rule of Christ: Dimensions of Baptist Spirituality* (Regent's Study Guides, 14; Oxford: Regent's Park College, 2008), 1-23, and the whole of this volume.

[6] E. Glenn Hinson, 'Baptist Approaches to Spirituality', *Baptist History and Heritage* 37.2 (Spring, 2002), 6-31 (6).

[7] See in particular the collection of essays in Gary A. Furr and Curtis W. Freeman (eds), *Ties that Bind: Life Together in the Baptist Vision* (Macon, GA: Smyth & Helwys, 1994), with its threefold focus on conversionist, contemplative, and corporate spirituality; also Christopher J. Ellis, *Gathering: A Theology and Spirituality of Worship in Free Church Tradition* (London: SCM Press, 2004).

missing spirituality,[8] and Molly Marshall has called for Baptist seminaries and colleges to redress this neglect by reintroducing spiritual formation into ministerial and theological preparation.[9]

Influences on Baptist Spirituality

What, then, have been the major influences on Baptist spirituality? Glenn Hinson has identified four major traditions, chief among which is Puritan-Separatist spirituality,[10] which was itself influenced by the contemplative tradition associated with such figures as Bernard of Clairvaux and Jan van Ruysbroeck, and is exemplified by John Bunyan.[11] Second is a conversionist spirituality which grew out of the two Great Awakenings, with a key figure being Jonathan Edwards, and finding expression in such Baptists as John Gill, Andrew Fuller, and William Carey, and the great missionary tradition which Fuller and Carey pioneered.[12] Third is a pragmatic spirituality which Hinson identifies in, for instance, the Southern Baptist Convention's concerns for public professions of faith and financial contributions,[13] and observes that this displays influence from contemporary business models.[14] Finally, there is a seeker spirituality with its emphasis on the inner life not outer commitment, and in which the subjective approach to religion is evident in the concern for the value of 'spirit' over institution.[15]

Other scholars identify different combinations of traditions. In another study, Hinson notes Richard J. Foster's identification of six traditions of spirituality which appeal to many Baptists: the contemplative, holiness, charismatic, social justice, evangelical, and incarnational traditions,[16] and Hinson notes how individual Baptists

---

[8] Ian. M. Randall, 'The Myth of the Missing Spirituality: Spirituality among English Baptists in the Early Twentieth Century', in Philip E. Thompson and Anthony R. Cross (eds), *Recycling the Past or Researching History?: Studies in Baptist Historiography and Myths* (Studies in Baptist History and Thought, 11; Milton Keynes: Paternoster, 2005), 106-27.

[9] Molly T. Marshall, 'The Changing Face of Baptist Discipleship', *Review and Expositor* 95.1 (Winter, 1998), 59-73 (66-67).

[10] E. Glenn Hinson, 'Reassessing the Puritan Heritage in Worship and Spirituality: A Search for a Method', *Worship* 53.5 (September, 1979), 318-26, 'Baptists and Spirituality: A Community at Worship', *Review and Expositor* 84.4 (Fall, 1987), 649-58, and 'Baptist Approaches to Spirituality'.

[11] Hinson, 'Baptist Approaches to Spirituality', 7-11. In this article, Hinson explores the influence of Puritans, Anabaptists, and the Great Awakening on the development of Baptist spirituality.

[12] Hinson, 'Baptist Approaches to Spirituality', 12-18.

[13] Cf. Marshall, 'Changing Face of Baptist Discipleship', 59-60.

[14] Hinson, 'Baptist Approaches to Spirituality', 18-24, and 'Baptists and Spirituality', 657.

[15] Hinson, 'Baptist Approaches to Spirituality', 24-27.

[16] Hinson, 'Baptist Approaches to Spirituality', 25-27. See Richard J. Foster, *Streams of Living Water: Celebrating the Great Traditions of Christian Faith* (San Francisco, CA: HarperCollins, 1998), 23-272.

and Baptist groups have been attracted to one or another of these approaches.[17] Molly Marshall identifies the various influences on Baptist spirituality as Lutheran, Reformed (often in the form of Puritan spirituality), Wesleyan, Anabaptist,[18] and even what she calls 'the *Zeitgeist* of the late twentieth century with its urgent spiritual quest'.[19] From these she identifies four types of Baptist spirituality (which she also speaks of in terms of discipleship): conversionist, charismatic, crusading (or prophetic), and contemplative spiritualities.[20] Graves extends the list of traditions that have shaped Baptist spirituality, including Puritans, Anabaptists, Calvinists, Evangelicals, Holiness, Modernists, Liberals, and Fundamentalists,[21] while others focus on one specific form of spirituality or another: for instance, Timothy George and Nigel Wright have both focused on the Anabaptist tradition,[22] while David Bebbington and Ian Randall[23] have explored the holiness tradition.[24] Recognition of all these influences confirms Randall's assessment of evangelical spirituality, that it

---

[17] Hinson, 'Baptist Approaches to Spirituality', 27.
[18] Marshall, 'Changing Face of Baptist Discipleship', 61-66.
[19] Marshall, 'Changing Face of Baptist Discipleship', 61.
[20] Marshall, 'Changing Face of Baptist Discipleship', 68-69.
[21] Graves, 'Centered Hearts, Circled Hands', 79.
[22] Timothy George, 'The Spirituality of the Radical Reformation', in Jill Raitt, Bernard McGinn and John Meyendorff (eds), *Christian Spirituality: High Middle Ages and Reformation* (World Spirituality; London: SCM Press, 1989 [1988]), 334-71; and Nigel G. Wright, 'Spirituality as Discipleship: The Anabaptist Heritage', in Fiddes (ed.), *Under the Rule of Christ*, 79-101.
[23] D.W. Bebbington, *Evangelicalism in Modern Britain: A History from the 1730s to the 1980s* (London: Unwin Hyman, 1989), 151-80, and *Holiness in Nineteenth-Century England* (The 1998 Didsbury Lectures; Carlisle: Paternoster Press, 2000); and Ian M. Randall, 'Capturing Keswick: Baptists and the Changing Spirituality of the Keswick Convention in the 1920s', *Baptist Quarterly* 36.7 (July, 1996), 331-48; and Charles Price and Ian Randall, *Transforming Keswick: The Keswick Convention, Past, Present and Future* (Carlisle: OM Publishing, 2000).
[24] It is also worth mentioning at this point that another key influence on Baptist spirituality has been the ecumenical movement. E.g., in Britain in the mid-twentieth century prominent Baptists, such as Neville Clark, Stephen F. Winward, Alec Gilmore, and later Paul Sheppy and Christopher J. Ellis, were among those involved in the Joint Liturgical Group, formed in 1963, who, with others, rediscovered and reintroduced liturgical thinking into Baptist worship. Not only did this focus on baptism and eucharist, but also prayer, Bible reading, hymnody and psalms, and the 'spiritual disciplines'. See Ian M. Randall, *The English Baptists of the Twentieth Century* (Didcot: The Baptist Historical Society, 2005), 320-24; and also Anthony R. Cross, *Baptism and the Baptists: Theology and Practice in Twentieth-Century Britain* (Studies in Baptist History and Thought, 3; Carlisle: Paternoster Press, 2000), *passim*.

is 'considerably richer and more dynamic than has sometimes been thought';[25] an observation that is equally applicable to Baptist spirituality.

Taking a different and complementary tack, Graves employs a biographical approach which focuses on prominent Baptists and their life and thought.[26] In doing so he focuses on three common themes found in each of them:

> *Jesus* as the interpretive source or guide for one's religious experience; *Conversion*, a spiritual-ethical transformation of the whole person from the inside out, as the heart of one's religious experience; and *Prayer* as the means of ongoing nurture of both root and fruit for the one transformed.[27]

But what is perhaps surprising from a people named after this rite, is how rare baptismal accounts and reflections on them are in Baptist autobiographies and biographies.

This dovetails with another approach that is particularly helpful to the study of baptismal spirituality. Stanley Grenz believes that 'there is a typically Baptist vision of spirituality, a Baptist way of going about the task of being Christian',[28] which lies 'in a unique blending of certain emphases into a specific approach to the quest for holiness and Christlikeness that typifies Baptists in general'. The strength of this approach lies in the fact that Grenz eschews 'a scholarly treatment of the subject', a 'purely academic approach', because it misses 'the ethos of the quest as practiced by Baptist people'.[29] He writes, 'The line of thought I offer is induced – almost simplistically[30] – from my own quest for spirituality fostered by, and nurtured within an unabashedly, unashamedly Baptist context.' It is 'an admittedly subjective attempt to come to grips with what to me is the specifically Baptist approach to the age-long quest to know God and grow in godliness'.[31] 'To know God and grow in

---

[25] Ian M. Randall, *Evangelical Experiences: A Study in the Spirituality of English Evangelicalism 1918–1939* (Studies in Evangelical History and Thought; Carlisle: Paternoster Press, 1999), 5.

[26] Graves, 'Centered Hearts, Circled Hands', 80. His three biographies, 81-98, are of Harry Emerson Fosdick, Rosalee Mills Appleby, and Howard Thurman.

[27] Graves, 'Centered Hearts, Circled Hands', 81 (italics added).

[28] Stanley Grenz, 'Maintaining the Balanced Life: The Baptist Vision of Spirituality', *Perspectives in Religious Studies* 18.1 (Spring, 1991), 59-68 (59).

[29] Cf. Ian Randall, *What a Friend we have in Jesus: The Evangelical Tradition* (Traditions of Christian Spirituality Series; London: Darton, Longman and Todd, 2005), 15, 'Evangelicals hold to ... a personal relationship with Jesus Christ ... It is also a spirituality of ordinary people.' This, too, applies to Baptists.

[30] Cf. Hinson, 'Baptists and Spirituality', 649, 'Broadly speaking, Baptists have exhibited a preference for a relatively simple and uncomplicated piety both corporately and privately. In public worship they usually include most of the same basic elements – prayer, Bible reading, sermon. All observe the two major "ordinances" – baptism and Lord's Supper – but in practice Baptists ascribe greater importance to scriptures and sermons than they do to the ordinances. Personal piety consists essentially of Bible reading and simple, direct prayers.'

[31] Grenz, 'Maintaining the Balanced Life', 60.

godliness', I believe, is effectively Grenz's working definition of spirituality, and is one with which many Baptists would agree. This approach has a strong appeal to Baptists with their emphasis, exemplified in believer's baptism, on the necessity of personal faith in Christ, and that through conversion (and in many cases on the condition of baptism) the believer enters the church.[32]

Employing the categories advanced by Ernst Troeltsch, Grenz observes that Baptists live within the tension between a sect-type spirituality that encapsulates the ethos of believers' church separatists while sharing certain features of other mainline denominations, specifically a church-type ethos. The genius of the Baptists, he argues, is their striving 'to be true to a basically sectarian vision, while responding to the lure of being a church'.[33] He expands on this:

> the genius of the Baptist vision of spirituality lies in the attempt – sometimes successful, sometimes thwarted – to maintain a delicate balance between, or to hold in creative tension, two sets of seemingly opposite principles: the inward versus the outward and the individual versus the corporate.[34]

It follows that because spirituality is generated 'from within the individual, inner motivation is crucial'. For Baptists, therefore, 'mere outward form does not constitute spirituality' because without the inward vitality the outward act is dead ritual. Outward adherence to ecclesiastical dictums is not personal spirituality, which is 'a matter of inner motivation'.[35] Further, faith is a matter of experience, transforming life. Personal conversion is an experience that is foundational to the Christian life and leads to a personal spiritual walk. While spirituality is a matter of the heart, the Christian life is also one of discipleship, which is the translation of the inner commitment into outward action. Discipleship can be summed up as the imitation of Christ, a daily walk, and this in turn determines Baptist ecclesiology.

---

[32] Cf. H. Wheeler Robinson, *The Life and Faith of the Baptists* (London: Methuen, 1927), 84, 'The Baptist stands or falls by his conception of what the Church is; his plea for believers' baptism becomes a mere archæological idiosyncrasy, if it be not the expression of the fundamental constitution of the Church. We become members of the living Body of Christ by being consciously and voluntarily baptized in the Spirit of Christ – a baptism witnessed by the evidence of moral purpose and character as the fruit of the Spirit.'

[33] Grenz, 'Maintaining the Balanced Life', 60-61, quotation from 61. Here he is using the classifications of Ernst Troeltsch, *The Social Teaching of the Christian Churches* (2 vols; London: George Allen & Unwin, 1950), as applied to Baptists by A.C. Underwood, *A History of the English Baptists* (London: The Baptist Union Publication Department, 1947), 15-20. For a critique of this view, see Paul S. Fiddes, 'Church and Sect: Cross-Currents in Early Baptist Life', in Anthony R. Cross and Nicholas J. Wood (eds), *Exploring Baptist Origins* (Centre for Baptist History and Heritage Studies, 1; Oxford: Regent's Park College, 2010), 33-57, who argues that the more appropriate classification is Troeltsch's 'free-church' type, which is closer to church than sect.

[34] Grenz, 'Maintaining the Balanced Life', 61.

[35] Grenz, 'Maintaining the Balanced Life', 62.

Salvation is not to be found in the church but in Christ, and a believer joins the church to share with the people of God in the mandate given to the church.[36]

This explains the attitude of the majority of Baptists to the rites of the church. On the one hand, they reject the sacramentalism of the mainline churches, but, on the other, unlike the Quakers, they do not totally reject the sacraments, a term which the majority of them avoid, preferring instead the word ordinances.[37] Generally they avoid religious rituals, and baptism and the Lord's supper are for them mere signs, symbols of personal obedience to Christ. In their rejection of the ordinances as means of grace Baptists on the whole deny any mediation of grace through their performance. Rather baptism and communion are acts of obedience to Christ's command. For the majority of Baptists they are baptized because Jesus was himself baptized and they are to follow his example. 'The ordinances, therefore, are outward acts of imitation of Jesus which reflect one's obedient response to Christ. They are means to express outwardly what is already inwardly true.'[38]

The second creative tension with which Baptists seek to live is that between the individual and the corporate.[39] Grenz notes that Baptists understand the Christian life as an individual matter with both conversion and growth in the faith being primarily the task of the individual. This rules out the possibility of infant baptism because there is no such thing for Baptists as vicarious saving faith. In the same way that the church cannot mediate grace and eternal life, neither can it mediate spirituality. In their separation from state churches, the first Baptists 'inaugurated a radical shift in the relationship of soteriology and ecclesiology, exchanging the priority of the church for the priority of the believer'. The church is no longer seen as antedating and constituting the believer, rather it is converted individuals who constitute the church 'which is the product of the coming together of the saved for the purpose of fostering growth toward spirituality within each other. The church, therefore, is a

---

[36] Grenz, 'Maintaining the Balanced Life', 62-64.

[37] Hinson, 'Baptists and Spirituality', 654, 'Baptist spirituality has obviously been more Bible and sermon-centered than liturgical and sacramental as in the Roman Catholic, Orthodox, or Anglican traditions. Indeed, most Baptists have hesitated to employ the word *sacrament* when they spoke of baptism or the Lord's Supper, preferring the term *ordinance* instead. Most have probably leaned toward Huldrych Zwingli's representational theory in their understanding of the ordinances, despite the fact that they drew most of their theology from John Calvin. Some Baptists, especially in England, however, have also followed Calvin's doctrine of the Lord's Supper with its emphasis on real presence and do not hesitate to speak of sacraments. Accordingly, they have referred to both baptism and Lord's Supper as "means" of grace rather than only "signs" of grace' (italics original). For examples of this, see the essays in Anthony R. Cross and Philip E. Thompson (eds), *Baptist Sacramentalism* (Studies in Baptist History and Thought, 5; Carlisle: Paternoster Press, 2003); and Anthony R. Cross and Philip E. Thompson (eds), *Baptist Sacramentalism 2* (Studies in Baptist History and Thought, 25; Milton Keynes: Paternoster, 2008).

[38] Grenz, 'Maintaining the Balanced Life', 63-64, quotation from 64.

[39] Of this Randall, *Evangelical Experiences*, 188, states that during the inter-war period 'Many Baptists sat somewhat uncomfortably between corporate and individualistic approaches to spirituality', and, I believe, this is still so.

voluntary association of individual believers.'[40] That said, however, 'In the Baptist outlook ... the individual is dependent on the group', for all believers need the encouragement and admonition that they both receive from and give to each other.[41] Grenz seeks to redress these tensions by balancing 'the priority of the individual with a turn in the opposite direction, to a corresponding emphasis on the corporate dimension of the Christian life'.[42] In short, 'Baptists understand spirituality in terms of the balanced life.'[43]

Grenz's personal and subjective approach harmonizes with Randall's when he notes the variety of understandings of spirituality within the Christian traditions – Baptists among them[44] – and accepts those which combine theological reflection *and* Christian experience.[45] He is particularly drawn to Martin Luther's phrase *sapientia experimentalis*, '"knowledge by experience", to convey the inner aspect of Christian faith'. 'This perspective', Randall maintains, 'means that spirituality is not taken to refer exclusively to the life of prayer or the spiritual exercises. Academic study of spirituality involves critical historical analysis of a broad range of "lived experience".' He, therefore, rejects looking at theology 'in an abstract fashion' and instead focuses on 'how doctrinal convictions both shaped and were shaped by concrete experience'.[46] To this end, he adopts the analytical framework proposed by Philip Sheldrake, that spirituality is 'concerned with the conjunction of theology, prayer and practical Christianity'.[47] He immediately comments on how the various Evangelical movements he examines

> espoused a theology of the way God relates to human beings, taught that there should be an experience of God which was both individual and communal, and had explicit guidelines or held implicit assumptions about the way faith should be practised. It has been common to study church history through the lens of developments in doctrine or

---

[40] Grenz, 'Maintaining the Balanced Life', 64-65, quotation from 65.

[41] Grenz, 'Maintaining the Balanced Life', 67.

[42] Grenz, 'Maintaining the Balanced Life', 66.

[43] Grenz, 'Maintaining the Balanced Life', 68. Cf. Graves, 'Centered Hearts, Circled Hands', 99, who concludes his study of Fosdick, Appleby, and Thurman with the observation that 'They shaped their appropriations of larger cultural and theological trends with a balance between individual autonomy and communal ethics – a balance consistent with Baptist values.'

[44] Randall, *Evangelical Experiences*, 174-205.

[45] Randall, *Evangelical Experiences*, 1-2.

[46] Randall, *Evangelical Experiences*, 2, gets the phrase from Bengt Hoffman, 'Lutheran Spirituality', in Robin Maas and Gabriel O'Donnell (eds), *Spiritual Traditions for the Contemporary Church* (Nashville, TN: Abingdon Press, 1990), 122-37 (147).

[47] Philip Sheldrake, *Spirituality and History: Questions of Interpretation and Method* (London: SPCK, 2nd edn, 1995), 60. See Randall, *Evangelical Experiences*, 2, and *What a Friend*, 22, in both of which he uses Sheldrake's first edition of 1991.

changes in ecclesiastical institutions. The procedure adopted here seeks to give weight to experience and how it interacts with theology and practice.[48]

In a similar fashion, this short paper sets out to do two things: combine aspects of Baptist baptismal theology with the personal testimonies given by those baptized immediately prior to their baptism, or their later reflections on that experience.[49]

The Personal Testimony and Baptismal Spirituality

The words of Andrew Fuller speak for many Baptists when, in his 1802 circular letter to the Northamptonshire Association, he draws attention to 'the *influence* of this ordinance [of baptism], where it produces its proper effects, in promoting piety in individuals, and purity in the church'.[50] It is on this dimension of spirituality that the remainder of this paper focuses.

The personal testimonies of baptismal candidates occupy a key place within the baptismal service,[51] and provide a window into Baptist spirituality. Their strength is also their weakness: they are reflections of a believer's experience of conversion and walk with God, their discipleship. Frequently lacking in theological sophistication,

---

[48] Randall, *Evangelical Experiences*, 2.

[49] This presents several immediate methodological problems for the present study's focus on *baptismal* spirituality: such testimonies are given before the act of immersion and, as such, have usually been written before the actual event; and such testimonies are not easy to come by. The first matter is obviated to some degree when baptism is itself seen as an event, an entire service in which the grace of God is acknowledged and celebrated and the baptized respond in personal faith within the setting of the fellowship at worship. The second matter means that such testimonies are unevenly spread geographically and chronologically. Those comments said, it is nevertheless a worthwhile exercise to examine the range of baptismal experiences.

[50] Andrew Fuller, 'The Practical Uses of Christian Baptism' (1802), in A.G. Fuller (ed.), *The Complete Works of the Rev. Andrew Fuller, with a Memoir of his Life* (London: William Ball, 1841), 728-30 (728, italics original). On Fuller's spirituality, see Michael A.G. Haykin, '"Hazarding all for God at a clap": The Spirituality of Baptism among British Calvinistic Baptists', *Baptist Quarterly* 38.4 (October, 1999), 185-95 (188-93), and Michael A.G. Haykin (ed.), *The Armies of the Lamb: The Spirituality of Andrew Fuller* (Classics of Reformed Spirituality; Dundas, ON: Joshua Press, 2001).

[51] Paul Beasley-Murray, *Radical Believers: The Baptist Way of being the Church* (n.pl. [Didcot]: The Baptist Union of Great Britain, 1992), 14, 'it is customary in many Baptist churches for baptismal candidates to give personal "testimonies" to God's saving power in their own lives: for, although baptism itself is a confession of faith, it is considered good to give opportunity for candidates to articulate this confession and tell what Christ means to them.' M.E. Aubrey, *A Minister's Manual* (London: The Kingsgate Press, rev. and enlarged edn, n.d. [1940]), 33, advocates a personal testimony but also notes that under the strain of the event, some 'sensitive candidates' might wish to make their verbal testimony by means of responding to a question.

what they lack in theological insight they tend to make up for in heartfelt conviction. As Hinson remarks,

> Somewhat restricted theology notwithstanding, baptism has figured significantly in Baptist corporate and individual life. Since baptism is administered on the basis of individual decisions, persons baptized have normally attached considerable significance to that special 'moment' in their lives and have looked back to it as a special marker on their spiritual journey. The large number of anecdotes connected with baptism in Baptist lore attests the high level of importance it may have in corporate experience.[52]

Hinson argues that Baptists have tended to over-emphasize a conversionist theology resulting in a weakened commitment to the devout life, and that their preoccupation with winning converts has too often 'overshadowed concern for deepening and conserving commitment and growth in grace'. They have also succumbed to an excessive individualism, and thereby left spiritual development to the responsibility of individual believers,[53] with little place for the corporate dimension of being a Christian. Similarly, Randall notes that evangelical spirituality is susceptible to tension between the individual and corporate priorities,[54] and this is clearly seen in baptismal testimonies. Testimonies also reflect the different influences we have already seen have contributed in shaping baptismal spirituality, as well as the baptismal beliefs of local congregations and their ministers.[55] There is much more to baptismal spirituality than is discussed here, but this is offered as a brief sketch of aspects of a Baptist baptismal spirituality.

Baptism is an act of worship, and by that fact is a matter of spirituality. Robert Robinson records 'a private baptism'[56] in Cambridge in 1767, when, following the sermon, the candidates each stood and said, '*I believe that Jeſus Chriſt is the Son of God, and into this profeſſion I deſire to be baptized*', then everyone knelt down 'and

---

[52] Hinson, 'Baptists and Spirituality', 654-55.

[53] Hinson, 'Baptists and Spirituality', 656. Cf. the testimony of a Baptist man aged thirty-eight: 'I knew in my heart it was *something I must do*, but did not attach to it the feeling of "wonderful" that lots of people called it. Baptism was *only a follow-up to giving my life* which was the really wonderful thing', in John Finney, *Finding Faith Today: How Does it happen?* (Swindon: British and Foreign Bible Society, 1992), 109 (italics added).

[54] Randall, *Evangelical Experiences*, 5.

[55] Ellis, *Gathering*, 206, 'There are tantalizingly few descriptions of how people were baptized in the early period of Baptist history.' It is also worth commenting that, as Haykin, '"Hazarding all for God at a clap"', 194 n. 11, notes, 'Detailed accounts of outdoor baptisms ... are rare.' However, see Robert Robinson, *The History of Baptism* (London: Thomas Knott, 1790), 540-50; C.H. Spurgeon, *C.H. Spurgeon: Volume 1. The Early Years 1834–1859: A Revised Edition of his Autobiography, Originally Compiled by his Wife and Private Secretary* (London: The Banner of Truth Trust, 1962), 148-50; and Roger Hayden, 'Believers Baptized: An Anthology', in Paul S. Fiddes (ed.), *Reflections on the Water: Understanding God and the World through the Baptism of Believers* (Regent's Study Guides, 4; Oxford: Regent's Park College, 1996), 9-21.

[56] By this I believe Robinson means one 'in the church' as opposed to 'in public'.

the adminiftrator in the name of all adored God'.[57] It is also an act of devotion. As John Clifford recorded in his diary's account of his baptism on 16 June 1851, 'I was a mere boy, and in the presence of that crowd, my father and mother looking on with emotions that can only be understood by a father who has seen his own children baptized and make a public avowal of discipleship to Jesus Christ I bore my testimony *to what I felt of love and devotion to the Lord Jesus Christ.*'[58]

In his discussion of balancing the inward and the outward dimensions of Baptist spirituality, Grenz describes the belief that 'religion is a matter of the heart' as 'a non-negotiable Baptist principle'. In a way that is similar to both Augustine and Jonathan Edwards, Grenz observes that Baptists understand religion to be more than intellectual assent in that it encompasses the 'affections'. Christianity is more than intellectual assent to doctrines, which, though important, 'is not enough'. Rather,

> Faith must entail a personal commitment that becomes the ultimate focus of the believer's affections. Convictions must not only be lodged in one's head; they must penetrate the whole person, so that they become near and dear to one's *heart*. In Baptist jargon, 'head-religion must become heart-religion.'[59]

This ties in with the Baptist conviction that conversion must always be personal,[60] that 'true Christianity is a matter of personal commitment'.[61] At the third general meeting of the Western Association held at Taunton, Somerset, from 18–20 July 1654, a series of issues were discussed and resolutions made.

---

[57] Robinson, *History of Baptism*, 544 (italics original). This account follows immediately after the account of the baptismal service presided over by Robert Robinson and Andrew Gifford at Whittlesford, which is dated by the St Andrew's Street church book as 1767. See *Memoirs of the Protestant Dissenting Church of Christ, Usually Denominated Baptists: voluntarily congregated out of several parishes; and assembling for divine worship at their meeting-house in St Andrew's parish, Cambridge*, entry for April 10th [1767], recorded in L.G. Champion, L.E. Addicott and K.A.C. Parsons, *English Baptist Records: 2. Church Book: St Andrew's Street Baptist Church, Cambridge 1720–1832* (n.pl.: Baptist Historical Society, 1991), see 40-42.

[58] James Marchant, *Dr. John Clifford, C.H.: Life, Letters and Reminiscences* (London: Cassell, 1924), 14-15 (italics added).

[59] Grenz, 'Maintaining the Balanced Life', 61 (italics original). See the whole of his discussion on 61-62; also Marshall, 'Changing Face of Baptist Discipleship', 64, 66 and 67; and Graves, 'Centered Hearts, Circled Hands', 88 n. 54, 90, 91, 92, 94 and 97-98. Hinson, 'Reassessing the Puritan Heritage', 321, identifies '"heart religion" authenticated in reformed lifestyle or the practice of religion' as a major legacy of the Puritans to the Baptists. He adds, 'In effect, the Puritans put *practice* before anything else' (italics original). See also 322 and 323-24.

[60] Grenz, 'Maintaining the Balanced Life', 62, 'A personal conversion *experience* is foundational to the Christian life' (italics original).

[61] Grenz, 'Maintaining the Balanced Life', 65.

Query 4. Whether any are to be received into the church of Christ only on a bare confession of Christ being come in the flesh and assenting to the doctrine and order laid down by him?

The answer given illustrates Grenz's insistence that 'mere outward form does not constitute spirituality', that the outward act *must* be accompanied by inner vitality, and that faith *must* be personally experienced. The West Country Baptists resolved,

> Answer: they may not be admitted on such terms without a declaration of *an experimental work of the Spirit upon the heart*, through the word of the Gospel and sutable [sic] to it, *being attended with evident tokens of conversion*, to the satisfaction of the administrator and brethren or church concerned in it ...[62]

This is why Baptists reject the idea of vicarious faith. For example, twelve-year old Laura Cross confesses, 'I've grown up in a Christian family and so far as I was concerned I was a Christian, my parents are Christians and I go to church every sunday [sic], so that must mean I was one too. but [sic] I was wrong. I was only part way there.'[63] She, as do all others, needed to come to her own personal faith in Christ.

The personal nature of this relationship with God is at times revealed through a personal experience of God, and sometimes this takes the form of audible encounters with God. Laura recounted that a week before her baptism 'God called my name', something she recalled he had done when she was eight, at which time she 'began thinking about being baptised', though did not at that time feel ready.[64] Her uncle, David Cross, who had also been brought up in a Christian family, had made a commitment in his teens, but then backslid for some twenty-five years. After nearly dying three times on a holiday in the USA, he heard God speaking to him and this moved him from his previous atheism then agnosticism to kneel in prayer one night. He prayed for three things, all of which happened the next day. On his return home, he started to attend Banbury Baptist Church, where he 'was immediately made welcome and shown generous hospitality.' He had 'many intellectual objections' and 'such an overwhelming guilty conscience' that he felt in the middle of a spiritual battle. Each week these 'obstacles were addressed and dismissed', the final hurdle being cleared by his middle brother Paul's personal testimony. Unable to sleep and crying in prayer, David heard God speak a second time, asking him what he was waiting for.[65] Martin, admitted that he was worried that although he was being

---

[62] B.R. White (ed.), *Association Records of the Particular Baptists of England, Wales and Ireland to 1660: Part 2. The West Country and Ireland* (London: The Baptist Historical Society, 1973), 56 (italics added).

[63] Laura Cross, baptized on Sunday 20 November 2005 at Radstock Baptist Church, Somerset. From a photocopy of her testimony in the author's possession.

[64] Laura Cross, testimony.

[65] David Cross, baptized on Easter Sunday 1997. His testimony is printed in *Together: The Magazine of Banbury Baptist Church* 40 (Pentecost, 1997), n.p..

baptized in water he 'would miss out on a touch from the Holy Spirit', even though he knew the minister would pray for this. However, during the service he had a picture from God while another candidate was being prayed for. A sky was completely covered with grey clouds, which then parted 'and the sunlight streamed through', and he felt excited. The next day he saw an image of 'an empty cross with flames burning out of the top of the upright' and since then reported, 'I have felt an amazing power inside me, growing and fading repeatedly but getting stronger each time.'[66]

Conversion and baptism can also be occasions of healing, cleansing and forgiveness (cf. Acts 2.38; 22.16; 1 Cor. 6.11), and new birth (cf. Jn 3.5; 2 Cor. 5.17; 1 Pet. 1.3). Joelene Sedgewick had made a commitment when she was young during a time her family was going through difficulties. Struggling with depression and a daughter who was diagnosed as autistic, she started to go to church with her mother. There she was prayed for with the laying on of hands, after which she came off her medication and her depression lifted. The reason she was baptized, she declares, was 'to become closer to the Lord. I am having my sins washed away and being reborn again to be free of sin. I love and believe in the Lord. God gave his only Son, [sic] Jesus was crucified so that our sins can be forgiven. I would like to thank the Lord for being with me always, supporting me and guiding me to him and Barton Baptist Church today.'[67] Susan says that 'The most important thing since my baptism is the feeling which I now have of being cleansed. The relief was wonderful and the release was tremendous!'[68] Following the second time God spoke to him, David asked him into his life 'and received the full gift of God's love and forgiveness in an experience I simply am unable to put into words'. His testimony closes, 'Since my rebirth my life has almost totally changed. I have witnessed God in action in my own life and others and I have experienced both answers to prayer and healing and I thank God from the bottom of my heart.'[69]

More commonly, however, the experience is less 'supernatural'. Susan recalls that 'On the day of my baptism, during the prayer time before the service, I had a real sense of being filled spiritually, of being in God's holy presence.'[70]

Awareness of being in a spiritual battle is not uncommon. As well as experiencing opposition and persecution, believers often discover new spiritual resources and strength with which to face them. In his autobiography, agricultural labourer, militiaman and later Baptist deacon, Joseph Mayett of Quainton, Buckinghamshire, talks of his Methodist parents' opposition to baptism by immersion, though this

---

[66] 'Martin', in Stephen Gaukroger, *Being Baptized: The Handbook to Believer's Baptism* (Bletchley: Scripture Union, 2nd edn, 2003), 11-12.

[67] Joelene Sedgewick, baptized on Sunday 8 April, 2012 at Barton Baptist Church, Torquay. See "'I am being baptised to become closer to the Lord'", <http://www.baptist times.co.uk/>, Monday 20 April 2012.

[68] 'Susan', in Gaukroger, *Being Baptised*, 9-10 (p. 10).

[69] David Cross, testimony.

[70] 'Susan', 9.

changed when the Baptist minister, John Davis, began to preach at their home.[71] Both parents became convinced of their need of believers' baptism and, in time, convinced Joseph of his need, too. However, about a week before they were to be baptized the devil

> stirred up my father to oppose it and although the[y] had Both given in their experience and were both accepted by the Church he declared that he would not go himself nor let her but the devils design was frusterated [sic] here also for on the saturday night before the ordinance he was struct with a thought that he was wrong in what he had done and on Sunday the 4th of october 1801 he acknowledged he was wrong and they both set out to go to waddsdon hill ...

Joseph accompanied them and when they were baptized he says, 'I thought it seemed as though they were taken into heaven and I was shut out ...'[72] Earlier, Joseph had recorded that when he had begun to reform his life, read his Bible and regularly attend worship, he had felt he could 'go through fire and water for the sake of the gospel neither did the persecution of the world affect me for my old Companions began to observe a moral Change in me and began to pour contempt upon me and upon Religion ...'[73] But the day after his parents' baptism, he reports that his

> old Companions began to pour out all the Contempt upon me as the[y] Could devise and one of them that had formerly reproved me for my wickedness began to persecute me worse than the others but this I did not mind for I was like too many others I thought I was Certainly something better/than I was before here I thought I Could stand anything for the sake of the gospel and felt myself willing to suffer anything so that I Could but go to heaven at last and my zeal was such that I began to reprove others for their sin ...[74]

Further, opposition for faithfulness to scripture and its Lord has, historically, often led to overt persecution – and in many parts of the world still does.[75] Perhaps the best-known early example of this is can be seen in the publication of Daniel Featley's *The Dipper Dippt* in 1645.[76] It is noteworthy that the frontispiece to the

---

[71] Ann Kussmaul (ed.), *The Autobiography of Joseph Mayett of Quainton (1783–1839)* (Buckinghamshire Record Society, 23; Cambridge: Cambridge University Press, 1986), 13.

[72] Kussmaul (ed.), *Joseph Mayett*, 17-18.

[73] Kussmaul (ed.), *Joseph Mayett*, 17.

[74] Kussmaul (ed.), *Joseph Mayett*, 18. Joseph was baptized at some point, as he refers to a young man 'Baptized with me', 66, but no detailed account is given.

[75] For European examples of such, see Ian M. Randall, *Communities of Conviction: Baptist Beginnings in Europe* (Schwarzenfeld: Neufeld Verlag, 2009), *passim*.

[76] Daniel Featley, *The Dippers Dipt. Or, The Anabaptists Dvck'd and Plvng'd Over Head and Eares, at a Diſputation in Southwark* (London: Printed for Nicholas Bourne, 1645). See, e.g., Haykin, '"Hazarding all for God at a clap"', 186-88, specifically on the scandal of believers' baptism; and Gordon Kingsley, 'Opposition to Early Baptists (1638–1645)',

first edition has the image of the devil breathing, presumably fire, onto the Anabaptists and holding a banner with the words 'The Difcription of the feverall Sorts of Anabaptists. With there manner of Rebaptizing' over a scandalously portrayed baptismal scene in which at least two topless women are being immersed. By the second edition of 1646 the image of the devil has been replaced by an eye from which the words 'VIDEO RIDEO' ('I see, I laugh') are emanating.[77]

The Baptists' emphasis on the personal all too often has spilled over to the individualistic. This is reflected in the fact that the most popular baptismal hymn for twentieth-century Baptists was 'O Jesus I have promised'.[78] The personal, therefore, must be balanced by the corporate, for, as Robert Walton expresses it, 'Christianity is not individualistic: it is personal. Individualism is a mere difference from others; a fully personal life is a growth in stature brought about by contact with, and appreciation of, the lives of others.'[79] New Testament baptism is clearly an initiation into the church, the body of Christ (1 Cor. 12.11), and this is reflected in Baptists eschewing 'private' baptism. Rather, baptism – whether in the church building or in public – is a part of the worship of the people of God. As the baptisms are conducted, the church is there. Some churches invite the congregation in part (just the children) or in total to gather around the baptistery.[80] The administrator of baptism – usually the minister – is often accompanied by another – a deacon, elder, or youth leader – and together they represent the church, as well as Christ, when they receive the candidate(s) in the water. Susan recalls, 'The two ministers in the water welcomed me with open arms. This was very symbolic – I felt I was being received by Jesus.'[81]

Yet baptism is not solely a profession of faith – though that it most assuredly is – but can also be an experience of the divine. Spurgeon recounted his baptism at Isleham Ferry near Cambridge on 3 May 1850:

> ... I attended the service previous to the ordinance, but all remembrance of it has gone from me: my thoughts were in the water, sometimes with my Lord in joy, and sometimes with myself in trembling awe at making so public a confession. There were first to be baptized two women – Diana Wilkinson and Eunice Fuller ... The wind blew down the river with a cutting blast, as my turn came to wade into the flood, but after I had walked a few steps, and noted the people on the ferry-boat, and in boats, and on either shore, I felt as if Heaven, and earth, and hell, might all gaze upon me, for I was

---

Baptist History and Heritage 4.1 (January, 1969), 18-30 and 66, on baptism and persecution more generally.

[77] I am grateful to Dr Larry J. Kreitzer for this observation. In the 1646 edition this image is no longer a frontispiece but is positioned on 17, though by the 1660 edition it is back as a frontispiece. Presumably the depiction of the devil backfired on Featley and he was forced to change it.

[78] See Cross, *Baptism and the Baptists*, 404.

[79] Robert C. Walton, *The Gathered Community* (London: Carey Press, 1946), 127.

[80] This was, e.g., my practice at Calne Baptist Church, Wiltshire, in the mid-1990s, and is the practice at Radstock Baptist Church, Somerset.

[81] 'Susan', 9.

not ashamed, there and then, to own myself a follower of the Lamb. My timidity was washed away; it floated down the river into the sea, and must have been devoured by the fishes, for I have never felt anything of the kind since. Baptism also loosed my tongue, and from that day it has never been quiet. I lost a thousand fears in that River Lark, and found that 'in keeping His commandments there is great reward'. It was a thrice happy day to me. God be praised for the preserving goodness which allows me to write of it with delight so long afterwards![82]

The day after her baptism, Heather, Martin's wife, wrote to her minister, Stephen Gaukroger, expressing her feelings of joy. 'Today I feel completely overawed and not really here. I feel so full of God that I'm ready to burst. I seem to be walking round with a permanent grin, feeling shaky with a strange yet peaceful agitation about me.' She asked him, 'what is this? Has the Lord been so good as to baptise me in his Spirit? ... Thank you, thank you for yesterday. It was the most wonderful experience of my life ... I shall never forget it ... Thank you for the most precious gift anyone could be given ...'[83] Four months later she wrote again: 'things are *still* amazing! This was not a stupendous "quick-then-over" experience but an ongoing one – God is refilling me with his Spirit almost daily ...' Her prayer life was now 'in a completely new dimension', praying in tongues had 'become so natural and lovely' and she was 'so aware of the Lord's presence so often now'. She closes, '[the Lord] is no longer just a part of my life but *all* of it'.[84]

The seven contributors to *Under the Rule of Christ* propose that Baptist spirituality 'in all its diversity, is characterized by living "under the rule of Christ"', and that while this is affirmed by all Christian spiritual traditions there is a particular sense in which Baptists and their way of being the church holds to this. For Baptists, spirituality has been shaped by their ecclesiological understanding that the local church is under 'the direct rule of Christ without intermediate authorities'.[85] This is reflected not just in the use of the trinitarian baptismal formula (Mt 28.19), but in the understanding that baptism means immersion into the life of God.[86] Marshall

---

[82] Spurgeon, *Spurgeon: The Early Years*, 149-50. Though representing Spurgeon's mature reflections on his baptismal experience, the essential accuracy of his account is argued for by Peter J. Morden, *'Communion with Christ and his people': The Spirituality of C.H. Spurgeon* (Centre for Baptist History and Heritage Studies, 5; Oxford: Regent's Park College, 2010), 80-84. It is worth noting that Spurgeon's theology of baptism was not as rich rich as his own personal experience of baptism, and was also non-sacramental. This latter point is discussed by Morden, *'Communion with Christ and his people'*, 84-89. See also the works cited in n. 97 below.

[83] 'Heather', in Gaukroger, *Being Baptised*, 10-11 (10).

[84] 'Heather', 11 (italics original).

[85] 'Preface', in Fiddes (ed.), *Under the Rule of Christ*, vii-ix (viii).

[86] Cf., e.g., George R. Beasley-Murray, *Baptism in the New Testament* (Exeter: The Paternoster Press, 1972 [1962]), 91, who recognizes the Semitic nature of the phrase 'into the name of' and that as such baptism sets people 'in that relationship which one has in view in the performance of it'. As such baptism in the name of the Trinity 'sets the baptized in a definite relation to God; the Father, Son and Holy Spirit become to the baptized what their

similarly asserts that 'we must maintain that spirituality is thoroughly Trinitarian, depends upon the designation of the human being as the creation of God, and is a relational movement between the human and the divine'.[87]

Having made a commitment to Christ as a teenager but then losing her faith when her father died suddenly, former paralympic swimmer Danielle Swann started attending Headington Baptist Church at the invitation of two friends. Feeling 'instantly welcomed by everyone', it was during an Alpha Course that she chatted to one of the ministers and from that day she turned back to God. The close of her testimony reveals the personal dimension of the believer's new relationship with God. 'Being baptised has given me the chance to follow God every day and hopefully make myself a better person. Knowing he is by my side feels like a father figure back in my life again. My dad was there for me whenever I needed him; I now know that God has taken over his role.'[88]

'For Baptists the church is a fellowship, a community of persons who take seriously their own responsibility to become spiritual and at the same time conscientiously engage in the task of fostering spirituality as a corporate people ... For the walk is the path of spirituality they tread individually together.'[89] This is highlighted in the testimony of thirteen year old Len Radley. Through the church's youth work he made 'a personal commitment to God with the help of the leaders', and 'saw and felt the power of God's love' for himself and everyone around him. In his testimony he expressed thanks especially for Andy, Duane and Will 'for guiding me, supporting me and putting up with me', and hoped that as he learns more he can show God's love to others. 'Knowing God through reading the Bible and praying and feeling his love and acceptance from the people around me have given me the strength to try new things and to stand up for myself.' He then closed, 'I want to thank God for what he has done for me and ask Him to accept my commitment to Him as I come to be baptised here.'[90]

---

name signifies' and that baptism in the triune name makes the baptized 'over to God'. See the development of this view by Paul S. Fiddes, *Participating in God: A Pastoral Doctrine of the Trinity* (London: Darton, Longman and Todd, 2000).

[87] Marshall, 'Changing Face of Baptist Discipleship', 61.

[88] Danielle Swann, baptized in February 2012 at Headington Baptist Church. See 'British Paralympics triple medallist takes to the waters again', <http://www.baptist times.co.uk/>, Tuesday 29 March 2012.

[89] Grenz, 'Maintaining the Balanced Life', 68. He continues, 'Baptists understand spirituality ... as the inward conviction of the heart warmed by the regenerating power of the Spirit, an inward conviction, however, which must be given expression by a life of discipleship as the believer seeks to live in imitation of the beloved Master who is likewise the living and present Lord. This Christian spirituality is an individual project, in the process of which the believer must dedicate all personal resources, but which requires as well personal participation in the corporate body, the fellowship of Christ.'

[90] Len Radley, baptized on Easter Sunday 2012 at Hertford Baptist Church. See 'I saw and felt the power of God's love for me and everyone around', <http://www.baptist times.co.uk/>, Tuesday 22 May 2012.

This testimony also supports Hinson's assertion that the central components of Baptist spirituality are worship, Bible reading, singing, baptism, the Lord's supper, prayer, and the sermon.[91] Not only do they appear as important in Len's coming to and growth in faith, but they also figure prominently in baptismal services. The baptisms themselves occur within the worship of the gathered community of believers (and sometimes, when in public, with non-Christian onlookers), in which the reading and preaching of the word (often containing if not comprising a biblical explanation of the meaning of baptism, and/or an evangelistic sermon) are central components, in which singing is prominent (often chosen by the candidate(s)[92]), and, not infrequently, lead into celebration of the eucharist. There is also a tradition of scripture passages being given to each candidate while in the water.[93]

For instance, on 10 April 1767, the church that is now St Andrew's Street Baptist Church, Cambridge, baptized twenty-five men and women from its own fellowship and that at nearby Walden. Conducted in the open air at Whittlesford in front of 'hundreds of spectators', Dr Andrew Gifford, from the Eagle Street Baptist Church, London, ascended a moveable pulpit near the river, and 'after singing and prayer, preached a suitable sermon on the occasion from Psalm cxix.57'. The men then 'retired to one room, the women to two others' while the baptizer, the Rev. Joseph Gwennap, minister of the Walden church, prepared to immerse them. 'After about half an hour' (presumably the length of the sermon), Gwennap, dressed 'as usual' (presumably his normal daily clothes), went down to the water, where he was joined by the men, 'two by two', dressed in their daily clothes. They were followed by the women, 'two by two'. Gwennap then 'sang an hymn at the water-side, spoke about 10 minutes on the subject, and then taking the oldest man of the company by the hand, led him to a convenient depth in the river.' He then pronounced, 'I baptize thee in the name of the Father, and of the Son, and of the Holy Ghost' and 'immersed the person once in the river'. The minister of the Stone Yard Meeting, Robert Robinson, stood in a boat and with others led the other candidates into the river, then wiped their faces after their immersion and helped them out. Then 'Mr Gwennap added a few words more after the administration at the water-side, and concluded with the usual blessing.'[94]

---

[91] Hinson, 'Baptists and Spirituality', especially 651-56.
[92] Gaukroger, *Being Baptized*, 45-46.
[93] William G. Channon, *Much Water and Believers Only* (London: Victory Press, 1950), 63, who remarks, 'In all my years of Christian service I have had good reason to remember my promise. It has often helped me on my way – "Let us not be weary in well-doing: for in due season we shall reap, if we faint not" (Gal. 6:9).' This was also the practice in my home church, New Road Baptist Church, Bromsgrove, Worcestershire, in the late 1970s to early 80s.
[94] *Memoirs of the Protestant Dissenting Church of Christ*, entry for April 10th [1767], in Champion, Addicott and Parsons, *Church Book: St Andrew's Street Baptist Church*, 41-42. Robinson's account of this baptism, which differs in some details from that of the church book, is recorded in his *History of Baptism*, 541-43.

The majority of Baptists repudiate the term 'sacrament', preferring instead 'ordinance' with its connotation of obedience to the command of Christ to be baptized.[95] In March 1770, Andrew Fuller witnessed the baptism of two young people, and '(having never seen that ordinance before,)' he commented how he 'was considerably affected by what I saw and heard. The solemn immersion of a person, on a profession of faith in Christ, carried such conviction with it, that I wept like a child, on the occasion.' The words of Psalm 111.10, he stated, 'left a deep and abiding impression on my mind'. Now fully persuaded that this was the apostolic form of baptism and that every Christian 'was bound to attend to this institution of our blessed Lord' that 'About a month after this, I was baptized myself, and joined the church at Soham, being then turned of sixteen years of age.'[96] Similarly, in a letter to his father, the young Charles Haddon Spurgeon wrote,

> From the Scriptures, is it not apparent that, immediately upon receiving the Lord Jesus, it is a part of duty openly to profess Him? I firmly believe and consider that baptism is the command of Christ, and shall not feel comfortable if I do not receive it. I am unworthy of such things, but so am I unworthy of Jesu's love. I hope I have received the blessing of the one, and think I ought to take the other also.[97]

It is not only important for Baptists that Jesus commanded his disciples be baptized (M. 28.19), but also the fact that he was himself baptized (Mt. 3.13-17; Mk

---

[95] See the discussion of this by Grenz, 'Maintaining the Balanced Life', 63-64, who is summarizing here the 'general' view of Baptists. His own sacramental theology is set out, e.g., in 'Baptism and the Lord's Supper as Community Acts: Toward a Sacramental Understanding of the Ordinances', in Cross and Thompson (eds), *Baptist Sacramentalism*, 76-95.

[96] Letter III, dated 'Jan. 1815', to 'My dear Friend', in John Ryland, *The Work of Faith, the Labour of Love, and the Patience of Hope, illustrated; in the Life and Death of the Rev. Andrew Fuller, Late Pastor of the Baptist Church at Kettering, and Secretary to the Baptist Missionary Society, from its commencement, in 1792* (London: Button & Son, 2nd edn, 1818), 20-28 (22).

[97] C.H. Spurgeon, letter to 'My Dear Father', dated 'Newmarket, January 30th, 1850', in Spurgeon, *The Early Years*, 111-12. Morden, *'Communion with Christ'*, 78, notes that Spurgeon's 'baptism as a believer took place at a crucial, formative time in his Christian journey ... setting the trajectory of his subsequent Christian life'. His mature understanding of baptism, as well as his theology of conversion, 'was closely bound up with his own experience', his baptismal theology being 'especially revealing of the store he set on committed Christian discipleship'. On Spurgeon and baptism, see Stanley K. Fowler, *More Than a Symbol: The British Baptist Recovery of Baptismal Sacramentalism* (Studies in Baptist History and Thought, 2; Carlisle: Paternoster Press, 2002), 79-83; Tim Grass and Ian Randall, 'C.H. Spurgeon on the Sacraments', in Cross and Thompson (eds), *Baptist Sacramentalism*, 55-75; and Peter J. Morden, 'C.H. Spurgeon and Baptism Part 1: The Question of Baptismal Sacramentalism', *Baptist Quarterly* 43.4 (October, 2009), 196-220, and 'C.H. Spurgeon and Baptism Part 2: The Importance of Baptism', *Baptist Quarterly* 43.7 (July, 2010), 388-409, and *'Communion with Christ and his people'*, 77-105.

1.9-11; Lk. 3.21-22; and Jn 1.29-34). This in and of itself is another powerful reason for believers' baptism, for in being baptized the believer is following in the footsteps of Jesus.[98] We have already encountered this in several testimonies, and it is also found in Baptist hymnody. For example, the baptismal hymn by Baptist minister Frederick Arthur Jackson (1867–1942), written in 1932 while at Campden, Gloucestershire, opens,

> Master we Thy footsteps follow
>   We Thy word obey,
> Hear us, Thy dear Name confessing,
>   While we pray.[99]

Grenz notes that the majority of Baptists

> have a special understanding of the nature of the outward acts they are called to perform. These acts are not a means to obtain God's favour. Rather, they derive their significance from the fact that they are related to the believer's desire to follow in the footsteps of Jesus. The spiritual life is above all the imitation of Christ, and discipleship means seeking to follow the model set forth by Jesus himself, for true Christians will reflect in their lives the character of Jesus.[100]

What Baptists must not forget is that following Christ is also a corporate matter, for in baptism the believer becomes a member of the community of disciples, who, together, are on the journey of faith.

Christopher Ellis discusses the differences between Baptists on the relationship between baptism and church membership; whether baptism is an initiation into the church or a prerequisite for membership in a local church. Those who advocate the latter 'see no need to associate the rite with the reception of the baptized person into church membership'. The emphasis, then, is on baptism as a testimony to the gospel, the candidate's faith, and their obedience to the command and following of Christ's example. Such tend to emphasize baptism as an ordinance and repudiate any sacramental connotations.[101] Ellis provides a simple order illustrating this position.

---

[98] Grenz, 'Maintaining the Balanced Life', 63. Also Wright, 'Spirituality as Discipleship', 88-89 and 95-97.

[99] F.A. Jackson, 'Master we Thy footsteps follow', #484, *The Baptist Church Hymnal (Revised)* (London: Psalms and Hymns Trust, rev. edn 1933), on which see #484 in Hugh Martin (ed.), *A Companion to the Baptist Church Hymnal (Revised)* (London: The Psalms and Hymns Trust, 1953), 127.

[100] Grenz, 'Maintaining the Balanced Life', 63. Baptist sacramentalists, of course, concur, however they see baptism as so much more than simply following Christ.

[101] As we have see, Hinson, 'Baptist Approaches to Spirituality', 25-27, following Richard Foster, identifies six traditions that appeal to many Baptists, among them the incarnational tradition which 'revolves around the sacramental life'. Hinson comments, 26-27, that 'this tradition links experience of God through material media and elevates the liturgy and sacraments in the religious sphere but also in everyday life'. Again following

Opening worship
Prayer
Scripture reading
Sermon
Hymn
Baptism
    Introduction
    Testimonies of the candidates
    Baptism
    Appeal to others in the congregation to respond in faith to the gospel
Closing hymn
Benediction.[102]

In more recent years,[103] another form of service has become common among British Baptists and includes baptism–reception into membership–celebration of the Lord's supper, often with the laying on of hands.[104] In all these various patterns the same components recur: the gathered community of believers, worship, Bible reading and proclamation, singing, testimony (usually incorporating both baptismal interrogations and personal testimony), reception into membership and celebration of

---

Foster, positive aspects of this tradition are that it underscores God's presence in all aspects of earthly existence, it roots us in everyday life, makes work meaningful, corrects Gnostic dualism between spirit and matter, beckons us Godward, emphasizes the body as the means through which God is daily experienced, as well as its concern for all creation. Negatively, it can tend to idolatry and seek to manipulate God through externals. Additional to those works cited elsewhere in this chapter dealing with Baptist sacramentalism, see Philip E. Thompson, 'Towards Baptist Ecclesiology in Pneumatological Perspective' (PhD dissertation, Emory University, 1995), *passim*; Fowler, *More Than a Symbol*; Brian Haymes, Ruth Gouldbourne and Anthony R. Cross, *On Being the Church: Revisioning Baptist Identity* (Studies in Baptist History and Thought, 21; Milton Keynes: Paternoster, 2008), *passim*; Anthony R. Cross, *Should we take Peter at his word (Acts 2.38)?: Recovering a Baptist Baptismal Sacramentalism* (Centre for Baptist History and Thought Studies Occasional Papers, 1; Oxford: Regent's Park College, 2010); and Brandon C. Jones, *Waters of Promise: Finding Meaning in Believer Baptism* (Eugene, OR: Pickwick Publications, 2012).

[102] Ellis, *Gathering*, 207-208.

[103] On the variations of twentieth-century practices, see Cross, *Baptism and the Baptists*, 395-405, and on the laying on of hands, 447-48. See the whole of the discussion of 'The Practice of Baptism: 1900–1999', 386-453.

[104] See, e.g., Neville Clark, *Call to Worship* (Studies in Ministry and Worship, 15; London: SCM Press, 1960), 54-59, on what he calls 'The Liturgy of the Baptized'; Alec Gilmore, Edward Smalley and Michael Walker, *Praise God: A Collection of Resource Material for Christian Worship* (London: The Baptist Union, 1980), 137-40; *Patterns and Prayers for Christian Worship: A Guidebook for Worship Leaders* (Oxford: Oxford University Press, 1991), 93-107; Christopher J. Ellis and Myra Blyth, *Gathering for Worship: Patterns and Prayers for the Community of Disciples* (Norwich: Canterbury Press, 2005), 67-80; and Ellis, *Gathering*, 209.

communion. However, as Ellis notes, this is a more sacramental approach which 'implies an ecclesiology in which it is incomprehensible to see someone as a Christian and not recognize their belonging to the Christian Church'. Baptism is into Christ and initiation into the body of Christ.[105]

Many Baptists tend to see conversion as a crisis experience, a sudden punctiliar event when they 'accept Jesus Christ as their personal Lord and Saviour',[106] and it is this which is seen as the requirement for baptism.[107] As such it is separated from baptism and is not seen as a means of grace.[108] In more recent years, however, many

---

[105] Ellis, *Gathering*, 208-11, quotation from 208. Cf. John Weaver, 'Spirituality in Everyday Life: The View from the Table', in Fiddes (ed.), *Under the Rule of Christ*, 135-67 (137), 'Our commitment to the world of the everyday, begun in baptism, is continued in our celebration of the Lord's Supper, which has both an individual and a corporate dimension.' Morden, '*Communion with Christ*', 78-79, notes how Spurgeon's approach to conversion had a strong stress on communion with Christ and that baptism also reveals much about Spurgeon's ecclesiology in which 'commitment to the church, the body of Christ, was essential. The Christian life, rightly conceived, was not a solitary affair. Rather, it had to be lived out in the midst of Christ's people.'

[106] Bill J. Leonard, 'Getting Saved in America: Conversion Event in a Pluralistic Culture', *Review and Expositor* 82.1 (Winter, 1985), 111-27 (124), 'for many Southern Baptists [and other Baptists, too] the language of Calvinism and the theology of Arminianism are united in the transaction of conversionistic individualism. Conversion is less a process of experience with grace than an event which satisfies a salvific requirement'. Marshall, 'Changing Face of Baptist Discipleship', 68, concurs. However, it is important to note that for the majority of Baptists conversion is the necessary prerequisite for baptism, and not a part of the process of becoming a Christian. On the latter, see Beasley-Murray, *Baptism in the New Testament*; Robert H. Stein, 'Baptism and Becoming a Christian in the New Testament', *Southern Baptist Journal of Theology* 2.1 (Spring, 1998), 6-17, and 'Baptism in Luke-Acts', in Thomas R. Schreiner and Shawn D. Wright (eds), *Believer's Baptism: Sign of the New Covenant in Christ* (NAC Studies in Bible & Theology; Nashville, TN: B&H Academic, 2006), 35-66; and Anthony R. Cross, 'The Evangelical Sacrament: *Baptisma Semper Reformandum*', *Evangelical Quarterly* 80.3 (July, 2008), 195-217. This view is advocated by those who hold to a biblical and evangelical form of sacramentalism.

[107] Cf. Hinson, 'Baptists and Spirituality', 650, 'Baptists have not developed an initiation process equal to the early Christian catechumenate or a monastic novitiate, but they have not lacked concern for spiritual formation. Insistence upon believers' baptism grew out of a concern for a "regenerate church membership," something Baptists failed to see in the established churches in England and the American colonies. Only those who freely and of their own accord resolved to become Christians, they asserted, were suitable candidates for baptism.'

[108] See Grenz, 'Maintaining the Balanced Life', 63, 'In general Baptists eschew religious ritual. Not slavish adherence to rites, but doing what Jesus would do is their concept of true discipleship. Consequently, historically they have not been sacramentalists. For them baptism and the Lord's supper are symbols of a personal obedient response to Christ more than some magical means of grace. In fact, contemporary Baptists so eliminated any vestiges of sacramentalism, that most would deny that any grace whatsoever is mediated through these rites.' Baptist sacramentalists, however, do not believe in the mechanical, *ex opere operato*

have begun to recognize that conversion is more of a journey,[109] a process,[110] of becoming a Christian.[111] This is illustrated in Laura's testimony, which mentions other themes we have already discussed. Three years after God had first spoken to her, she was invited by a friend to attend a youth group for younger pre-teens and teens where she realized 'they all had something I didn't. And I was determined to have that something.' This led her to a questioning of her faith, attendance of the youth work for older teens, and a meeting in Bristol. The significance for her of the latter lay in that 'It was so much bigger than anything I'd been to before. There were so many young people there.' It was here that she came to realize 'God cared for us, and how he made us in his image', and 'that there was someone who loves me so much that he gave his life for me'. This knowledge, she explains, 'changed me'. At the speaker's invitation she stood to be prayed for along with others wanting 'to give their heart to God'. 'So I stood. [sic] and knowing how emotional I get, I cried, but I was so happy, because I'd really found God, and I gave my heart to him.' The impact of the Bristol youth evening was repeated when she attended the 2005 Baptist World Centenary Congress when 'there were just so many ... from all over the world'. It was at this gathering that she 'really began to see & feel what it was really like to love and Praise [sic] God.' On the last day of the Congress, the young people were 'asked who would like to go out and live [their] lives serving God', and she stood and then knelt. Later that summer, attending Soul Survivor with a group from the church, she felt 'touched by God' and 'laughed, cried, shook & was over powered by God & his holy Spirit' and even spoke in tongues. And all these had led her to the baptistery.[112]

---

operation of baptism or the Lord's supper. See, e.g., John E. Colwell, *Promise and Presence: An Exploration of Sacramental Theology* (Milton Keynes: Paternoster, 2005), 72, who affirms that baptism is 'a means of grace through which *God has promised* to mediate ... grace in Christ to us by his Spirit. It is *the promise of God (and nothing else)* that establishes baptism as the primary defining sacrament of the Church' (italics added). On 133, he reiterates, 'Baptism is a sacrament; it is a means of grace; it is a human event through which a divine event is promised to occur.' See the whole chapter which discusses baptism, 109-34. Cf. also Paul S. Fiddes, '*Ex Opere Operato*: Re-thinking a Historic Baptist Rejection, in Cross and Thompson (eds), *Baptist Sacramentalism 2*, 219-38.

[109] E.g., Paul S. Fiddes, 'Baptism and Creation', in Fiddes (ed.), *Reflections on the Water*, 47-67 (55-56), also in Paul S. Fiddes, *Tracks and Traces: Baptist Identity in Church and Theology* (Studies in Baptist History and Thought, 13; Carlisle: Paternoster Press, 2003), 107-24 (115-16); and *Believing and Being Baptized: Baptism, so-called re-baptism, and children in the church* (Didcot: The Baptist Union of Great Britain, 1996), 9-12.

[110] E.g., Paul S. Fiddes, 'Baptism and the Process of Christian Initiation', *The Ecumenical Review* 54.1 (January–April, 2002), 48-65; Cross, 'Evangelical Sacrament', 206.

[111] The classic Baptist explication of this is, of course, John Bunyan's *The Pilgrim's Progreſs from this World, to That which is to come: Delivered under the Similitude of a Dream Wherein is Diſcovered, The manner of his ſetting out, His Dangerous Journey; And ſafe Arrival at the Deſired Countrey* (London: Printed for Nath. Ponder, 1678).

[112] Laura Cross, testimony.

The final dimension of baptismal spirituality we will examine here is drawn out by Grenz when he explains that 'Baptists espouse the principle that each believer is to be involved in the task entrusted to the people of God, and thereby to be personally engaged "in the work of the Lord."'[113] Spurgeon is not the only one to have experienced an enablement to serve God when baptism loosed his tongue. The day of his baptism, John Clifford said,

> marks definitely the accession of great power to my conscience, a quickening of my sense of obligation such as does not characterise any single day since: and hence every recurrence of 16th June is to me a most memorable time,[114] because it recalls that baptism into a quickening of the conscience, which set me, in full dependence upon God, to a full-hearted determination to obey Him ... to bear a continuous witness for Jesus Christ.

His baptism led him to a moral imperative to live each day for Christ: 'I was known from that day, through the factory where there were hundreds of folk at work, as one who had lifted the Christian flag'. If he were untrue, false or dishonest he 'damaged my Church', if he lost his temper, or was not genial, kind or considerate, then he 'injured that Church', and this consciousness of this responsibility 'for keeping that flag aloft' drove him to God 'so that every morning I sought, with the utmost earnestness, that I might be kept through the day from doing anything that would discredit Christ, whose name I had professed, and the Church into which He had bought me.' Clifford's biographer, James Marchant, adds, 'His soul, lit by the light of Heaven, and brought to the burning point of public testimony in his baptism, was now turned Godward and his life's career determined.'[115] Similarly, Wang, a businessman from China declares, 'Before I return to Beijing I want to be baptised to show that I will follow God through my whole life. I love him and want to be in union with him.'[116] Heather says, 'I do long to get out there and be of real service to my Lord, to give my life to seeking and doing his will',[117] while Laura believes that 'because of all God has done in my life I am declaring my love for him. I am being baptised because I love God, I want to live for him. I'll do whatever he says, and go where he sends me. and [sic] that is why I'm being baptised today!'[118] In short, 'A key meaning of "spirituality" is ... a heightened sense of the presence of God which is inseparable from the mission of God.'[119]

---

[113] Grenz, 'Maintaining the Balanced Life', 67.

[114] Richard Bowers, a Downs Syndrome man, celebrates the anniversary of his baptism at Bloomsbury Central Baptist Church, London, each year. For his account of his baptism, see Hayden, 'Believers Baptized', 16-17.

[115] Marchant, *Dr. John Clifford*, 15.

[116] 'Wang', in Gaukroger, *Being Baptised*, 8-9 (9).

[117] 'Heather', 10.

[118] Laura Cross, testimony.

[119] Fiddes and Finamore, 'Baptists and Spirituality: A Rule of Life', 3.

A Few Concluding Reflections

Many Baptists have rejected the sacraments of baptism and eucharist because of what they see as the corruption of the New Testament rites in the direction of understanding them in terms of their magical efficacy. Yet they have, at the same time, replaced them with what John Colwell calls 'pseudo-sacraments', such as altar calls, the signing of decision cards, repeating the sinner's prayer,[120] and the invitation.[121] Such an abandonment of the biblical sacraments in general and baptism in particular is contrary to all they believe about the place of scripture in Baptist life, thought, and practice.[122] For those who hold to the view that baptism is merely an ordinance, a symbol of what has *already* taken place, there is little to find by way of baptismal spirituality, for all that the New Testament ascribes to faith *and* baptism[123] has then to be ascribed to conversion *alone*. However, the revival and resurgence of Baptist sacramentalism recognizes baptism as a 'means of grace',[124] a place where God meets the believer who comes in faith that they will both meet with and experience the saving, loving, gracious, and all-powerful God. William Carey called on Baptists not just to attempt great things for God, but to expect great things from God.[125] Whatever tradition Baptists come from – merely symbolic or sacramental – they need to come with expectant faith that the baptismal waters are a true place of the divine–human encounter. In Paul Fiddes' words,

> The baptismal pool may be pictured as a meeting-place between the believer and the triune God. Emil Brunner envisaged baptism as a place of 'divine–human encounter', a 'two-sided happening' involving 'personal correspondence'.[126] The Baptist New Testament scholar George Beasley-Murray uses the term 'trysting-place';[127] although a

---

[120] John E. Colwell, *Living the Christian Story: The Distinctiveness of Christian Ethics* (Edinburgh: T&T Clark, 2001), 154 and 48.

[121] Hinson, 'Baptist Approaches to Spirituality', 14, sees one of the weaknesses of a conversionist spirituality as 'a shift from the goal of Christian life and the way to the goal to an almost exclusive concern for the gateway to the way, that is, conversion'. This is confirmed by his observation that 'the invitation has replaced baptism as the dominant sacrament ("means of grace") in Baptist churches in the South. As in frontier revivals, the object is to get people to respond to the exhortation. Not much attention is given in many churches to the personal account of religious experience; it suffices to come forward and declare oneself. When linked with the assurance "Once saved, always saved," nothing more need be done.'

[122] Cf. Christopher Ellis, 'Baptism and the Sacramental Freedom of God', in Fiddes (ed.), *Reflections on the Water*, 23-45 (28), 'Baptists will want all theological claims to be tested by Scripture alone'.

[123] See Cross, 'Evangelical Sacrament', 206-208.

[124] Cf. Anthony R. Cross and Philip E. Thompson, 'Introduction: Baptist Sacramentalism', in Cross and Thompson (eds), *Baptist Sacramentalism*, 1-7.

[125] See Brian Stanley, *The History of the Baptist Missionary Society 1792–1992* (Edinburgh: T&T Clark, 1992), 14. Stanley notes that the text of the sermon has not survived.

[126] Emil Brunner, *The Divine–Human Encounter* (London: SCM Press, 1944), 128-35.

[127] Beasley-Murray, *Baptism in the New Testament*, 305.

somewhat archaic form of expression (I have previously used *rendez-vous* myself),[128] it does catch an essential dimension of what the meeting is about. It is about love and faithfulness; it is like a 'tryst' between two lovers. The term has its limits, however, in that this meeting is never entirely private but always in the context of the community; it is in the company of others that the believer comes to meet God – Father, Son and Holy Spirit – with her trusting love, however weak it is. God meets her in everlasting love, to transform her life. The New Testament thus speaks of this meeting with a profusion of pictures of God's grace; it is a moment of new birth (Jn. 3:5; Tit. 3:5), forgiveness and cleansing from sin (Acts 2:38; 1 Cor. 6:11; Heb. 10:22), immersion in the Holy Spirit and the receiving of spiritual gifts (1 Cor. 12:13; Acts 2:38; 10:47), deliverance from evil powers (Col. 1:13), union with Christ (Gal. 3:27), adoption as a child of God (Gal. 3:26), and membership in the body of Christ (1 Cor. 12:13; Gal. 3:27-28).[129]

As such, baptism is an intensely spiritual experience.

The purpose of this exploration in Baptist spirituality has been to honour the ministry of a friend and colleague whose work has greatly benefitted myself and many others, of our own Baptist and Evangelical tradition, but further afield, too, not just through his research and teaching, but through his wisdom and counsel, and also to explore ways in which experience interacts and dovetails with theology and practice – for these are not separate components of being a Christian. And Ian Randall's concluding comments on F.B. Meyer seem a fitting conclusion to this paper.

> In all his active promotion of holiness, Meyer was also reflective, and tried to bring together a framework of theology and of spirituality. The vision he promoted through Keswick and tried to realize himself was one in which inner devotion, a commitment to active service, and the work of theological thought were brought together in a balanced and integrated spiritual life.[130]

---

[128] Fiddes, 'Baptism and Creation', 57, also in Fiddes, *Tracks and Traces*, 107-24 (117).

[129] Paul S. Fiddes, 'Believers' Baptism: An Act of Inclusion or Exclusion?', in Fiddes, *Tracks and Traces*, 125-56 (128-29).

[130] Ian M. Randall, 'F.B. Meyer: Baptist Ambassador for Keswick Holiness Spirituality', *Baptist History and Heritage* 37.3 (Spring, 2002), 44-60 (59). See his detailed study, *Spirituality and Social Change: The Contribution of F.B. Meyer (1847–1929)* (Studies in Evangelical History and Thought; Carlisle: Paternoster Press, 2003).

CHAPTER 16

Bringing Good News to the Poor: An Evangelical Imperative

J. Andrew Kirk

Introduction

Go and tell John what you have seen and heard: the blind receive their sight, the lame walk, the lepers are cleansed, the deaf hear, the dead are raised, the poor have good news brought to them (Luke 7:22).

In recent years that part of the global Christian community that identifies itself as 'evangelical' has been seeking to understand better the relationship between various aspects of the Trinitarian God's call to mission. In particular, it has been concerned to grasp more fully the nature of the correlation between evangelism, as a personal invitation to believe and act on the truth about Jesus Christ, and its public ministries of seeking justice and extending compassion for suffering and vulnerable people. In other words, it has been attempting in theological reflection, and even more in missionary practice, to bring together the Church's evangelistic, prophetic and diaconic ministries so that they form a convincing united call to mission – distinguished, but not separate. The effort continues to be made in many circles to elaborate a notion of 'integral mission', that is a mission that is complete in giving due emphasis to all its constituent parts. The problem is that, whilst it is relatively easy to settle on the different forms of mission,[1] it is a much harder task to do justice to their unity.

Since the epic, ground-breaking Lausanne Congress on World Evangelisation (1974), the evangelical Christian world has been putting its mind to resolving this dilemma. Much has been written and some noble attempts have been influential in shaping the continuing debate.[2] However, no entirely satisfactory conclusion has yet

---

[1] See, for example, J. Andrew Kirk, *What is Mission?: Theological Explorations* (London: Darton, Longman and Todd, 1999); Stephen B. Bevans and Roger P. Schroeder, *Constants in Context: A Theology of Mission for Today* (Maryknoll, NY: Orbis Books, 2005).

[2] For example, 'Transformation: The Church in Response to Human Need' (The Wheaton '83 Statement), in Vinay Samuel and Chris Sugden, *The Church in Response to Human Need* (Grand Rapids, MI: Eerdmans, 1987), 254-265; 'The Iguassu Affirmation', in William D.

been reached. There is, for example, a tendency in some evangelical circles to think that integral mission is about redressing the balance between evangelism and social action by dwelling on, even giving preference to, the prophetic and diaconic dimensions of mission; presumably in the belief that the evangelistic will take care of itself. This has proved not to be the case; evangelism then tends to be neglected.

Without being presumptuous enough to think that I could possibly accomplish what so many have found so problematical to resolve, I offer this essay as a theoretical framework for considering a way of approaching integral mission that, through God's particular concern for the poor, explores the nature of the 'whole gospel' for 'the whole person'. It is also designed to provide a biblical and theological foundation for making a practical Christian response to poverty as an integral part of the Church's mission, an inescapable element of its very *raison d'être*.

From the outset, we should remind ourselves that we are speaking of the poor as real people living in concrete situations all over the globe, not just about poverty as an abstract concept. Poverty is experienced by actual human beings, created in the image of God. Whether they live close by or at a distance, they are our neighbours (Luke 10:29-37). They belong to families like us; their needs are the same as ours. However, unlike many others, they have been born into circumstances that have given them little or no opportunity to escape from the humiliating cycle of poverty in which their community is trapped.

I will begin by highlighting three important aspects of this theme, which will set the direction for all that follows. First, the reality of the poor is taken seriously in the whole of the Bible. It might be an exaggeration to say that they appear on every page but, as we shall see, their plight is seen as a major concern in every strand of literature,[3] especially in the ministry of Jesus Christ himself; see, for example, Luke 4:18; 6:20; 11:41; 12:33; 14:13.

Secondly, from its very beginning the Church has shown a special care for the poor. Early in its life, the diaconal ministry was given prominence. The main task of the deacons was to attend to the sick and to aid the poor. In the second and third centuries, churches cared for the sick during plagues that afflicted significant portions of population in the Mediterranean basin. Later, 'monasteries were well known as places of hospitality and refuge during the cataclysmic events of the great migrations during the fifth, sixth and seventh centuries'.[4] Most of the oldest established educational institutions in Europe, sponsored by Christian communities, began their life by giving free tuition to the children of the poor. In its origins, the Pietist movement of the seventeenth and eighteenth centuries paid special attention

---

Taylor (ed.), *Global Missiology for the Twenty-First Century: The Iguassu Dialogue* (Grand Rapids, MI: Baker Academic, 2000).

[3] The Law, the Prophets, the Wisdom literature, the Gospels, and the Epistles.

[4] See Bevans and Schroeder, *Constants in Context*, 369.

to the social responsibility of Christians.[5] People like Philipp Spener and August Hermann Francke raised awareness among rulers, church leaders and ordinary people of their responsibilities towards those living in conditions of extreme poverty. Francke, in particular, created many institutions for the alleviation of poverty, not least those that promoted education. The modern mission movement has spent much time and energy in attending to excluded and oppressed peoples, such as lepers, outcasts, abandoned children and young girls exploited in religious prostitution.

Thirdly, in the last forty years or so, Christians of all persuasions have moved noticeably in thought and action from having a concern just to alleviate poverty to issues of justice and liberation. Thus, whilst continuing to serve the immediate needs of people for health care, adequate supplies of nutritious food and clean water, proper drainage, solid housing, ante-natal and post-natal care of young mothers, and for the acquiring of skills (such as carpentry, electrical work, agriculture, book-keeping, and clothes' manufacture), they have also stressed issues of economic exploitation, political corruption, lack of fair trade, long-term debt and the paucity of capital spent on infrastructures that will benefit marginalised communities. Charity has become a suspect word whilst justice is rhetorically approved.

The Nature of Poverty

As we live in a technical world, given to measuring reality by means of statistics, we tend to create definitions in terms of figures. Thus, to be categorised as poor, a person needs to belong to a household whose annual cash income is less than 50% of the national average.[6] Within this group there are further categories, of which the largest is called the 'ultra poor' or the 'vulnerable poor'. These are people who cannot work – the elderly, the disabled and children – or those who are dependent on seasonal work because they have no productive resources of their own (such as land, skills, capital or tools) to earn for themselves an adequate income.

Usually, the poor are spoken about in terms of *quantity of life* criteria; they are judged to be poor in terms of an absence of life-sustaining goods and services such as adequate food, housing, clothing and health-care. There are, however, also important *quality of life* factors, which are both the cause and the result of material deprivation. These can be thought of in terms of what is lacking in a given society: for example, proper access to decision-making processes, a rightly respected process of law in which there is redress against violence and bureaucracy, opportunities for education and training, a healthy environment, regular paid employment, physical

---

[5] See Jonathan Strom, Hartmut Lehmann and James Van Horn Melton (eds), *Pietism in Germany and North America 1680–1820* (Aldershot: Ashgate, 2009).

[6] J. Remenyi, *Where Credit is Due* (London: Intermediate Technology Publications, 1991), 3. Clearly, the national average depends on the relative wealth of the country in question. Thus, this indicator measures inequality rather than absolute poverty. An example of a standard measurement of poverty, applicable to all situations, would be a daily intake of food less than is required to sustain the human body (i.e., approximately 2,000–2,500 calories for an adult male).

and social security. Important as material circumstances are, social conditions may be even more fundamental in describing the character of poverty. 'By "the poor" is meant all suffering people condemned to live under inhuman conditions with little or no opportunity to influence their fate themselves.'[7]

So far, definitions of the poor tend to stress impersonal, external factors. However, when we turn to biblical references, we are confronted with a different set of criteria. Five different words in the Hebrew Old Testament are translated in the Greek version (the Septuagint) with the one word *ptōchos*, which is also the preferred designation of the poor in the New Testament. In each case, the word carries a strong ethical implication. The poor are needy, destitute, having to beg, because they have been dispossessed of their rightful place in the social community to which they belong:

> ... the word becomes generally synonymous with the socially poor, with those without land. That such poverty has been caused by disinheritance or unlawful injury and not by the person's own fault is shown by its being contrasted with violence, not riches.[8]

This is why God lays upon his people a special responsibility to ensure that there are no poor in the land (Deuteronomy 15:7-11). As poverty is caused largely by the desire of some to gain excessive riches at the expense of others, it can be ended by people's determination to share resources equitably. The poor exist, because they have been deprived by others of the means of livelihood.

Scripture recognises another kind of poverty – being 'poor in spirit' (Matthew 5:3). This is depicted in two contrasting ways. The poor are those who consciously yearn for God's coming reign of justice (*mishpat*) and well-being (*shalom*) and for God's gift of salvation from sin and failure. They are those who humbly cast themselves upon the unfailing care and compassion of God as the only one guaranteed to protect them from destitution and despair (Psalms 146:7-9; 147:6). However, those who ignore God and live for pleasure are also poor (Proverbs 21:17). They are those who trust in their possessions but are never satisfied (Luke 12:15). They accumulate wealth through excessively hard work or through speculative ventures, only to see it evaporate (Ecclesiastes 5:10-14).[9] Their lives are described as ultimately meaningless, a chasing after wind.

The Consequences of Poverty

The poor generally have no power in society to influence the economic and political decisions that could change their situation. They suffer the effects of the policies

---

[7] Risto A. Ahonen, *Mission in the New Millennium* (Helsinki: Finnish Evangelical Lutheran Mission, 2000), 236.

[8] H.-H. Esser, 'Poor (*ptōchos*)' in Colin Brown (ed.), *New International Dictionary of New Testament Theology*, Volume 2 (Carlisle: Paternoster, 1986), 821.

[9] The turmoil through which the banking system went during the last few months of 2008 shows the prescience of God's word.

decided and enacted by those who control the organs of power, the ruling classes. In ancient Israel, these were the retainers of the royal court, the large landowners, the money-lenders and the military. An unequal division of the means of production led to a stratified society with deep divisions between the permanently poor, the seasonal poor, the small landowners and artisans and those who had amassed considerable wealth for themselves and their families.

Poverty causes a waste of human resources. The poor are not allowed to benefit properly from their substantial contribution to the creation of wealth in society. They are not so much marginalised or peripheral, pushed to the very edge of society, as excluded:

> It is more clearly seen now that, from the point of view of the way economies are run today, the poor are unimportant, if not irrelevant. Whether they are inside or outside the system is of little consequence.[10]

Where societies recognise the plight of the poor and the obligation to save them from utter destitution through some kind of welfare scheme, they become a burden on the public finances, taking away resources that could be used to increase investment in productive processes or to lower the taxes on the rich.

The present situation is one of catastrophic proportions: perhaps some 75% of all human beings living on the planet are shut out from the normal life of a civilised society. We see them as effectively disabled by their economic and social circumstances, unable to participate meaningfully in the construction of a flourishing human community. This is one of the greatest tragedies of poverty: the knowledge that the presence of the poor does not count for anything, that, at best, they are the object of charitable donations; at worst, they are despised and condemned.

The Causes of Poverty

Ultimately, the fundamental cause of poverty is lack of income that would enable a person or household to acquire the necessities of life. This is why some economists insist that asking about the causes of poverty is the wrong question; rather, we should be investigating the reasons for an absence of wealth, or conversely we should try to discover the optimum conditions for its creation. This is a valid way of looking at the problem. However, it only moves the question one stage further back: what are the circumstances that prevent the majority of humankind from receiving an income sufficient to be able to afford the basic goods and services necessary for a dignified existence?

There is a tendency in the discussion of the causes of poverty to polarise around extreme positions and seek to gain the 'moral high ground' by means of rhetorical language and ideas. On the one hand, it is said that there can be no liberation from poverty unless one type of economic system is replaced by another. The existence of

---

[10] Kirk, *What is Mission?*, 99; see also Zygmunt Bauman, *Work, Consumerism and the New Poor* (Buckingham: Open University Press, 1998).

private property and the working of a competitive, profit-seeking, market economy inevitably produce inequality of opportunity and deny many people access to the benefits of wealth-creation. The system in practice discriminates against the weak, denies openings to the disadvantaged and prevents people escaping from the spiral of poverty. Even in nations where recently there has been a rapid increase in gross national product, such as Brazil and India, this has hardly affected the situation of the majority poor. The much vaunted 'trickle down theory' doesn't work, the extra wealth created does not percolate through all strata of society – not even crumbs fall from the rich persons' tables.

Poverty is caused, according to this reading of the situation, by the flight of capital from the South to the North, by the manipulation of markets by the economically powerful, by grossly unfair trading arrangements, by paralysing debt burdens and by the imposition of programmes of austerity by international financial institutions which further depress economic growth. Moreover, the present international economic situation is said to be morally repugnant, because it is based on self-interest, the necessity of ever higher levels of consumption and the unsustainable exploitation of the environment. *Indeed, it is difficult to see how two equally admirable goals are reconcilable: the drive to 'make poverty history' and the campaign to reverse the damage caused to the environment by rapid developmental processes.*

On the other hand, it is claimed that there will be no end to poverty unless individuals and communities change their attitudes. Poverty is primarily the result of deeply rooted cultural attitudes: for example, the acceptance of a fatalistic view of life, believing that the spirit world, rather than natural causes, is directly instrumental in creating ills, refusing to accept blame, practising nepotism and bribery, not pursuing a policy of thrift. Liberation from poverty, therefore, has to come through renouncing and removing the cultural and religious factors inimical to the creation of wealth. Wealth can only be created, thereby raising the levels of income, when there is a favourable environment (i.e., where the belief system is conducive) for creating a self-sustaining, productive capacity.

During the time of the cold war between East and West, it was difficult to move far beyond the ideological rhetoric of the extremes. Neither side seemed prepared to admit that there was any truth in the other's interpretation of the situation. The Old Testament Scriptures, however, with predictable realism, state that poverty may be the result of any of three circumstances. First, unfavourable natural events (storms, floods, soil erosion, drought, blight or insects) may lead to the failure of harvests (as in the case of Jacob and his family in the book of Genesis and Elimelech, the husband of Naomi, in the book of Ruth), or people become ill, or husbands die, leaving vulnerable widows and children behind. In a fallen world, unpredictable, calamitous events just happen. There does not appear to be any rhyme or reason. These natural events are much more serious, however, in places where marginal economies are already creating conditions of extreme vulnerability.

Secondly, the Wisdom literature in particular recognises that in some cases poverty is the result of the refusal to work. Some scholars have seen this alleged cause as an ideological defence by the prosperous, urban elite of their own wealth by arguing that poverty is the fault of those who prefer not to earn a living. More recently, some preachers have insisted that wealth and poverty are the direct result of either God's blessing or affliction, depending on the spiritual state of the people concerned. There appear to be some verses in the Psalms and Proverbs that might suggest such an interpretation. However, this prosperity teaching ignores the whole balance of scriptural teaching concerning the issues; it insensitively raises false expectations and promotes a highly distorted message about God and his offer of salvation.

To be sure, idleness, refusal to work and the squandering of resources may indeed be causes of impoverishment: 'Do not love sleep, or else you will come to poverty' (Proverbs 20:13); 'Laziness brings on deep sleep; an idle person will suffer hunger' (Proverbs 19:15); 'a little sleep, a little slumber, a little folding of the hands to rest, and poverty will come upon you like a robber' (Proverbs 24:33-34). At the same time, the Wisdom literature also recognises that people may be poor *in spite of* their hard labour: 'The field of the poor may yield much food, but it is swept away through injustice' (Proverbs 13:23). Often, it is not the lack of a desire to work but the absence of opportunities that bring deprivation.

Thirdly, by far the most acknowledged cause of poverty is exploitation of the socially and economically weak by those who have gained status and power in society. It is generally agreed among historians of ancient Israel that the beginning of a sharp differentiation of wealth began with the advent of the monarchy. Samuel was the first prophet to point out how poverty would be generated by exploitation. It would happen as the direct result of the centralisation of political power and the means of production through the creation of a standing army, the establishment of state industries, which took people from the land to work as wage-labourers, and taxation to maintain a state bureaucracy (1 Samuel 8:11-17).

The narrative makes explicit that the people of Israel in choosing to have a king, in order to be like all the other nations, had broken the terms of the covenant with the Lord. Subsequently, God sent prophet after prophet to denounce the injustices being committed against the majority of the population, to warn the rulers of the dire consequences of their policies and to announce the coming of a righteous king who would restore again the terms of the covenant and make an end to idolatry.[11] It is highly significant that

> the classical period of biblical prophecy corresponds to the time of the monarchy, from the tenth to the sixth centuries BC ... During the centuries of the monarchy, it was the

---

[11] See J. Andrew Kirk, 'Mission as Prophecy', in J. Andrew Kirk, *Mission under Scrutiny: Confronting Current Challenges* (Minneapolis, MN: Fortress Press, 2006), 157-160.

prophets who kept alive the tradition of Yahweh as the God who took the part of the poor in a society dominated by a ruling class dependent on the court.[12]

One might say that the coming of the monarchy brought with it a centralisation of economic and political power. The countervailing power was invested mainly with the prophets, who were independent of the royal court and risked their lives to remind the rulers of the nature and requirements of the God who had redeemed his people from slavery and given them the liberating laws of the covenant. Ultimately, the whole system of monarchy was brought to an end in the exile, from which Israel had to reinvent itself as a covenant people under Ezra and Nehemiah.

Economic Life as Intended by God

The biblical narrative recognises two opposite facts about the poor. On the one hand, their existence in every society seems to be endemic. So much so, that Jesus, echoing the statement in Deuteronomy 15:11, declared what appears to be obvious from human history, 'you always have the poor with you' (Mark 14:7 and parallels). We should not understand this verdict in fatalistic terms, as if the division of societies into rich and poor was somehow woven into the very fabric of human life; rather, it is to be seen as a comment on the reality of a world that has gone seriously wrong, perhaps in the manner of the observations of Qoheleth, the Teacher: 'If you see in a province the oppression of the poor and the violation of justice and right, do not be amazed at the matter' (Ecclesiastes 5:8).

On the other hand, there is what today we might call a 'vision statement' about God's final purpose to bring in a totally new ordering of human society in which all poverty and injustice will have been eliminated. The ultimate horizon, in which we are to view the issue of the poor, is God's mission to create 'new heavens and a new earth, where righteousness is at home' (2 Peter 3:13). Throughout Scripture we catch intriguing glimpses of what one day will be brought to pass, not just in the eschatological and apocalyptic passages of the two Testaments, but also in God's blueprint for the daily life of his people.

Thus, when reflecting on what God is calling his people to do today, the place to begin is with the pattern of economic life that God laid out for his people yesterday. Here, I will follow the excellent summary of the law set out by Christopher Wright.[13] He emphasises four distinct precepts.

i. The natural resources of the earth are designed for the well-being of all peoples

> Ownership of land and resources does not entail an absolute right of disposal, but rather responsibility for administration and distribution. The right of all to *use* the

---

[12] Jorge Pixley and Clodovis Boff, *The Bible, the Church and the Poor* (Maryknoll, NY: Orbis Books, 1989), 41.

[13] Christopher J.H. Wright, *Old Testament Ethics for the People of God* (Leicester: IVP, 2004), chapters 3 and 5.

resources of the earth seems to be morally prior to the right of any to *own* them for exclusive enjoyment.[14]

This principle can be illustrated by a story of the seventeenth-century European settlers in North America. When some of them encountered the indigenous population, one of their first questions was, 'who owns this land?' The reply 'no one' greatly surprised them, for they had completely failed to grasp the proper implication of the indigenous peoples' attitude to the land and property rights. For them, 'no one' meant 'everyone'. The immigrants interpreted the response to mean that they were free to possess it for themselves.[15] This was a fatal misunderstanding with disastrous consequences for future community relations and the continuing economic well-being of the indigenous community. A somewhat similar fate befell the indigenous population in Northern Argentina at the hands of the Creoles.

ii. Work is a God-given task

Part of the meaning of being created in the image of God is the ability and the call to follow God's creative activity, 'thinking, planning, deciding, executing, and evaluating'.[16] It has been suggested that the pattern of creation is that God worked for six days, putting in place all the elements that have made the world a wonderful place to live in; he rested on the seventh day. On the eighth day, and subsequently, humans took on the task of looking after the earth (Genesis 2:15):

> This means not only that we ourselves have the moral duty to work ... But it also surely means that we have a responsibility to enable or allow others to work.[17]

iii. Economic growth is a natural consequence of the abundant resources of the world

> Growth in numbers ... requires growth in material production and provision. God provided for that need ... through the astounding and incalculable riches of the legacy that God put at human disposal in the earth's crust, and ... through the equally incalculable endowment of ingenuity and adaptability God gave to human beings themselves.[18]

Within the economic activity of human beings, necessary both for survival and for material comfort and enjoyment beyond survival, the exchange and trade of commodities is a consequence:

---

[14] Wright, *Old Testament Ethics*, 148.

[15] For an account of John Locke's 'theological' defence of this land grab, see Michael Northcott, *An Angel Directs the Storm: Apocalyptic Religion and American Empire* (London: SCM Press, 2007), 47-49.

[16] Wright, *Old Testament Ethics*, 148.

[17] Wright, *Old Testament Ethics*, 148.

[18] Wright, *Old Testament Ethics*, 149.

Bringing Good News to the Poor

All such economic activity at every level comes within the sphere of God's concern and moral scrutiny.[19]

iv. *The products of economic activity are to be shared equitably among all people*

Just as the right access to and use of the *resources* of the earth is a shared right that sets moral limitations to the right of private ownership of resources, so too the right to consume or enjoy *the end product* of the economic process is limited by the needs of all.[20]

This means that

there is no necessary or 'sacrosanct' link between what one owns or invests in the productive process and what one can claim as an exclusive right to consume as income in return.[21]

In other words, the basic needs of the other always make a prior claim upon our conscience and action, before we spend on ourselves.

Responses to Poverty in Biblical Perspective

In the final part of his chapter on 'Economics and the Poor', Wright turns his attention to solving the perennial problem of poverty. He shows the importance of community solidarity, of welfare provision, of proper legal representation for the poor, of the inviolability of the family inheritance (as in the case of Naboth's vineyard, for example) and of the link between true worship and responsibility for equitable economic practices. He sums up the general biblical approach to the poor with three broad concepts: compassion, generosity and justice.

Compassion

Perhaps the major contribution of the prophets, and the major lesson we can learn from them in terms of the prophetic responsibility of the church today, lies in the fact that *they saw what was going on*.[22]

In other words, the plight of the poor must never be allowed to become invisible. Compassion means first that the poor are treated as full human beings. Exploitation of their labour power, because of their perilous circumstances, is abhorrent to God. Therefore, practices like child-labour, bonded labour and high interest loans have to

---

[19] Wright, *Old Testament Ethics*, 149.
[20] Wright, *Old Testament Ethics*, 149.
[21] Wright, *Old Testament Ethics*, 149.
[22] Wright, *Old Testament Ethics*, 176.

be eradicated. Compassion implies eternal vigilance against all forms of abuse, and the advocacy of laws that successfully protect the interests of the vulnerable. It has to be distinguished explicitly from paternalistic or condescending attitudes. The best way to achieve this is by supporting the poor in their struggle for recognition by helping them to gain a measure of control over their own destiny.

Generosity

In many ways this is the principal response that the New Testament gives to the question of the poor. The biblical teaching is set within the realities of the life of the early Christian community that emerges as a new, small religious group and makes its way within the spheres of power of the Roman and other empires. Although the system of wealth disparity based on the exploitation of markets and slave labour by Rome is seemingly denounced in the prophetic passage of Revelation 18, the first Christians were hardly in a position to challenge the economic injustices perpetrated by the system of empire, except (and it is an important exception) by living out a different kind of economic regime within their own community.

Jesus' teaching on wealth would have been a decisive factor in the way the early Christians approached economic matters. It may be summarised by considering some of the special material that Luke incorporates into his Gospel.

THE NAZARETH MANIFESTO (LUKE 4:16-21)

Jesus was anointed by the Spirit, in fulfilment of prophecies in Isaiah 61:1-2 and 58:6, 'to bring good news to the poor … to proclaim release to the captives and let the oppressed go free, to proclaim the year of the Lord's favour'. If not actually declaring the inauguration of a jubilee year of the remission of debts, there are certainly allusions to the provisions of the jubilee in his teaching here and elsewhere; compare Matthew 11:2-6, 18:21-35 and Luke 14:12-24.

THE BEATITUDES AND WOES (LUKE 6:20-25)

Luke's version of the Sermon on the Mount connects a great blessing for the poor, when the kingdom comes, with a reversal of fortune for the rich. The disciples are commended for acts of generosity (6:30-34). They are told that such attitudes towards the needy are the result of God's grace (*charis*): 'If you love those who love you, what *charis* is that to you? ... If you do good to those who do good to you, what *charis* is that to you?'

THE PARABLE OF THE RICH LANDOWNER (LUKE 12:13-21)

The story is designed to illustrate the folly of amassing wealth, as if this was the main purpose of life: 'Take care! Be on your guard against all kinds of greed; for one's life does not consist in the abundance of possessions.' Life and material goods are gifts from God. He will require of us an account of how we have used them.

HOSPITALITY TO THE POOR AND DISABLED (LUKE 14:12-14)
Generosity is measured by how we respond to those who could never repay our giving. If the giving is reciprocal, it becomes calculating in the expectation of a reward. True giving is unsparing and unselfish.

REBUKE TO THE PHARISEES (LUKE 16:14-15)
The Pharisees were castigated for scoffing at Jesus' assertion that human beings cannot 'serve God and wealth'. When the accumulation of wealth is made the object of existence it becomes the god whom we revere.

THE PARABLE OF THE RICH MAN AND LAZARUS (LUKE 16:19-31)
The point of this story is that the rich man did not live by the word of God in his relationship to the poor: 'They have Moses and the prophets; they should listen to them.' As he did not heed God's word (e.g., Deuteronomy 15:10-11), the rich person cannot expect to have fellowship with God when he dies.

THE EXAMPLE OF ZACCHAEUS (LUKE 19:1-10)
Zacchaeus, on the other hand, did listen to God's word. Once convicted of the deception and corruption by which he had become rich, he obeyed the injunctions of Deuteronomy 15:10-11 concerning generosity to the poor ('Half of my possessions I will give to the poor.') and those of Exodus 22:1-2 ('If I have defrauded anyone of anything, I will pay back four times as much').

Generosity was the key to the economic practices within the early Christian communities. From the sharing of material goods by the Christian believers in Jerusalem (Acts 2:44-45, 4:34-37), to the relief of the famine-stricken Christians in Judea by the church in Antioch (Acts 11:27-30), to the collection that Paul organised in the churches of Macedonia and Achaia (1 Corinthians 16:1-4; 2 Corinthians 8-9), the Christians showed that they strove to live according to the principle of generous giving that reflected the new life of the kingdom they were called to embody:

> Strive first for the kingdom of God and his righteousness, and all these things [food, drink and clothing] will be given to you as well (Matthew 6:33).

Generosity springs from the heart of people who know that they owe their salvation and new life to the generosity of God (2 Corinthians 8:9; James 2:5, 14-17; 1 John 3:16-18). The apostle Paul *even goes so far as to state that generous giving is a way of confessing the gospel (2 Corinthians 9:13) for it is a reflection of God's abundant grace in giving up his Son as a sacrifice for the world.* It is an excellent manifestation of the 'amazing grace' received by all whose lives have been transformed by knowing Christ in the power of his resurrection; it is also an expression of worship:

> You will be enriched in every way for your great generosity, which will produce thanksgiving to God through us; for the rendering of this ministry not only supplies the

needs of the saints but also overflows with many thanksgivings to God ... Thanks be to God for his indescribable gift! (2 Corinthians 9:11-12, 15).

Justice

Both the basis for and the meaning of justice spring from the nature of who God is. Justice is what God does, for justice is what God is ... So we know justice through God's acts of deliverance, through his laws and through the kind of relationships between human beings that he requires (see Micah 6:8; Isaiah 58:6; Psalm 72:1-4).[23]

The meaning of justice is best illustrated in the New Testament by the condemnation of exploitative practices made by James (5:1-6):

> ... the references to 'riches', 'gold and silver', 'treasure', 'luxury', 'pleasure' and 'fattened hearts', in the immediate context of defrauding workers of their wages, suggest not just that the wages have not been paid, but that the employers have made excessive profit out of the wealth created in their agri-business by not paying adequate wages.[24]

The point is that the just wage is an instance of the meaning of justice:

> The just wage is one that enables the worker to be respected as a member of the community, not dependent upon further welfare benefits, and which does not create enormous disparities of wealth among people. In this concept of justice there is a strong element of grace: the requirements of compassion take precedence over the requisites of the law.[25]

This means that doing what is legally required, for example to pay the minimum wage demanded by the law, is not necessarily the same as doing justice. Justice does not ask a question about profit margins, but about the dignified life of the worker in terms of earnings which enable him or her to afford all the basic necessities of life, not just food, clothing and accommodation, but also entry into the benefits of culture – education, access to the arts, sport and other recreation facilities. In other words, the just wage will probably exceed the minimum wage in most societies.

---

[23] Kirk, *What is Mission?*, 104.
[24] Kirk, *What is Mission?*, 107.
[25] Kirk, *What is Mission?*, 107. I believe that this may well be the right way to interpret the parable of the labourers in the vineyard in Matthew 20:1-16: the point of the story is not to underline the justice of a minimum hourly wage but the justice that sees the need of the family which the labourer needs to support by being hired for work. Thus, the pericope ends with the punch-line 'Are you envious because I am generous?'

Mission in Relation to the Poor

An option for the poor means that the Christian community mobilises its resources to inspire people to work for a society in which everyone's basic needs are met and in which the vulnerable – minority groups, children, women, the disabled, the elderly and the unemployed – live in hope and without fear.

As ending poverty is not a simple matter, including as it does intense debates about complex economic matters, Christians should beware of being overly idealistic or naïve about how this may be achieved. Above all, they should avoid ideologies (of whatever hue) which promise unqualified success if certain economic and political directions are taken. Overcoming poverty is not merely a matter of making the correct political decisions regarding the material conditions of life; it also has strong cultural, moral and spiritual dimensions. Poverty is about the situation of human beings, not just about abstract economic theories and structures.

Therefore I would argue that mantras about such matters as free markets, competition, entrepreneurship, the profit motive, structural adjustments, or about the collective ownership of the means of production and a centrally planned economy, spring from a simplistic analysis of the problems. This does not mean, however, that Christians should become cynical or despairing about the possibilities of substantial change. There is a divine obligation to care for the poor in the best ways possible; the best way being to bring about conditions in which they can escape the cycle of poverty. The specific contribution that the Church can make to ending poverty may vary according to circumstances but in general it will probably include the following:

Be a model of a sharing community
Churches will learn in practice the meaning of costly giving. Particularly in societies that are heavily oriented towards consumerism, Christians will need to learn a proper balance between spending surplus income on themselves and on others. Irrespective of the intense commercial pressures to 'shop until you drop', Christians should be conscious of what constitutes an acceptably modest lifestyle under the lordship of Jesus Christ. Teaching will include the meaning and blessing of generous giving. One might call this the practice of the 'widow's mite' (Luke 21:1-3).

Be an agent of empowerment
The general principle here is that of helping the poor in appropriate ways to be genuine shapers of their own history, sharing resources and skills in such a way that there is a genuine transference of power. Means are to be found to treat people as responsible agents and to give them the resources by which they can take their own economic decisions. On a small scale, one of the most successful ways of doing this has been the creation of micro enterprises by making available low interest loans for the creation of small-scale businesses or industries and imparting the necessary skills to enable them to be run successfully.

Be involved in political advocacy

Churches will either initiate or join forces with campaigns to rectify specific injustices and abuses: for example, the debt trap, bonded and child labour, discrimination against women (including unequal educational opportunities, female circumcision, the dowry system, the exposure of female babies and unequal pay), the tyranny of war lords, child soldiers, wage exploitation by multinationals. Advocacy will also involve a continuing struggle for fair trade, national debt relief, a vast reduction in the arms trade, ethical investment and an exposure of political and economic corruption by political leaders and businesses.

Good News for the Poor?

In his public ministry Jesus singled out the poor as the recipients of the good news (*ptōchoi euangelizontai* – literally 'the poor are evangelised', Luke 4:18). The phrase comes directly from one of the messianic passages in Isaiah. The extract speaks of the 'year of the Lord's favour' (Isaiah 61:2, Luke 4:19) and pictures this in terms of restoring to all God's people the enjoyment of a land rich in resources. The context is the end of exile and the repossession of the land God had given to his people as an inheritance. The year of the Lord's favour means a transformation of the people's life: liberation from captivity; freedom from alien domination and external pressures; the end of mourning (Isaiah 61:2-3), because children die young (Isaiah 65:20) or fathers and sons are killed in war (Isaiah 65:23), and the elimination of despair, because in captivity there appeared to be no future worth living for (Isaiah 61:3). In this year, as they rebuild the infrastructure of their country (Isaiah 61:4) and enjoy favourable trading relations with other peoples (Isaiah 61:6), prosperity will return to the whole people (Isaiah 61:9).

This vision of a community at peace with itself and with surrounding peoples is dependent on a number of factors being in place. First and foremost is the belief that God desires to bring complete well-being to his people. Secondly, there is the acceptance of the messenger, who has been specially anointed for the task of conveying the good news of the year of God's favour, and a positive reception of the message. Rejection of the one who bears God's word is a sure sign of continued opposition to God's covenant grace. Thirdly, the people are required to live in a particular way – in the path of righteousness (Isaiah 61:3) and justice (Isaiah 61:8). This way implies, among other matters, an acceptance of foreigners (Isaiah 61:5) who 'join themselves to the Lord' (Isaiah 56:6-8), a respect for the inviolability of family inheritances (the means of livelihood) (Isaiah 65:21-23), and a rejection of the temptation to gain wealth at the expense of others (Isaiah 65:22). Fourthly and crucially the members of the community are to acknowledge the sovereign rule of God (Isaiah 61:10-11) by repudiating all forms of idolatry (Isaiah 65:11-12). This is to be one nation consciously and consistently 'under God'.

This vision is the good news that is proclaimed to the poor. Clearly it is good news, for it heralds an end of all those circumstances that contribute to poverty. In biblical terms, the state of affairs that produces deprivation and misery is first and foremost the rejection of the ways of the Lord: injustice is the fruit of idolatry (Romans 1:18 – *asebeia* [ungodliness] precedes *adikia* [injustice]). The good news is that the sovereign reign of God will be restored and with it his absolute requirements of right relationships between people (Micah 6:8). It is for this reason that the poor are blessed (Luke 6:20-21), for the coming of the kingdom of God means that their suffering will be at an end.

However, the blessings of the kingdom or righteous rule of God the Father exercised through God the Son in the power of God the Holy Spirit, can only be available to those who are 'poor in spirit' (Matthew 5:3), those who, in the words of Micah, walk humbly with their God' (Micah 6:8), or in the words of Isaiah 'are contrite and humble in spirit' (Isaiah 57:15). No longer will there be any poor in the land, when God is allowed to walk without let or hindrance with his people. This is, of course, an eschatological vision, when God finally makes all things new (Revelation 21:3-4). So, the Christian community's main contribution to making poverty history is to bring the whole gospel to the whole world and to live it out in the midst of a corrupt and suffering generation.

Conclusion

'Bringing good news to the poor' may be a biblically coherent way of dealing with the inherent tendency to separate out different features of the task of mission and of restoring the unity. On the one hand, it unites the commission 'to remember the poor' (i.e., the economically vulnerable, the materially destitute and the physically and emotionally violated) and to proclaim salvation to 'the lost' (identified as those who, like sheep, 'have gone astray', turning away from God to their own ways (Isaiah 53:6; Luke 15:6, 9, 24; 19:10). On the other hand, it highlights the imperative for Christians to be engaged in Christ's mission to 'bring forth justice to the nations' (Isaiah 42:1; 49:6), insisting that poverty is a political matter that calls for deeply costly shifts in the way power is exercised in contemporary societies.

In the perspective of the whole Bible, the poor are both the materially, educationally and culturally deprived, and the spiritually ignorant and rebellious. The poor may be those who live in shanty towns or those who live in luxurious villas, absorbed by their own interests, morally bankrupt and spiritually diminished. The good news of the kingdom of Jesus Christ, the saviour, applies in different measure to both of them. Responding to the grace-filled rule of Christ over the world for which he gave his life means both turning from a self-centred, selfish existence that ignores God's claims on one's life, solidarity with those pushed to the margins, and striving for societies, communities and families where poverty is eliminated.

Bringing 'good news to the poor', therefore, is integral mission, for it addresses the call to proclaim forgiveness of sin to those willing to turn from it (whatever their material circumstances), costly discipleship in the service of the weak and vulnerable (following in the way of Christ) and the challenge of promoting justice for those on the edge of existence. There is no escaping the fact that each of these aspects of mission is part of the one gospel. The absence of any one implies a truncated gospel and an inadequate evangelism. For those who boldly claim to be gospel people the imperative is inescapable.

CHAPTER 17

Struggling with Female Happiness: God's Will and God's Blessing in Primary Evangelical Theology

Lina Andronovienė

Happiness and Society

Togetherness, foreverness means nothing less than happiness.[1]

Happiness[2] is a popular word today – especially in a woman's world.[3] The word happiness keeps appearing in pop songs, in virtually every woman's magazine and in a whole array of self-help literature. Even governments are coming to acknowledge happiness as an important issue to consider in politics and policy-making. Of course, this is by no means a novelty for a world shaped by the Enlightenment but the current interest in happiness is in many ways unprecedented. Whereas a few decades ago the King of Bhutan's attention to 'gross national happiness'[4] would have been a piece of exotic news, now there are initiatives such as the New Economics Foundation's The Happy Planet Index 2.0 which encourages a 'radical departure

---

[1] Winfred Lovett, 'Happiness', recorded by Soul II Soul, *Keep On Movin'* (1989).

[2] As a concept happiness seems to be hopelessly polymorphous and a whole cluster of terms is used to clarify exactly what is being meant: 'quality of life', 'life satisfaction', 'wellbeing', 'goodness of life', 'fulfilment', 'flourishing', etc. Some researchers have been employing 'hedonia' and 'eudaimonia' to distinguish between psychological, subjective wellbeing reflecting someone's state of mind and meaningful, satisfying life in its long-term perspective. See, e.g., Edward L. Deci and Richard M. Ryan, 'Hedonia, Eudaimonia, and Well-being: An Introduction', *Journal of Happiness Studies* 9.1 (2008), 1–11. The distinction may be expressed by considering the difference between a person who is referred to as 'happy' (e.g., because they ate a cake a minute ago, or are known to be of optimistic disposition) and a conversation about a 'happy life' which has much more to do with a complexity of well-being – including, but not limited to, feelings and circumstances – and a concern for life which can be called meaningful. It is this latter meaning to which I am leaning.

[3] Although there are many commonalities between the way women and men experience and perceive happiness, this article will focus on the woman's experience.

[4] See, e.g., the website of the Centre for Bhutan Studies, <www.grossnationalhappiness.com/> (accessed 6 July 2012).

from our current obsession with GDP' as the indicator of human satisfaction with life.[5]

Discussions on happiness typically acknowledge a variety of avenues leading to personal wellbeing. Perhaps the clearest example, as well as a source, of this insistence is found in the comparatively contained, yet highly influential field of positive psychology – a field that is interested in what contributes to healthy and positive expressions of life.[6] The interest in such a 'psychology of happiness' arose out of frustration with the preoccupation of standard psychology with the anomalous and pathology. An impressive number of books written by positive psychologists for the general public have become bestsellers and have been translated into various European languages, followed by references and quotations in the popular media, perhaps especially notably magazines.

One source of a happy life is especially prominent, particularly in popular discussions, and certainly dominates all other motifs of happiness as far as a woman's life is concerned. I have explored this motif to a greater extent elsewhere,[7] but briefly put, it centres on the idea of coupledom. This idea may or may not be expressed in the form of marriage, but it is guided by a perception that 'being a couple' is necessary and, indeed, so crucial to happiness that even an unsuccessful attempt ought not stop one from trying again – and, if needed, again. Public policies also tend to follow this perception, as do scientists. DePaulo and Morris, writing specifically regarding the American society, see this perception arising directly from what they call the 'Ideology of Marriage and Family' – an ideology which 'has gone largely unrecognized and uncontested'. They point to, and provide a critique of, the bias in much social science that there is a direct link between coupledom and happiness.[8] Uncoupled people – even ostensibly happy single people – are likely to be viewed with suspicion or pity. If a single woman appears happy, 'she [must nevertheless be] unhappy. Although you wouldn't tell that just by looking.'[9]

There are, of course, alternative views being affirmed and saluted, even if they are largely perceived as 'complementary' or 'alternative' in relation to coupledom. One of these is motherhood. In some ways, this motif can be seen as forming one larger domain – 'satisfaction domain' as it would typically be called by sociologists – with the practice of coupledom, and therefore as functioning as a single factor which may

---

[5] New Economics Foundation, 'The Happy Planet Index 2.0: Why good lives don't have to cost the Earth', <http://www.happyplanetindex.org/public-data/files/happy-planet-index-2-0.pdf> (accessed 3 June 2011), 3.

[6] For an introduction to positive psychology, see Shane J. Lopez and C.R. Snyder (eds), *Oxford Handbook of Positive Psychology* (Oxford: Oxford University Press, 2009).

[7] Lina Andronovienė, 'Transforming the Struggles of Tamars: Singleness in Intentional Baptistic Communities' (PhD thesis, International Baptist Theological Seminary, Prague, 2012).

[8] Bella M. DePaulo and Wendy L. Morris, 'Singles in Society and in Science', *Psychological Inquiry* 16.2–3 (2005), 57-83, esp. 58, 65-80.

[9] 'Kodėl mes norime ištekėti?' [Lithuanian], < http://gyvenimas.delfi.lt/love/article.php?id=20037881> (accessed 7 June 2011; translation mine).

be termed, albeit loosely, 'family', encompassing both romantic/sexual relationships and progeny. 'Almost all of us dream about one and the same thing: a beloved next to us and healthy and smart children.'[10] Thus the happiness of a sexual partnership is expected to become a gate into the happiness of motherhood – although the link has been significantly weakened by the rising numbers of single mothers.

A third prominent element of a good life is some form of personal development.[11] As personal development encourages celebrating different ways of shaping one's identity, it does not necessarily rule out the first two paths – finding a partner and having a child – yet it does suggest that other ways are possible.[12] Expressions of personal development are countless indeed: from the trendiness of yoga or joining a local reading club to the whole health, beauty and diet industry, time management, or career ambitions.

Other motifs could be explored such as money/pleasure,[13] health[14] or spiritual affiliation,[15] and indeed the insight that a happy life necessarily involves a good balance between different sources of happiness.[16] No doubt all these factors do play a role. However, in spite of the validity of other avenues, at the present time none of them seem to be as pervasive as coupledom. I have proposed elsewhere that insights into other forms of fulfilment suffer from insufficient attention to the necessity of a

---

[10] «Неполноценная женщина?» Клуб одиноких и независимых женщин [Russian], <http://newwoman.ru/club1.html> (accessed 6 July 2010; translation mine). For another example, consider the way a Cambridge University sociological study is reported in a news portal for working mums: 'Happiness linked to family and loved ones', <www.workingmums.co.uk/working-mums-magazine/news/958243/happiness-linked-to-family-and-loved-ones.thtml> (accessed 7 July 2011).

[11] For an example of a website dedicated to personal development, see the website of a personal development coach, Jane C. Woods, 'Women's Personal Development', <www.changingpeople.co.uk/> (accessed 1 July 2011).

[12] John R. Gillis, *A World of Their Own Making: Myth, Ritual, and the Quest for Family Values* (Cambridge, MA: Harvard University Press, 1997), 233.

[13] On economic and leisure satisfaction in terms of gender differences see, e.g., a Danish study by Jens Bonke, Mette Dedding and Mette Lausten, 'Time and Money: A Simultaneous Analysis of Men's and Women's Domain Satisfactions', *Journal of Happiness Studies* 10 (2009), 113-31.

[14] The importance of this motif usually grows with age, as health deteriorates; see Dana Kotter-Grühn *et al*, 'What is it we are longing for?: Psychological and demographic factors influencing the contents of Sehnsucht (life longings)', *Journal of Research in Personality* 43.3 (2009), 435. Another side of the issue is the way happiness seems to be conducive to one's health.

[15] See, e.g, Eduardo Wills, 'Spirituality and Subjective Well-Being: Evidences for a New Domain in the Personal Well-Being Index,' *Journal of Happiness Studies* 10.1 (2009), 49-69.

[16] E.g., M. Joseph Sirgy and Jiyun Wu, 'The Pleasant Life, the Engaged Life, and the Meaningful Life: What about the Balanced Life?', *Journal of Happiness Studies* 10 (2009), 183-96. A commonly suggested triad of 'satisfaction domains' is marriage, economic wellbeing and health; see, e.g., Anke Plagnol, 'Subjective Well-being Over the Life Course: Conceptualizations and Evaluations', *Social Research* 7.2 (2010), 749-68.

larger framework – the visionary and the corporate dimensions of human life.[17] What seems to happen is that the motifs of happiness most widespread in and practiced by popular culture end up serving the function of the corporate and the visionary. This, as I argue next, may also be true for those who profess to be the followers of Christ, but who are also easily caught in these popular perceptions.

Oh I'm happy in Jesus[18]

If you're happy and you know it, clap your hands.[19]

On the surface, there may not seem to be a strong connection between the hermeneutics of happiness in the culture at large and the evangelical ideas about happiness. The little rhyme above assumes that those who sing it in the church context *are* happy, and the reason for their happiness arises out of their connection with God through Jesus. As Ian Randall notes, the double emphasis on 'happiness and holiness', so prominent in the Wesleyan tradition, has certainly become a mark of evangelicalism.[20] Such an understanding of the source of happiness would be corroborated by various hymns and praise songs as well as sermons and other occasions for propositional teaching on happiness. In the evangelical world the culture's insistence on the necessity of being coupled in order to be happy stands in the light of the gospel: happiness, or blessedness, depends on Jesus, not on family circumstances.

Yet a closer look beyond the 'sanctioned' talk about happiness – the 'between-the-lines' comments in sermons, testimonies and informal conversations – suggests that the way that evangelical Christians *really feel* about the elements necessary, or highly conducive to, happiness, is at worrying odds with their official theology. The common perception of happiness in the churches is rather similar to that of the culture at large.

---

[17] Andronovienė, 'Transforming the Struggles of Tamars', ch. 5.
[18] Eddie Robinson, 'I'm Happy in Jesus', recorded by Dottie Peoples, *On Time God* (1995).
[19] The lyrics of this popular children's song, especially suitable for Sunday school and camp times, are anonymous and exist in several variants, although the tune traces back to Isaak Dunayevskyi's song 'Molodezhnaya' featured in the Soviet film of Grigoryi Aleksandrov, 'Volga-Volga' (Moscow: Mosfilm, 1938). There are rumours on the internet that the tune is based on a Latvian folk melody, but I have not been able to establish this.
[20] Ian M. Randall, *What a Friend We Have in Jesus: The Evangelical Tradition* (London: Darton, Longman and Todd, 2005), 116.

Marriage, Family, and the Will of God

During a prayer at church celebrating wedding anniversaries, the person praying says a special prayer for all the people that are still single and lonely.[21]

Of course, it takes some careful listening and 'translation' of the churchly language to see the connection; something which at times has been called a theology of convictions. I will comment on the convictional approach later, but here will simply note that, in the case of exploring happiness, it starts with a recognition of the importance of the language of the 'will of God'. A widely expressed variant of the hermeneutics of happiness in evangelicalism has to do with the notion of blessing as a consequence of being in God's will. While charismatic movements such as Word of Faith, Full Gospel and other expressions of prosperity gospel provide an ultimate example of such a view, they are certainly not the only examples. After all, it makes a lot of sense to suggest and to believe that God desires and grants the best for his children.

The real issue here, however, is what is understood to be 'the best'. The 'staple' elements, for a female believer especially, centre on a successful ('happy') marriage, problem-free children and perhaps an overall comfortable life surrounding these aims, such as economic blessings. Such a view is, at times, defended on biblical and/or theological grounds[22] and may also be combined with the pagan idea that God has chosen a particular individual to be one's marital partner. Once 'baptised', this idea becomes the notion that God blesses his faithful children by helping them to find their other 'half' – a term which abounds in church contexts.[23] Indeed, what Ronald Rolheiser observed about American culture is generally true throughout the West,[24] 'No possibility of real happiness is seen outside [marriage].'[25] There is a deep-seated conviction that, despite what the apostle Paul may have had to say about singleness and marriage, it is much nicer to be in the latter position. The words of a pastor of an evangelical church of a Pentecostal flavour express it well.

---

[21] A true story recounted by Jonathan Acuff, 'Surviving church as a single', <www.jonacuff.com/stuffchristianslike/2009/06/550-surviving-church-as-a-single/> (accessed 25 March 2011).

[22] Al Hsu, *The Single Issue* (Leicester: IVP, 1998), 72.

[23] Hsu, *The Single Issue*, 73. The idea that human beings cannot help but look for 'their other half' can be traced back to Plato's *Symposium*. Such a search, Aristophanes argued, is the longing for the bliss of fulfilment. Plato, *Symposium* (trans. Benjamin Jowett, available online via Project Gutenberg, <www.gutenberg.org/dirs/etext99/sympo10.txt> (accessed 27 January 2007).

[24] By 'the West' I mean regions and cultures nurtured by western civilisation, marked by the imprint of the classical culture of Greece and Rome, the experience of Christendom and the worldview shaped by Enlightenment philosophy.

[25] Ronald Rolheiser, *Forgotten Among the Lilies: Learning to Love Beyond Our Fears* (New York, NY: Galilee/Doubleday, 2005), 51.

> It is better; it's Paul isn't it, that says it's better to be single um so um, so I think it probably is. But then having said that I think it's really good it's just fun – it's great to be married um, and I think it's a natural thing and I think, you know, you'd expect for most people to get married in the end.[26]

Thus 'never mind how much we intone that singleness is great, the general attitude is that marriage is better'.[27] The institution of marriage is still very much a necessary element in an evangelical happiness package, in contrast to much of contemporary society which expects not so much marriage as '*any* kind of a sexual relationship'.[28] It is the same dominant understanding of a satisfying life in popular culture that is mirrored in the church.

The same could be said about the motif of happiness through motherhood. Mary Grey, a Roman Catholic feminist, contends that although there have been vocal voices within culture contesting and deconstructing this doctrine, 'motherhood is still the official ecclesial discourse for women'.[29] Women can still be seen to be saved through childbearing (including the still existing literal interpretation of that expression within some conservative evangelical enclaves in the territory of the former Soviet Union).[30] For some of those who are denied such an opportunity, the struggle may be hard indeed.

> Coping with the stigma of being childless, as well as not being married, can be intolerable for some women. Motherhood is so powerfully associated with being a true woman that some single women today are deliberately choosing to have children.[31]

Such a move is certainly not encouraged, but privately people might acknowledge that they 'do understand' these single mothers.

---

[26] Quoted in Kristin Aune, 'Singleness and Secularization: British Evangelical Women and Church (Dis)affiliation', in K. Aune, S. Sharma and G. Vincett (eds), *Women and Religion in the West* (Aldershot: Ashgate, 2008), 63.

[27] Lauren F. Winner, 'Solitary Refinement', *Christianity Today* 11 June 2001, 36.

[28] One of the respondents in Philip B. Wilson, *Being Single: Insights for Tomorrow's Church* (London: Darton, Longman and Todd, 2005), 110. Cf. also Steve Chilcraft, Sheena Gillies and Rory Keegan, *Single Issues: A Whole-church Approach to Singleness* (Warwick: CPAS, 1997), 5, 'Outside the church, people think you're strange because you are not having sexual relationships. Inside the church, you're labelled strange because you're not married.'

[29] Mary Grey, *The Wisdom of Fools?: Seeking Revelation for Today* (London: SPCK, 1993), 35.

[30] Coming from that part of the world, I have personally encountered such a view, with the appropriate quotation from 1 Timothy 2:11-15, on a number of occasions, even if it is becoming considerably rarer.

[31] Linda Harding, *Better Than or Equal To?: A Look at Singleness* (Milton Keynes: Word Publishing, 1993), 79-80.

If I did have a child out of wedlock, it wouldn't have been from a lack of desire to do it the Proper Way, and I suspect some people might even sigh with relief, wondering why I'd never married and glad to know I was Normal after all.[32]

Alternatives?

Is there an alternative and, if so, how does it compare with the motif of personal development as a way into happiness? There is indeed an approach in church life and in theology which seeks to subvert the very idea of happiness on the basis that happiness is not a Christian concept.[33] Contrary to the Wesleyan idea, here holiness becomes the centre of personal development, and is set in contrast with happiness as a worldly desire.[34] Although such a standpoint takes seriously Christ's invitation to 'deny oneself' (e.g., Mt. 16:24), it can easily miss the loving nature of God, and is often expressed in lifeless and joyless concentration on duty and the fear of God: a 'happiness police' of some sort.

The other alternative that, at least to me, seems to be the most hopeful and the most faithful to the evangelical message, is the one that, with the songs and the sermons, confirms that happiness for Christians is indeed necessarily linked to Jesus, yet also recognises the problem which lies not with one's life which does not seem to correspond to the common understanding of happiness, but precisely with that common perception of happiness. It confirms that God desires our utmost happiness but contests the belief that the present understanding of happiness is correct. It claims that true happiness comes from God even if it may not 'feel' like happiness, at least to start with. In other words, it underscores the need to discover a different way of being happy, 're-learning' happiness.[35] On such a view, the term most likely to be preferred for considering human flourishing would be 'the meaning of life'. I will return to its exploration as a source for a more faithful hermeneutics of happiness.

---

[32] Kathy Keay, *Letters from a Solo Survivor* (London: Hodder and Stoughton, 1991), 66-67. There are, of course, also the cases of adoption and foster care.

[33] For consideration of the roots of such a theological stance, see, e.g., Adrian Thatcher, 'Religion, family form and the question of happiness', in John Atherton, Elaine Graham and Ian Steedman (eds), *The Practices of Happiness: Political Economy, Religion and Wellbeing* (London: Routledge, 2011), 149-52.

[34] David K. Naugle, *Reordered Love, Reordered Lives: Learning the Deep Meaning of Happiness* (Grand Rapids, MI: Eerdmans, 2008), 12.

[35] A number of authors on Christian spirituality point to the error of the perception of happiness in today's church; see for instance Rolheiser, *Forgotten Among the Lilies*.

On our Convictions

Where is the front line for each of us: in our hearts; in the society; in the church itself?[36]

But first something more needs to be said about the method employed here. The premise I have been following is that attention must be paid not (only) to the examples of explicit and intentional teaching by way of sermons, Bible studies or seminars, but also to testimonies, well-meant advice, songs, gossipy comments on the lives of others and other elements which make up the complex fabric of church life: something that can be termed first-order theology.[37] Yet is it really sensible to try to discern what is being conveyed 'in between the lines'? After all, there are solid theological treatises on the true nature of happiness, all good examples of sound theology. Observing church culture, doing first-order theology, on the other hand, can be messy, depressing and hardly ever definitive.

However, I would side with those who argue that exploring such primary expressions of theology is indispensable for the theological task. Such an approach is also known as convictional theology, understood as a commitment to a careful examination of deeply-held beliefs of people and communities. On the basis of that examination and in relation to their professed theology, the discussion then can be steered further, hopefully to some sufficiently realistic transformation. James W. McClendon, my guiding voice in such convictional theology, described it as a three-fold task of theology: to describe, analyse, and evaluate 'the convictions of a convictional community, including the discovery and critical revision of their relation to one another and to whatever else there is'.[38]

---

[36] Waldemar Zorn, «Слово редактора. Новости с фронта». *Вера и жизнь* 4 (2006), <www.lio.ru/archive/vera/03/02/article06.html> (accessed 18 March 2010; translation mine).

[37] Second-order theology then engages in making sense, analysing and appraising the first-order material and the convictions expressed therein. As an example of an exploration of the sung expressions of the convictions of a particular community of faith, see my article 'As Songs Turn into Life and Life into Songs: On the First-Order Theology of Baptist Hymnody', in Keith G. Jones and Parush R. Parushev (eds), *Currents in Baptistic Theology of Worship* (Prague: International Baptist Theological Seminary, 2007), 129-41.

[38] James W. McClendon, Jr, *Systematic Theology:* Volume 1. *Ethics* (Nashville, TN: Abingdon, rev. edn, 2002), 23. There are different ways of describing realities which here are termed 'convictional', and examples can be encountered in different fields of inquiry. See, for instance, Ron Ritchart's usage of terms such as 'dispositions', 'inclinations', 'mental models' or 'fixed and developed beliefs' from an educationalist perspective, in his *Intellectual Character: What It Is, Why It Matters, and How to Get It* (San Francisco, CA: Jossey-Bass, 2002); or Charles Taylor's 'basic' (or 'fundamental') 'orientation' in *Sources of the Self: The Making of the Modern Identity* (Cambridge, MA: Harvard University Press, 1989), e.g., 29-30.

Different, and even conflicting, convictions can coexist in a particular convictional set[39] because they are fostered by different groups that influence the person (or the community).[40] An example of this would be a tension between certain Christian and patriotic convictions.[41] Indeed, convictions are not necessarily logically ordered and some convictions will be much more central than others. Convictions that are more at the centre of the convictional web, and therefore related to a greater number of other convictions, would result in an especially significant change when altered. It is in this context that a profound change of convictions can be called 'conversion', although this is not likely to be an acceptable concept when used outside the religious context.[42] Yet as far as the church goes, Darrell L. Guder has rightfully pointed out the need for a *continuing* corporate conversion of the church.[43] My argument is that such conversion may be in order in relation to the current evangelical perception of what constitutes a happy life.

The perception of happiness in evangelical primary theology is a prime case of a convictional clash. It is helpful to recognise that the Christian understanding of happiness and a good, meaningful life does not emerge exclusively out of the Christian narrative; it will always be related to the particular context which helps shape that understanding. Where the problem lies is in the assumption that the theology of happiness centring around marriage and family *is* Christian through and through and, by implication, a good one. Churches which cannot see the cultural influences which shape their life are unable to see where change is needed, and even less to bring about such change. They may fiercely cling to what they consider to be Christian language and Christian practices, but these will be either neutralised by the much greater loyalty to culture's gods or subverted to serve the purposes of this religion and to reflect its narrative.[44]

---

[39] On convictional set, see James M. Smith and James W. McClendon, Jr, *Convictions: Defusing Religious Relativism* (Valley Forge, PA: Trinity Press International, 1994), 91-101.

[40] E.g., Willem F. Zuurdeeg, *An Analytical Philosophy of Religion: A Treatment of Religion on the Basis of the Methods of Empirical and Existentialist Philosophy* (London: George Allen & Unwin, 1959), 40-44.

[41] As Zuurdeeg, *Analytical Philosophy*, 41, aptly notes, much of Christianity seems to be unaware of such a tension or conflict. Such unawareness, 41-42, does 'not so much reveal an admirable naïveté as a misleading glossing over of a factual situation: man [sic] is a complicated and ambiguous being, not all of a piece, but full of contradictions and conflicting loyalties. The suspicion widely felt, that being a Christian requires a considerable amount of hypocrisy, is connected with the awareness that so many "Christians" share in the "naïve" denial of man's [sic] ambiguity.' Such hypocrisy is 'a laudable attempt to construct a respectable façade behind which he can live his real life in peace'.

[42] McClendon and Smith, *Convictions*, 7-8.

[43] Darrell L. Guder, *The Continuing Conversion of the Church* (Grand Rapids, MI: Eerdmans, 2000).

[44] Jonathan R. Wilson, *Living Faithfully in a Fragmented World: Lessons for the Church from MacIntyre's After Virtue* (Christian Mission and Modern Culture Series; Harrisburg, PA: Trinity, 1997) 31. Wilson, 34, draws attention to the practice of worship and how significantly the practice would be altered if the *de facto* purpose of human life and the

Evangelical Happiness

Our need for God is sensed in our restlessness, but the goodness of other things keeps us hoping that we shall find fullness of life in the world.[45]

As was noted earlier, one of the ways to deal with this convictional clash would be to insist even more strongly on separating the notions of happiness and the will of God. In some ways, such an exercise may help to clarify the different meanings attached to the term 'happiness'. It is certainly true that some of the hedonistic shades of the term would stand in direct opposition to the classical Christian notion of the will of God. However, what would not stand is an insistence that Christians are not supposed to be interested in happiness. At least for the children of the western culture, Christian or otherwise, happiness, with all its multiple interpretations, is something which 'is consistently described as the object of human desire, as being what we aim for, as what gives meaning and order to human life'.[46]

Between First-Order and Second-Order Theology: The Case of Billy Graham

Having observed the first-order theology 'on the ground', I turn now to the popular writings of someone who has had a tremendous impact on evangelicals throughout the world, the Rev. Dr Billy Graham.[47] His writings stand in between the primary expressions of evangelical convictions and reflections on the convictions that *ought* to mark evangelical witness. One of Graham's works which has been translated into many languages and enjoyed great popularity, including secret publishing and circulation in countries under communist regimes, was a book called *The Secret of Happiness*.[48] It explores a particular biblical passage from an evangelistic, rather than a scholarly or spiritual perspective. By focusing on a biblical text, Graham has been especially appealing to evangelical communities for whom focus on the Bible represents one of their key identity features.[49]

---

narrative supporting it would be perceived as, for instance, that of being part of a happy nuclear family.

[45] Diogenes Allen, *Love: Christian Romance, Marriage, Friendship* (Cambridge, MA: Cowley Publications, 1987), 122.

[46] Sara Ahmed, 'The Happiness Turn', *New Formations* 63 (2007–08), 7.

[47] For a biography of Billy Graham, see William Martin, *A Prophet with Honor: The Billy Graham Story* (New York, NY: William Morrow, 1991).

[48] Billy Graham, *The Secret of Happiness* (Milton Keynes: Word Publishing, 1986 [1955]). As a young child, I witnessed its publication by *samizdat* into Lithuanian.

[49] Cf. Randall, *What a Friend*, ch. 2. Even those in academia, sceptical as they were of writings of such order, could admit that Graham's sermonic practice was able to make Christ visible 'in such a way that [the hearers/listeners] are not listening to ancient history but are entering into personal spiritual encounter with the Word made flesh': Ronald E. Osborn, review of *The Secret of Happiness: Jesus' Teaching on Happiness as Expressed in the Beatitudes* by Billy Graham, *Encounter* 17.2 (1956), 202.

The Secret of Happiness starts with a definition of happiness as something deep, secure, permanent – and for Graham, that certainly means rooted in God and God's goodness.[50] Graham also laments the state of the Christianity of his day which 'has become well versed in Christian terminology, but is remiss in the actual practice of Christ's principles and teachings'.[51] His response is an invitation to 'retrace our steps to the source' and to return to a life of Christlikeness.[52]

The chapters of the book follow the individual Beatitudes of Matthew 5:3-10, exploring the features of those who can be called μακάριος – 'happy', 'contended', 'joyful', 'blessed'. Graham explores happiness through poverty in spirit; happiness while mourning; happiness through meekness; happiness through hunger; happiness through showing mercy; happiness in purity; happiness through peacemaking; and happiness in persecution. The book concludes with a chapter illustrative of the primary audience for which Graham was writing, with 'steps to happiness'.

Although simplistic in his argumentation, Graham discusses the concrete virtues befitting the vision of the Kingdom of God. According to Graham, the Beatitudes must be the core text for those who claim to follow the One who uttered these words. This is important, because in spite of its clearly central role in Christian theology, the Sermon on the Mount has been overlooked both in the teaching and the practice of churches for much of the history of the church.[53] Granted, Graham takes up only the introductory part of the sermon, the Beatitudes, but this is a start nevertheless.

Yet how is it that these same evangelical communities who were familiar with Graham's *The Secret of Happiness* and, it must be assumed, the Sermon on the Mount itself, have been so quick to adopt a stance towards happiness which disregards the Sermon on the Mount? I would suggest that, as they stand, Graham's virtues as secrets of happiness still suffer from a lack of grounding in a fuller story of salvation. They largely miss the *'they'*, the third person plural of the Beatitudes themselves. Graham offers his insights from the Beatitudes as 'a formula for personal happiness'.[54] Surely, he thinks that living out the Beatitudes can 'transform the world in which we live',[55] but such an application is secondary to their personal significance. What is omitted is the thrust of the Sermon on the Mount being lived out in a community where such humility, such poverty, such hunger and thirst for righteousness are worked out together and in a variety of ways. No wonder, then, that the remainder of the Sermon on the Mount (Mt. 5:11–7:27), with its second

---

[50] Graham, *Secret of Happiness*, 14-19.

[51] Graham, *Secret of Happiness*, 9.

[52] Graham, *Secret of Happiness*, 10.

[53] As Glen H. Stassen and David P. Gushee, *Kingdom Ethics: Following Jesus in Contemporary Context* (Downers Grove: IVP, 2003) xi, note, such 'evasion ... has seriously malformed Christian moral practices, moral beliefs and moral witness ... When Jesus' way of discipleship is thinned down, marginalized or avoided, then churches and Christians lose their antibodies against infection by secular ideologies ...'

[54] Graham, *Secret of Happiness*, 9.

[55] Graham, *Secret of Happiness*, 9.

person plural '*you*', is ignored. Without such a community, the practice of the sermon can easily become the project of a madman.

If the Beatitudes are indeed to be the manual for happiness, the sermon's larger context in the story of Christ and his church has to be kept in mind. Only then can the virtues which Jesus calls for in the Beatitudes be embodied and developed in Christian practices and embedded in the Christian narrative.[56] Otherwise, taken as an abstraction, they can easily morph into the world's order of things – where the 'will of God' becomes surprisingly similar to my own wants which in turn very much mirror the common views of happiness. The second-order theological reflections that follow are aimed at addressing this concern and the need.

Where God's Will might Lead: The Meaning(s) of Life

At this point, I return to a more comfortable synonym for happiness in the Christian language: that of the 'meaning of life'. This term is considerably less polymorphous than 'happiness' and has enjoyed much more respect in Christian circles. However, there is a danger that the phrase may remain abstract, without any applicable meaning. The task of the church includes the task of concretising such a meaning for a particular time or place; a task which demands much more attention within church life – songs, sermons, occasional remarks, non-verbal cues – so that meaning-making can become a deeply integrated practice. Sure, the meaning of life must be about following Jesus and doing God's will. As the famous formulation of the *Westminster Shorter Catechism* puts it, the human being's 'chief end' is 'to glorify God, and enjoy him forever'. This, of course, echoes the Thomistic understanding of the end of the human being – and that being's complete happiness – in the contemplation of God.[57] This is how far the account goes much of the time. Yet the question often remains as to how it is to be embodied, not in a high moment of singing praise on a Sunday morning, or upon hearing a moving sermon, but in a day-to-day working out of one's life.

Of course, certain instructions are likely to be given: one is to have one's daily devotional time of reading the Scriptures and praying, to listen to God's voice in order to understand the specific will of God, and so on. Yet these elements may not be sufficient in providing a framework for life which would be strong enough to resist mirroring dominant cultural understandings of requirements for happiness, and to sustain one when life gets hard or different from one's expectations. Thus, although it is certainly true that the meaning of the Christian life involves doing the will of God by following the risen Christ, further exploration is needed about how

---

[56] Here I largely follow the framework proposed by Alasdair MacIntyre; see his seminal *After Virtue* (Notre Dame, IN: University of Notre Dame Press, 2nd edn, 1984); for a further elaboration on the contribution of MacIntyre's work for Christian ethical thinking, see Nancey Murphy, Brad J. Kallenberg, and Mark Thiessen Nation (eds), *Virtues and Practices in the Christian Tradition: Christian Ethics after MacIntyre* (Notre Dame, IN: University of Notre Dame Press, 1997).

[57] Thomas Aquinas, *Summa Theologiae* I-II, 3.

this is worked out: smaller, yet concrete meanings that would sustain Christian life in a variety of situations. The ease with which the plural of the phrase –'meanings of life' – can be employed is another reason why it is a helpful term; 'happinesses' does not quite work and the ever-singular 'happiness' fails to convey the plurality of its expression.

David Schmidtz provides a helpful metaphor to illustrate such plurality which is worth quoting at length.

> Life is a house. Meaning is what you do to make it a home. Giving life meaning is like interior decorating. It is possible to overdo it, so that the walls become too 'busy'. But if our walls are bare, the solution is not to stare at bare walls, or philosophize about their meaning, but to put up a few photographs, making the walls reflect what we do, or care about, or making them reflect our judgment about what is beautiful or worth remembering. Activity can be meaningful, and philosophical reflection can be meaningful activity if done in the right way and if kept in its place – if we take it seriously without taking it too seriously or taking it seriously the wrong way. We need not be afraid of bare walls or deceive ourselves about their bareness. Neither is there any reason to dwell on the 'fundamental underlying' bareness of walls we have filled with pictures. If we do that, we are not being deep. We are pig-headedly ignoring the fact that the walls are *not bare*. We are failing to take our pictures seriously, which is metaphorically to say we are failing to take seriously what we do with our lives. We are saying, what would be the meaning of this life (the wall) if the activities that make it up (the pictures) were not real? But they *are* real.[58]

Just as with interior decorating, so with meanings: they involve intentions and choices of some sort.

> Persons can choose to see their lives (or other lives) as meaningful. The less inspiring corollary is, persons also can choose to see their experiences, and by extension their lives, and other lives, as meaningless.[59]

Yet the restlessness and the anxiety about life-meanings which visits many human beings from time to time can help them to improve in their decoration practice. The dynamic and creative nature of meaning-making also has to do with the positive angle of the aforementioned restlessness.

> To be happy with things as they are is to risk detaching oneself from God's project ... A theological understanding of human happiness will need to embrace some notion of

---

[58] David Schmidtz, 'The Meanings of Life', in Leroy S. Rouner (ed.), *If I Should Die* (Boston University Studies in Philosophy and Religion, 22; Notre Dame, IN: University of Notre Dame Press, 2001), 184 (italics original).

[59] Schmidtz, 'Meanings of Life', 181.

continual struggle rather than being posited on the completion of a discrete process of change.[60]

Such an awareness also helps to stop the obsession with 'happy endings' and instead turns our attention, as Malcolm Brown puts it, to 'happy middles'.[61] That said, the choice involved in meaning-making also entails accepting the limitations of the circumstances: one may miss either some pictures or more space to hang them. It entails working with what is there, rather than with what is not.

The meanings of life become an especially important synonym of happiness when viewed from the perspective of the end of life. A deep sense of happiness must include making peace with the prospect of death, imminent for all sooner or later.[62] The reminder of death gains its full meaning in the light of the message of the resurrection and of the life which awaits its fulfilment at the dawn of a new age, even if very little can be intelligibly said of that age. That 'not yet' aspect of the realm of God is also true of happiness. It is also, in all its varied expressions, both common to all human beings and unique to the Christian experience, a foretaste of what is yet to come.[63]

Experiences of such a foretaste come about in the relation of Christ's disciples to one another. Some may argue for the meaning of life based on a principle or an idea, yet ideas and principles come to us through language which has been passed down by others. Another objection to the relationality of meaning would lie in the suspicion of the fleeting nature of situations and relationships. However, this is where a theology of Christian community formation has a strong contribution to make: what is at stake is not just any relationship, but relationships that are aligned to the visionary thread of life: not just any group of persons, or even an interest-based club, but a community sharing the same convictional set. When one such member moves away and joins another faith community elsewhere, the change is likely to be painful and involve aligning to a different group of particular people with particular characters, but the common vision provides sufficient stability in one's set of meanings of life without shaking all the pictures off the walls.

Such a communal framework also enables bestowing meanings when a particular member loses hold of them: 'meaning can be our gift to each other', in the words of Schmidtz.[64] Such meaning, received as a gift, can be especially poignant in times of crises. Paul Fiddes comments, 'As [God's] story of suffering is retold in the preaching and worship of the church it gives new words to those whose meaningless suffering has struck them dumb.'[65] In the case of a female disciple of Jesus

---

[60] Malcolm Brown, 'Happiness isn't working, but it should be', in Atherton, Graham and Steedman (eds), *Practices of Happiness*, 76.

[61] Brown, 'Happiness isn't working', 84.

[62] I thank Lydie Kucová for helping me to reflect on this issue.

[63] Elaine Graham, 'The "virtuous circle": Religion and the practices of happiness', in Atherton, Graham and Steedman (eds), *Practices of Happiness*, 233.

[64] Schmidtz, 'Meanings of Life', 181.

[65] Paul S. Fiddes, *The Creative Suffering of God* (Oxford: Clarendon Press, 1988), 173.

struggling with the contrast between the shape of her life and the dominant – and hoped for – version of happiness, the community of other disciples is the arena where her own meaning-making is worked out.

Thus, our personal anguish, questions and hopes in relation to our happiness, or the meaning of our life, begins to bring fruit and fulfilment when complemented by another two threads – the social and the visionary.[66] Beside the bodily strand, our personal lives, there is the strand of community, or the corporate personality of what we call a local church; and to these two the strand of the anastatic, or resurrection ethics, must be added, colouring and aligning the other two strands with the vision of the newness of life through Christ. These constituents are interwoven in a variety of ways,[67] but all three have a role to play in the experience of happiness, bringing meanings into life. That is especially true for women experiencing the enormous pressure of the popular versions of happiness: only in such a three-stranded context the Christian talk of life in abundance (following Jn 10:10) or of *shalom* can actually be meaningful.[68]

---

[66] I borrow the metaphor of the three strands from McClendon; for a concise description, see James W. McClendon, Jr, *Systematic Theology: Volume 2. Doctrine* (Nashville, TN: Abingdon Press, 1994), 109. McClendon discusses organic, social and 'anastatic' ('resurrection') ethics as a way of organising a reflection on Christian life with its challenges and opportunities. For the third strand, I employ Parush R. Parushev's term 'visionary' to describe the realm of human life which has to do with the vision 'of construing the world according to ... [the] best aspirations' of its holders. As Parushev notes, a convictional perspective will want to ask not only 'what' is being said but also 'why' it is being said (or indeed, why certain things are left unsaid). See his 'Convictions and the Shape of Moral Reasoning', in Parush R. Parushev, Ovidiu Creangă and Brian Brock (eds), *Ethical Thinking at the Crossroads of European Reasoning* (Prague: International Baptist Theological Seminary, 2007), 37.

[67] McClendon, *Ethics*, 78.

[68] I am grateful to Parush Parushev for sharing this insight.

CHAPTER 18

Hearing what is Written to Recover our Future

Simon Jones

Silent and Solo Reading

On a recent visit to the National Gallery in London, I stood for a while in front of Rogier van der Weyden's *The Magdalen Reading*. It is part of an altar piece (since mostly lost) that now serves as a study of evangelical contemplation. The sumptuously dressed saint is pictured looking down at a book resting in her hand, silently reading, a sign of Bible-focused piety. Her green gown and bejewelled underdress, glimpsed below her knees, suggest a certain wealth; the alabaster jar at her side is proof of her identity: she is the sinful woman who wept in gratitude and washed Jesus' feet with her tears, anointed them with costly perfume and received his forgiveness. As a result she has devoted herself to holy living, rooted in the reading of what we take to be a Bible or book of hours.

The work is, of course, a complete fiction. Mary of Magdala was almost certainly illiterate (something she shared with almost all the first followers of Jesus, as I shall demonstrate below), did not live in a lavish wood-panelled apartment and would not have had access to the kind of cloth-bound book that she is reverently holding in Van der Weyden's portrait. But as we gaze on it, we are confronted with an almost stereotypical image of devotion that has captured the imaginations of believers for generation upon generation: the individual believer reading her Bible in the sanctity of her own living room. Silent and solo reading is perhaps the central image of the individualism often seen to lie at the heart of Protestant, evangelical faith.

What follows arises from a concern that has nagged away at me for a long time. It was touched on in my recent MA that explored aspects of the history of Pauline Christianity.[1] I am glad to have the opportunity to explore further a single aspect of that work, namely the literacy of those first communities of Jesus followers and what that meant for the way they appropriated Scripture. But the concern has been around for longer than that project. As a young believer, I was taught never to attend church

---

[1] Simon Jones, 'The Church in Your Workshop?: The Economic, Physical and Social Location of the Early Pauline Communities' (unpublished Archbishop's Examination in Theology MA, 2011). I would not have completed this work without Ian Randall's constant encouragement to stick to my guns and work in the history of the New Testament period. This makes him indirectly responsible for the book that I wrote alongside the MA research, *The World of the Early Church: A Social History* (Oxford: Lion Hudson, 2011).

without a Bible in hand, one in which I could make notes in the margins to show that I was advancing in understanding of God's Word. I stood in a long line of young disciples. In the mid-sixteenth century, William Cecil advised his son 'to procure expositions of the New and Old Testament "to be bound in parchment and to note the same books with your pen".' A century later, Oliver Heywood was similarly advised to 'labour to get every day some sanctified thoughts and write them in a book'.[2]

To those discipling me, I stood in an even longer line of young learners: I was frequently reminded of the Beroean believers who searched the Scriptures to see if what Paul was saying was indeed true (Acts 17:11).[3] This individualistic approach to the appropriation of Christian truth was, I was told, rooted in the very Scriptures I was urged to read on my own. It was never in doubt, as I was finding my feet in the faith, that my ability in reading was essential to my sanctification. Even as a teenager, I wondered at the link between reading and sanctity, troubled by the fact that some of my peers seemed excluded from the world of faith I was exploring by their inability or unwillingness to read.

David Cressy demonstrates that such a view has always been at the heart of some branches of Protestant Christianity. 'The person who could read was better equipped to prepare for salvation than his illiterate fellow Christians and was more likely, in the view of protestant divines, to lead a life of duty and godliness.' Even better, Cressy goes on to say, was the person who could write as well. 'He could set down his own ideas, his accounts, his reports, his instructions and communicate them over distance and time.'[4] Puritan divines were full of advice on how the literate could advance in their faith. So, Nicholas Brownde, writing in the 1590s, says, 'so many as can read, let them do it on the Lord's day, and they that cannot, let them see the want of it to be so great in themselves that they bring up their children into it'. And George Swinnock, writing in 1663, mourned the fact that 'many for want of reading have lost their precious souls', adding, 'alas the people perish for want of knowledge. And how can they know God's will that cannot read it?'[5]

Illiteracy

The trouble is, not everyone could read. Cressy suggests that it is likely that at best a third of men could sign their names in the 1640s – slightly more in the urban areas and the south of England, fewer in the countryside and the north. Literacy was better among the better off, worse among the poorer sections of society and worst of all among the labouring poor in the countryside. Eric Ives posits a slightly higher

---

[2] David Cressy, *Literacy and the Social Order: Reading and Writing in Tudor and Stuart England* (Cambridge: Cambridge University Press, 1980), 6.

[3] We shall return to this verse in due course.

[4] Cressy, *Literacy*, 1.

[5] Nicholas Brownde, *The doctrine of the Sabbath* (1595), 202; George Swinnock, *The Christian Man's Calling ... the second part* (1663), 22-23; both quoted in Cressy, *Literacy*, 3.

number: 'male literacy in London may have reached 40 per cent' at the start of the sixteenth century, he says.[6] By the middle of the century, most gentlemen and merchants could sign their name, usually taken as indicating an ability to read since penmanship is harder to master than reading. Few of the rural poor would have been able to read and therefore would not have benefited from the growing quantities of devotional literature in English, 'although where a person could read and did own a primer, others might gather round to listen'.[7] Keith Thomas suggests that the very poor had no time for reflection on their lives, for reading or intellectual discourse at any level. 'For many, the quest for subsistence was so all-absorbing that larger questions about how they should live seldom arose: mere life was a more urgent matter than the quality of life', he says.[8] In other words, those living at or below subsistence did not have time to read or gather in groups to be read to. So while there is some dispute about the precise numbers, there is no doubt that literacy was achieved by a minority through the entire early modern period.

This fact was recognised even by godly preachers, so they urged ministers to find ways of helping the non-reading majority to acquire the saving knowledge of the gospel. Christopher Haigh notes that Theologus, the divine in Arthur Dent's *The Plain Man's Pathway to Heaven*, knew 'that congregations must first be taught the basic principles of Christian religion by a question and answer method of rote learning. The minister was not only a preacher, he must be a teacher – a catechist.' And Richard Bernard in his *The Faithful Shepherd* agreed: 'preaching doth little good without catechising'.[9] Cressy notes that 'The protestant revolution notwithstanding, it was not necessary to be literate to be devout, and entry into the kingdom of heaven was not conditional on being able to read.'[10] It wasn't just the likes of Thomas More who argued this. Richard Steele, a restoration divine whose sermons were models for many late seventeenth-century preachers, said, 'though you cannot read a letter in the book, yet you can by true assurance read your name in the Book of Life, your scholarship will serve ... if you cannot write a word, yet see you transcribe the fair copy of a godly, righteous and sober life, and you will have done well'.[11] Haigh draws our attention to the fact that 'reading was often a group activity' and so a group might gather with a minister present to go 'over a sermon to make sure they had thoroughly understood it'; he suggests that many early seventeenth-

---

[6] Eric Ives, *The Reformation Experience: Living through the turbulent 16th Century* (Oxford: Lion, 2012), 42; but this is almost certainly a figure for reading only, rather than both reading and writing.

[7] Ives, *Reformation Experience*, 42-43.

[8] Keith Thomas, *The Ends of Life: Roads to Fulfilment in Early Modern England* (Oxford: Oxford University Press, 2009), 2. For a full discussion of the measurement of literacy in early modern England, see Cressy, *Literacy*, 42-174.

[9] Christopher Haigh, *The Plain Man's Pathways to Heaven: Kinds of Christianity in Post-Reformation England* (Oxford: Oxford University Press, 2007), 26.

[10] Cressy, *Literacy*, 15.

[11] Richard Steele, *The husbandsman's calling ... being the substance of XII sermons preached to a country congregation* (2nd edn, 1672), quoted in Cressy, *Literacy*, 15.

century divines would hold gatherings in their homes where more in-depth Bible study could take place.[12]

Reading Together

Ian Randall and others have drawn our attention to an alternative model of early evangelical life that, while lauding literacy and revering texts – especially the text of Scripture – also saw the Christian life as fundamentally communal. At a gathering where one or two could read, the Bible could be studied, appropriated by each individual to be lived out in a way that was accountable to the group of which each was a member. This way of learning – that is perhaps not exclusively Baptist – had its roots in earlier renewal movements and, I will argue, in the first communities of Jesus' followers to which the New Testament bears witness – and so could be a road worth exploring by those seeking to renew Baptist and evangelical life in our own day. Perhaps we need to be exploring ways of developing a communal hermeneutic of listening.[13]

Writing about the Lollards of the fifteenth and early sixteenth centuries in England, Susan Brigden notes that while many adherents were from 'the higher ranks of society', most were artisans and thus unlikely to be able to read and write.[14] She notes that Lollards met 'to read the scriptures', adding that

> Reading the Bible aloud and evangelising the Christian message was the purpose of the Lollard assembly, and if some, perhaps most, were illiterate, it hardly mattered, for those who could not read could listen. This was a society used to committing words to memory. Lollards became deeply versed in the texts.[15]

She tells the story of a thirteen year old who could recite the Gospels and Epistles by heart. The owners of books could not necessarily read them. One Robert Benet sold a good portion of his property to buy a copy of *The Four Evangelists*. 'He could not read it', notes Brigden, 'but kept it safe in his belt, and Thomas Capon, the stationer who sold it to him, taught him its truths.'[16]

Texts like Benet's were dangerous. Many Lollards who were burned for their beliefs had their books burned with them as the authorities sought to control the spread of ideas. It was for this reason that even as late as the early 1530s, English church courts were prosecuting people for having vernacular translations of Bibles, parts of Bibles, mass books and missals under a 1409 prohibition of such literature.

---

[12] Haigh, *Plain Man's Pathways*, 113.

[13] See Stuart Murray, *Biblical Interpretation in the Anabaptist Tradition* (Studies in the Believers' Church Tradition, 3; Kitchener, ON: Pandora Press, 2000), 157, who describes these churches as 'hermeneutic communities'.

[14] Susan Brigden, *New Worlds, Lost Worlds: The Rule of the Tudors 1485–1603* (Harmondsworth: Penguin, 2001), 86.

[15] Brigden, *New Worlds*, 86-87.

[16] Brigden, *New Worlds*, 87.

But these prosecuted people stood near the start of a long line of Christian groups for whom direct access to the Word of God in Scripture was 'a kind of sacrament'.[17]

The Hutterites were another. Born of the scattered flock of the Anabaptist Balthasar Hubmaier, which settled on the estate of a sympathetic landowner in what is now the Moravian town of Slavkov, the Hutterites were organised into an effective community by an artisan, Jakob Hutter. Diarmaid MacCulloch suggests that the *Bruderhof*, as their community was called, with its pooling of skills and resources, its focus on farming and craft trades, anticipated the *kibbutz* movement in modern Israel.[18] It might be more obvious to suggest that its organisation and life grew out of their reading of the New Testament with its description of the radical community that formed after the Day of Pentecost in Jerusalem. The community 'paid much attention to communal upbringing and education of all children: this was the first society in Christian Europe to expect everyone to read and write'.[19] They anticipated the strong emphasis on literacy that Puritans of all stripes manifested through the sixteenth and seventeenth centuries. It was the outworking of the dream which Erasmus of Rotterdam had that the Bible would be available in every language of Christendom and beyond: 'I wish even all women to read the gospel and the epistles of Paul', he wrote, adding, 'I wish that the husbandman may sing parts of them at his plough, that the weaver may warble them at his shuttle, that the traveller may with their narratives beguile the weariness of the way.'[20] At the time, of course, most ploughmen and weavers – and certainly all but a handful of elite women – were unable to read a word, let alone a Gospel or a New Testament Letter.

Many works on the history of the radical movements in the European Reformation, preferring to note the theological, social and ethical distinctives of the various groups, do not dwell on literacy rates – if they mention them at all. The likelihood is, however, that barely three in ten of the adherents of these movements would have been able to read, which makes the descriptions of their gatherings suggestive of fresh lines of enquiry.

Ian Randall has pointed out that of five crucial theological convictions of early Anabaptist and Baptist life, a particular way of reading the Bible was primary. From Hubmaier on, all practices and beliefs were weighed against Scripture, which meant that all instruction was to be rooted in 'the written divine word'.[21] Randall notes, 'what is significant about his approach is that those present would "instruct one another" from the Bible'.[22] He goes on to suggest that eighty years later, as the first English Baptists were coming together in Amsterdam, the same approach to learning

---

[17] Brigden, *New Worlds*, 87.

[18] Diarmaid MacCulloch, *Reformation: Europe's House Divided 1490–1700* (London: Allen Lane, 2003), 170.

[19] MacCulloch, *Reformation*, 170.

[20] Cited in David Daniell, *William Tyndale: A Biography* (New Haven, CT: Yale University Press, 1994), 67.

[21] Hubmaier cited in Ian M Randall, 'Tracing Baptist Theological Footprints: A European Perspective', *Perspectives in Religious Studies* 36.2 (2009), 133-48 (134).

[22] Randall, 'Tracing', 135.

was being utilised. He cites the words of Hugh and Anne Bromhead, members of John Smyth's congregation, who report that 'we begin with a prayer; after read some one or two chapters of the Bible, give the sense thereof and confer upon the same'. Commenting on this, Randall argues that the congregation is here discovering the power of the Bible and they are discovering it by listening to it being read and then discussing how what they have heard will make them better disciples of Jesus.[23]

The Jesus Movement

I want to suggest that the roots of such a way of being church, where texts were important in a community in which most could not use texts, are to be found in the earliest years of the Jesus movement. Furthermore, it seems to me that the recovery in our day of the vitality enjoyed by our early forbears might lie in a rediscovery of communal ways of hearing Scripture.

Like those on the radical edge of the Reformation in Europe, the earliest followers of Jesus were most likely craft workers gathering in homes and workshops in the back streets of Roman cities where Paul had preached the gospel. An examination of the economic, physical and social location of these groups suggests that they comprised artisans who lived at or a little above the margins of subsistence. There is a growing consensus among New Testament historians that these early groups were small – maybe twenty to thirty – and that they gathered in the workshops where they will have worked as artisans – potters, cabinet makers, leather workers, tent makers and the like. Most of these people would have been poor – there were certainly no members of the imperial elite among them – and thus lacking in any formal education. It is likely that very few were literate and even fewer would have been able to cope with a text as sophisticated as anything that now appears in the New Testament.[24]

And this begs a vital but still little asked question. Why is it that churches made up of mainly poor craft workers were in some senses literary communities, when production and enjoyment of literature was an almost exclusively elite occupation? We know Paul mainly through the Letters he wrote to his churches; we know of the life and beliefs of these communities through these written sources. How was it that these poor and socially marginalised groups were shaped in their lives of discipleship by literary texts that few of them could read?[25] And did the way these groups organise themselves, using elite forms for egalitarian ends, unleash something essential for the development of the church in every age?

---

[23] Randall, 'Tracing', 135-39.
[24] See Jones, *World*, 13-73, 143-65, and *Workshop*, for detailed bibliography.
[25] See Harry Y. Gamble, *Books and Readers in the Early Church: A History of Early Christian Texts* (New Haven, CT: Yale University Press, 1995), 2, 'To what extent were early Christians actually capable of writing and reading? The question has rarely been raised and has never before been explored by historians of early Christianity.'

Literacy

To answer these questions, we first need to ascertain the levels of literacy in the Roman Empire in the first century AD. The question of literacy in the ancient world is a contested one among historians. Keith Hopkins, in common with the majority of historians who have reviewed the evidence, argues that between 10–20% of males around AD 100 would have been able to read and write – and far fewer females.[26] Most literacy was basic and functional rather than rhetorical and literary – the latter being the almost exclusive preserve of the elite minority. Hopkins argues that below the elite there was a group of middling land owners, merchants, professionals, such as lawyers, some administrators, army officers and veterans, and school teachers who would have had functional literacy. These people were concentrated in the urban centres of the Empire, many of which feature in the New Testament. He stresses that the emerging Christian movement did not attract people from the ruling elite – its message was not supportive of their social position – but he argues that the writings of the second-century Apostolic Fathers display the marks of elite writing.[27] The New Testament, he suggests, is written in a less literary style but still with flourishes of rhetoric and inventive prose structures. He argues that maybe 20% of Christian males were literate by the turn of the second century, of which 2% were fluent and skilled literates. He further asserts that by AD 100 there might have been 7,000 Christians across the Empire (barely 0.01% of the population of roughly sixty million). This suggests that only forty-two males out of 420 who would have had literacy at any level, would have been able to read and understand Paul's letters.[28]

For their part, New Testament scholars have tended to take the findings of historians or the claims of contemporary (and therefore exclusively elite) writers on trust. Those who follow the historians argue that literacy rates were generally low, while those who follow elite (and especially Jewish) sources generally pitch literacy rates much higher. The most recent major study of ancient literacy is by William Harris. He suggests a literacy rate of no more than 15% for males in Italian cities in the first century AD.[29] Harris tends not to take a single measure of literacy, however, arguing that it is essential to ask what were the uses of literacy in the ancient world. He points out that reading and writing were distinct skills and that signature literacy – the ability to write one's name – did not necessarily suggest a higher level of literacy than just having the ability to read. The elite – roughly 1–3% of the population of the Empire – used literacy for the arts and entertainment as well as commercial and legal transactions. An elite male unable to read would have been thought an oddity.[30]

---

[26] Keith Hopkins, 'Christian Number and its Implications', *Journal of Early Christian Studies* 6.2 (1998), 185-226 (207).

[27] Hopkins, 'Christian Number', 209-10.

[28] Hopkins, 'Christian Number', 212.

[29] William V. Harris, *Ancient Literacy* (Cambridge, MA: Harvard University Press, 1989), 267.

[30] Harris, *Ancient Literacy*, 248.

Harris takes on the argument of some historians that increased commercial activity, legal processes and the explosion in memorial inscriptions, not to mention the extensive graffiti found in Pompeii, all suggest that literacy rates were much higher than he holds.[31] In matters of law, for example, Harris shows that engaging in legal processes did not require literacy as there were scribes and clerks who would deal with documents on your behalf.[32]

> Most epitaphs were inscribed by skilled masons, who in many cases probably contributed to the formulation of the text, and this leads inevitably to the conclusion that an epitaph is far from guaranteeing that the deceased or even his or her survivors were themselves wholly literate.[33]

All it demonstrated was that such people had money to pay a mason and the desire to be memorialised. Many monuments and inscriptions were not designed to be read by the masses but to leave them in awe of the status of the one who caused the monument to be raised. Letters again were invariably written by a scribe or secretary – as was the case for Paul – and only sent over long distances because the sender could not go in person.[34] Letters were designed to be heard by the recipients rather than read directly by them, even where the recipients would have been capable of reading the content for themselves. As Botha says, 'one must reckon with the letter as having been prepared for a careful oral performance, and … that eventually the letter was delivered like a proper speech'.[35]

This all suggests that a movement of the economically poor and socially inferior like the first followers of Jesus would have contained few people able to read Paul's Letters or the Gospels. Hopkins argues that if the average Christian gathering had twenty male members in it, only two of them would have been able to read at the level required to tackle a Pauline Epistle. It is likely, he suggests, that the bearers of these Letters would have had an important role in reading and interpreting them to their recipients. It is entirely possible that these men were the freed slaves of better-off households in which they had been taught to read and write so that they could administer the master's affairs. Such freedmen often formed the backbone of the mercantile organisations that elite families invested in but could not run. But such men could also have been skilled artisans with a head for business and some literacy and numeracy skills that would have helped them to prosper, who would have been

---

[31] E.g. in Craig A. Evans, *Jesus and His World: The Archaeological Evidence* (London: SPCK, 2012), ch. 3, which begins by not contesting Harris' overall conclusions before suggesting literacy rates were almost certainly higher than he allows!

[32] Harris, *Ancient Literacy*, 203-205.

[33] Harris, *Ancient Literacy*, 222.

[34] Harris, *Ancient Literacy*, 229.

[35] Pieter J.J. Botha, 'Letter Writing and Oral Communication in Antiquity: Suggested Implications for the Interpretation of Paul's Letter to the Galatians', *Scriptura* 42 (1992), 17-34 (24).

attracted to the Christian movement of which Paul – a literate and literary tent maker – was a leading member.[36]

Justin Meggitt, who does not discuss what the existence of Paul's Letters might tell us about the economic location of the Jesus movement, is probably right, however, to refute the suggestion of Judge, supported by Malherbe, that Paul could have earned some of his living as a sophist.[37] His argument is that sophists were members of the social elite. A stronger argument would be that there is simply no evidence for Paul earning a living by teaching anywhere in his Letters; he only refers to working with hands and receiving the odd gift (for example 1 Thess. 2 and Phil. 4). But none of this accounts for the fact that he communicated with his churches through writing Letters; a fact that suggests that he expected that there would be at least one person in the receiving churches who would have been able to read the Letter he had sent – even allowing for the fact that the Letter bearer would, in the first instance, have read and explained the Letter. That such skills are rare in the churches is alluded to by Cox who points out that when Paul is describing the typical worship gathering of the churches, he does so in terms of the gifts of the Spirit, of which reading is not one (see 1 Cor. 12 and 14). 'The gift of the Spirit does not enable one to read: a gift of the Spirit does not replace an education!'[38] Someone, however, was required to read Paul's teaching on the gifts to the Corinthian congregations, possibly Sosthenes (the bearer of the Letter[?], see 1 Cor. 1:1), Chloe, Stephanas, Crispus, Gaius or Erastus, the handful of named people whose economic location might suggest an ability to read and write.

Materials

Producing written materials in the ancient world was expensive. Harris notes that in Egypt papyrus seems to have cost 'four drachmas a roll, and a single sheet might cost two obols – this at a time when skilled labourers earned about six obols a day, unskilled three. The price is analogous to one of, say, thirty to thirty-five dollars for

---

[36] Hopkins, 'Christian Number', 211-13. Harris, *Ancient Literacy*, 251, suggests that literacy was not essential for getting on in business, citing the example of P. Annius Seleucus, a freedman earning some 100,000 sesterces a month, who had to have a slave read and write for him because 'he did not know letters'.

[37] Justin J. Meggitt, *Paul, Poverty and Survival* (Edinburgh: T&T Clark, 1998), 78-79; on 117 n. 207 he suggests that letter writing was common across all classes within the Roman Empire, but offers no evidence for such a sweeping assertion. See Edwin A. Judge, *The Social Pattern of the Christian Groups of the First Century: Some Prologemena to the Study of New Testament Ideas of Social Obligation* (London: Tyndale, 1960); and Abraham J. Malherbe, *Social Aspects of Early Christianity* (Eugene, OR: Wipf and Stock, 2nd edn, 2003), esp. ch. 2, for the position he is attacking.

[38] Claude E. Cox, 'The Reading of the Personal Letter as the Background for the Reading of the Scriptures in the Early Church', in Abraham J. Malherbe, Frederick W Norris and James W. Thompson (eds), *The Early Church in its Context: Essays in Honour of Everett Ferguson* (Supplements to Novum Testamentum, 90; Leiden: Brill, 1998), 74-91 (81).

a sheet of paper today.'[39] Richards suggests that the Epistle to the Romans would have taken two to three days to write – Paul dictating to a secretary who would have the quality of handwriting needed to ensure the Letters' recipients would have been able to read it.[40] This would obviously have been time when Paul could not be focused on making tents. Or would it have been possible for him to dictate a Letter while sewing a seam? As to the monetary cost, Richards points out that we have insufficient evidence for a precise calculation, though it is possible to produce a rough estimate. 'A standard papyrus roll cost about four denars.'[41] Such a roll would have been made by joining together twenty sheets of papyrus on which a secretary writing with a medium size hand – in contrast to Paul's large hand (Gal. 6:11) – would have been able to fit about thirty lines of writing. On these calculations, Romans was 979 lines long – taking up thirty-three papyrus sheets (one and half standard rolls) and therefore costing in paper alone some six denars.[42]

On top of the raw material costs, we have to add the cost of the secretary. The going rate, according to evidence from Oxyrhynchus, was between twenty and twenty-eighty drachmas per 10,000 *stichoi* (lines of written text), the best part of a month's work. This leads Richards to conclude that Romans would have cost twenty denars to produce.[43] The question, of course, that is impossible to answer is whether Paul would have incurred these secretarial costs at all. If a member of his mission team acted as his secretary, then notionally, producing Letters was part of his role. Of course, there was a 'cost' involved in employing him in such a task since he would still need to eat, but he would not be generating any income. If one dinar is a day's wage for a labourer, then the raw material costs alone for producing Romans would have been the equivalent of a week's work. Add to this the three days' work in producing the text itself and it suggests that only people with a moderate surplus could have contemplated writing such letters. Those scrabbling for a living at or below subsistence would not have had nine days' worth surplus to spend on producing Letters of such length and complexity.

The Next Best Thing

But why would an economically pressed group with few literate members have gone to the trouble and expense of producing texts that only a handful of its adherents could read? The answer seems to lie in the role of texts in ancient communication. We have already noted Harris' assertion that letters were only used where the sender wanted to get a message to someone who was too far away for a personal visit. The letter, being read to its recipient, was a performance of what the sender wished to

---

[39] Harris, *Ancient Literacy*, 195.

[40] E. Randolph Richards, *Paul and First Century Letter Writing* (Downers Grove, IL: IVP, 2004), 163-65; for the argument that Paul used secretaries, see 32-93.

[41] Richards, *Paul*, 166.

[42] Richards, *Paul*, 165-67; the precise calculations are mine.

[43] Richards, *Paul*, 169, who assumes that this covers the cost of one copy to be sent and another to be kept by Paul. He works on the basis that three denars equalled four drachmas.

say, the next best thing to them being physically present. This seems to be in Paul's mind when he speaks of being present in spirit when his verdict on the man having a sexual relationship with his father's wife is performed to the Corinthians house churches (1 Cor. 5:3); his presence is embodied in the Letter being read.

In this respect Paul might well be standing firmly in his Jewish tradition. Levels of literacy among first-century Jews in both Judea and the diaspora have almost certainly been exaggerated. The claims of elite Jewish writers, such as Josephus, that all Jewish boys learned to read in the synagogue, need to be set against the evidence amassed by Harris and Hopkins that literacy levels across the Empire were 15% at best. Dewey, surveying the evidence, argues that literacy among the Jews would have been as dependent on social status as it was elsewhere in the Empire. So, the elite – chief priests, scribes and some higher status Pharisees – would have been literate, but the vast bulk of the populace would not have been. Their knowledge of the texts on which their tradition was based would be derived from hearing the scrolls read in synagogue and temple and from travelling teachers and story tellers who performed parts of the sacred texts.[44]

The narrative of Jeremiah committing his message to Judah to writing on a scroll is instructive here. The story, told with much rhetorical flourish in Jeremiah 36, begins with Jeremiah dictating the words to Baruch who faithfully writes them in ink (Jer. 36:18). It seems that only Baruch and Elishama, the king's secretary, could read what was written. Baruch reads it to worshippers assembled in the temple, Elishama to the king and his cabinet. Everywhere it is read, there is heated discussion of it. Even the king senses the power of the written text (even though he probably cannot read it) as he cuts it up and burns it. God tells Jeremiah to re-write it with additions, an indication that the text carries an authority beyond the personal presence of the prophet himself. It certainly seems to have had that effect among the exiles in Babylon who at some stage decided to keep the scroll and allow it to shape their lives as God's people. In a similar way, Paul's Letters embody his presence and the sacred tradition of the Jesus movement that needed to be heard and acquired by all its adherents.

Paul Achtemeier stresses that 'no writing occurred that was not vocalised'.[45] Everything written was dictated – either to oneself or a secretary – and what was written was then performed aloud for its intended audience. Even when one was alone, one read aloud (see Acts 8:30). For this reason, Achtemeier suggests that 'the

---

[44] Joanna Dewey, 'Textuality in an Oral Culture: A Survey of the Pauline Traditions', *Semeia* 65 (1994), 37-65 (44, 46). Evans, *Jesus and His World*, 74, puts the counterargument suggesting that the quantity of scrolls surviving from the first century suggests a higher level of literacy in Judea than in other parts of the Roman world. But even if every synagogue had a scroll of every book of the Hebrew Scriptures, that says nothing about literacy rates. Each meeting place could have had one or two males whose literacy meant they could cope with the scrolls in question.

[45] Paul J. Achtemeier, 'Omne Verbum Sonat: The New Testament and the Oral Environment of Late Western Antiquity', *Journal of Biblical Literature* 109.1 (1990), 3-27 (15).

NT must be understood as speech'.[46] But it was speech specifically intended to be heard by groups of people rather than individuals. The gathering of Jesus' followers in Corinth and Thessalonica, Philippi and Rome to hear a Letter of Paul performed and to join in the discussion of it became a vital event in which their lives of discipleship were shaped. 'Ancient communication, including reading and writing, was an oral, collective activity and not the private, silent experience that we consider it to be ... Greco-Roman communication was connected to the physical presence of people and to living speech to an extent that is consistently underestimated today.'[47]

It is instructive, therefore, that there are few references to reading but many to hearing in the New Testament. Most of the references to reading are in situations where Jesus is encountering the elite, the priests and scribes (e.g.. Mt. 12:3, 5; 19:4; 21:16, 42). Whereas when Jesus is addressing his disciples and the crowds, he speaks about them hearing the Law (e.g.. MT. 5:21, 27, 28, 33, 38, 43); he tells his audience to build their lives on what they hear (Mt. 7:24, 26), and many parables end with the words 'let the one with ears, hear'. Paul talks about reading only in relation to the reading of the Law in synagogues (e.g., 2 Cor. 3:14, 15) and in reference to his Letters being read in gatherings of Jesus followers (Col. 4:16; 1 Thess. 5:27). The isolated reference to the public reading of Scripture in 1 Timothy 4:13 is moot because of the doubts over authorship and because, even assuming the Letter is Pauline, it begs the question of whether anyone in a craft worker assembly would have had access to a copy of the Scripture that they could read. So is 'public reading' a way of expressing the idea that there should be some performance of Scripture, maybe those sections of the Hebrew Bible that point particularly to the coming of Jesus, by someone in the gathering who has memorised them?

Joanna Dewey points out that the reading of Scripture is not attested as part of the Christian gathering until the middle of the second century. 'The only reading done during worship in Paul's churches was the reading – or rather performance – of Paul's letters.'[48] These letters, of course, contained considerable quantities of direct quotes from and allusions to the Hebrew Scriptures; indeed Paul's purpose in much of his writing was to show how the story told by those Scriptures reached its dénouement in the coming, cross and resurrection of Jesus, Israel's Messiah. So Dewey's assertion that Scripture is not central for Paul might be somewhat wide of the mark. Paul does indeed share the Hebrew Scriptures' view of God and history, as well as their apocalyptic viewpoint, as Dewey notes, because he believes that Jesus is the fulfilment of these texts, something the texts he produced seek to show.[49]

More common in Paul is that people 'hear' his Letters and the gospel contained in them and in the preaching of him and his team. The key verse is Romans 10:17 which tells us that 'faith is from hearing and hearing is through the word of Christ'

---

[46] Achtemeier, 'Omne Verbum Sonat', 19.

[47] Pieter J.J. Botha, 'Greco-Roman Literacy as Setting for New Testament Writings', *Neotestamentica* 26.1 (1992), 195-215 (207).

[48] Dewey, 'Textuality', 52.

[49] Dewey, 'Textuality', 52-53.

(author's own translation). Arthur Dewey renders the verse, 'Trust, thus, comes from actually hearing, hearing through the word of Christ', arguing that we have here

> the outline of a communication system (vv. 14-15), founded upon the relationship of trust (vv. 14, 16). At the same time, it is quite significant that Paul even brings the written word into this oral chain of communication. It is, thus, not simply a sharp dichotomy of orality vs literacy; rather a fascinating dialectic is underway.[50]

He points out that Romans 10 is a rehearing of Deuteronomy 30 in the light of the coming of Christ that is read by a single member of the congregation receiving the Letter and heard afresh by everyone else.

Similarly, the author of Hebrews urges his audience to 'hear' God's voice. Three times he quotes Psalm 95 in a way that indicates that he expects the recipients of this Letter to 'hear' God's voice as it is performed in their gatherings. And the same is true of the author of Revelation who speaks blessing on those who hear his words (Rev. 1:3) and urges each of the churches addressed in the seven letters to hear what the Spirit is saying to them (Rev. 2:7, 11, 17, 29; 3:6, 13, 22), before, in the conclusion, warning his hearers not to add or subtract from the scroll they have heard read to them (Rev. 22:18-19).

Symposium

All this suggests there was a context within which the first followers of Jesus commonly heard these words. It seems that quite quickly the new movement adopted the symposium, a gathering to eat and engage in philosophical conversation that was favoured by the elite of the Empire, as the pattern for their gathering. Inscriptions from across the Empire and descriptions from elite written sources indicate that such gatherings followed a pretty strict pattern. Food would be served to invited guests and when everyone had eaten, wine and water would be brought, a libation offered to the deity favoured by the host, after which the guests would begin a conversation about a philosophical or topical issue which would last until it was time to go home. Sometimes there was singing – mainly of religious songs that honoured the household or city gods – and sometimes the conversation would be prompted by a special guest or by a new publication, some or all of which would be read before the guests were offered the chance to discuss it.[51]

Most of the early followers of Jesus would not have been regular attendees at such events. They might, by virtue of association membership, enjoy one banquet and symposium a year. But it was a form of gathering with which they were familiar – even if only because they had served at one as a domestic slave or heard of it being

---

[50] Arthur J. Dewey, 'A Re-hearing of Romans 10:1-15', *Semeia* 65 (1994), 109-27 (114).

[51] Full details of the symposium can be found in Dennis E. Smith, *From Symposium to Eucharist: The Banquet in the Early Christian World* (Minneapolis, MN: Fortress Press, 2003), esp. ch. 7. A more popular account of the likely influence the symposium form had on early Christian gatherings can be found in Jones, *World*, 77-83, 106-108, 132-38.

hosted by their patrons. So, at the end of the working day, a group of Jesus followers would meet in the largest workshop the group had access to or in the home of a wealthier member of their group, to share food and to hear about the faith. It is likely that Paul is describing such a Christian symposium in 1 Corinthians 11–14.

This was where non-literate craft workers were able to access the texts that underlay their new faith. These texts were 'performed' so that they could be heard and discussed. What Paul describes in 1 Corinthians is a gathering where everyone is encouraged to participate, regardless of gender, educational attainment, social status or income. The Christian symposium was where each spoke the truth in love to the others (Eph. 4:15-16) so that all would be built up in their understanding of the faith and their ability to live in their working lives outside the gathering. It was in the symposium that the Letters from Paul were heard and discussed, where complex literary texts were appropriated by non-literate people in such a way that they shaped their lives of discipleship.

Harris points out that 'It is Christian writings which suggest a coming change in the religious importance of the written word.'[52] While other religious groups communicated with each other by letter, it was the Christians who gathered the Letters which its leading figures had sent, attaching special importance to them. 'Something of the kind was happening by the 50s and 60s, for otherwise letters of Paul would probably not have survived. The forcefulness of his writings may in fact have contributed to the new development.'[53] Harris suggests that 'the written word thus came to exercise religious power in a somewhat novel way'.[54] It could be argued that this was happening concurrently with the scattered Jewish communities, following the disasters of AD 70 and 135, gathering their sacred texts into the canon that would guide and shape their community life.

Conclusion

It seems, therefore, that Dewey is right to stress that it is the performance of Paul's texts within the gatherings of his communities that was determinative in the shaping of the lives of his hearers. Discipleship was formed and resourced by these texts being heard in groups of followers of Jesus. And it is this pattern of using texts that seems to have been the powerhouse of the movement of which Paul is the centre. Texts are not read privately nor are they interpreted individualistically, but they are heard together, debated, argued over and so shape the lives of those interacting with them.

So, instead of holding the Beroeans up as models of those who search their Bibles on their own to see if a teaching is true, let us restore them to their place as forerunners of those who debate the message with each other – and in their case, the messenger. As Roy Ciampa argues, the meaning of ἀνακρίνοντες in Acts 17:11 is

---

[52] Harris, *Ancient Literacy*, 220.
[53] Harris, *Ancient Literacy*, 220-21.
[54] Harris, *Ancient Literacy*, 221.

that they interrogated Paul to see if what he said made sense against their understanding of the Scriptures as they had heard them – probably in the setting of a symposium.[55] Ciampa argues that there is nothing in this text that suggests the Beroeans were reading Scripture on a daily basis. Rather, 'they were asking Paul questions about the Scriptures and how his teaching cohered with what they knew about them', adding that

> the way Luke depicts the Beroeans' behaviour would be perfectly consistent with a scenario according to which they were mainly illiterate and had little direct access to the scriptures. In that case the ancient reader (sic) of Acts would understand that they were simply asking Paul questions about the scriptures based on the knowledge they had gained through their exposure to previous preachers and teachers and synagogue readings.[56]

If Ciampa is right, the Beroeans are the first example of congregational hermeneutics in action. They stand in a long line of disciples who together explore the meaning of the Scriptures and how they apply to the life of discipleship on which they have embarked. Many Anabaptist groups followed similar practices. Stuart Murray cites an early Swiss Brethren tract that said

> When brothers and sisters are together, they shall take up something to read together. The one to whom God has given the best understanding shall explain it, the others should be still and listen.

It also stressed that Christian love meant that if someone had a word for the congregation, they were to share it. Murray comments,

> It appears from this tract and other sources that contributions might include reading texts of scripture, expounding them, asking and answering questions, prophesying, and discussing what has been said.[57]

It goes without saying that such a gathering has strong echoes of the one described by Paul in 1 Corinthians 11–14 which has been a template for renewal movements throughout history.

There has been much discussion over recent years about how renewal will come to the church if we recapture the vitality we read of in 1 Corinthians 12–14. Such discussion is usually centred on recovery of the charismatic gifts, especially tongues and prophecy. Perhaps we need to learn from our Anabaptist and Baptist forebears that a recovery of the Christian symposium described in 1 Corinthians 11–14 could be the key to renewing our life and structures in our generation. Here is the marriage

---

[55] Roy E. Ciampa, '"Examined the Scriptures"?: The Meaning of ἀνακρίνοντες τὰς γραφὰς in Acts 17:11', *Journal of Biblical Literature* 130.3 (2011), 527-41.

[56] Ciampa, '"Examined the Scriptures"', 541.

[57] Murray, *Biblical Interpretation*, 161, and references there.

of food and conversation, rooted in the Word of God, at which all are welcome and in which all can participate regardless of their ability to handle complex texts.

Select Bibliography of the Writings of Ian M. Randall

1993
'A Christian Cosmopolitan: F.B. Meyer in Britain and America', in G.A. Rawlyk and M.A. Noll (eds), *Amazing Grace: Evangelicalism in Australia, Britain, Canada, and the United States* (Grand Rapids, MI: Baker, 1993), 157-82

'"Mere Denominationalism": F.B. Meyer and Baptist Life', *Baptist Quarterly* 35.1 (January, 1993), 19-34

'Spiritual Renewal and Social Reform: Attempts to Develop Social Awareness in the Early Keswick Movement', *Vox Evangelica* 23 (1993), 67-86

'Early English Baptists and Religious Liberty', *Anabaptism Today* 4 (October, 1993), 10-15

1994
'Cultural Change and Future Hope: Premillennialism in Britain following the First World War', *Christianity and History* 13 (1994), 19-27

'"Incarnating the Gospel": Melbourne Hall, Leicester, in the 1880s as a model for holistic ministry', *Baptist Quarterly* 35.8 (October, 1994), 393-406

1995
Quest, Crusade and Fellowship: The Spiritual Formation of the Fellowship of the Kingdom (Horsham: Fellowship of the Kingdom, 1995)

'The Social Gospel: A Case Study', in J. Wolffe (ed.), *Evangelicals and Public Zeal Evangelicals and Society in Britain 1780–1980* (London: SPCK, 1995), 155-74

'Southport and Swanwick: Contrasting Movements of Methodist Spirituality in Inter-War England', *Proceedings of the Wesley Historical Society* 50.1 (1995), 1-14

'Conservative Constructionist: The Early Influence of Billy Graham in Britain', *Evangelical Quarterly* 67.4 (October–December, 1995), 309-33

'British Churches and the Second World War', *Transparant* 6 (1995)

1996
Called to One Hope: 150 years of the Evangelical Alliance (n.pl.: n.p., 1996)

'Schism and Unity: 1905–1966', in S. Brady and H. Rowdon (eds), *For Such a Time as This: Perspectives on Evangelicalism, Past, Present and Future* (London: Scripture Union, 1996), 163-77

'The Role of Conscientious Objectors: British Evangelicals and the First World War', *Anabaptism Today* 11 (1996), 9-15

'"Life-Changing": The Oxford Group as a Movement of Spiritual Renewal', *Christianity and History Newsletter* 16 (1996), 18-41

'Evangelicals and the First World War', *Anabaptism Today* 11 (February, 1996), 9-15

'"Capturing Keswick": Baptists and the Changing Spirituality of the Keswick Convention in the 1920s', *Baptist Quarterly* 36.7 (July, 1996), 331-48

'The Truth Shall Make You Free: The Growth of the Anglican Evangelical Group Movement', *Anglican and Episcopal History* 65.3 (September, 1996), 314-56

1997

'"How to Work a City Church": Christ Church, Westminster Bridge Road from the 1890s to the 1920s', *The Journal of the United Reformed Church History Society* 5.10 (1997), 576-92

'"Old Time Power": Relationships between Pentecostalism and Evangelical Spirituality in England', *Pneuma* 19.1 (Spring, 1997), 53-80

'"Ideas have Wings": Ernest Payne and Anabaptism', *Anabaptism Today* 16 (October, 1997), 11-16

'"The Tried People of God": Strict Baptist Spirituality in Inter-War England', *The Strict Baptist Historical Society Bulletin* 24 (1997), 16-33

'Evangelicals and Social Reform', *Light and Salt* 9.2 (1997), 1-4

1998

'*Entire Devotion to God*': Wesleyan Holiness and British Overseas Mission in the Early Twentieth Century (Ilkeston: Wesley Fellowship, 1998)

'Evangelicals and Catholics Together?', *Priests and People* 12.1 (1998), 8-13

'"Full Salvation": Expressions of Traditional Wesleyan Holiness in the Early Twentieth Century', *Methodist History* 36.3 (April, 1998), 176-90

'The Pentecostal League of Prayer: A Transdenominational British Wesleyan Holiness Movement', *Wesleyan Theological Journal* (Spring 1998), 185-200

1999

Evangelical Experiences: A Study in the Spirituality of English Evangelicalism, 1918–1939 (Paternoster Biblical and Theological Monographs; Carlisle: Paternoster Press, 1999)

Pathway of Power: Keswick and the Reshaping of Wesleyan Holiness (Ilkeston: Wesley Fellowship, 1999)

'Austere Ritual: The Reformation of Worship in Inter-War Congregationalism', in R.N. Swanson (ed.), *Continuity and Change in Christian Worship* (Studies in Church History, 35; Woodbridge: The Boydell Press, 1999), 432-46

'"Arresting People for Christ": Baptists and the Oxford Group in the 1930s', *Baptist Quarterly* 38.1 (January, 1999), 3-18

'The Waldensians and the Healing of the Wounds of History', *Anabaptism Today* 21 (Summer, 1999), 12-19

With M.J. Quicke, '"The Real Wants of the Age": Spurgeon's College, London', *American Baptist Quarterly* 18.2 (1999), 118-30

2000

Educating Evangelicalism: The Origins, Development and Impact of London Bible College (Carlisle: Paternoster Press, 2000)

With Charles Price: *Transforming Keswick* (Carlisle: OM Publishing, 2000)

'Connecting Radical Church Life to the Riches of the Past', in Alan Kreider and Stuart Murray (eds), *Coming Home: Stories of Anabaptists in Britain and Ireland* (Kitchener, ON: Pandora, 2000)

'Graham Scroggie and Evangelical Spirituality', *The Scottish Bulletin of Evangelical Theology* 18.1 (Spring, 2000), 71-86

'"Outside the Camp": Brethren Spirituality and Wider Evangelicalism in the 1920s', *Brethren Archivists and Historians Network Review* 2.1 (2000), 17-33

'Spirituality and Theological Education: A Case Study', *LBC Review* (2000), 4-11

'"Pious Wishes": Baptists and Wider Renewal Movements in Nineteenth-Century Europe', *Baptist Quarterly* 38.7 (July, 2000), 316-31

'"The Things which shall be Hereafter": Strict Baptist Views of the Second Coming', *The Strict Baptist Historical Society Bulletin* 27 (2000)

'"We All Need Constant Change": The Oxford Group and Mission in Europe in the 1930s', *European Journal of Theology* 9.2 (2000), 171-85

2001

With David Hilborn: *One Body in Christ: The History and Significance of the Evangelical Alliance* (Carlisle: Paternoster Press, 2001)

'Theological Education in the Evangelical Context', in S. Sannikov (ed.), *The History of Christianity and Present Epoch* (Odessa, Ukraine: n.p., 2001), 114-25

'Unity Truly of the Universal Christian Faith', *Anabaptism Today* 26 (Spring, 2001), 5-12

'"The Blessings of an Enlightened Christianity": North American Involvement in European Baptist Origins', *American Baptist Quarterly* 20.1 (March, 2001), 5-26

'"To Anglicize, Gallicize or Americanize": The Evangelical Alliance and Europe, 1840s–1940s', *Journal of European Baptist Studies* 1.3 (May, 2001), 39-49

'Word and Spirit: Evangelical Spirituality', *Partnership Perspectives* 17 (2001)

2002

'"Days of Pentecostal Overflowing": Baptists and the Shaping of Pentecostalism', in D.W. Bebbington (ed.), *The Gospel in the World* (Studies in Baptist History and Thought, 1; Carlisle: Paternoster Press, 2002), 80-104

'"Every Apostolic Church a Mission Society": European Baptist Origins and Identity', in Anthony R. Cross (ed.), *Ecumenism and History: Studies in Honour of John H. Y. Briggs* (Carlisle: Paternoster Press, 2002) 281-301

'F.B. Meyer: Baptist Ambassador for Keswick Holiness Spirituality', *Baptist History and Heritage* 37.2 (Spring, 2002), 44-60

2003

Spirituality and Social Change: The Contribution of F.B. Meyer (1847–1929) (Studies in Evangelical History and Thought; Carlisle: Paternoster Press, 2003)

Edited, *Baptists and the Orthodox Church: On the Way to Understanding* (Prague: IBTS, 2003)

With Brian R. Hoare: *More than a Methodist: The Life and Ministry of Donald English* (Carlisle: Paternoster Press, 2003)

'"Great National Crisis": New Road and the World Wars', in R. Chadwick (ed.), *A Protestant Catholic Church of Christ: Essays on the History and Life of New Road Baptist Church, Oxford* (Oxford: New Road Baptist Church, 2003), 259-83

With Tim Grass, 'Spurgeon and the Sacraments' in A.R. Cross and P.E. Thompson (eds), *Baptist Sacramentalism* (Studies in Baptist History and Thought, 5; Carlisle: Paternoster Press, 2003), 55-75

'Unity in the Gospel: Catholic Evangelical Relationships', *One in Christ* 38.1 (2003), 16-30

Articles on 'Samuel Chadwick', 'T.D. Harford-Battersby', 'Jan Hus', 'F.B. Meyer', and 'Graham Scroggie', in T. Larson (ed.), *Biographical Dictionary of Evangelicals* (Leicester: Inter-Varsity Press, 2003), 133-35, 288-89, 321-22, 428-30, and 593-95

2004

'American influence on Evangelicals in Europe: A Comparison of the Founding of the Evangelical Alliance and the World Evangelical Fellowship', in H. Krabbendam and D. Rubin (eds), *Religion in America: European and American Perspectives* (Amsterdam: VU University Press, 2004), 263-74

'"A Good Bench of Bishops"?: Early Baptist Superintendency' in S. Murray (ed.), *Translocal Ministry* (Didcot: Baptist Union, 2004), 33-43

'When the Spirit Comes in Power' (Keswick Lecture) in A. Hull (ed.), *Out of Control?: God's Sovereignty in an Uncertain World* (Milton Keynes: Authentic, 2004), 73-90

'Evangelicals, Ecumenism and Unity: A Case study of the Evangelical Alliance', *Evangel* 22.3 (Autumn, 2004), 62-71

Editor, *Journal of European Baptist Studies* 4.3 (May, 2004)

2005

A School of the Prophets: 150 Years of Spurgeon's College (London: Spurgeon's College, 2005)

The English Baptists of the Twentieth Century (A History of the English Baptists, 4; Didcot: Baptist Historical Society, 2005)

What a Friend we have in Jesus: The Evangelical Tradition (London: Darton, Longman and Todd, 2005)

'The Myth of the Missing Spirituality: Spirituality among English Baptists in the Early Twentieth Century', in P.E. Thompson and A.R. Cross (eds), *Recycling the*

Past or Researching History?: Studies in Baptist History and Myths (Studies in Baptist History and Thought, 11; Carlisle: Paternoster, 2005), 106-27

'Pro-Existence Not Co-Existence: The Baptist World Alliance in the 1980s', in R.V. Pierard (ed.), *Baptists Together in Christ 1905–2005: A Hundred-Year History of the Baptist World Alliance* (Falls Church, VA: Baptist World Alliance, 2005), 194-234

'Evangelicals and European Integration', *European Journal of Theology* 14.1 (2005), 17-26

'History's lessons for the great leap forward', *Talk: The Mainstream Magazine* 5.2 (Summer, 2005), 4-7

'"The Breath of Revival": The Welsh Revival and Spurgeon's College', *Baptist Quarterly* 41.4 (October, 2005), 196-205

'"The Low Condition of the Churches": Difficulties Faced by General Baptists in England – the 1680s to the 1760s', *The Pacific Journal of Baptist Research* 1.1 (2005), 3-19

'Baptist spirituality' and 'Evangelical spirituality', in P. Sheldrake (ed.), *New SCM Dictionary of Christian Spirituality* (London: SCM, 2005), 142-44 and 289-91

2006

The Bible is Central: Cliff College and the Evangelical Tradition (Weston-Super-Mare: The Flame Trust, 2006)

Edited, with T. Pilli and A.R. Cross, *Baptist Identities: International Studies from the Seventeenth to the Twentieth Centuries* (Studies in Baptist History and Thought, 19; Milton Keynes: Paternoster, 2006)

With John Charles Pollock: *The Keswick Story: The Authorized History of the Keswick Convention-Updated!* (Fort Washington, PA: CLC, rev. edn, 2006)

'"To Equip and Encourage": The Life of Harold H. Rowdon', in N.T.R. Dickson and T. Grass (eds), *The Growth of the Brethren Movement: National and International Experiences. Essays in Honour of Harold H. Rowdon* (Studies in Evangelical History and Thought; Milton Keynes: Paternoster, 2006), 3-10

'"Look to Jesus Christ": English Baptists and Evangelical Spirituality', *American Baptist Quarterly* 25.1 (Spring, 2006), 8-26

'Christ comes to the Heart: Moravian Influence on the Shaping of Evangelical Spirituality', *Journal of European Baptist Studies* 6.3 (May, 2006), 5-23

'English Baptists of the 20th Century', *Baptist Quarterly* 41.7 (July, 2006), 389-408

'Evangelical Spirituality and the Church Catholic', *The Way* 45.3 (2006), 95-112

'A Missional Spirituality: Moravian Brethren and Eighteenth-Century English Evangelicalism', *Transformation* 23.4 (October, 2006), 204-14

'Editorial', *Journal of European Baptist Studies* 7.1 (September, 2006), 4

'Tomáš Garrigue Masaryk (1850–1937): European Politician and Christian Philosopher', *Political Theology* 7.4 (October, 2006), 441-59

'"To be occupied with God": John Stott on Worship', *Anvil* 23.4 (2006), 247-57

2007

Edited, with A.R. Cross: *Baptists and Mission: Papers from the Fourth International Conference on Baptist Studies* (Studies in Baptist History and Thought, 29; Milton Keynes: Paternoster, 2007)

'"The world is our parish": Spurgeon's College and World Mission, 1856–1892', in Randall and Cross (eds), *Baptists and Mission*, 64-77

'Anabaptism and Mission: The British Experience 1980–2005: A Baptist Perspective', in W.R. Shenk and P.F. Penner (eds), *Anabaptism and Mission* (Erlangen: Neufeld Verlag, 2007), 145-65

'Eastern European Baptists and the Evangelical Alliance, 1846–1896' in S. Carrado and T. Pilli (eds), *Eastern European Baptist History: New Perspectives* (Prague: IBTS, 2007), 14-33

'Charles Haddon Spurgeon, the Pastors' College and the Downgrade Controversy', in K. Cooper and J. Gregory (eds), *Discipline and Diversity* (Studies in Church History, 43; Woodbridge: The Boydell Press, 2007), 366-76

'"A Mode of Training": A Baptist Seminary's Missional Vision', *Transformation* 24.1 (2007), 2-13

'"To give the first place to spiritual fervour": Priorities for Seminary Education, *Journal of European Baptist Studies* 7.2 (January, 2007), 5-20

'"Der geistlichen Leidenschaft den ersten Platz einräumen" – Prioritäten in der Seminarausbildung', *Theologisches Gespräch*, Heft 3 (2007), 107-24

'Mission in Post-Christendom: Anabaptist and Free Church Perspectives', *Evangelical Quarterly* 79.3 (July, 2007), 227-40

Article on Gilbert Kirby in C. Binfield and J. Taylor (eds), *Who they were in the Reformed Churches of England and Wales, 1901–2000* (Donington: United Reformed Church History Society, 2007), 125-26

2008

Spiritual Revolution: The Story of OM (Milton Keynes: Authentic, 2008)

Edited, with K.G. Jones, *Counter-Cultural Communities: Baptistic Life in Twentieth-Century Europe* (Studies in Baptist History and Thought, 32; Milton Keynes: Paternoster, 2008)

'Baptist Revival and Renewal in the 1960s', in K. Cooper and J. Gregory (eds), *Revival and Resurgence in Christian History* (Studies in Church History, 44; Woodbridge: The Boydell Press, 2008), 341-53

'Dietrich Bonhoeffer's Christology', in Petr Jandejsek (ed.), *Christological Handbook* (Prague: Jabok, 2008), 104-108

'"Live much under the Shadow of the Cross": Atonement and Evangelical Spirituality', in D. Tidball, D. Hilborn and J. Thacker (eds), *The Atonement Debate* (Grand Rapids, MI: Zondervan, 2008), 293-310

'The Baptist Convictions of Martin Luther King Jr (1929–1968)', *Journal of European Baptist Studies* 9.1 (September, 2008), 5-21

2009

Communities of Conviction: Baptist Beginnings in Europe (Prague: European Baptist Federation/Schwarzenfeld: Neufeld Verlag, 2009)

One of the editors and contributor of 30 entries to J.H.Y. Briggs (ed.), *A Dictionary of European Baptist Life and Thought* (Studies in Baptist History and Thought, 33; Milton Keynes: Paternoster, 2009)

'Catholicity and Particularity in the Ecclesial Thinking of Early English Baptist Confessions of Faith', in L.J. Koffeman (ed.), *Christian Traditions between Catholicity and Particularity* (Frankfurt am Main: Verlag Otto Lembeck, 2009), 85-100

'Part of a Movement: Nigel Wright and Baptist life', in Pieter J. Lalleman (ed.), *Challenging to Change* (London: Spurgeon's College, 2009), 143-62

'"Take my Life": Evangelical Spirituality and Evangelical Identity', in Mark Smith (ed.), *British Evangelical Identities Past and Present: Volume 1. Aspects of the History and Sociology of Evangelicalism in Britain and Ireland* (Studies in Evangelical History and Thought; Milton Keynes: Paternoster, 2008), 215-37

'Tracing Baptist Theological Footprints: A European Perspective', *Perspectives in Religious Studies* 36.2 (Summer, 2009), 133-48

'Lay People in Revival: A Case Study of the "1859" Revival', *Transformation* 26.4 (October, 2009), 217-31

'"A fence of scholasticism around the ministry"?: Theological Education among English Baptists, 1900–1950s', *Perspectives in Religious Studies* 36.4 (Winter, 2009), 461-75

2010

Rhythms of Revival: The Spiritual Awakening of 1857–1863 (Milton Keynes: Paternoster, 2010)

Baptists, the Gospel and Freedom of Conscience (50th Anniversary Lecture of the Strict Baptist Historical Society; Dunstable: Strict Baptist Historical Society, 2010)

'Conscientious Conviction': Joseph Angus (1816–1902) and Nineteenth-Century Baptist Life (Centre for Baptist History and Heritage Studies Occasional Papers, 2; Oxford: Centre for Baptist History and Heritage, 2010)

'Recovering Evangelical Spirituality', *European Journal of Theology* 19.1 (2010) 33-44

'Outgrowing Combative Boundary-Setting: Billy Graham, Evangelism and Fundamentalism', *Evangelical Review of Theology* 34.2 (April, 2010), 103-18

'"Counsel and Help": European Baptists and Wider Baptist Fellowship', *Journal of European Baptist Studies* 11.1 (September, 2010), 25-35

2011

'Baptist–Anabaptist Identity among European Baptists since the 1950s', in J.H.Y. Briggs and A.R. Cross (eds), *Baptists and the World: Renewing the Vision*

(Centre for Baptist History and Heritage Studies, 8; Oxford: Centre for Baptist History and Heritage and Baptist History Society, 2011), 133-51

'Lloyd Jones and revival', in A. Atherstone and D. Ceri Jones (eds), *Engaging with Martyn Lloyd-Jones* (Nottingham: Apollos, 2011), 91-113

2012

Religious Liberty in Continental Europe: Campaigning by British Baptists, 1840s–1930s (The Whitley Lecture 2012; Centre for Baptist History and Heritage Studies Occasional Papers, 4; Oxford: Whitley Publications, 2012)

'Baptist Growth in England', in David Goodhew (ed.), *Church Growth in Britain: 1980 to the Present* (Farnham: Ashgate, 2012), 59-76

'Five things from early Baptist life', in Andy Goodliff *et al.*, *Beyond 400: 40 Baptist Voices in the 400th Year* (n.pl.: www.beyond400.net, 2012), 46-47

'Seedbed for Baptist Leadership: The Baptist Students' Federation from 1947 to the 1970s', *Baptist Quarterly* 44.6 (April, 2012), 324-43

'Nineteenth-Century Bible Society Colporteurs in Eastern Europe', *Journal of European Baptist Studies* 12.3 (May, 2012), 5-25

General Index

Achtemeier, Paul 302
action 46-50
Adamow, Poland 86
Adams, Stephen 220
African Independent or Initiated Churches 139
Agapemonites 73
Agbebi, Mojola 139
Albik, Archbishop 5
Alexander V 4, 5
Alf, Gottfried F. 86
Alison, James 230
American Bible Societies 137
Anabaptism/Anabaptists xxiii, 1, 10-15, 20, 21, 53, 231, 237, 306
  Mennonites 11, 20, 107, 109, 215
  Swiss Brethren 306
Andel, Adrian van 88
Angus, Amelia 141
Angus, Isabel 141
Angus, Joseph 141
Antichrist 178, 179
anti-Semitism 172, 175
Arminianism/Arminians 18, 19, 20, 21, 29, 44, 56, 255n
Arminius, Jacob 19
Arndt, Johann 166
Ashworth, Graham 211
Askew, Barbara 218
Association of the Friends of Israel 168
assurance 20, 37, 41-46, 49, 51
atonement xxiii, 18, 23, 27, 38, 45, 225
Augustine 7
Awakening Movement, the 165

Babcock, S.H. 126
babies 61
Baedeker, Friedrich 108, 116
Bamber, Theo 206
Band of Hope 125

baptism 24, 27, 77, 81, 86, 105, 139, 183, 235-59
  baptism in the Spirit 214
  believer's baptism 53-68, 73, 77, 239, 247
  believers' baptism 80, 82, 88
  credobaptists 40
  infant baptism/paedobaptism 53-68, 240
  modes of baptism
    immersion 53-68, 246
    pouring 61, 62
    sprinkling 59, 60, 61, 62
  paedobaptists 40, 54, 55, 59, 61, 62, 63, 64, 65, 66, 67
Baptist Associations
  Devon and Cornwall Association 217
  London Baptist Association 77
  Northamptonshire Baptist Association 242
  Northern Baptist Association 220
  Western Association 244
  Yorkshire Baptist Association 217
Baptist churches
  Altrincham Baptist Church 203
  Banbury Baptist Church 245
  Barton Baptist Church 246
  Bloomsbury Baptist Church, London/Bloomsbury Central Baptist Church 154, 155, 156, 159, 160, 257n
  Broadmead Baptist Church, Northampton 216
  Charlotte Baptist Chapel, Edinburgh 141
  Chatsworth Baptist Church, West Norwood 72
  Dedworth Green Baptist Church, Windsor xx
  Dublin Street Baptist Church, Edinburgh 134

Duke Street Chapel, St James's Park 77
Eagle Street Baptist Church, London 251
East Street Baptist Chapel, Bristol 125
Fishergate Baptist Church, Preston 141
Gorsley Baptist Church 203
Headington Baptist Church 250
Jozsef Street Baptist Church, Budapest 186
Keila Baptist Church 106, 107, 108, 111, 116, 117
Lewin Road Baptist Church, Streatham 203
London Road Baptist Church, Lowestoft 152, 153
Metropolitan Tabernacle, London 150
Moscow Central Baptist Church 183
Native Baptist Church, Lagos 139
Odesa Baptist Church 198
Old King Street Baptist Church, Bristol 118, 125
Prescot Street Baptist Church, London 54, 55, 57, 58
Queensberry Street Baptist Church, Old Basford 151
Ramsden Road Baptist Church, Balham 152, 153
Šárka Valley Community Church (Baptist), Prague xxii
Soham Baptist Church 252
St Andrew's Street Baptist Church, Cambridge (Stone Yard Meeting) 251
St Mary's Baptist Church, Norwich 149
Tabita Baptist Church, Brno 90, 94
Tyndale Baptist Church, Bristol 126, 135
Upton Vale Baptist Church, Torquay 215
Walden Baptist Church 251
Wraysbury Baptist Church xx

Baptist colleges
Acadia Divinity School 197
Baptist College of Victoria 141
Baptist Seminary, Budapest, the 186
Baptist Seminary, Hamburg 90
Baptist Theological Seminary, Rüschlikon 184, 197, 199
Bristol Baptist College 119, 211
Estonian Baptist Preachers' Seminary/Baptist Theological Seminary 107, 112-14, 116, 117
German Baptist Seminary, Hamburg 197
International Baptist Theological Seminary, Prague xxii, 14
International Baptist Lay Academy, the 199
Japan Baptist Seminary 143
Newton Theological Institute/Andover Newton Seminary 114, 142
Northern Baptist College 218
Northern Baptist Seminary, Chicago 198
Rangoon Baptist College 143
Regent's Park College (Stepney College) xx, 58, 93, 197, 205
Serampore College 33
Shanghai Baptist Theological Seminary 142
Southern Baptist Theological Seminary, Fukuoka 143
Spurgeon's College/Pastor's College xx, xxi, xxii, 72, 78, 141, 202, 207, 216, 219
Summer Institute of Theological Education (SITE) 184
Tartu Theological Seminary 113, 198
Baptist confessions 16-32
Declaration of Principle 203, 204
Baptist identity 217, 221
Baptist organizations
Bible Translation Society (Baptist), the 138
Czechoslovak Baptist Publication Society 94, 95

General Index

Estonian Baptist Literature Society 107
Hungarian Baptist Aid 194
Hungarian National Baptist Youth Committee 186
London Baptist Board 58
London Education Society, the 58
London Society for Itinerancy 57
Baptist Response-Europe 192
Baptist Revival Fellowship, the 162, 203, 205, 206
Baptists xx, xxi, 17, 18, 19, 20, 21, 23, 29, 30, 48, 53, 67, 69, 75, 76, 78, 83, 92, 111, 115, 119, 126, 131, 137, 138, 147, 149, 154, 158, 162, 165, 180-201, 202-22, 235-59, 295, 296, 306
   American Baptists 143, 144
   Armenian Baptists 198
   Association of Baptists in Israel 200
   Czech Baptists 85-102
   Estonian Baptists 198
   European Baptist Federation, the 180-201
   General Baptists 17, 21, 23, 26, 28, 30, 31
   German Baptists 86
   Grace Baptists 17
   Independent Baptists xix
   Irish Baptists 220
      Irish Baptist Network 220
   Lithuanian Baptist Christians 198
   New Connexion of General Baptists 18
   Northern Baptists 142
   Particular Baptists 17, 18, 21, 22, 24, 27, 28, 29, 30, 31, 39, 55, 57, 133
      Particular Baptist Fund 57
   Polish Baptists 198
   Southern Baptists 142, 143, 199, 255n
   Strict Baptists 17, 24, 82
   Swedish Baptists 199
   Telegu Baptists 144
   Baptist Unions and Conventions

   All-Union Council of Evangelical Christians-Baptists 183, 184, 188, 196, 197, 198
   Baptist Union of Estonia 107, 112
   Baptist Union of Great Britain (and Ireland) xx, xxiii, 17, 77, 78, 83, 93, 135, 139, 148, 156, 158, 159, 162, 203, 204, 205, 206, 207, 208, 209, 211, 212, 213, 215, 217, 219, 220, 221, 222
   Baptist Union of Romania 200
   Baptist Union of Yugoslavia 195
   Brethren Union of Chelčický (Baptist Union of Czechoslovakia) 92, 93, 96, 97, 98, 99, 100
   German Baptist Union 184
   Hungarian Baptist Union 194
   Lebanese Baptist Convention 200
   Natal Telegu Baptist Association 145
   Northern Baptist Convention 92, 93, 94
   Polish Baptist Union 197
   Russian Baptist Union 198
   Southern Baptist Convention 200, 236
   Union of Evangelicals Christian Baptists, the 196
Baptist World Aid 193
Baptist World Alliance 92, 183, 191, 197, 198, 200
Barber, Peter 189, 199
Barbour, Thomas S. 135, 140
Barnardo, Thomas 80
Barth, Karl 31, 32
Baxter, Richard 51, 53, 60, 69
Bayly, Lewis 41
Beasley-Murray George R. 207, 258
Beasley-Murray, Paul 202, 204, 210, 214, 216, 219
Bebbington, David 34, 35, 36, 39, 40, 45, 49, 71, 131, 164, 237
Belben, Howard 210
Benet, Robert 295
Bengel, Johann Albrecht 165
Beresford Chapel, Walworth 78, 80

Bernard of Clairvaux 236
Bernard, Richard 294
Bethel Chapel, Isle of Man 81
Bethesda Chapel, Sunderland 74, 75, 77, 79
Bethesda, Bristol 78
Beyerhaus, Peter 170
Bible Christian Chapel, Bedminster 122, 124
Bible Christians 119, 121, 122, 128, 131, 132
Bichkov, Alexei 198
Birrell, Augustine 129
Black, Cyril 203, 207, 208
Bohemian Unity of Brethren, the 10
Boniface IX, Pope 4
Booth, Abraham 53-68
Botha, Pieter J.J. 299
Bourne, F.W. 122, 123
Bowers, Richard 257n
Bowes, John 81
Bowman, Elizabeth 56
Braght, Thieleman J. van 11
Brandýs nad Orlicí 87
Brethren xix, 69, 74, 75, 76, 77, 78, 79, 80, 81, 82, 83, 154
    Plymouth Brethren 76, 77
Brigden, Susan 295
Briggs, John H.Y. 208
Bristol Charity Organisation Society 127
British and Foreign Bible Society 137, 168
Brokenshire, Rev. 124
Bromhead, Anne 297
Bromhead, Hugh 297
Brooks, Thomas 43, 44, 50
Brown, A. Douglas 151, 152, 153, 154, 155, 156, 157, 159, 160, 161, 162
Brown, John 34
Brown, Malcolm 290
Brown, Raymond 202, 203, 204, 211, 213, 214, 219
Brownde, Nicholas 293
Brunner, Emil 258
Bryan, R.T. 142
Bucer, Martin 223

Bunyan, John 33-52, 235n, 236
Burford, Samuel 57
Burget, Cyril 98
Burroughs, Edward 41
Butt, Clara 125
Butt, Hugh 206

Callenberg, Johann Heinrich 168
Calvin, John 223, 224, 225, 240n
Calvinism/Calvinists 16, 17, 18, 19, 21, 22, 23, 24, 25, 26, 28, 29, 32, 39, 40, 56, 68, 237
    high Calvinism 19
    hyper Calvinism 31
    moderate Calvinism 30, 31
    New Calvinism 16, 30, 32
    Synod of Dort 17
Campbell, Alastair 214, 216, 218
Campbell-Bannerman, Henry 129
Čapek, Norbert 90, 91
Capon, John 205
Capon, Thomas 295
Carey, William 23, 49, 50, 57, 133-34, 143, 144, 236, 258
Carlile, J.C. 157, 158, 159
Carson, Don 16
Carter, Grayson 69
catholicity 40, 41, 71
Cecil, William 293
Channon, William G. 251n
Chapman, Ian 198
Charismatic Renewal/Movement(s)/Charismatics xx, 30, 53, 204, 205, 209, 211, 212, 214, 216, 281
Chelčický, Petr 92
Chesterton, Ridley 158
children 18, 24, 27, 64, 65, 66, 244
Christian Endeavour 171
Christian Literature Society for China 135
christological controversy 206-208
church and state 14, 53, 89, 97
Church Growth Movement 208, 209
Church of England/Anglicans 41, 49, 57, 59, 66, 69, 73, 74, 80, 154
    High Anglicans 134
Church of Scotland xix, 134

General Index

church, the 231-34
Ciampa, Roy 305, 306
Clement VII, Pope 4
Clifford John 113, 156, 244, 257
Coffey, David 204, 205, 215, 218, 219, 221
Collier, Thomas 28, 29
Collins, Iain 219
Colwell, John E. 258
Community of Protestant Churches in Europe (Leuenberg Church Fellowship) 164
Congregationalists 24, 75, 76, 81, 88
conversion 239, 240, 246, 256, 285
    conversionist theology 243
convictional theology 284, 285, 286, 290
Council of Constance 7-9, 12
Cox, Claude E. 300
Cressy, David 293, 294
Cross, David 245, 246
Cross, Laura 245, 256, 257
Cross, Paul 245
cross, the 36, 37, 38, 40, 45, 157, 160, 169, 170, 232, 234
Crouch, Douglas 72
Cuff, William 148
Czech Brethren xxii

d'Ailly, Pierre 9
Darby, John Nelson 77, 173, 175
David, John 247
Delitzsch, Franz 168
Denham, W.H. 33
Dent, Arthur 41, 294
Deuster, Wilhelm 177
Dewey, Arthur J. 304, 305
Dewey, Joanna 303
Disciples of Christ 79
discipleship 239, 242, 275, 305
dispensationalism/dispensational-premillennialism/dispensationalists 173, 174, 175
Dissent/Dissenters 40, 58
    Calvinistic Dissent 44
Doddridge, Philip 64
Doggart, A.R. 162

Downgrade controversy 70, 71, 72, 213
Dresser, Madge 119
Driscoll, Mark 16
Dutton, Anne 235n

Eastman, Michael 212
ecclesiology 27, 69, 71, 74, 75, 81, 83, 100, 239, 240, 241, 245, 249, 253, 255n
ecumenism 82
    anti-ecumensim 17
Edinburgh Castle People's Mission Church, London 80
Edwards, Jonathan 17, 40, 47, 48, 236, 244
Edwards, Peter 67, 68
Ellis, Christopher J. 253, 255
English, Donald 209, 215
Enlightenment, the 45, 46, 55, 225, 226, 231, 233, 234, 277
Enquiry Room, the 160
Episcopius 63
Erasmus of Rotterdam 296
eschatology 46-50, 76, 173-77, 229
    postmillennialism 46, 47, 48, 49, 50
    pre-millennialism/premillen-nialists 78, 206
Estonian Bible Society 109
Estonian Sunday School Union 115
evangelical theology 285
evangelicalism xx, xxi, xxiii, xxiv, 14, 15, 18, 33-52, 79, 119, 153, 223-34, 237, 260, 280, 281, 282, 283, 295
    charismatic evangelicalism 213
    quadrilateral
        activism xx, 36, 49, 50, 51, 105, 116, 164
        biblicism 36-37, 39, 51, 164
        conversionism 39-40, 164
        crucicentrism 37-39, 164
    evangelical organizations
        Conservative Evangelicals in Methodism 209

Estonian United Evangelical Believers' Educational Society 107
Evangelical Alliance xxii, xxiii, 70, 71, 75, 110, 114, 116, 117, 165, 206
Evangelical Church of Czech Brethren ('Away from Rome' movement), the 91
Federation of Free Evangelical Congregations, the 165
Fellowship of Independent Evangelical Churches 70, 75, 83
German Evangelicals 164-79
Group for Evangelism and Renewal 210
Lausanne Congress on World Evangelisation 260
Lausanne Covenant 203
National Association of Evangelicals, the 164
evangelical groups
Evangelical Anglicans 134
evangelical Calvinism 49
evangelical ecumenism 41
evangelical Nonconformity 119
evangelical seceders 69
evangelicals xix, 33-52, 69, 84, 103, 104, 115, 117, 118, 134, 157, 202-22, 235, 295
evangelism 39, 76, 77, 83, 105, 116, 147, 157, 196, 209, 260-76
evangelists 72, 77, 82, 142
Eve, John 39

Featley, Daniel 247
Fellowship Movement, the 165
Fiddes, Paul S. 197, 216, 258, 290
Findlay, D.J. 77, 81, 82, 83
Forlong, Gordon 76, 78, 80
Foster, Richard J. 216, 236
Foundationalism 223-34
Fountain Trust, the 214
Fox, William 58
Franck, Sebastian 11
Francke, August Hermann 165, 262
Free Church of Scotland 88
Free Churches 165
Free Reformed churches 89
freedom of conscience 13, 15, 95, 97, 167
Fuller, Andrew 26, 38, 39, 40, 48, 49, 50, 133, 236, 242, 252
Fullerism 40
Fuller, Eunice 248
Fullerton, William Young 140
Fundamentalism 237

Gaukroger, Stephen 249
George, Timothy 237
Gereszenyi, Sandor 188
German Christians 169
Gero, Julia 199
Gerzsenyi, Laszlo 199
Ghiletchi, Valeriu 193
Gifford, Andrew 251
Gifford, John 36, 41, 42
Gill, John 39, 40, 236
Gilmore, Alec 182
Gladstone Street Bible Christian Church, Bristol 128
Glover, Richard 126, 135
Glover, T.R. 148
Goldie, Archie 193
Goncharenko, Evgenii 189
Gooch, Henry Martyn 75, 114, 116
Gooch, William Fuller 71, 72, 75, 77, 81, 82
Goodland, Patrick 203, 204, 209, 215, 219
Goodspeed, Malcolm 219
Gotch, Frederick 119
Gotch, Mary 126
Govett, Richard 73, 79, 81, 82
grace 17, 19, 20, 22, 25, 26, 28, 30, 57n, 65, 66
Graham, Billy 99, 207, 209, 286-88
Graham, Jim 211
Grange, Peter 204, 219
Graves, Brian 235, 238
Green, Bernard 212
Gregory XI, Pope 4, 5
Grenz, Stanley J. 238, 239, 240, 241, 244, 245, 253, 257
Gribben, Crawford 42, 43, 47

General Index

Griffith, Terry 216
Grudem, Wayne 16
Guder, Darrell L. 285
Gwennap, Joseph 251

Haigh, Christopher 294
Haldane, James 80
Haldane, Robert 80
Haliburton, Gordon 140
Hall, Mrs 128
Hamburg 93
Hammond, Dr 64
Hancock, W.C.R. 212
Hannam, June 119
happiness 277-91
Harper, David 220
Harris, Harriet 223
Harris, Howell 44
Harris, William 298, 299, 301, 302, 305
Havel, Vaclav 190
Hawkins, Anne 43
Hayford, J.E. Casely 140
Hayford, Joseph de Graft 139
Hayford, Mark Christian 139, 140, 146
Haymes, Brian 217, 218
Hegel, G.W.F. 229
Helwys, Thomas 19, 20
Henry, Matthew 54, 60
heretics 9, 10, 11
hermeneutics 175, 281, 283
Highgate Road Chapel, London 77, 80
Higman, W. 123
Hilborn, David xxii
Hill, Philip 206
Hinson, E. Glenn 235, 236, 243, 251
Hitler, Adolf 172, 176, 178
Hled'sebe 89
Hobhouse, Charles 129
Hoburg, Christian 167
holiness 43, 232
Holiness tradition 237
Holocaust, the 169, 170, 177
Hopkins, Keith 298, 299, 302
Houston, Tom 211
Howells, George 52

Hubmaier, Balthasar 10, 11, 296
Hulett, James Liege 144, 145
Hulse, Erroll xix
human depravity 17, 18, 19, 27
Humphrey, F.J.H. 158, 160
Hurditch, C. Russell 77
Hus, Jan 1-15
Hussites 1-15
  utraquism 7, 14
Hutterites 296

individualism 240, 241, 243, 255n
indulgences 5
infants 20, 25, 27, 29, 31, 64, 65, 66
interdenominationalism 84
Ives, Eric 293
Ivimey, Joseph 37, 49

Jablonec nad Nisou 91
Jackson, Frederick Arthur 253
Jerome of Prague 3, 12
Jersák, Jan 87
Jews 164-79
Jingan, Dong 142, 146
John Paul II, Pope 14
John Street Chapel, London 76
John XXIII, Pope 5, 8
Jones, Keith G. 219
Jones, Leif 129
Jowett, J.H. 149
Judson, Adoniram 143

Kalmus, Ain 109, 113
Karel, Zygmunt 184
Kargel, Johann 103, 104, 108, 116
Karlsson, Birgit 199, 200
Karu, Tõnu 108, 114
Kaups, Richard 107
Kelly, James 115
Kemp, Joseph 141
Kešjar, Michal 98
Keswick
  Convention/Movement/teaching xxii, xxiii, 103, 105, 116, 147, 149
Kicin, Poland 86
Kiffin, William 40
Killingray, David xx
King, Geoffrey 206

King, Martin Luther, Jr 186
Kinkeard, Maurice 220
Kiss, Emil 188
Knappe, Magnus 86
Komendant, Gregory Ivanovich 196
Korjus, Tabea 115
Kreider, Alan 215
Künneth, Walter 170, 171, 179
Kurówek 87

Lagergen, David 188
Lampeter Brethren, the 73
Lang, G.H. 78, 79
Lansdowne Hall, West Norwood 71, 75, 79, 81, 83
Lattik, Jaan 109
Lewis, Walter O. 113
Liberal Party/Liberalism 127, 129, 237
  Women's Liberal Association 124, 132
Lieven, Natalie 108
Lincoln, William 78, 80, 82
Lloyd-Jones, Martyn 206, 210
Lockhart, David 134
Lodge Street Congregational Church, Bristol 125
Lodz 89
Lollards 295
Lombard, Peter 7
Lord's Supper 65, 68, 72, 77, 78, 82, 110, 240, 251
  closed communion 40
  eucharist 251, 258
  holy communion 65, 74, 81, 82, 255n
  infant communion 65
  Lord's Table 40
  open communion 80
Lotz, Denton 192, 193
Luiken, Jan 11
Lumpkin, W.L. 18
Luther, Ludvig 107
Luther, Martin 1, 2, 3, 7, 12, 13, 167, 223, 241
Lutheran
  Church/Lutherans/Lutheranism 13, 89, 92, 164

Macalpine, George W. 134, 138
MacCulloch, Diarmaid 296
Mainstream 202-22
Malherbe, Abraham J. 300
Manila Manifesto, the 177
Manna Ministries 212, 219
Marchant, James 257
Markham, Maurice 210
Marnham, Herbert 139
Marsh, F.E. 77, 79
Marshall, Molly 236, 237, 249, 250
Marshman, Hannah 33, 34, 46, 49, 51, 52
Marshman, Joshua 33, 49
martyrs 11
Marx, Karl 178
Masaryk, T.G. 92
Matthias of Janov 3
Mayett, Joseph 246, 247
Mazowiecki, Tadeusz 190
McBain, Douglas 203, 204, 205, 209, 215, 217, 212, 213, 214, 219, 221
McCaig, Arcibald 141
McClendon, James W., Jr 284, 291n
McMillan, David 220
McRae, Andrew 197
means of grace 230, 240, 255, 258
Meereis, August 87, 89
Meggitt, Justin 300
Merrion Hall, Dublin 75
Methodist
  Church/Methodists/Methodism 40, 165, 209, 210, 215, 247
  Primitive Methodists 119, 128, 131, 154
  United Methodist Church 166
Methodist Revival Fellowship 210
Meyer, F.B. xxi, xxiv, 139, 149, 150, 235n, 259
Michaelis, Walter 171, 177, 179
Milicz, Jan 3
Millward, Craig 217
Misselbrook, Lewis 211
missiology 135
mission xxi, 23, 34, 46-50, 86, 89, 96, 116, 135, 146, 167, 222, 257, 260-76
  Great Commission, the 64, 169

General Index

mission agencies
  American Baptist Foreign Missionary Society 135, 138, 140, 141, 142
  American Foreign Mission Boards 92
  Anglican Bristol Missionary Society 126
  Baptist Foreign Mission Board of Canada 138
  Baptist Missionary Society 49, 50, 52, 57, 126, 135, 137, 138, 139, 140, 141
  Baptist Zenana Mission 126, 138, 141
  Berlin City Mission 172
  Berlin Society for the Promotion of Christianity among the Jews, the 168
  Bohemian Baptist Mission 90
  China Inland Mission 137
  Evangelical-Lutheran Central Association for Mission among Israel, the 168
  Evangelistic Mission 77
  Foreign Mission Board of the General Conference of Free Baptists 138
  Foreign Mission Board of the National Baptist Convention 138
  Foreign Mission Board of the Southern Baptist Convention 137
  Foreign Mission Committee of the Church of Scotland 137
  Foreign Mission Committee of the United Free Church of Scotland 137
  German Baptist Foreign Mission 138
  Indian Baptist Mission 145
  London Missionary Society 50, 137
  Missionary Society of the Seventh Day Baptists 138
  Seaman's Mission Society 105, 106
  Southern Baptist Convention-International Mission Board 193, 201
  Southern Baptist Foreign Mission Board 197
  Telegu Baptist Home Missionary Society 143, 144
  Victorian Baptist Foreign Mission 138, 141
  Wesleyan Methodist Missionary Society 137
mission halls 78, 79, 81, 122, 123
mission to the Jews 164, 168, 169, 170
missionaries 88, 93, 94, 142, 143, 146
Modernism 237
Molnar, Enrico 14
Montacute, Paul 193
Moody, D.L. 71
Moore, Harry 184
Moorshead, R. Fletcher 141
Moravian Church 89
Moravian Diet 13
More, Thomas 294
Morgan, George 82
Morgan, R.C. 72, 82, 84
Morley, Samuel 81
Mott, John R. 136
Müller, George 74, 77, 78
Murray, Stuart 306

National British Women's Temperance Association 119, 128
Nazism 170, 172, 176, 177, 178, 179
New Frontiers International (Coastlands) 17, 204, 217
Newton, B.W. 77, 78, 82
Newton, John 44
Nicholls, Brian 219
Nicolay, Baron Paul 116
Niem, Dietrich von 5
Nikolaev, Sergei 183
Noel, B.W. 76
Nonconformists 118-32
  Nonconformist conscience 127
Novatian 61
Novotný, Henry 87-90, 92, 94

Novotný, Joseph 92, 94
Nunn, Roger 217

Oetinger, Friedrich Christoph 165
Offor, George 34, 51
Old Catholic Church 89
Oldham, J.H. 136
Oncken, Johann Gerhard 85, 184
Ondra, Karl 87, 89
open membership 80
ordinance(s) 54, 60, 62, 82, 240, 253, 258
original guilt 31
original sin 18, 19, 20, 25, 27, 31
Orthodox Churches 89, 134
    Eastern Orthodoxy xxiii
    Greek Orthodoxy 14, 61
    Russian Orthodoxy 61
Owen, John 40, 50

Packer, J.I. 216
Pain, Alan 214, 215
Pannenberg, Wolfhart 229-30
Panton, D.M. 79
Papp, János 186
Paradise Chapel, Chelsea 78
Parker, G. Keith 193
Parks, R. Keith 197
Parushev, Parush R. 291n
Pashkovism 108, 117
Pawson, David 209
Payne, Ernest A. 181, 206
Peacock, David 215
Pearce, Edith 118, 128-30, 131, 132
Pearce, Joseph 128
Pelagianism 21
Pentecostalism/Pentecostals 53, 134, 281
Perkins, William 43
Pernstejna, Jan z 13
persecution 89
perseverance of the saints 17, 20, 22
Peters, Gerhard 91
Peterson, Eugene H. 7
Phillips, Thomas 149, 150, 154, 156, 159, 161
Pietism/Pietists 63, 103, 166, 169, 172, 225, 261

Piper, John 16
Podin, Adam 103-17
Podin, Emilie 115
Podin, Karlis 104
Podin, Lize 104
Podin, Samuel 113
Poole-Connor, E.J. 70, 75, 79, 80, 81, 82, 83
Popkes, Wiard 192
Pospišil, Jan 195
prayer 7, 48, 49, 150, 153, 155, 156, 157, 158, 210, 241, 251
Prayer Call, the (1784) 154
preaching 7, 15, 38, 49, 120, 121, 124, 157, 158, 251
predestination 16-32, 57n
    elect, the 43
    election 16-32, 57n
    predestinarianism 44
Presbyterianism/Presbyterians xix, 16, 24, 81, 154
    United Presbyterians 77
Priestley, Joseph 65
Prince, H.J. 73
Procházka, Henry 93, 98
Puritanism/Puritans 35, 39, 44, 45, 46, 47, 50, 52, 207, 224, 225, 226, 237, 293

Radcliffe, Reginald 72
Radley, Len 250
Radstock, Lord 72
Ramsbottom, Jack 220
Randall, Ian M. xix-xxiv, 14, 15, 16, 53, 84, 133, 147, 149, 177, 201, 206, 235, 237, 241, 243, 259, 280, 295, 296
Randall, Janice xix, xx, xxii, xxiii
Rangiah, John 143-46
Rees, Arthur Augustus 73, 74, 79, 82
Reformation, the 35, 164, 224, 226, 297
Reformed Church 88, 92, 164
Reformed tradition 16, 30, 52, 89
religious freedom 13, 95, 195
reprobation 21, 24, 28, 29, 31
Restorationists 78
revivals 147-63, 210

General Index

East Anglia Revival 154, 158, 159
Evangelical Revival 35, 50, 56
Great Awakenings, the 236
Lowestoft Revival 147, 151-61, 162
Welsh Revival 147, 149-51, 154, 159, 162
West Coast revival 103
Rhinish-Westphalian Association for Israel, the 168
Řičař, Jan 98
Richard, Timothy 135, 138
Richards, E. Randolph 301
Roberts, J.E. 161
Robinson, Edward 119, 120, 121, 125, 126
Robinson, H. Wheeler 162
Robinson, Katherine 118, 119, 120, 121, 125-27, 131, 132
Robinson, Robert 243, 251
Rogaczeswki, Jerzy 185
Rokytnice u Vsetína 91
Romaine, William 73
Roman Catholic Church/Roman Catholics/Roman Catholicism 3, 6, 11, 14, 62, 63, 88, 92, 95, 98, 164, 167, 190, 230, 282
Room of Quiet, the 160, 161
Rosenberg, Alfred 170
Roseweir, Clifford 204
Roxborough, Bob 215
Rushbrooke, James Henry 92, 93, 113, 162
Russell, David S. 181, 182, 203
Ruysbroeck, Jan van 236
Ryland, John, Jr 48

sacrament(s) 7, 61, 65, 240, 258, 296
  pseudo-sacraments 258
  sacramentalism 240, 255
  sacramentalists 55n
Salvationists 154
Sangma, Thang Khan 142
Sankey, I.D. 71
Sannikov, Sergey 198
Savoy Conference 24
Schmidt, Peter 107
Schmidtz, David 289, 290

Scofield Reference Bible 173, 175
Scott, Thomas 51
scripture 230-31, 234
  sola Scriptura 224
Searle, Roy 220
sectarianism 69, 70
  non-sectarianism 69
Sedgewick, Joelene 246
Selina, Countess of Huntingdon 56
Sell, Alan P.F. 18
seminaries/colleges/universities
  Aoyama Gakuin school, Tokyo 143
  Bethel Seminary 17
  Cimze Seminary, Valga 104
  Cliff College 210
  Colby College, Maine 143
  Comenius Protestant Theological Faculty, Prague, the 99
  Evangelical Seminary, Wroclaw, the 184, 185
  Fuller Theological Seminary 17
  Moody Bible Institute 143
  Prague Theological Seminary 93, 97
  Rochester Theological Seminary 139
  Union Theological Seminary 114
  Wheaton College xxiii, 17
Separatists/separatism 19, 20
sermons 251, 280, 284
Shakespeare, J.H. 159
Sheldrake, Philip 241
Shergold, James 122
Shoreditch Tabernacle 148
Sigismund 8, 12
Simmons, O. Errol 199
Smail, Tom 213
Smith, J. Denham 75
Smyth, John 19, 297
social action/concern 49, 209, 261
Social Service League 127
Society of Friends/Quakers/Quakerism 21, 41, 119, 154, 216, 240
soteriology 240
  salvation history 176, 177
Sou, L.T. Ah 143

Sovereign Grace Advent Testimony, the 78
Spalatin, Georg 1
Spanu, Paulo 192
Spener, Philipp Jacob 165, 166, 167, 168, 262
spirituality xxi, xxiii, 2, 16, 34, 77, 97, 106, 131, 148
   Anabaptist spirituality 237
   baptismal spirituality 235-59
   charismatic spirituality 236, 237
   contemplative spirituality 236, 237
   conversionist spirituality 236, 237
   crusading (prophetic) spirituality 237
   Evangelical Alliance spirituality 106, 108
   evangelical spirituality 84, 236, 237
   holiness spirituality 103, 236
   incarnational spirituality 236
   Keswick spirituality 84, 116, 259
   Lutheran spirituality 237
   pan-evangelical spirituality 109
   pragmatic spirituality 236
   Puritan spirituality 43, 237
   Puritan-Separatist spirituality 236
   Reformed spirituality 237
   sect-type spirituality 239
   seeker spirituality 236
   social justice spirituality 236
   Wesleyan spirituality 237
Spurgeon, Charles Haddon 34, 37, 39, 44, 45, 46, 51, 71, 76, 78, 88, 140, 161, 235n, 248, 252, 255n, 257
Spurgeon, Thomas 78, 150
Spurr, Frederic C. 155, 160
St Chrischona, Basel 88
St George's Cross Tabernacle, Glasgow 77, 80
St Stephen's Church, Norwich 73
Stackelberg, Nicolaus von 106
Steele, Anne 235n
Steele, Richard 294
Stephens, J.R.M. 138
Stephens, James 77, 78
Stern, Klara 178

Still, William xix
Stockmayer, Otto 105
Stoecker, Alfred 172
Stott, John R.W. 209, 214
Strong, Augustus H. 139
Ströter, Ernst 116
Surrey Chapel, Norwich 73, 79
Sutcliff, John 48
Švec, Stanislav 99
Swann, Danielle 250
Swinnock, George 293

Taborites 10
Talbot Tabernacle, Notting Hill 75, 76, 78, 79
Talpos, Vasile 196, 199
Tammik, Emilie 106
Tärk, Osvald 114
Taylor, David 219
Taylor, James Hudson 137
Taylor, Jeremy 65, 66
Taylor, Michael 207
temperance movement 118, 119, 122, 123, 130
Terrett Memorial Hall 124
Terrett, Sarah 118, 119, 120, 121-25, 128, 130, 131, 132
Terrett, William 120, 121, 123, 124
Tersteegen, Gerhard 165
Tertullian 63
Tervits, Janis 198
testimonies 155, 242-57, 280, 284
Thomas, Keith 294
Thompson, Arthur 208, 219
Thompson, Ralph Wardlaw 137
Tidball, Derek 219
Tilney, Mary 41n
tolerance 10
Tom LaHaye 173n
Transfer Movement, the 91
Tregelles, S.P. 77, 78
Trinity, the 170, 260
Troeltsch, Ernst 239
Turner, Harold 147
Tuskegee Institute 140

Üxküll, Woldemar von 106, 116
undenominationalism 69-84

General Index

Unitarianism/Unitarians 131, 19
United Free Church of Scotland 134, 135
unity 18
Unity Chapel, Bristol 77, 78, 79
Universities' and Colleges' Christian Fellowship 17
Urban VI, Pope 4

Vaculík, Karel 91
Varley, Henry 76, 77, 79, 80, 81
Vavrišovo 92
Vellacott, Humphrey 214
Venema 65
Venn, Henry 57
Viczian, Gábor 188
Viczián, János 186, 194, 199
Vikýřovice 95
Virgo, Terry 217
Voke, Stanley 215

Waldhauser, Conrad 3
Walker, Mr 62
Wall, William 61
Walter, Karl Heinz 191, 192, 193, 194, 195
Walton, Robert 248
Warneck, Gustav 135
Wattville Street Undenominational Church, Handsworth, Birmingham 79, 80
Wellings, Martin 209
Wenceslas, King 4
Wesley, Charles 44, 54, 225
Wesley, John 44, 53, 225, 232
Wesleyanism 280, 283
West London Tabernacle (Free Chapel) 76, 79
West, W.M.S. 211, 217
Western Schism 4
White Ribbon Army, the 119, 121-25
White, Barrington R. xx, 205, 211, 218

White, F.J. 142
White, Frank H. 78, 80
Whitefield, George 41, 44
Whitley, W.T. 141
Wiazowski, Konstanty 184
Wieske, Günter 184
Wilkinson, Diana 248
Wilkinson, Mrs 130
Williams, Edward 67
Williams, Garry 35
Williamson, Andrew Wallace 134
Wills, Monica 127
Wilson, Charles Edward 140
Wimber, John 216
women's suffrage 130, 132
Working-Group of Jews and Christians, the 169
World Council of Churches 135
World Missionary Conference, Edinburgh (1910) 133-46
World's Sunday School Association 115, 116, 117
Worthing Tabernacle 72, 83
Wright, Christopher J.H. 269
Wright, Nigel G. xx, xxiv, 219, 237
Wümpelmann, Knud 185, 186, 188, 191, 192, 197, 198
Wyclif, John 3, 4, 6, 7, 8, 11, 12

YMCA 137
Yugoro, Chiba 142
Yuille, George 137

Zajic, Archbishop 5
Zeitgeist (twentieth-century) 237
Zelów 87
Zinzendorf, Nikolaus Ludwig, Count 165
Zionism 173
Zwingli, Huldrych 12, 223, 240n
Żyrardow 89

Spurgeon's College

Spurgeon's College was founded in 1856 and is one of the leading theological colleges in the UK. It offers a range of courses from lay training through to doctorates; the BA, MTh and MA are validated by the University of Manchester. The College trains women and men for mission and ministry from a wide range of denominations and from every continent, regardless of age and background.

Spurgeon's College
189 South Norwood Hill
London, SE25 6DJ
United Kingdom.
Tel: 020 8653 0850
Fax: 020 8771 0959
College web site: www.spurgeons.ac.uk
Spurgeon's Online Learning site: www.spurgeonsonline.org.uk

Welcome to College

'We continue today with the same generous evangelical vision that Charles Spurgeon himself had to offer training for mission and ministry that is both relevant and practical.'

Dr Nigel Wright, Principal

A member college of the Baptist Union, a member of the Evangelical Alliance and a member of the Micah Network. Registered Charity number 1096721 and a Company Limited by Guarantee number 4418151 registered in England.

Baptist Historical Society

What this Society does

We are here to help Baptists understand their heritage and history. We provide an appropriate academic opportunity for those who wish to study the life of Baptist churches, people and ideas, so that Baptists can 'articulate and discover the faith by which we all live' (Brian Haymes). We are interested in collecting primary Baptist information for the national Baptist collection in The Angus Library and Archives, Regent's Park College, Oxford (www.rpc.ox.ac.uk), and finding such resources in local churches, record offices and any in the possession of private individuals.

Series

History of the English Baptists
A full history of English Baptists is within the 'century' volumes listed below.

B.R. White
The English Baptists of the 17th Century
Enlarged revised edition 1994, 176pp
ISBN 0980903166218

Raymond Brown
The English Baptists of the Eighteenth Century
1986, viii + 187pp
ISBN 0980903166107

J.H.Y. Briggs
The English Baptists of the Nineteenth Century
1994, 432pp
Pb ISBN 0980903166188

Ian M. Randall
The English Baptists of the Twentieth Century
2005, xxvi + 600pp
Pb ISBN 9780903166356

English Baptist Records
Series Editor: Roger Hayden

Transcribed by L.G. Champion
No. 1. The General Baptist Church of Berkhamsted, Chesham and Tring, 1712–1781
1985, xiv + 166pp
Pb ISBN 0903166097

Transcribed by L.G. Champion and K.A.C. Parsons
No. 2. Church Book: St Andrews Street Baptist Church, Cambridge 1720–1832
1991, xl +196pp
Pb ISBN 0903166143

Transcribed and edited by S.L. Copson
No 3. Association Life of the Particular Baptists of Northern England 1699–1732
1991, x + 153pp
Pb ISBN 0903166151
A set of volumes 1 to 3 is available for £25

Individual Volumes

Geoffrey R. Breed
Particular Baptists in Victorian England and their Strict Communion Organizations
2003, xiv + 348pp
Pb ISBN 0903166348 [Only available from Dr Roger Hayden—see below]

Sharyl Corrado and Toivo Pilli (Eds)
Eastern European Baptist History: New Perspectives
International Baptist Seminary, Prague, 2007,
Pb ISBN 80-87006-02-X [Only available from Dr Roger Hayden—see below]

Kenneth Dix
Strict and Particular
English Strict and Particular Baptists in the Nineteenth Century
2001, xii + 337pp
Pb ISBN 9780903166317 [Only available from Dr Roger Hayden—see below]

Stephen Greasley
Recording your Church's History
2009, 12pp
[Only available from Roger Hayden—see below]

Bernard Green
Crossing the Boundaries: A History of the European Baptist Federation
1999, xiv + 243pp
Pb ISBN 0903166291

Bernard Green
European Baptists and the Third Reich
2008, xii + 270pp
Pb ISBN 9780903166386 [Only available from Dr Roger Hayden—see below]

Bernard Green
Tomorrow's Man: A Biography of James Henry Rushbrooke
1997, 228pp
Pb ISBN 978090366294
Hb ISBN 0903166275

Roger Hayden
Continuity and Change: Evangelical Calvinism among 18th century Baptist Ministers trained at Bristol Baptist Academy, 1690-1791.
2006, xiv + 273pp
Pb ISBN 139780903166379 [Only available from Dr Roger Hayden—see below]

Roger Hayden
English Baptist History & Heritage (Second Edition)
Published by Baptist Union of Great Britain, 2005, xvi + 286pp
Pb ISBN 0901472794 [Only available in UK, for overseas and trade orders visit the Baptist Union of Great Britain's website, see below]

Susan J. Mills
Exploring History
Probing the Past: A Toolbox for Baptist Historical Research.
2009, 199pp
Pb ISBN 978-0-903166-39-3 [Only available from Dr Roger Hayden—see below]

Michael Walker
Baptists at the Table: The Theology of the Lord's Supper amongst English Baptists in the Nineteenth Century
1992, xii + 212pp
Pb ISBN 9780903166164

W.M.S. West
Baptists Together
2000, vi + 143pp
Pb ISBN 0903166305 [Only available from Dr Roger Hayden—see below]

John H.Y. Briggs and Anthony R. Cross (eds)
Baptists and the World: Renewing the Vision
Papers from the Baptist Historical Society Conference, Prague, Czech Republic, July 2008
2000, xiv + 228pp
Pb ISBN 9781907600050 [Only available from www.rpc.ox.ac.uk and select 'Publications']

Baptist Quarterly
The journal of the Society contains articles on history, theology and general topics, together with reviews of recent books. Published four times a year, each issue being around 52pp, and an index is produced alternate years.
ISSN 0005 – 576X
Sent free to members.

Cumulative Indices
The updated CD Rom is now available. It contains
- *Transactions of the Baptist Historical Society* Vols 1–7
- *Baptist Quarterly* Vols 1–41

All these in ASCII txt format and volumes 40 and 41 are also in Rich Text Format.

Web: http://www.baptisthistory.org.uk/

To order any Baptist Historical Society Publications
Retail sales in Great Britain:
Baptist Union Publications Department, Baptist House,
PO Box 44, 129 Broadway,
Didcot, Oxon,
OX11 8RT, UK.
www.baptiststore.co.uk

Trade and Overseas Sales:
Revd Dr Roger Hayden,
15 Fenhurst Gardens,
Long Ashton, Bristol.
BS41 9AU. UK
rogerhayden@tiscali.co.uk

For information on membership of the Baptist Historical Society contact:
Steve Langford: adm@baptisthistory.clara.co.uk